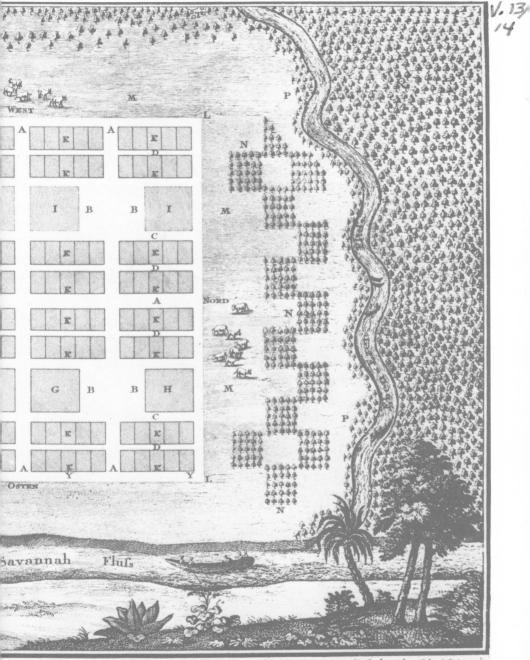

...ten, *13te Continuation, Erster Theil* (Halle and Augsburg, 1747).
...on, University of Georgia Library.

Detailed Reports on the
Salzburger Emigrants
Who Settled in America . . .
Edited by Samuel Urlsperger

GEORGIA SALZBURGER SOCIETY MUSEUM BUILDING
(Drawn by John Courtney LeBey)

Detailed Reports on the Salzburger Emigrants Who Settled in America . . .

Edited by Samuel Urlsperger

VOLUME THIRTEEN, 1749

Translated by
DAVID ROTH
GEORGE FENWICK JONES
Edited by
GEORGE FENWICK JONES

VOLUME FOURTEEN, 1750

Translated by
EVA PULGRAM
MAGDALENA HOFFMAN-LOERZER
GEORGE FENWICK JONES
Edited by
GEORGE FENWICK JONES

THE UNIVERSITY OF GEORGIA PRESS
ATHENS AND LONDON

The paper in this book meets the guidelines for permanence
and durability of the Committee on Production Guidelines for
Book Longevity of the Council on Library Resources.

Printed in the United States of America

93 92 91 90 89   5 4 3 2 1

Library of Congress Cataloging in Publication Data

(Revised for volume 13–14)

Urlsperger, Samuel, 1685–1772.
    Detailed reports on the Salzburger emigrants who settled in America.

    (Wormsloe Foundation. Publications, no. 9–   )
    Vol. 6 translated and edited by George Fenwick Jones and Renate Wilson.
    Vols. 7, 9 translated and edited by George Fenwick Jones and Don Savelle.
    Vol. 8 translated by Maria Magdalena Hoffmann-Loerzer, Renate Wilson, and
George Fenwick Jones.
    Vol. 13 translated and edited by George Fenwick Jones and David Roth.
    Vol. 14 translated and edited by George Fenwick Jones, Eva Pulgram, and Mag-
dalena Hoffman-Loerzer.
    Translation of Ausführliche Nachricht von den saltzburgischen Emigranten, die
sich in America niedergelassen haben.
    Vols. 1–5 issued in series: Publications (Wormsloe Foundation)
    Includes bibliographical references and indexes.
    Contents: v. 1. 1733–1734. v. 2. 1734–1735. v. 3. 1736. —[etc.]— v. 13. 1749—
v. 14. 1750.
    1. Salzburgers—Georgia—History—Sources. 2. German Americans—Georgia—
History—Sources. 3. Lutherans—Georgia—History—Sources. 4. Ebenezer (Ga.)—
History—Sources. 5. Georgia—History—Colonial period. ca. 1600–1775—Sources.
6. Stockbridge Indians—Missions—History—Sources. 7. Indians of North America—
Georgia—Missions—History—Sources. I. Jones, George Fenwick, 1916– . II.
Wilson, Renate, 1930– . III. Savelle, Don. IV. Series: Publications (Wormsloe Foun-
dation); no. 9, etc.
F295.S1U813   975.8'00436   67-27137
ISBN 0-8203-1120-0 (alk. paper) (vols. 13–14)

British Library Cataloging in Publication Data available

Vols. 1–5 were published as part of the Wormsloe Foundation
Publications series.

To Amy Lebey

Detailed Reports on the
Salzburger Emigrants
Who Settled in America . . .
Edited by Samuel Urlsperger

VOLUME THIRTEEN, 1749

Contents

Introduction
by George Fenwick Jones

xi

Daily Reports of the Year 1749

1

Songs Sung by the Salzburgers
in the Year 1749

157

Cumulative Index to
Volumes I through XII

159

Notes
for the Year 1749

181

Index
for the Year 1749

189

 *Introduction*

This and the following four paragraphs are taken from the introduction to a previous volume of this series and therefore need not be read by those who have already read them or who are otherwise familiar with the history of the Georgia Salzburgers. For those who come new to the field, the following resume should suffice; those who wish more detail may consult the *Salzburger Saga.*[1] When the Lutherans were expelled from Salzburg in 1731, not all the exiles went to East Prussia and other Protestant lands in Europe: a small number, some two hundred, were taken to the colony of Georgia, then in its second year. Georgia, the last of Britain's thirteen North American colonies, was founded according to the grandiose schemes of a group of benevolent gentlemen in London, called the Trustees, who wished to provide homes for impoverished Englishmen and persecuted foreign Protestants, to protect the more northerly colonies from the Spaniards in Florida, and to provide raw materials for English industry.

The first Salzburger transport, or traveling party, consisted of recent exiles who had been recruited in and around Augsburg, a Swabian city just north of Salzburg. This group arrived in Georgia in 1734 and settled some twenty-five miles northwest of Savannah, where they founded a settlement which they named Ebenezer. By the time the second transport arrived a year later, the land that had been chosen had proved infertile and the stream on which it was built, Ebenezer Creek, had proved unnavigable. When a third transport arrived in 1736, composed mostly of Upper Austrian exiles, the survivors at Ebenezer joined them on the Red Bluff on the Savannah River, bringing the name of the earlier settlement with them. The original site,

---

[1]George F. Jones, *Salzburger Saga.* Athens, Ga.: U. of Ga. Press, 1983.

which became the Trustees' cowpen or cattle ranch, was henceforth called Old Ebenezer.

A fourth and last transport, consisting of Salzburger exiles who had been sojourning in Augsburg and other Swabian cities, arrived in 1741. The Salzburgers were joined by Swiss and Palatine settlers from Purysburg, a Swiss settlement a short way down the Savannah River on the Carolina side, and also by some Palatine servants donated by the Trustees. Finding insufficient fertile land on the Red Bluff, many Salzburgers moved their plantations to an area along Abercorn Creek where the lowland was flooded and enriched each winter by the Savannah River. This explains the terms "the town" and "the plantations." After some gristmills and sawmills were built on Abercorn Creek, it was usually called the Mill River (Mühl-Fluss).

Despite appalling sickness and mortality and the hardships incident to settlement in a wilderness, the Salzburgers were the most successful community in Georgia. This relative success was largely due to the skill, devotion, and diligence of their spiritual leader, Johann Martin Boltzius, the author of most of these reports. This young divine had been trained at the University of Halle in eastern Germany and had taught in that city at the Francke Foundation, a charitable institution that was to have great influence on the development of Ebenezer. Although Boltzius was at heart a minister, his secular responsibilities in Georgia moulded him into a skillful administrator, economist, and diplomat. A few of the reports were written by Boltzius' admiring younger colleague, Christian Israel Gronau, who officiated whenever Boltzius was away in Savannah or elsewhere until his untimely death in 1745.

Boltzius' journals were edited contemporaneously by Samuel Urlsperger, the Senior of the Lutheran clergy in Augsburg. Comparison of the original manuscripts surviving in Halle with Urlsperger's published edition shows that he took considerable liberty in deleting unpleasant reports and suppressing proper names, which he replaces with N. or N.N. So far as we know, the original documents for 1749 no longer exist, so there is no way to know how much Urlsperger changed or deleted; but there is reason to believe that Boltzius made an entry for every day, as he

had been instructed to, and that Urlsperger made major deletions for both diplomatic and economic reasons. In some cases
he simply consolidated the material for two or more days into
one. Urlsperger's deletions are very illogical: he often deletes a
name in one passage even though it appears in another and can
be easily recognized.

The present volume for the year 1749 shows the Salzburgers
well established and busy consolidating their position. Their
farms were steadily spreading southeastward, the entire "Mill
District" had been occupied, and Boltzius was now negotiating
for more land in the fertile area south of Abercorn. With the
increased number of horses and plows, "European" crops like
wheat, barley, rye, and oats were flourishing; and the Salzburgers were well able to feed themselves. Emphasis was now shift-
ing from subsistence farming, which had been the Trustees' first
goal, to commercial enterprises such as silk culture and the timber trade, which would bring monetary returns. Consequently,
Boltzius now reports more fully on silkworms, mulberry trees,
and sawmills than on crops.

While the Salzburgers had sufficient land, and nearly enough
horses, they lacked hired hands, who were greatly needed because the early settlers had lost most of their children to disease
and had no staff for their old age. Boltzius was not yet persuaded that Negro slavery was the answer to this need, and he
was still pleading for the Trustees to bring indentured servants
from Germany. This request was finally honored in the early autumn of 1749, when Peter Bogg, the master of the *Charles Town
Galley,* brought a shipload of "Palatines," many of them from
Wurttemberg. Unfortunately for Ebenezer, these were not
really indentured servants. A number were free men, who had
paid for their passage; and of these all but one family preferred
to move on to South Carolina, where they had been promised
provisions for their first year. The remainder were redemptioners, who, unlike indentured servants, were free to redeem themselves by finding an employer who would advance them 6 L for
their passage. This the wealthy in Savannah did, with the result
that Boltzius did not always get the cream of the crop or had to
take the large families, who would be expensive to support until

the children came of working age. He did, however, wrest the Schubdrein brothers from the Anglican minister Bartholomäus Zouberbuhler, who had crossed on the *Charles Town Galley* with them and had seen their worth. Despite Boltzius' initial disappointment with many of the young servants, who were mostly tradesman apprentices and wished to practice their professions rather than work as field hands, and who liked the innocent pleasures of this world, most of these servants served their masters well and eventually became respected members of the congregation and the forebears of many Georgia families. Several, however, absconded and moved to Congrees in South Carolina without serving out their time.

This volume follows in the same format as its predecessors, except that, at the suggestion of two reviewers of a previous volume, Biblical verses are identified, when recognized, for the benefit of our un-Biblical younger generation. At this time I wish to thank Pastor Helmut Beck, the Moravian minister at Hamburg, for his help in various matters, such as identifying hymns and hymn-verses.

ACKNOWLEDGMENTS

This volume of the *Detailed Reports* is cordially dedicated to "Miss Amy" Lebey and her family for reasons poignantly expressed as follows by the board of the Ebenezer Trustees:

"At the March 12, 1928, gathering of the Salzburger Society, Mrs. William George Gnann (nee Pearl Havilla Rahn, 1881– 1973) accepted the new office of genealogist, "to which she will devote her whole time." The monumental result of that effort is the *Georgia Salzburgers and Allied Families*, compiled, edited, and published by Pearl Rahn Gnann, copyright 1956.

"Miss Pearl's mantle was taken up by her daughter, Naomi Amanda Gnann (Mrs. Charles LeBey), now known to many as "Miss Amy." Amy Lebey's corrections and new materials were published in March 1970 and again in 1976, in her first and second revisions of her mother's book. A third revised printing was made in 1984. Although she worked in The Best Laundry and reared two daughters, her research and publishing did not keep her from serving as the Society's genealogist and as Curator of the Museum.

"While gathering the supplementary material, "Miss Amy" has always enjoyed the energizing efforts of her husband, "Mr. Charlie." Although Charles had prepared for a career in electrical engineering at Georgia Tech, after marrying Miss Amy he became the manager and then the owner of her family's The Best Laundry; but in essence he had married Miss Amy's work with the Salzburgers. In addition to always assisting Amy, he served as president of the Salzburger Society, and for fifteen years he was the treasurer.

"His brother, John Courtney LeBey, who married Amy's sister, Louise, is an architect of some note. His career has earned him a Governor's Fine Arts Award for his contributions to architectural restoration in Georgia. He is a Fellow of the American Institute of Architects and is on the National Board of Restoration; and many church buildings across Georgia and South Carolina reveal his skill. To the Georgia Salzburger Society he has given endless hours of architectural guidance on the Fail House, and for Richard Kessler he has designed the cemetery gate and fence as well as the cottages on the New Ebenezer Family Life Center. In September 1971 he designed and donated the museum building, patterned after the eighteenth-century Orphanage at Ebenezer, as a memorial to his wife, Louise, who had died in January 1969.

"Beyond the books and the buildings, the Lebeys serve year after year in a variety of ways. Miss Amy and Mr. Charlie are constantly donning Salzburger costumes and meeting individuals and groups at the church and the museum to share their knowledge, dedication, and enthusiasm.

"Amy LeBey's life parallels that of the Georgia Salzburger Society. For all that she has accomplished, alone or with the help of Charles and John, and for all her known and anonymous deeds, the Salzburger Society dedicates this volume."

This volume was funded by contributions from many members of The Georgia Salzburger Society:

MRS. RAY B. ANSLEY
R. L. ARMSTRONG, JR.
MRS. HELOISE ARNSDORFF

RUSSELL E. BAINBRIDGE
GERTRUDE T. BEASLEY
MRS. LEO G. BECKMANN

Michael and Cindy R. Bignault
Claire Z. Billings
Carol C. Bland
Erma L. Bourne
Mr. and Mrs. Marvin Brown
Ethel Rahn Brunson
Rebecca Burgstiner
Jean Burkhalter
Farris Cadle
Gail, Blaney & Callie Carter
    (In Memory of Mrs. Rena
    Falligant Travis)
Mrs. Miriam H. Conant
William H. Cone
James Corey
Marion A. Crawford
Martha Alice Crookshank
Rev. and Mrs. Raymond E. Davis, Jr.
Dr. Heinz J. Dielmann
    and Dr. Frances B. Dielmann
Mrs. Hilda Ruth Morgan Dugger
    and Mr. and Mrs. J. H. Dugger
Mr. and Mrs. Irby S. Exley
    (The Edward Wilkes Exley
    Foundation, Inc.)
Hilde Shuptrine Farley
Frances S. Frye
Mr. and Mrs. J. W. Garland
Lawton D. Geiger
Miss Essie Gnann
H. C. Goldwire
Fred E. Groover
W. Clifford Groover
Mrs. Catherine S. Hardman
Clarence E. Hester
Mr. and Mrs. Marion C. Jaudon

F. D. Johnson
Richard C. Kessler
Barbara Klingelsmith-Geisert
Dr. and Mrs. F. Leslie Long
Ruth Exley McCormick
James E. Martin
Lena and Alvah D. Mikell
Mrs. G. Philip Morgan, Sr.
Mr. and Mrs. Hollis Morgan
Helene E. Ott
Mrs. Dianne Gnann Perry
Holmes C. and Isabel Posser
Mr. and Mrs. Milton H. Rahn
Eveline Fountain Reiser
John C. Rentz
Mr. and Mrs. Stanley Rich
Harold C. Schwanebeck
W. L. Schwanebeck
Dr. H. S. Shearouse
Mrs. Paul Shearouse
Mrs. Frances Shropshire
    (In memory of Great-
    grandfather, William
    Remshart)
Mr. and Mrs. Hubert O.
    Shuptrine
William T. Smith, Jr.
Isabell Arnsdorff Sowell
Thomas E. Stonecypher
Virginia B. Strickland
Charlton W. Tebeau
Col. William L. Travis
Mr. and Mrs. Jeffrey Tucker
George Zeigler
Evelyn Zittrauer
A. L. Zittrouer

I.N.I.A.[1]
Daily Reports Of the Year 1749

JANUARY

Sunday, the 1st of January. May the name of the Lord be praised for all spiritual and physical benefactions which He has so generously shown not only in previous years but also for those which He has once again begun to show us on this New Year's day. Yesterday during the evening prayer meeting, He bestowed on us a new awakening to faith and evangelical Christianity through His words, "And of his fullness have all we received, and grace for grace."[1] On this day during Holy Communion and in prayer, we felt His merciful presence deeply. It has been, to be sure, very cold today as in previous days. But this kept no one from the sermons and evening prayer meeting. My dear colleague, Mr. Lemke, preached in Savannah and administered Holy Communion to the Germans there, while I performed the official duties here. At the beginning of the service, after the prayer, we sang the inspiring and rousing *Ach möchte ich meinen Jesum sehen, der meine Seele so herzlich liebt* which I gave as a New Year's gift to my dear congregation. I also wished them true desire, honest intention, and the Christian attitude of a believing soul that are so excellently expressed in it.

Tuesday, the 4th of January. This morning we consecrated Michael Rieser's new house with song, God's word, and prayer. A few pious women from the city also attended. The head of the house, a young and once capricious man, finds himself currently in a serious struggle for penitence and is in need of instruction from the gospels to awaken and strengthen his belief. Therefore, the passage Luke 19:1 ff. is appropriate not only for the present time and the matters we have preached publicly in the past but also for the spiritual well-being of this man, especially because it concerns not only the sinner but also the Healer of sinners. In contemplating this gospel story, it correctly states: "Here the heart of Jesus openeth for all them which recognize their loss in pain and penitence."

Wednesday, the 5th of January. Because the three families who live on Ebenezer Creek can only rarely attend the evening prayer meetings on account of their household chores and the long way they must travel, I have begun to hold a Bible study this week at their request from eleven to twelve o'clock. Henceforth, with the help of the Lord, this will take place twice a week if no more important business prevents me.[2]

Thursday, the 13th of January. Since the beginning of the new year we have had continued cold winter weather, frost, ice, and snow. No one can remember ever having experienced it's like in this country.

Sunday, the 15th of January. The weather has become bearable on this second Sunday after the celebration of the epiphany of the Lord. An Englishman was traveling from the Ogeechee River to Old Ebenezer with his wife and children, and he came to our town because there was no food in Old Ebenezer. Because he had no money he wanted to trade clothing to buy supplies for himself and his children. We gave him some supplies out of sympathy. He couldn't describe the poverty which drove him away from the Ogeechee River, where many slave owners are already settled.[3] Now he is going to Augusta. Nothing can be earned there; and his crops in the lowland were spoiled by water. This is new evidence that wherever there are blacks, white people who can't afford them find it difficult to get along. However, many are so blind that they insist on having black slaves whether they can afford them or not. Since S. B. and H. have gone to Carolina, they have fared worse rather than better (even if one just looks at the material aspect).[4] The eyes of many people of our town have been opened, and they are beginning to recognize their advantages more so than before. It is no small blessing that they always have the opportunity to work for an hourly wage or earn money with their crafts in Ebenezer.

Monday, the 17th of January. The majority among us have gotten very well settled in on their plantations; and it seems they lack nothing in a material way but good servants, with whom they would be able to feed themselves better than with Negroes.

Tuesday, the 18th of January. Mrs Riedelsberger became seriously ill, which is why she summoned me. She is experiencing the same things as other honest souls under the similar circumstances. The sins of her youth occur to her and become magnified, and when she does not feel the faith and comfort of the Holy Ghost from the gospels, she becomes humble and subject to the law.[5] What I read to her yesterday and today from the gospel appears to have made a salutary impression on her troubled, burdened soul.

After the unusually cold weather, some people have now come down with fever, stitches in their sides, colds, and sore throats. I am also experiencing this; however, thank God, it is bearable. Mrs. Kalcher had another serious onset of her old sickness and predicted her own death last evening. Indubitably, she is, just like Mrs. Riedelsberger, a precious jewel in the eyes of God. At times she has very serious pangs of conscience. It serves, however, for her better purification and earnest penetration into Christ, the only Savior from sin.

Wednesday, the 19th of January. General Oglethorpe's company captain, George Cadogan, spent several hours in our town on his way to Augusta to inspect his soldiers. He told me that Major Horton had become seriously ill with fever in Savannah. He also told me that the officers and other men who own land and slaves near Frederica and the Ogeechee River have collected a sum of money through subscription in order to construct a roadway and footpath from the Ogeechee to Savannah through a long swamp so that one can travel to Savannah comfortably in three hours to bring their produce to market. Savannah will remain the capital of this colony.[6] We have it easier in that we can take our things down river in small and large boats. A small boat carrying four hundredweight or a little over can be taken down the river and back by one man. The roads in this land have been poorly made until now. This will improve in due time as the population, trade, and commerce increase. Because Negroes are already as good as permitted, there is no doubt that the colony will be filled with people.

Two weeks ago, the pious Mrs. Kornberg had a miscarriage, in addition to her many domestic troubles. When I visited her yesterday, I found that she was in good health, thanks to the good care of her Christian friends. She was in a fearful state of mind especially because of the following verses: "Your iniquities have separated between you and your God," etc. Likewise, "Ye know that no murderer hath eternal life abiding in him."[7] I opened the Bible to the chapter about the cities of refuge for the unintentional manslaughterer and suggested she appropriate this prefiguration in our *Little Treasure Chest*.[8] For this she was very eager.

Friday, the 21st of January. God has visited N. N. /Bacher/ with various physical trials to humble and cleanse him of his sins and imperfections. He has a truly pious wife, who, indeed, has her tribulations but is very patient and allows everything to turn out for her good. What will become of him remains to be seen. He has many very good natural gifts and could be of good use for many things in our town if his disposition were only more reserved, humble, and gentle.

The pious Mr. Glaner is still a widower; he holds his pious and now deceased housekeeper and wife in devoted remembrance and makes an effort to follow in her footsteps. He appreciates the advantages given us here by a merciful God, who has given the Salzburgers more here than they had hoped for in their homeland. He told me about his landlord's son in Salzburg, who wished many times to be able to be in a situation where he could put his Bible in his knapsack and travel wherever he would like to. God granted him his wish. About one of his other friends he said that he would steal away from the other boys and take his Bible into a barn, bury himself in the hay near a wall where the sun shone through an opening, and read his fill of the holy word without being caught. He could not even trust his brothers about his recognition of the truth; but God in His wisdom gave him two brothers similarly disposed, so that they are now one heart and soul.

Saturday, the 22nd of January. I received a letter yesterday

dated the 31st of October from our dear brother, Pastor Brunnholtz, from Philadelphia; it was a pleasure to receive it after having to wait for such a long time. I answered it immediately. His
correspondence is a blessing. He has again had a high fever
which brought him close to death; but our merciful God has
brought about his recovery, even though he was weak while writing the letter. To the great sorrow of God's servants in Philadelphia, a pious, agreeable, and learned Swedish provost who
arrived there a short time ago died recently. And a young preacher from St. Gall, just arrived and eager to travel to his parish,
had the misfortune to shoot himself in the chest with his own
flintlock as a result of carelessness, and this caused a lot of dis-
may. At the solemn consecration of St. Michael's Lutheran
Church in Philadelphia the righteous and industrious catechist,
Mr. Kurtz, was ordained as a teacher and preacher by several
assembled preachers; and the ceremony was attended by the
aforementioned Swedish provost. The other servants of god,
such as Mr. Mühlenberg and Mr. Handschuh, are still healthy
and are in harmony with helping Mr. Brunnholtz and are in
blessed harmony. This we like to hear.

Sunday, the 23rd of January. After I had been with dear
Glaner the day before yesterday, he became suddenly so sick
with fever that he did not expect to survive the next day. I was
called to him yesterday evening shortly before the repetition
hour. My dear colleague took over for me so that this necessary
and useful hour would not be canceled. He lay on his bed in
great pain and sickness. He had a dangerous and unusual attack,
but his heart was happy in the Savior. He longed to be freed and
to be with the Lord and his deceased wife. This morning he was
a little better; and he said to me: "Our dear savior does not want
to take me yet. I would gladly have died." Yesterday he showed
me as well as he could how he wanted his worldly possessions
distributed since he had forgotten something; and he arranged
it today. Because he has neither children nor relatives, he
thought generously of widows and orphans, and the rest he left
up to my discretion.

Thursday, the 27th of January. On the 24th of this month an express messenger came on horseback from Savannah bringing the sad news that our great friend and benefactor Major Horton died at two o'clock in the afternoon of a dangerous fever. With moving and emphatic words, I was asked to come immediately, without delay, and hold the burial in the English fashion because their regular preacher is away and because they find the preacher from Frederica, currently in Savannah with his Indian family, disgusting and objectionable.[9] This is also why he has not received permission to preach in Savannah on Sundays. Gratitude and respect for the deceased benefactor and obligation to the authorities required me to ride down there and endure the uncomfortable cold and stormy night rather than miss the prearranged burial time. It was not my intention to replace the English pastor, but merely to show final honors to the deceased like others attending the burial. However, my reasons for not being able to serve the Englishmen in an official capacity were refuted by counter arguments and the agreeable way they implored me; therefore, I had to acquiesce to their wishes.

Mr. Stephens, the president and colonel, an eighty year old gentleman, provided the greatest impetus to the matter by not only persuading me verbally but also with a little letter with which I can sufficiently protect myself from any accusations and judgments of the preacher from Frederica. God has granted me his merciful support in this matter. Through this, also others who looked askance at me without cause were placated. I was able to recognize this through their words and behavior toward me after the burial.

The funeral was held in accordance with the social standing of the major and was probably not inexpensive. It proceeded very orderly and piously, both in regard to the procession of the wealthy and those of lesser social position following the coffin into the church, as also in the churchyard and back to the house of Mr. Habersham, the merchant, the place from which the body was carried. When I last dined with the major on the 10th of this month, he recalled several different, witty epitaphs, which he had collected in England, in Latin and English, in prose and verse. As well, he led a philosophical discourse concerning clear conscience and joyful death. Who would then have thought that, of all those gathered at the table, indeed in the entire land, he would be the first to exchange time for eternity. He did not think he would die, but he fought with death for almost two days, and he did not die easily.

Major Horton was only forty-two years old and his premature death was greatly mourned by all who knew him. He resolved to support Ebenezer's best intentions in London as best he could. He planned to travel there at the beginning of April. He admonished me several times to remind him in writing of many things because he wanted to repeat everything in our favor. He wanted to meet the court chaplain Mr. Ziegenhagen, whom he holds in high esteem; and he wanted me to help arrange a meeting between the two of them. It was to have been to our advantage. Therefore, on the twelfth of this month I wrote to our worthy court chaplain and sent him a copy of the restrictions on slavery that were prepared here. But now I have to write again to tell him that death has disrupted the major's plans. My moral in this stands in Psalms 146: 3–6.

The 29th of January. This year we have had continually the kind of weather which is to be expected in winter. The wind blows mostly from the west and east and occasionally from the north. It is mostly dry and cool during the day and cold and chilly, but bearable, during the night. It appears that our merciful God wants to give us a fruitful year. The water in the river is not too high and not too low. Therefore, all our mills are running at full capacity and as desired, bringing profit to our inhabitants as well as to those of Purysburg, Savannah, and Frederica.

From Pennsylvania we have received the news that last fall's crops were very damaged, and almost ruined, by excessive rain. Therefore, the price of wheat flour which is sent from there and New York to our colony and Carolina has risen greatly; one hundred pounds costs us twenty-six shillings Sterling, and we aren't even able to get enough to fill our needs. Our nice Indian cornmeal is now in great demand, and that is a blessing for us. Not even the poorest among us lack bread and other healthy foods, which perhaps others in the land do not have. A good amount is being exported from here. Our miraculous God, who afflicted

us with work and suffering after our fall from grace, has visited
us with good measure; however, He gives us much edification,
comfort, and blessing from His words and providence, so that
we are sincerely content with His merciful guidance. We praise
him publicly and privately for the many spiritual and physical
advantages He has given us.

Especially on Sunday does God let His kindness become great
by letting us consider His holy word in great quietude, in unity
of spirit, and in great edification in our two comfortable houses
of worship; and He has also shown noticeable blessing in our
common prayer and song. The devotion and edification are fur-
thered by the fact that all our dear members are supplied with
Bibles and hymnals. We are waiting with longing for the crates
of books and medicines from Halle, in which there are some
Bibles and hymnbooks, which we need for the grown children,
of whom some have graduated from school. May our dear God
awaken one or another benefactor, who will help us procure a
good number of Bibles and Halle hymnbooks.

Sunday, the 30th of January. Glaner, a righteous Israelite, has
been seriously ill. But God blessed the use of medication for his
recovery, for which he is very thankful to Him, even though he
had wished to die. He also told me of the many physical kind-
nesses shown him by God on both healthy and sick days in his
own home. In addition, he recalled the speech of his deceased
wife, in which she heartily mourned those who have passed on
previously. He was told by our herdsman that a short time ago an
Englishman from Pennsylvania came on horseback with wife
and children to our cowpen dreadfully in need of food and
clothing and then proceeded to Savannah.

This same man was at our mill last week and told us that Pennsylvania is overrun with people and that there is a food shortage.
He thought the people of this colony were better off than they.
We are not in need of anything except loyal servants, whom God
will bestow upon us in His time. Since then a well-to-do German
from Savannah, whose son and cousin left their service in this
colony to go to Pennsylvania with the permission of his master,
inquired into the conditions there with regard to both religious

and economic matters. He brought back a bad report. This discouraged those vacillating about moving there. In the past, it was always described as a true paradise.[10]

Tuesday, the 31st of January. Praise be to God for having helped bring another month to its conclusion. The pious Mrs. Riedelsberger, who went out today for the first time after her serious illness, said "Blessed be the Lord, who daily loadeth us with benefits, and the God of our salvation." Many of us can now say that. There are many among the men and women who have been dangerously sick this month with side-stitches and fever; God has helped so much that all seem to be out of peril now. This time, too, He has blessed the sickness so that His word has awakened their hearts, melted away evil, and brought forth a new resolution to live for the Lord alone. Today we had nice weather, as agreeable as usual in the spring. We could not have foreseen this from yesterday because it rained heavily for an hour, accompanied by a violent storm wind, which continued through the night. Yesterday, shortly before evening, we saw from the northeast to the northwest a rainbow, twice as beautiful as any I have ever seen. God remember us and bless us.

FEBRUARY

Wednesday, the 1st of February. The widow /Ursula/ Meyer, a Swiss, moved a short time ago with her daughter /Magdelena/ to a plantation below the mill, which her son-in-law bought from the wicked Michael R. /Rieser/, who moved away a year ago. The young man, also Swiss, is working for an Englishman in Mount Pleasant and is applying the money he earns to build this plantation. The daughter and mother are putting a lot of effort into raising cattle and planting crops. I saw their industriousness and good arrangements, but I fear they will lose more than they will gain because the husband, who is often not there, does not understand field work and husbandry and because the day laborers demand too great a wage, as is normal for this area. It is a quarter greater than the value of their work.

There is no easier way for a man to get into debt than to have to use day laborers on his plantation for building fences, cultivating, plowing, and other field and house chores because the wages are much too high. That is the reason why we don't have fields or plantations or even a productive garden.[1] Otherwise my colleague, like me, would be inclined to experiment with this and that thing, both necessary and curious, and to help our friends with the resulting experience. It is otherwise excellent and fruitful land. A man who has a little knowledge, industriousness, and experience could probably raise almost everything he plants.

I heard once from an intelligent English doctor that everything grows in this climate that grows in the West Indies. European plants grow better here than in the West Indies. The only resource missing is people. The Swiss woman mentioned above was sick, and she and her daughter were glad that I came to visit them and prayed and talked to them of God's word. What especially pleased me about the elderly mother is that she pitied and took in—for a small amount of money—the poor child of a soldier, whose mother died between Savannah and Ebenezer and whose father brought it here to be baptized.

Thursday, the 2nd of February. It is a pleasure for me to hold the edification hours on the few plantations along Ebenezer Creek; and I expect great use from this for eternity. Two men had things to attend to in the forest and could therefore not attend the lesson. Shortly before evening they told me they regretted this and promised not to let this hinder them in the future. I am preaching to them the same things we have heard in the prayer meetings and weekly sermons from the Old Testament, and now from the exemplary and instructive story of King Solomon.

Lechner,[2] the locksmith, was formerly an indolent man in mind and body and unknowledgeable in divine truths; but, since his serious and lengthy illness, he has become an entirely different man through the grace of God. He is resolved to save his soul; he shows great desire for God's word and complains bitterly that because of his weakness he is unable to retain as much as he would like. Despite his poor ability to read, he practices to learn the verses of the exordium which he often repeats when he sees me. He also experiences many difficult temptations[3] which lead him to prayer, from which he sometimes receives relief; however, sometimes he is praying to an iron wall. He said among other things: "When I am working alone in the forest, I often fall on my knees and complain to God of my hardship; sometimes afterwards my heart is relieved. When someone is working with me, however, I am too embarrassed."

Saturday, the 4th of February. Strong storm winds and cold temperatures followed the extraordinarily large and beautiful rainbow of the thirty-first. It seems we are getting one winter after another this year. This has kept the plum and peach blossoms from flowering as usual; otherwise, they would have been damaged by such weather as we have now.

Sunday, the 5th of February. Through the mercy of the Lord, this Esto mihi Sunday has been a blessed day. He has sent our souls much edification and happiness through the teaching of the cross and the ministration of Holy Communion, in which sixty-three people participated. We dealt with the regular gospel of the great blessing of the meritorious passion and death of Christ not only in the morning; we also dealt with it in the afternoon. My colleague began a contemplation of the Passion story from the gospel of St. Mark. This time is always very important and noteworthy; and we ask our true and exalted Holy Redeemer to preserve the pleasant stillness and send us many blessings for eternity from the story of all stories, from His passion and death and also from the edifying passion hymns.

Tuesday, the 7th of February. Last night the recently mentioned soldier's child, who was taken in to be raised by the widow Meyer, died and was buried this afternoon as is our custom in accordance with the wishes of the father. This time many members of our congregation are afflicted by a kind of chest disorder and side stitches, which also afflict the children. Our dear Lord has heard our pleading and blessed the diligence of Mr. Thilo and Mr. Meyer so that all appear to be recovering. May He make them, and all of us, thankful for the extended period of grace. It is no small blessing (this I often point out to our inhabitants) that we have two ministers, two school masters, two doctors, and two churches as well as complete freedom in religious and secular affairs, nourishment for body and soul in sickness and in health, and support from near and far in every possible way. How bad off are others in America in regard to the ministry, means of grace, doctors, and medicines. As a result, not a few people are demoralized in spiritual or secular matters, or they demoralize themselves!

Wednesday, the 8th of February. I have heard from Halle that the conferences held in the blessed orphanage, which began and ended with heartfelt prayer, were a blessed means of uniting in brotherhood and encouragement to a wise and loyal administration of the respective offices and stations, where also many misunderstandings were prevented. Therefore, we found it necessary, after the appointment of Mr. Meyer as justice of the peace and superior in Ebenezer, to start a like conference to be held weekly by Mr. Lemke, me, and Mr. Meyer. We beseech the Lord to bless this new arrangement and grant us the Holy Spirit to pray for our congregation, our authorities, and our benefactors and take measures to enrich the spiritual and physical well-being of our dear inhabitants. Amen, so let it be.

I had sent a knowledgeable and Christian-thinking Reformed man[4] the *Penitence Prayers* by the late Dr. Johann Schmid of Strassburg; and today he wrote me among other things this answer:

> Mr. Schmid is a very good writer but not quite as good as the late Professor Franke and Pastor Schubart, whom I esteem more than gold. Because I did not yet have the sermons of his which I have just received, I would—with heartfelt gratitude—like to keep them. If you could spare some more, I would like to pay for them, like all works of this very edifying preacher. More than two years have passed since I wrote to Hamburg about the works of Schubart. I also requested Francke's repentance sermons, and Freylinghausen's epistolary sermons; but, as yet I have received no answer.

Friday, the 10th of February. Our friend, Mr. Habersham, told me that Mr. Whitefield's wife has become seriously ill. He is very worried about her recovery. She is a godly and understanding woman who has a great love for the children and servants of

God. It was reported from Savannah that the body of Major Horton was exhumed and reburied by the new, not yet completed church in town. Doubtless people wished to do more honor to the already deteriorating body rather than let it decompose in a common church yard.

Mr. Habersham sent me a letter from a merchant from Port Royal who would like to buy a quantity of lumber from us at a fairly low price; and another captain in Savannah, who travels to the West Indies, is doing the same. As they are cut now, our boards are not known outside of Savannah and Purysburg; yet those who know them prefer them to the best boards sawn in Carolina and say they are so valuable they should be sent to England. They are not only composed of the best heartwood, they also have the most accurate as well as the cleanest cuts. They probably know in Savannah, however, that we have no one to take care of the sales for the boards. That's why they offer us the lowest price possible. If the boards became well known in Charleston, it would be easy for us in these peaceful times to get a merchant who would send new wares for lumber and other wood products.

The last two years of the flour and butter trade have brought great profit to Riedelsberger and the others who participated (almost the entire town). And what a fine profit our flour mills have enjoyed from it! We lend him our boat for a small interest charge for upkeep. He can take to Savannah in one trip at least 2400 pounds of flour, in addition to butter and live calves. Sometimes he brings back a cargo for his own small business or corn to mill for the inhabitants of Savannah. We usually have several thousand feet of lumber stored in Savannah and, when these are sold, we send more down. By doing this, those who operate the rafts easily and without danger are able to earn a lot. Because they must carry the boards up the steep sandy bluff at Savannah, which is very difficult work, the lumber is more expensive. The sawmill brings our poor people the most income.

Monday, the 13th of February. Our mills are special evidence of God's fatherly care over our congregation. Through them they are able to grind their grain, to sell some of their flour, and to earn a good bit of money at the mill. The sawmill requires a miller, an apprentice, and servant, two carters with two wagons and four horses, two men to cut the long logs in the forest, and some men to put the lumber into rafts and take them to Savannah. Also one occasionally needs men at the saw mill to stack the lumber and other wood products and to clean up. And how often something breaks or is lacking in such large waterworks, by which something can always be earned. Thank God, who until now has bestowed on us the means to give our people the opportunity to earn a living and give them cash for their work, which contributes greatly to their support and establishment.

We leaders of the congregation must pay cash for wood, wheat, meat, and other necessities, i. e. whatever we need in our household and for our livestock. We also have our houses repaired for cash because our poor people have not been well off enough yet to do something for nothing. God has bestowed on us some funds from our benefactors in Europe, so that we are able to acquire all the necessities that congregations are accustomed to contribute and to distribute the money among the members of the congregation. Otherwise, our salaries would not be enough. Our desire to improve our community, even in worldly goods, is so great that we like to spend our total wealth to further them, if we only had as much money as our desire is great.

Tuesday, the 14th of February. Today after the catechism class at the plantation, I had planned to go visit Mr. Brandner's oldest daughter,[5] who has become seriously ill with side stitches. I was, however, overjoyed to see her coming unexpectedly to school, even though she was still a little weak. With the other school children and her, I encouraged myself to praise God, who does great things everywhere, for the great and the small, both in body and in spirit. She is a fine, Christian, and diligent little girl, who serves her frail parents in many ways. She was born in Old Ebenezer and is, along with Kalcher's oldest daughter and Johann Martin Rheinländer (an orphan), one of the remaining children who were born there. What a goodly number of young people we would have if all, or only half, were still living. They were sent early to heaven and are better taken care of there than here.

Wednesday the 15th of February. At midday there arose a strong thunderstorm with much rain, which passed quickly. The wind came initially from the southeast; but, as it rained, it changed direction to the exact opposite, the northwest. At noon after the rain, the wind shifted its direction back and forth. Then more rain followed and another thunderstorm with lightning.

Friday the 17th of February. The old widow N.N. is losing a lot of strength now that she is already in her sixties. I advised her earnestly many times today to prepare for a blessed death through the grace of God more intensely by praying seriously and contemplating the divine word in order to be able to say as did the devout Simeon: "Lord, now dost thou let thy servant..." But beforehand one must truly be a servant of the Lord and in peace. To be sure, she acknowledges her mistakes and spiritual frailty, but I do not detect the care and dedication to reject these through the power of Christ. She lets herself be disquieted greatly by her own willfulness, is impatient about trifles, and does not take reprimands with love. She is attached to her two youngest children with too much love and causes herself much useless unrest. Among other things, I told her about the wish of Christ through Paul, Romans 16: 20.

Saturday, the 18th of February. Young N. has recovered from his serious sickness, and I instructed him and his wife through the word of God how best to use this new blessing of God's and the new period of grace in the most Christian way. He considers his repentance during the sickness to have been sincere. It will be shown in his life whether it is true. Many times I related to him the verse: "Behold thou art made whole: sin no more, lest a worse thing come unto thee." I have more hope for his wife than for him, that she will become a righteous person. Until now he has been like the son that said to his father: "Yes Lord," but did not go.

It has been almost a year since a German man named Straube from Vernonburg moved here with his wife and six small children.[6] They have established themselves here rather well during this time even though they arrived here with almost no food and clothing for the children. I didn't have a good feeling about these people, yet I helped them get shelter as best I could, and God blessed everything to their spiritual and physical benefit. They thank God warmly for His merciful guidance; they love His word, Holy Communion, public worship, and all good institutions. They also appreciate the advantages, spiritual and physical, in Ebenezer after experiencing the misery and tribulations of their previous home. We are hopeful that their children will turn out well.

Sunday, the 19th of February. In just a few days the Savannah River rose unexpectedly so high that it flowed over its banks and stopped the mills. We had never before noticed such a sudden rise in the river. It cannot be entirely a result of the last rainfall but also the result of the heavy rainfall we had eight to ten days ago as well as the melting of the snow.[7] The river also had the color of melted snow. Germans from Vernonburg came to our mill with a great amount of corn, but they were forced to leave it with us and return home without flour. We were sorry about that. I gave them a few books. A short while ago, before the water rose over the banks and by the mills, two Salzburgers took five thousand feet of lumber to Savannah. Last evening they returned safely. A knowledgeable merchant wrote me the following about our lumber: "the lumber brought down is overall as good as any I have ever seen." If only our inhabitants would reduce their daily wage in the mills somewhat so they could be sold more cheaply, we would get a crowd of buyers. We will see what we can do with them with admonitions.

Monday, the 20th of February. Last night we again had an unexpected sudden, passing thunderstorm with rain. We are having warm, spring weather. The peach trees are in full bloom and the blossoms of the white mulberry trees are also already bursting forth. From a man from Purysburg I heard that they have had a lot of rain in their region every week. Here the rain has been sparser. Nevertheless, the European crops such as corn, rye, barley, and peas are already standing so beautiful in the fields that we could not wish for anything better.

Tuesday, the 21st of February. While working in the house, the righteous widow Zant was suddenly overcome with a severe fever. For a long time she was out of her mind and unable to see and hear. Today to my joy I found her a little better, and I hope God allows her to remain with us and her two dear, gentle children a little longer. She belongs to the wise virgins who prepared well for the arrival of the Bridegroom. Her heart is full of recognition of divine blessings and praise of God's name. In her little room I felt at home during the discussions and prayer with her and her children. The merciful Lord let me feel especially His merciful presence and led me to a newer, stronger awakening.

Wednesday, the 22nd of February. With the return of our boat, Mr. Meyer received the news that the President of the Council and his Assistants are planning a large assembly at the end of the week. We have waited a long time for this. It was necessary for Mr. Meyer, as the representative of our community, to travel there already this evening to present the Council a few important matters about which I have written in a letter. We ask 1: that careful plans be made to exterminate the wild cattle near our cowpen as soon as possible according to the Trustees' urgent orders before greater harm comes to our poor people. When our domesticated cattle come in contact with the wild cattle, as often happens, we consider them as good as lost.

2: We have heard that a man from Carolina, or Virginia, has bought land in Abercorn and the surrounding region and would like to bring in a lot of cattle; this would obviously harm our poor people and other inhabitants of the region. Therefore, we ask the gentlemen to prevent this harmful matter according to their wisdom and power.

3: Not long before his death, Major Horton was helping us to get the entire stretch of land between Abercorn and Mount Pleasant at Palachocolas and from our settlement to the Ogeechee River. At the time and at my request, he obtained it at the Council assembly. Because he died, however, and we never received an actual assurance, I am now asking that we be able to occupy gradually part of the aforementioned with our older inhabitants, who are settled too closely together because of the lack of good land on this side of Abercorn Creek, and that we be able to inform our patrons and friends about this large and beautiful

district that belongs to Ebenezer. Perhaps it would be pleasing
for other Christian compatriots to move here and live with our
congregation separated from other people in the country.

This district is to a certain extent the heart of the colony because it lies between Carolina, Savannah, and the plantations on
the other side of the Ogeechee river. Those coming from Augusta or Carolina by land to Savannah or Frederica have to make
their way through this district of ours, not to mention that we
have desirable communication by water on all sides. If this district is given to us, we can prevent the slave owners from settling
in this region with their cattle. They have ruined the land and
pastures in other places; and they would do it here also. The
Uchee Indians, who have barely thirty men left in their tribe,
have not yet yielded a large section of this land because the gentlemen here, unmindful of the Trustees' express order, have
made no effort. Therefore, we ask that this be quickly remedied.

4: A young man from the last German servants[8] has honestly
served his time and would like to settle in our village, but he
heard from his brothers that because of the the councilmen I
would exclude him from all benefactions that are given to others
at the command of the Lord Trustees. I assure the leaders in my
letter that we gladly submit ourselves to their will and decree,
even regarding the settlement of our village. Therefore, we are
requesting that they advise us of their wish. The aforementioned young man would rather renounce all the Trustees' and
Councilmen's benefits than leave Ebenezer. God has drawn him
to Him here.

5: We would like to know whether the inhabitants may spin
their silk for the Trustees or whether they must send it to Savannah. Likewise, whether they would receive their payment
shortly after the delivery of the silk to encourage their industriousness and the continuation of their economy.[9] I have gotten
into such a fix in the last years that I had to borrow money with
bills of exchange to placate those who gave me the money in advance to pay for the silk for the Trustees. I would not get myself
into such a complicated situation again, but I fear that the production of silk will come to a standstill if the people are not paid
promptly.

6: Our people suffer for want of shelter when they go to Savannah. Their health suffers especially when it is cold because they cannot afford to stay at an inn. Firewood and warm places to stay are rare and expensive in Savannah. Therefore, we have resolved to build a firm, well protected hut with a kitchen on the bank of the Savannah River near Savannah, if the council will grant us a convenient place where we can easily land. I requested this in my letter. We could probably get an old house in Savannah, but it is cumbersome to carry the oars and supplies a long distance from the boat. Besides this, rents and weekly rates are demanded from the houses, which come to thirty shillings Sterling yearly. It is also more difficult to get wood the further one is from the landing.

We would bring the wood from Ebenezer. We will not be able to deliver the seven thousand feet of lumber which is being urgently requested by a captain because the river is too high and has overrun its banks. Presently there are five thousand feet of lumber sitting in Savannah, which cannot be sold cheaply because they were carried with great effort up the sandy bluff. On the other hand, the amount desired should be delivered into a ship lying before Savannah. If we had a convenient and secure wharf to store our lumber in Savannah, we would be able to serve the wishes of the captain and our own mills as well.

Monday, the 27th of February. On the 24th I went to Savannah in an official capacity to preach to the Germans and administer Holy Communion. In doing so, I felt God's assistance strongly. They came diligently on Friday and Saturday to the assembly to hear the words of preparation and they listened just as attentively to the word of the Lord which was preached to them three times on Sunday. May it grow roots below and bear fruit above.

MARCH

Wednesday, the 1st of March. The pious widow Bacher is often afflicted by God with sicknesses, which she counts among the Lord's many great blessings and for which she praises him childlike and humbly. She desires anxiously to be at home with the

Lord, yet she does not hold this sickness from which she has begun to improve to be the last. Her heart is full of peace, comfort,
and heavenly refreshment, which has taken over the old, fearful
person she once was. Among the married women here, she is a
very useful and almost indispensable person. We would have
many reasons to thank God if He let her remain with us a little
longer. Our wondrous God visits her younger daughter in her
marriage with physical afflictions, which are medicine for her
soul. My conversation and prayer with her made a great impression because her spirit was already prepared for the cross.

A good friend from Charleston wrote me among other things
that the measles are raging and that many people have died.
People are worried about a rebellion of the Negroes, which he
described in the following manner: "There was a great excite-
ment here because of a feared rebellion by the slaves, but I spec-
ulate that everything will be put to rest." This friend does not
think much of the conditions and restrictions on the introduction of Negroes, which have been made by and are under the
direction of the deceased Major Horton, because he knows from
experience how badly the people in this colony have kept the
decrees of the Trustees and the laws in Carolina which concern
the Negroes. Those who should enforce and uphold these laws
have a great number of Negroes themselves and transgress these
laws in any way that promotes their self-interests. He added that,
even if the aforementioned restrictions, limitations, and decrees
of the Trustees are upheld in the future better than before, he
cannot understand how poor white workers would benefit,
which one could call *bonum positivum*. If we could really hope that
something good could come of these restrictions on slaves, it
would only be a *bonum negativum* for the poor Protestant
workers. It would help them if the Trustees would find some
privileges and immunities for the poor people who support
themselves without Negroes.

Thursday, the 2nd of March. It has rained a lot for three days
in a row; and, because of this, the water has risen in the river and
into some settlements in the country. Last night a strong wind
arose which continued through the next day and eventually settled in the west. After this, the weather cleared and became cool.

The white mulberry trees are now starting to sprout leaves, and our inhabitants are getting ready to make silk. The silkworms are hatching without difficulty from the seeds or small eggs if one exposes the box or cloth to warm air. We have tried to delay the hatching of the eggs as long as possible because in this month we still tend to get severe frosts, which harm the delicate mulberry leaves (the only healthy food for the worms).

Completely unexpectedly the widow Bacher was afflicted by a new paroxysm of her sickness so violently that she herself as well as her family thought it would result in her departure from this world. Our dear God looked mercifully upon our pleading, and right noticeably blessed the medicine, especially the essentia dulcis. For this she, along with us, earnestly and humbly praised His sweet goodness. Her soul was full of impassioned desire for her Savior, and the powerful verse: "Who is he that condemneth? It is Christ that died"[1] was more precious than the most precious of life's ointments. We sang for her the beautiful song *Liebster Jesu in den Tagen dieser Niedrigkeit* from which God sent her edification and renewed strength.

Friday, the 3rd of March. Mr. Meyer received a good opportunity to travel with Christian people from our place to Charleston to solicit a merchant who might let us have the necessary supplies at a low price for our boards. For this purpose he took along also a sample of our boards, which are also valuable in the eyes of those who envy us, to send to England. Even though this opportunity came completely unexpectedly, I wrote a letter hurriedly to our dear friend, the court chaplain Ziegenhagen, and sent him our journals from the middle of January to the end of February so that our dear Fathers and friends may know how we are spiritually and physically. We are hoping for the crate from Halle and Augsburg and also for letters which we would answer immediately.

Sunday, the 5th of March. Yesterday in the late evening there was a lot of lightning in the west even though the sky was clear and full of stars. During the night a very strong wind arose which remained strong today. It was so cold that we anticipated frost or hoarfrost. We were pleased by this physical benefaction in no small way. The leaves on the mulberry trees and the vege-

tables in the garden are very delicate and would have been
ruined by the frost, to the detriment of the silk production and
the poor people. It appears as if this year we will have a lot of
mulberry leaves and from them a good harvest for the poor and
the sick. They view successfully produced silk as their harvest.

Monday, the 6th of March. Some of the soldiers who were in
our village previously came in a large boat from Frederica to pay
cash for corn, flour, meat, and other groceries they could get.
They also brought used clothing to sell to the people at a pass-
ably low price. If they are successful this time, as I hope, they will
return many times, which I view as a good beginning to a long-
desired, small commerce; and I am pleased with God's merciful
guidance. Our gristmills are also to be seen as an earthly jewel
amidst the desert not only because they entice many strangers
from this and the neighboring colony with its fruits but also because it provides a means for turning our grain crops advan-
tageously to money. And along with the flour, which is often sent
to Savannah, also other things for sale can be sent in the same
boat at the same cost.

If we did not have a mill, it would be difficult for our inhabitants to sell their Indian corn because the same corn is brought
from Carolina and Augusta to Savannah for sale. Because the
flour sells well, corn is bought with cash from the house, taken to
the mill, and shipped to Savannah and farther down to Frederica. From this the mills as well as the people on the boats
make a good profit. The man who sells the flour and other
things pays for the use of the boats so they can be repaired and
kept in good condition. In Europe they do not make as big a deal
of the mills as we rightly do with our two courses, the rice
stamps, and the sawmill. They are gifts of God and a blessed
means to let our people subsist more easily. Many here and in
other places would give up their planting and farming and fall
into an anxious way of life if they could not make their European and Indian corn into flour easily. Without mills, wheat and
rye would more or less disappear.

Wednesday, the 8th of March. The pious widow /Maria/ Lemmenhofer still lives in the house of her deceased husband /Veit/

alone without children or anyone else around her. She would rather suffer with her housekeeping and this and that hardship than exchange her isolation for comfort. She receives some support to ease her economic situation, as do other widows from the benefactions which God lets come from Europe for the needy members of the congregation. It is well spent on her. She is a good housekeeper, she is still not that old and she would still be a good help meet in marriage, yet she prefers to live alone. Following the example of her pious husband and his pious sister, Mrs. /Gertraut/ Glaner, she is preparing for a blessed death. She let me read to her a letter again, which was written many years ago by the aforementioned Mrs. Glaner from Memmingen (at that time Gertraud Lemmenhof) to her deceased brother. From this God also bestowed a blessing on me. Just such a blessing happended to me today in a very edifying and congenial letter, which Mr. Michaelis wrote to me from the office of the esteemed court chaplain Ziegenhagen at the end of 1741. What a wonderful letter to read again. May the Lord annoint him with His spirit and make him a blessing for his church.

Thursday, the 9th of March. Today, which according to the old style is the spring equinox,[2] we had a lot of rain again and a strong wind during the night. The weather is very beneficial and the European crops are beginning to come forth, whose growth was stifled by the long hard winter. Because they have not been able to grow high, they have been less damaged by the severe frosts. The deer and hares have done a lot of damage especially now and again to the European peas. Also, in the well-protected herb garden we would have been able to keep only little, were we not able to catch them[3] with a certain, easily constructed machine. The hares are smaller than those in Europe and do not taste as good.

Friday, the 10th of March. A year ago the pious Ruprecht Steiner's wife became seriously ill. Even though an herbal remedy helped her a little, the cause of the disease was not eradicated. As a result she looks more dead than alive. She has three children and a difficult household to maintain and cannot take her medicine as she should. Therefore, it is no wonder that it has not taken effect. She is an honest woman, who lives in poverty of spirit and longs for her Savior.

Saturday, the 11th of March. A young, pious housewife told me, praise God, that her husband has recently begun to straighten up. However, one thing still hurts her greatly: from Germany he brought the bad habit, which he occasionally gives in to, of going away from his family and being with others, where he spends his precious time talking about unnecessary temporal things. I directed her to faithful and continuous prayer. God, who has already answered many of her prayers, can also grant her that which she would like changed in her husband. I also offered her and her husband alike, who usually likes to read, some edifying books. There are a few others among us who have the same bad habit of getting together evenings to talk extensively about such useless things. In doing this, they neglect the diligent practice of home worship. For a long time I have wished to have enough copies of the *Glaucha House-Church Order* so that I could give the father of every household a copy.[4] We have some copies of this little book in the congregation, which we justly deem as valuable.

Sunday, the 12th of March. It has again rained consecutively for several days and has intermittently stormed a lot. During the night, the wind changed from the south to the west, bringing us a severe storm and cold dry weather. We have not let ourselves be kept from public worship of God's word, prayer, and song either on this Sunday Judica or on days past by the cold weather, which our loyal God blessed for our preparation for eternal life and tomorrow's day of remembrance and thanksgiving.[5] To date, during the evening prayer meetings and weekend sermons, we have contemplated in sequence the edifying and mysterious subject matter of the Old Testament's public religious celebrations and Solomon's zeal in worshiping God. This has fit well into our intentions and present situation.

Monday, the 13th of March. Fifteen years ago, after we had survived a dangerous and troubled journey, God brought us to this colony and Old Ebenezer, where we lived as pilgrims and strangers for two years in great isolation, not without troubles, for the salvation of our souls. Two years later, our dear God directed the hearts of the Trustees and Mr. Oglethorpe to let us move from this inconvenient and barren place to a better place, namely the present place of our pilgrimage, where our merciful Father in heaven has shown us immeasurable goodness in spiritual and physical ways. Therefore, it is meet and right for us to celebrate every year at this time a festival of remembrance and thanks, to the glory of God and the edification of adults and children, as we again did today in peace, health, and good weather. After the prayer and the reading of a chapter in the Bible, we sang again at the beginning of the service the beautiful song written around the 107th Psalm and our situation: *Auf, Ebenezer! werde heut zu Gottes Lob erwecket.* The texts from which I preached this morning and afternoon were taken from The Book of Psalms 22: 4–6 and John 10: 27–30.

Wednesday, the 15th of March. Paul Müller's wife recently spoke to me in passing and asked me if I would not visit her and her family on the family's plantation. I had the time today for this, and the opportunity. To be sure, her husband had to do some necessary work in the fields, but with her and her children I was able to talk about that which served to instruct and edify them. After I reminded the child of the verses to be learned in the ABC Primer, she brought her catechism and asked me to listen to her repeat the first two sections by heart. This I did willingly, and I received edification myself from her edified recitation. The dear Lord has made the sick and very dear and helpful Mrs. Bacher well again so that she was able to celebrate the festival of remembrance and thanks. This meant a lot to her. She is now occupied with putting her house spiritually and physically in order as dictated by God's will and word because she suspects she will not live long and soon will die. It is easy to get along with her. She has a very honest, God-devoted nature, which is why everyone finds her dear and worthy.

Friday, the 17th of March. Our soldiers heard from those who were at our mill that it is time for the day of the Irish patron saint, which they celebrate in Frederica in a bacchanalian fashion.[6] They let themselves be induced to drink more rum and brandy than is permitted within the limits of moderation, even though they forced themselves not to make excessive shouting for fear that I would find out about it. However, I did find out about this disorderly conduct; and I spoke about it with the corporal, who promised not to let anything of the like happen again, in default of which I would write to their captain in Augusta. They like being in our settlement and do not want to give occasion for me to complain about them. I have lent them some good English books, from which the corporal should read them something.

The widow Graniwetter had the opportunity to marry here, but decided not to, for which she had good cause. She is content to be a widow, and she knows how to cite many refreshing examples of God the Father's care for her and her two small children. On her plantation she plants all kinds of produce as well as cotton and flax; she buys wool and makes clothing for herself and her family. With God's blessing she is able to get along easily. In Germany spinning and knitting were her profession, in which she is very skilled. For our widows and weak people, making silk is an easy and profitable activity this year since they collected more mulberry leaves than in previous years. I heard complaints that the silkworm eggs are not hatching and will not produce new worms. They do not know the cause of this. I do not know where to get help, unless perhaps such a thing can be got in Purysburg for money. This is a trial for our good people. A year ago they had enough worms but not enough leaves because the trees were either frozen to death or damaged.

Saturday, the 18th of March. Two well-mannered youths among us, who no longer have any parents, let themselves be persuaded to engage themselves to the Trustees' harmful cowpen in Old Ebenezer for six months in order to earn some good money quickly. Because this service was coupled with apparent danger for the soul and Christianity and more is to be lost than gained, I advised them against this change and made other better suggestions. It appears they will remain here. For young people this country is very dangerous because there is great freedom, and the inducement to sin and vanity is manifold. Most craftsmen one finds in Europe are of no value here. Youths are taken in by the false freedom so that they are not able to endure the many consecutive years with a master needed to learn something useful. Therefore, it so happens that we are in need of many necessary tradesmen. And, because these young fellows do not like to do field work and farming, they grasp at all sorts of means for earning their clothes and living. Those kinds of work with the least amount of effort and the highest pay are the most dangerous in this country.

Sunday, the 19th of March. In both the Jerusalem Church and the Zion Church the Passion of Christ will be contemplated mornings and afternoons and repeated catechistically. In this activity Christ lets us feel His support and blessing generously, for which we humbly praise Him in the congregation and at home. After such instruction, he who still has a callous, unbelieving heart and still continues his sinful life, for which Christ atoned so dearly, hardens himself more and more and makes himself more incapable of repentence and faith. Unfortunately, we are not devoid of such people, whom we tolerate and view with pity.

Monday, the 20th of March. Our merciful God has allowed me to know through many people that yesterday's proclamation of Christ's disgrace and suffering in and outside of Jerusalem was a holy blessing to many people for their souls. One told me as he was working that he was among the soldiers (because something was mentioned about Christ's atonement for society and for the sins of soldiers) and had sinned greatly. He has it now in mind "Ye must be born again." His wife is working on him according to her recognition, which he recognizes as a blessing.

Tuesday, the 21st of March. Yesterday evening during the prayer hour, two Germans came up from Savannah to fetch one of us ministers to baptize two children and to marry a young couple. Even though we would rather be spared from travel because this is the week to prepare for the last supper and the Easter celebration, we were not able to refuse the wishes of these people or postpone the trip. So, my dear colleague went down there with them this morning because I had business to do with some disorderly people, who had registered for Holy Communion, and other necessary business. One serves everyone in the country with one's office, with good books, and in other ways when opportune or inopportune, even if one does not notice much success. This should not tire us of doing good because there is still time.

With these men I received the written plenipotentiary power from Council in Savannah to exterminate the wild cattle. No other people have permission to do this except those who have lost cattle and have cattle in the same regions where there are wild cattle. The hides must be sent to Savannah, or to a justice of the peace, to determine whether wild or tame cattle have been shot. If by accident it happens that a branded cow is shot (because many tame and wild oxen and cows joined the wild ones some years ago), the owner must be compensated. The meat of the slaughtered animal can be used as our people wish. As it was this spring with our silk, in whose production our inhabitants are very diligent, it should be decided if our women will be paid promptly, no matter whether they spin it here, or whether the cocoons must be brought to Savannah. The gentlemen wish to give no answer, rather there is deep silence. In a letter sent to Savannah I asked Mr. Meyer to speak with the president and clear this matter up after his return from Charleston.

Wednesday, the 22nd of March. During the holidays the locksmith S. /Schrempf/ came from Carolina again to hear God's word and take Holy Communion. He is very serious about spending time with his own kind in our settlement. It would be a great act of God's grace were he able to be with those of his confession and compatriots again. We would like to take him in. The other two people, H. /Held/ and B. /Bishop/, who had also moved to Carolina, have asked through S. in a letter to be taken in by our congregation. They will be content with the very least after comparing the advantages here and having sufficiently witnessed what advantages Ebenezer has for spirit and body. It is a special divine dispensation that these three families became aware of the great detriment caused by their moving away. This made a deep impression on those who had a mind to move away because of other's lightmindedness and ingratitude, and it both shamed and strengthened them.

Thursday, the 23rd of March. Mr. Meyer returned yesterday before evening from Charleston and was unable to find a merchant for the benefit of the sawmill. I hope that the trip was not entirely for nothing. At least it was useful in letting us find out the price of boards in Charleston, and enabling us to price ours accordingly in Savannah.

Friday, the 24th of March. Today we celebrated Good Friday, the greatest day of reconciliation in the New Testament. We were edified greatly by the important and marvelous story of the death and burial of our mediator Christ through God's grace. We also held Holy Communion for sixty-six people, of whom five were of our confession in Carolina. Yesterday we had a half holiday because the usual sermon for Holy Communion, along with its preparation and the confession, was preached then. A man who needs to come around seriously to God missed this sermon unwittingly to work in the woods. He regretted it sincerely though, with tears in his eyes. It would have been easier for him to lose the money he earned that week than to sin by missing the sermon and confession by working at an inopportune time. I tried to comfort his downcast soul.

Sunday, the 25th of March. God has ended Lent in quietude and with His blessing. He did not allow Satan to enter and inflict trouble upon us internally or externally. I was informed about two couples who were living in discord. This caused some neighbors and kinsman to be offended and saddened. However, today this has been resolved, for which I praise God. A pious, sickly woman told me, to the praise of God, that she received a beautiful treasure during Passion week from the sermons, hymns, and readings of her husband. She thinks she will probably die soon; and she is looking forward to it more than to a regal life of pleasure. She has two still unreared children; she is not worried about them though. Another woman came depressed to me and could barely talk because she was crying so. God recently reawakened her again during a prayer hour, and touched on her own conscience during the sermon on good and bad consciences. She complained bitterly about the callousness in her heart, which would not become softer through either prayer or tears. I advised her to endure with God's word and prayer and warned her against being unfaithful to the seeking mercy of God. I also gave her the verse: "Truly God is good to Israel, even to such as are of clean heart."[7]

Monday, the 27th of March. Yesterday and today we celebrated Easter in good health, in good weather, in peace, and to
the edification of our souls. In prayer we often presented the
proclaimed word to our living Savior and hope by His goodness
that He let us see some fruits in this period of grace.

Tuesday, the 28th of March. In more than fourteen days it has
not rained. To be sure, it looked like rain today and a few times
before, but the rain clouds gradually dispersed. The earth is
very dry. Because the water has been too high on the river, the
sawmill has been unable to cut wood for a few weeks. Today,
however, it was working again. Mr. Lemke received the Carolina
newspapers from a good friend in Charleston, in one of which
for the current month we found this month's prices for boards
which are sold to the ships headed to the West Indies. It is usually said that the boards in Carolina are cheaper than those
which can be bought from our mills, but from this newspaper as
well as from previous ones it seems to be the other way around.
Our congregation would profit greatly if we were able to get
such a good price for our boards, which according to knowledgeable people are better because of the quality of the wood
and the cut. We are only lacking a clever, willing man from our
congregation to strike up trade. It would improve conditions
here in many ways. They know in Savannah that we do not know
what to do with our boards. Therefore, they pay for them only as
much as they want.
they want.

Wednesday, the 29th of March. God blessed me today with
heartfelt joy with the children at the plantation school as I filled
in for the schoolmaster. This I would like to do more often if my
office, and the time set aside for other duties, would permit it.
As I came back from the school and other business, I found a
saddened woman waiting for me whose conscience had been
wounded by the arrow of the Lord Jesus and who found herself
burdened by her many sins. She said that she had no rest day
and night and could not get any comfort from God's word. In
her eyes, her ingratitude toward God and Christ, who had loved
her unto death, was great and frightening. I gave her instruction, and I promised to visit her diligently. She and her family

have been at our place about a year, and she has proven diligent with God's word and prayer. She appreciates greatly the good which God shows in our settlement.

This afternoon three male children were baptized in Jerusalem Church. One of them belonged to Balthasar Bacher, whose wife gave birth last night. The other two belonged to an Englishman who was traveling upriver to Savannah Town, and later on to North Carolina with his wife and a Negro boy. One of the children was one year old and the other was two and a half. After the only preacher in North Carolina died, an honest man who travelled around the country like Mr. Whitefield, the state was left without a preacher or someone to care for their salvation. While traveling to the new territory on the Ogeechee River, he would have liked to have his children baptized. But he did not meet up with any preachers.

Because he does not like the land on the Ogeechee, where for years many have settled from Carolina and Virginia, he is moving back, despite the cost and difficulty to North Carolina, where he has better land and pastures. Supplies were in abundance there because almost everything grew one could desire. It was only problematic that one was not able to turn produce and work readily into money because the ships only come as far as Virginia. The inhabitants of North Carolina had to be happy when the gentlemen from Virginia bought their produce and goods. He told me that the people around Frederica and on the new plantations and on the Ogeechee River almost starved because of a great lack of food and because they could get neither Indian corn, nor flour, bread nor meat for money. The land and the pastures were good, but they were lacking a pine forest. As a result they had few summer pastures because the cattle will eat the cane, which comprises great portions of the surrounding areas, only out of necessity. He liked our region and the diligence of our inhabitants a lot. May God let us acknowledge the exemplary spiritual and physical advantages we enjoy here, which one can recognize through God's dispensation and the example of this man and his believable tale (because similar conditions were known before).

I was amazed when, a few weeks ago, a boat from Frederica

came to the mill and bought one hundred bushels of corn and had some ground. I did not know that the shortage in those areas was so great. Also, one cannot find much in Carolina because the last ships took so much away. Our pine forest has been scorned by some ignorant people among us as well as other places. What a great blessing it is to us has become evident over a period of time. When it has been plowed and fertilized in the third year, the earth produces not only agricultural crops and healthy trees but it also provides the horses and cattle with pleasant grass during the summer, and beautiful, straight-growing, long timber from which we can cut boards, other wood for building purposes, and masts for ships.

We admonished our people, on the advice given us by Mr. N.N. and General Oglethorpe, to spare as much construction wood and other useful wood as possible because the wood they find no use for now will surely be used by those who follow. In Charleston they would hardly believe that all the boards were cut from the same beautiful pine as the sample of wood we sent. It has very delicate annual rings or veins and is very durable. If enough people were here, we could make turpentine from the rich trees in the pine forest; and from the resinous pinewood and the old trees lying around we could make pitch and tar.

Friday, the 31st of March. After waiting for such a long time, our dear God blessed us with a wonderfully fruitful rain accompanied by some large, but sparse, hail. It thundered a lot as it rained, and we received the first thunderstorm of the spring. The European crops, the wheat, rye, barley, and peas needed the moisture urgently; also we hope it will promote the growth of the leaves on the mulberry trees, which have not filled out and made such a good appearance as they did two years ago. These trees were damaged a year ago by the late frost and they have still not been able to recover. Some of the trees' growth has been stunted. Today we had a strong westerly wind that is drying things out. Our people have noticed that, during this season, when the silkworms are being raised, a kind of black worm similar to the caterpillars are eating away a great portion of the young corn, cabbage, lettuce, cotton etc. With the silkworms these will also take their end.

APRIL

Saturday, the 1st of April. N.N. seems to have injured his lung by getting overheated and then cooling off too quickly, from which he has become seriously ill. He has a righteous wife; but even in healthy days he, to be sure, was a diligent reader of the Bible and a good churchgoer but at the same time a very indolent Christian. Now God has awakened him, and he has proven himself to be devoted and interested in the things which I told him and in the things we prayed today.

Sunday, the 2nd of April. Yesterday evening I received a nice and edifying letter from Pastor Brunnholtz in Philadelphia, in which he wrote many good things about God's servants, that they are not only healthy but also are working with His blessing and are standing as one with the Lord. The two former catechists, Mr. Schaum and Mr. Kurtz, who were recently ordained as ministers, are taking their positions seriously. Dear Mr. Handschuh is still clearing up the confusion in Lancaster, in which the Herrenhüter have made all kinds of dissensions. He is still able to do some good, even if he had not imagined so many difficulties. Some distinguished merchants have not only realized the necessity of a true conversion to God's word with increased conviction, they are also starting, more so than previously, to reconcile themselves to the order of grace. Mr. Vigera resides with Mr. Brunnholtz now and is teaching school to a fairly large number of pupils. He also wrote me a few lines, from which I recognize his poverty of spirit and the fruit of the office and example set by Pastor Brunnholtz. He sent us spelt as seeds, which never arrived.

Monday, the 3rd of April. Yesterday after the midday service a man from our congregation came to me with his wife. In previous days and on Saturday during the night she has been restless because her conscience has been awakened. She spends her time in crying and prayer but refrained from going to the public service because she did not want her profuse crying to burden anyone. If her husband had not persuaded her to attend the midday service, she would not have attended this service either. I prayed with both of them and admonished them to use God's word and prayer diligently. I also consoled her with the gospel. She was then able to recognize the friendly heart of the Lord Jesus toward his crying, suffering disciples in the exordium verses of John 14:19, as well as the catechismal repetition, and the sermon was about the gospel for that time, Quasimodo Sunday, which was contemplated this morning and afternoon.[1]

Wednesday, the 5th of April. What we were unable to secure from the President and the Council in Savannah in regard to getting a convenient place for us to ship or sell our lumber and other products on the bluff near Savannah, our friend Mr. Habersham was able to secure for himself. He is allowed to build such a facility on the bank near Savannah at a convenient location. He writes me that he will construct the building large enough so that there is enough room for our people to store their boards and woodwork securely. He will order a ship from London in less than a year with all sorts of wares to bring him trade with the Indian merchants (which one calls Indian Trade in English and which has been done solely by the people of Charleston), which also is easy to start up if he gets cheap products first hand. We will be able to have our beautiful boards ready for loading, if not to England, then certainly to the West Indies.

It will be a great advantage to the entire northwest region of this colony when we get shipping trade in Savannah because the inhabitants will be able to bring and sell their products, even if they are just small things such as garden produce and edibles. If one did not know what trading in this country can earn when done cleverly, prudently, and happily, one could learn this by the example set by the two young business partners Habersham and Harris. A few years ago they had nothing of their own but began with borrowed money. Now they have not only built a great deal and respectably, they can also order their own ship from London. On one of the ships now in Savannah they are loading ten thousand feet of lumber from our sawmill and shingles which are made in Savannah.

This I see as a grave mistake and the main reason why it is not easy to populate this colony with whites, because the merchants sell their wares at too high a price and demand the greatest profit at once. On the other hand, they pay the whites as little as possible for their work. Because there are few whites and many jobs in the country, the daily wage is high. The merchants, however, add more to the price of the wares and are not affected by the high wages. On the other hand, those who are not merchants and need labor feel the high wages all the more and are not able to hold their own very long.

Thursday, the 6th of April. Yesterday and the night before it rained, and since then it has become very cold as if it were late fall again. This wet weather came with the new moon; therefore, it is assumed that we will get a lot of rain this month. Our inhabitants' silkworms have developed for the most part to where they will start spinning their cocoons and making their silk. And, because they eat more at this time in one day than in the entire first four weeks, this wet weather, although normally fruitful, is very inconvenient for the gathering of leaves, which should be given the worms dry, with as little moisture as possible. Those who have many worms hardly know what they should do.

As far as I see and hear, the production of silk is not only very useful but also easy and pleasant if the people have enough white mulberry trees near by and have clean, spacious chambers or rooms. It is not as demanding or nerve-racking or burdensome a process as is claimed in some books and written reports we have received. If at the time when they are still dormant and have shed their brown skins it rains a few days, or if it is too hot the day and night before they spin their cocoons, they cause a lot of trouble and often die. It also appears as if they cannot take severe thunderstorms.

Because I know that some of our worthy patrons and friends are served by news about our external and physical circumstances, I have had no reservation thus far to incorporate the same in our journal as they come up. What appears to be superfluous and minimal to one person is perhaps not so to another man.

Friday, the 7th of April. Young Meyer's wife /Elizabeth/ is very joyous that our dear Lord has freed her and her husband from the temptation to leave Ebenezer and has bestowed on her, since he has moved into town, the great benefaction of the daily evening prayer meeting. She boasted that she received blessing and edification from the 17th chapter of St. John. To maintain and promote this edification, I lent her the explanation of the High Priest's prayer to Christ, which was written by the same Pastor Freylinghausen.[2]

Saturday, the 8th of April. The widow Ursula Meyer has become seriously ill, of which I learned only today. For her sake I traveled to her plantation, which is a good distance; and I found that God blessed this illness because of her atonement and strict adherence to Christianity. This brought her tears of joy, and she was greatly pleased by my encouragement and prayer. She received much edification and spiritual use from the biography of a pious child. Among us she is a very helpful woman, serving the people in the congregation in many different ways.

The assumption that we would have a lot of wet weather with the changing of the moon had no foundation. Yesterday the rain tapered off; and yesterday and today we have had dry, pleasant weather. Only in the evenings is it cold, but it is bearable and healthy. Since the new moon the wind has been blowing from the northwest. The silkworms' growth has been hindered in cold rooms.

Sunday, the 9th of April. In one of his previous letters to me, a pious German man from Carolina asked to have either the late Professor Francke's *Penitential Sermons* or Pastor Freylinghausen's *Epistle Sermons* for his neighbor's and his own edification.[3] Because I promised to lend him the *Penitential Sermons* for a while, his latest letter evidences his great pleasure and uses the following expressions:

> If God is willing and I am still alive, I would like to send it back
> as quickly as possible with thanks; but I fear it may not happen
> so quickly. Because I cannot bring it upon myself to read such
> an edifying piece of literature just for my own sake, I would
> like to read it aloud in public, may it please the Almighty.

I had lent him the *Penitential Sermons* of Dr. Johann Schmid,[4] the theologian from Strassburg, which he has returned with the following comment:

> I have often found that the erudite Pastors are not always the most edifying preachers. They are so rich in explications of the Holy Scripture that the best is given the least space (I think application is the soul of the sermon). I love sermons which strongly penetrate one's innermost Christianity so that almost the entire sermon is almost like application, or at least a great part of it. It is more important for a sinner who is desirous of being healed to hear edifying teachings and applications rather than extensive explanations, the different opinions of the scholars, and quotations from the original texts.

Monday, the 10th of April. The diligent and pious widow Graniwetter has been seized every year by spiritiual confusion and depression. Once again she is in this condition. The cause was her servant boy, who ran away yesterday with his two brothers to Carolina during divine services. She greatly needed him to take care of household matters, and up until now has always served her well. That is why the news of his unexpectedly running away affected her deeply. These three boys served among us in good places and with Christian people.[5] The parents, who have long been freed from the Trustees' servitude in Savannah, are moving, as did the runaway oldest son, to Carolina. They instigated, for certain, the running away of their children. The majority of the German servants are unscrupulous people who are ungrateful for the goodness they enjoy from this land and from our office. Even though, as is to be expected, Mrs. Graniwetter's spirit is still in disorder, she still works industriously and fairly well, while quoting pure, edifying things, among which sometimes there are silly, absurd questions.

Tuesday, the 11th of April. Three days ago we sent an urgent message to Savannah with a letter to the President, Colonel Stephens. In it was asked in the name of the inhabitants to permit the spinning of silk on the two machines given us by the Trustees. Mr. Meyer and I have obligated ourselves to have everything under our supervision so that the silk bought by the

Trustees will not be damaged in any way. Today we finally received permission from the Council, which will please our people, who would otherwise have had to send their cocoons down to Savannah with expense and difficulty and probably with loss and consequent diminution of their industry. Now it is not as it was a few years ago when the boats left empty for Savannah when they could easily have taken the silk along. Now they are loaded with wheat and other things to sell in Savannah or Frederica. Therefore, every week around this time, express boats must be rented, as the silk is gradually completed, to send the silk. Thanks to God, who has granted us this wish.

Friday, the 14th of April. I received word from Savannah that General Oglethorpe's regiment was disbanded and that only three companies were kept on, partially in Frederica and partially in Charleston. On the other hand, the soldiers in Charleston should be dismissed. Therefore, the garrison in our village will also be terminated. The soldiers would probably like to stay with us; however, they do not serve us very well because they are not as orderly as the last soldiers were. With the death of Major Horton, those who support slavery have lost a large part of their hope and comfort. And now they have also lost the comfort of the hope that Oglethorpe's troops would prevent their slaves from going over to the Spaniards. Only one company will remain in Frederica; the other two will go to Carolina. These soldiers will probably not prevent it if the blacks want, as they do in Carolina, to go to Augusta[6] or want to run over to the French.

Sunday, the 16th of April. The wife of the German who moved up here from Vernonburg a year ago[7] is taking her conversion very seriously. And she likes it when I visit her on her plantation regularly, instruct her in God's word, and pray with her. God has already drawn her to Him, as she tells me, through the work of my deceased colleague /Gronau/ in Savannah. And even though He continued His act of merciful work thereafter, a true conversion never took place. Now she is serious about it. She uses the means of salvation and a good opportunity for illumination and conversion, on both Sundays and weekdays, diligently and with benefit. She sees it as a special benefaction of God that she has come here to God's word and ministry because others in this land must do without this. She has six small, well-mannered and industrious children, yet some are sickly and the oldest daughter is somewhat weakminded.

Monday, the 17th of April. A rich and well-known planter near Charleston heard from someone that we have a costly eye lotion, namely *essentia dulcis ad oculos*.[8] He hoped to use this on his eyes, which have been blind for two years. Therefore, he let the captain at Palachocolas ask me for a small vial. Because he has now regained the use of one eye by using this medication, he sent a slave on horse via Palachocolas to me with the request that I provide him once again with this eye lotion. This I could not do for certain reasons. I have already written recently and again pointed out that there are a doctor and a surgeon in our settlement, two skilled and careful men, to whom he should go regarding his illness.

Tuesday, the 18th of April. Yesterday afternoon we had a heavy rain accompanied by a thunderstorm with lightning and hail which lasted late into the night, longer than is usual for this time of year. The hailstones we have had thus far are occasionally large, but widely scattered, and do little damage. Heavy cloudbursts flatten the long grains more than the hail. In summer we usually have many thunderstorms and short rains which end when the thunderstorms pass. This morning it was cold after the rain. The weather this spring has been fertile, for which we hear Christians praise and thank God. The damage which has been caused to the Indian corn by caterpillar-like worms is tolerable. Also field mice have damaged sweet potatoes and seed corn in the ground on some plantations.

After our people were granted permission to wind their silk, they have been very busy preparing the silk machine's old masonry.[9] The second machine, which I had manufactured like the model we received from London, was set up in the same kitchen next to a beautiful copper boiler in order to help facilitate the spinning of the silk. Yesterday afternoon Mr. Meyer's first bit of silk was weighed, and with it we made a start at silk spinning. The young women are gaining great proficiency in spinning silk; and, because of their great diligence in this useful and important activity, they deserve more encouragement than they have received thus far. The reward which the Trustees ordered for them is not yet paid. It will probably be the case with the current silk.

Thursday, the 20th of April. Some of our residents have business to take care of for a few days at our communal cowpen; and they brought back the news that on the evening of the 17th during the heavy rain and thunderstorms, there was hail almost the size of chicken eggs. Some of the cattle which were hit received large contusions on their hides. We thank God that our fields have been missed by such a hail storm; otherwise, the rye, wheat, and barley would look sad. Most of the rye finished blooming, and the wheat is beginning to produce ears. Since then it has been so cold both by day and by night the likes of which have not been felt since the end of February. The wind comes one moment from the northeast, and the next it blows from the east southeast. A knowledgeable mathematician,[10] who prepares calendars, imparted to me the following observations about the weather in this country.

> Concerning the weather in general, the sky is usually clear, especially in summer. In fall, spring, and winter it vacilates quickly between warm and cold. Consequently in spring, summer, and fall, but rarely in winter, there are fairly strong thunderstorms; yet they are no stronger than those in Canton Appenzel in Switzerland, where I lived. Hail storms are rare, and in the last twelve years in this region I have not experienced one yet that has caused great damage, though I have heard about the large hail stones which have fallen in this country.

> The winds are inconsistent in this country, not only in their direction but also in their strength and weakness. For example, it may blow more or less strongly for an hour and shortly thereafter it is calm again. When the west wind blows, it is mostly clear and nice, but in winter cold. The south- and northeast winds are almost the same, but these winds are unable to sustain good weather for long. If we have bad weather and the wind changes to the west, the weather will clear. The windier it is, the less rain can be expected. And if a wind arises while it is raining, the rain's duration is shortened. When it rains, it is usually very heavy but it never lasts long except in winter when it can rain for more than a day so that the water of the main

river rises so high that it overflows the banks and greatly harms the cattle and horses which feed both in summer and winter in the low lands next to the river.

Seldom do we have snow, and even more rarely does the snow remain on the ground longer than twenty-four hours. Up in the mountains where the Savannah River originates, there is a lot of snow and when it melts it causes high water and flooding. My plantation lies on the Savannah River one hundred hours away from the sea. About three hours upstream is a waterfall caused by high cliffs, and boats can only go this far. From this point the Savannah River goes up for another one hundred hours inland. Last winter was the coldest that I have experienced in this country. It seldom happens that the earth remains frozen for an entire day where the sun shines on it.

Friday, the 21st of April. The woman who was unsettled and fearful a while ago because of her sins and requested my consolation and help through prayer told me today along the way how much mercy the Lord showed her last Monday. He assured her heart of His forgiving her sins and He sent her a genuine emotional spiritual peace. Her fear and unrest increased anew on Sunday after the evening prayer meeting and stayed with her through the night. She and her family continually sought the heart and countenance of God in Christ, our mediator, which she finally found to the great joy of her heart. Our dear Lord especially blessed her in her fear with the 3rd chapter of Zephaniah.

Saturday, the 22nd of April. Our dear God has afflicted the pious and diligent Brandner with physical frailty for a long time. To be sure, he is not bedridden; but his strength has been so reduced that he can barely manage his work and the difficult housekeeping.[11] In the congregation he is a helpful and useful man, who is well established on his plantation near Zion Church. He takes medication, but it has had little or no effect as of yet. Some illnesses appear wondrous and are perhaps not as usual in Europe. Regarding this, a doctor would have a good opportunity to reflect, do experiments, and in the interest of sound medical advice, start corresponding and discussing with other experienced men, if not in America, then in Europe.

Sunday, the 23rd of April. Yesterday late in the evening I received a friendly letter dated November of last year from Mr. Whitefield in London. He took it badly that I had sent him a long letter to London three years ago discussing the harmfulness of the slave import, defending the actions of the Trustees, and refuting his arguments in favor of importing slaves.[12] He also adds that it is forgiven and forgotten. He is still of the opinion that Georgia cannot develop without Negroes; and he said that, right while writing the letter, he had heard that slaves were allowed in Georgia. I was not happy to hear this and neither were the Salzburgers. It would have been better to hear that the Trustees with God's help had been able to make it possible to settle this country with white Protestant people, for it lies between the Spanish and the three colonies of South Carolina, North Carolina, and Virginia which are full of slaves.

Tuesday, the 25th of April. Yesterday it rained mildly several times; and in the evening a severe thunderstorm arose with heavy rains, which, however, only lasted a few hours into the evening. The wind changed direction from the southeast to the exact opposite northwest; notwithstanding this, it became very hot around noon. The weather is very beneficial; and the European crops such as the wheat, rye, and barley are growing well. They are already sprouting ears on which kernels are starting to form. The wheat has the appearance again as if the stalks wish to turn brown, as it happened a few years ago to the detriment of our people. We must commend this to God, who does nothing without reason. Some attribute this harmful rust to the heavy night dew and the ensuing heat during the day; but others attribute it to the short, light rains, after which the sun shines strongly after the clouds disperse. Still others believe the nearby swamps or low lying rice paddies and the harmful fog cause it. This malady seldom strikes all the fields and only a few districts. Our good people are often tested in many ways and have difficult moments with their farming. They often need to be called out to from God's word: "Cast not away therefore your confidence, which hath great recompence of reward."

Wednesday, the 26th of April. Last week during a certain rather difficult task at which a number of men had to be present a certain disorderliness took place which had to be investigated and settled today by Mr. Meyer, the justiciary.[13] I was present but only to give this judicial investigation and settlement greater esteem and to promote with my warnings and admonitions both true confession and Christian cautiousness and to encourage them to realize the men's behavior towards their superiors and each other and finally to pour out my heart to God alongside them. As far as I can tell at present everything went well. Hopefully this investigation will make a good impression on the future behavior and cautiousness of the men, who run riot when given the opportunity or when they come together. I do not doubt that, in this way, all the bitterness against me will be prevented, if the justiciary treats the issue in accordance with his secular offices; while I remain within the bounds of my ecclesiastical office. The guilty will be treated less severely, and they will be easily convinced that their salvation is the purpose for observing external public order. This may also be one of the reasons why the priests and levites in the Jewish community had to run the judicial offices.

As long as the honorable, elderly Thomas Jones was the storehouse supervisor and member of the Council in this country, we enjoyed his great love and friendship. He also thought of us fondly in London after his departure. However, it has amazed me that he has not written us for such a long time, and others of his friends can hardly understand this. That notwithstanding, he is held in blessed remembrance on account of his fear of God, righteousness, and kindness towards me, my late colleague, and the congregation. From the bottom of my heart I wish him spiritual and physical well-being. Just as I used to write him occasionally and give him news about our circumstances, I began again today to write in order to renew our mutual remembrance and friendship. His speeches and conversations were always so edifying and impressive that I shall never forget this dear man. It makes heaven attractive to think that it is the general gathering place of all God's children and that nothing there can disturb their joy and their blessed communion.

Thursday, the 27th of April. It was not pleasant news for our soldiers that General Oglethorpe's regiment was disbanded and that not more than a single company will be left in this colony. They must prepare themselves to move away from here at any minute. They would have liked to stay here, and therefore they have bought land and planted several acres with Indian corn, squash, and melons, and set up an orderly household. Now they are busy getting buyers for that which they have cultivated and plowed so that they may be able to get some benefit from their efforts. Soldier's wives are usually of the worst kind; however, it must be that the English women are better, or there is another reason that they have shown themselves respectable among us and hard-working. They all show me much love and would not do anything that could cause me sadness or unrest. We had to let them have their days of celebration, such as St. George's Day, St. Patrick's Day, and St. David's Day, which were celebrated without excess.

The widow Graniwetter, who was recently in a confused state of mind, is feeling better today. But she feels strongly the difficulties of her husbandry because her servant /Lorentz Richard/ ran away, a happy child of thirteen who was well taken care of and very useful to her.

Friday, the 28th of April. Shortly before the weekly sermon on the plantations, five honorable Salzburgers came to me, namely Leimberger, Ruprecht Steiner, Matthias Brandner, Simon Reuter, and Thomas Gschwandl and expressed with words and gestures their worry, sadness, and apprehension about the arrival of news that the Lord Trustees have finally been persuaded to approve the introduction and use of Negroes. They testified together that they have only now begun to regret having moved to this faraway land and believed that their brothers in Prussia were happier than they are, even though they live next to a popish land,[14] for they do not have to live among thieving and cunning Negro heathens but among whites. They feared the introduction of slaves would cost them not only their grazing pastures, physical subsistance, and temporal possessions but also the well-being of their children, whose salvation is more important than all physical advantages.

Where Negroes take over,[15] there is an increase in the repression of the poor, the difficulty of earning a living, the insecurity of the belongings in the homes and the produce in their fields; and there is an increase of vexations and the shameful mixing of blacks and whites, not to mention the danger of the French, Spanish, and Indians. If they knew of a place within the King's territory which had a provision against the introduction of slaves, and they were allowed to move there without opposition, and if they were given some help toward their new and difficult beginning, they would not hesitate for the sake of their children and other important reasons to emigrate again rather than live among Negroes. If they had been told this in Germany, no one could have persuaded them to move here. Should the Salzburgers' worthy benefactors know what the Negro problem is in this country, they would not hold this worry and resolution against them.

If nothing else could be done to protect them, I would like to request that the Lord Trustees grant our congregation the entire stretch of land from Abercorn to Mount Pleasant and from Ebenezer to the Ogeechee River and not allow any slave owners to settle in this district for fear of openly damaging people, cattle, and crops. They could not buy any Negro slaves and they could not treat them in the way that necessity and convention appear to require because of their lazy, thieving, rebellious manner. If others in their neighborhood had Negro slaves, then they too would go to ruin and see their children and possessions placed in danger. This is not solely their opinion but also the opinion and the will of many of their brethren in the congregation.

It would be a great favor to them if I were to report their request, which they would gladly sign, to Senior Urlsberger and the Trustees. In answer I told them that I believe their complaint and worry are well founded, also that I had tried to present as clearly as possible to the Trustees, Fathers, and benefactors the great harm which poor whites would suffer through the introduction of slaves. I said not only that little had been done but that I had also incurred the wrath of many people in this land and perhaps in England because the young Stephens and the merchant, Robert Williams, who now resides at Port Royal, blamed me before Parliament that I am turning the inhabitants against using black slaves and I had my evil purpose in this. I do not want to get myself more involved. Therefore, I said, I have given the task of representing their wishes to the justiciary Meyer and my colleague, both of whom realize, discover, and oppose the harmfulness of the Negroes as well as I. They will write a petition in the name of the Salzburgers on the basis of the aforementioned matter. I have promised to make known their aversion against using Negroes and the reasons for this to our kindly and sympathetic Court Chaplain Ziegenhagen, which is accomplished with this entry.

I must praise the goodness of God, who has given me ample time and strength so far to catechize the children in the school on the plantations with the beautiful booklet printed in Wernigerode *The Dogma of Penitence and the Forgiveness of Sins,* which we finished today.[16] I was especially aiming at the adults, who should be preparing to take Holy Communion. Yet even the little children were able to understand something of it for their own edification. May our merciful God give His gracious prosperity to that which has been sown and nurtured until now, so that all our beloved children may become and conduct themselves as the possibility and necessity was convincingly presented to them from this book and God's word. I am now planing to make this *Catechism* the basis of our catechizing despite its being preached by my colleague Lemke in church as a catechism for the congregation.

I hear and see with joy that the production of silk in our settlement has happily gotten under way, even though the mulberry trees have not completely recovered from the severe, late frost a year ago and fewer than usual leaves have come forth. Mr. Meyer has already weighed more than four hundred and fifty pounds of silk produced by our own inhabitants, and there is still a good quantity expected. Three young women, along with some helpers who run the machines, spin the silk with such agility and accuracy that one is unable to watch without being amazed and joyful. In the last two years they have brought this to perfection. I hope that the Lord Trustees will not let me suffer deep sorrow for having encouraged these industrious and skillful people to this work in their name and having them receive no compensation for it. The ten pounds Sterling given two of these women a year ago by the Lord Trustees have still not been paid.

MAY

Monday, the 1st of May. At the end of last month my office required me to travel to Savannah to preach the gospel to the German people of both confessions and to administer Holy Communion to our co-religionists.[1] From this I returned toward noon happy and healthy. To be sure, I was sick when I went down there; but, as I worked, our dear Lord gave me special strength and bestowed upon me great joy and comfort through His word and the pious behavior of my congregation. On Saturday, the 29th of April, to my surprise, I was unexpectedly handed a friendly letter from General Oglethorpe from which I could still richly recognize his continuing love and concern for our congregation. He was displeased the Regiment posted for the protection of Frederica and other towns was disbanded.

Tuesday, the 2nd of May. Yesterday during the night it thundered loudly but it did not rain. Yet this afternoon it thundered, lightninged, and rained as hard as it has ever done so in the past. At the same time there were very high winds, and we are worried that the heavy rain will beat down the long wheat and rye. Some of the barley is ripe and is being harvested, and such is the case also with some peas. It is a great pleasure for me to watch the industriousness of our people, which God has crowned with His prosperity. If they only had a little more help. For example, if every one had an honest servant or maid, how much good they would accomplish and how little they would complain about the intense heat. Today it was exceptionally hot, however, later we had a thunderstorm which cooled things off. These changes often come about during the heat of summer. Now that the days are beginning to turn hot and there is much work in the fields, the production of silk is at an end. One harvest occurs after the other: in fall turnips, squash, Indian corn, beans and rice; in the spring, silk; in May, barley and peas; and soon thereafter, rye and wheat and simultaneously peaches, which God will give us this year in great quantities.

Here in this country there is not only excellent fruit to eat (or fruits, since there are many different kinds); one can also distill brandy for which purpose some residents have made stills. They want to support themselves in every way possible. What I wonder about the most is this: that in this colony so few attempts have been made to plant vineyards. It must be good for growing wine because grapes grow wild on dry as well as the wet soil. The wild grapes are so sweet and good tasting that one must marvel. A Portuguese Jew, who seems to be a swindler, made a good start a few years ago planting a vineyard at the Trustee's expense. However, he ran away, and then everything was destroyed. After that, Germans and Swiss have planted vineyards. Because they planted them, cut them, and did other things as in Germany, nothing came of it.

I had neither the people nor the money to continue my vineyard, and I also had to let it die. One cannot even get workers for money, and daily wages are so high that one cannot experiment or even flirt with the idea. The planting of vineyards here has been just like building mills: some did not have the money to continue the building already started, and others were ruined by later construction workers because the workers here are very uncertain.

A Swiss near Savannah recently requested me to help him get some mill stones because he wants to build a mill. If the good people only knew, not only what the construction but also the upkeep of a mill costs they would not let themselves get so deep into debt that there is no way out. First of all, it is impossible in this flat, low land to have the mill run the whole year round. Sometimes there is so little water in the river that it hardly flows, and we also get high tide and low tide, but much more so near Savannah and Purysburg. Secondly, there are too few inhabitants and consequently not enough to grind. Few put much stock in the European seeds, whose growth is uncertain; and the slave owners let their Negroes crush, pick, and grind as much corn as they need on their iron and stone mills. Their staple food is crushed or broken corn, rice, and potatoes. When the German grains are gathered and threshed, we have the most work for our mills; at other times, however, they are inactive. The planned change in Frederica, the dismissal of the regiment, is also detrimental to our people because they will now have less opportunity to sell their corn and flour. Our beautiful sawmill is starting to make money, which is helping maintain the other mills. We are content if this preserves there two things; namely that our residents are able to earn money from it and that they will be able to keep the mills in order from their earnings.

Wednesday, the 3rd of May. The wife of our town's schoolmaster is an honest soul who carries the cross for her Savior, willingly and in many honorable ways. Today she complained to me that she has been plagued with difficult temptations and that many times while working and in prayer terrible, sinful ideas pierce her heart like arrows. This causes her to fear and cower because she has earned God's wrath and hell. Nothing could have been more beneficial for her than to be delivered from this suffering by a holy death, which would also rid her completely of these temptations.

A short while ago, God sent her such joy through the gospel in the Holy Spirit that it was indescribable how well she felt; now she is unable to explain in words the suffering she feels internally to anyone. Still our heavenly Father treats her very mercifully in that He comforts and inspires her with gospel verses, some of which she recited for me. I prayed with her, instructed her in God's word, and directed her to chapters 52 and 53 in Johannes Arnd's *True Christianity*.[2] She is also physically weak and can barely manage her work. It is a merciful work of God that her husband, who is also too weak for field work, receives a salary as schoolmaster.

This evening before the prayer meeting we received two packets with letters from Europe, from which we were able to praise God and strengthen our faith. May He be praised heartily for preserving the life and health of the Fathers, benefactors, and friends of His church as well as our well-being, and for strengthening their faltering health. May he also be praised that the hearts of the Lord Trustees continue to be mercifully inclined toward us, as has been mercifully shown in a letter from the Secretary, Mr. Martyn, as well as toward the esteemed court chaplain Mr. Ziegenhagen, who promises to do the best for us in every way possible, even if Negroes are imported.

We are hopeful about the loyal servants requested a while ago. It appears that in Germany there is no shortage of those who would allow themselves to be sent to us here under good conditions. If they are honorable and cheerful, they will not regret this. From a catalogue of an esteemed friend, Mr. Albinus, I see that two of our packets, one from February and one from June of 1748, were lost at sea. I checked and the loss is bearable. It concerns only the short journals of those months mentioned and the copies of some letters sent previously, which happily have already arrived. What was written us by our friends and Fathers has always arrived.

Thursday, the 4th of May. Today we celebrated the ascension of Christ. On this day our dear God has sent us great goodness through His word and through prayer. During the evening prayer meeting we praised our heavenly Father in the name of Jesus Christ for the spiritual and physical benefactions which He has shown us so generously so far and again recently through the letters we received. We requested God's rich blessing for the esteemed Fathers and benefactors in return for their love and beneficence.

The visit and comfort of a woman, who was mightily awakened by our dear God through the Holy Ghost to earnestly achieve her salvation, was a great blessing to me. God disclosed the spiritual enemies, which until now have done so much harm; and, because she did not treat honestly the great mercy she received in the past, about which she was deeply saddened and feared that he may abandon her as a lost soul and show her no more mercy, which is why she greatly lamented the condition of her soul. She has a great love of God's word and work and diligently practices her prayer.

Friday, the 5th of May. Since the 2nd of this month we have had cool weather and a lot of rain. Especially yesterday before sundown, it rained harder than it usually does into the night. The strength of the downpour has let up, but not the rain. A light wind arose around noon and lasted until evening.

Through all the rain there were no thunderstorms. The crops on the wet low land may suffer damage, if not prevented by our wondrous and kindly God. Most people find the low land good and choose it, if they can, for their plantations. Based on experience, however, I am not of this opinion. The high land, although not as rich, yields very well if one fertilizes or improves it in the third year. And even if the year is wet or dry, the harvest is not affected.

Saturday, the 6th of May. Last evening and last night it rained considerably after which the wind changed to the west, bringing us clear, dry weather again. Our soldiers have their orders now to go to Frederica on the boat from Augusta. One of the soldiers had settled separately on a piece of land near the town because he was willing to lead an orderly, withdrawn, and diligent life. He also asked me to help him get permission to take land after they are discharged. He likes our people, our way of life, and our arrangements. His neighbors have liked him as well. I told him he should consider well that he will have to adopt our way of life. If that is his intention I would promote his cause rather than hinder it. There is no doubt that he will get his discharge and permission to settle among us because the Secretary of the Lord Trustees has written me that those soldiers who want to acquire land and farm it will receive five pounds Sterling as an encouragement as well as provisions for a year.

Two men from the Council in Savannah have orders to be present when the soldiers are discharged to provide as many as are willing to remain in the country under the aforementioned condition. The King and the Lord Trustees intend not only to give these people an orderly way of life and through this to direct their livelihood but also, in their scheme of things, to settle this colony with whites.

Monday, the 8th of May. Certain things regarding the best interests of our congregation require Mr. Meyer and me to travel to Savannah. I also intend to recover my strength because I have felt weak these past few days. The weather is good for traveling because it is dry and cool. The Europeans would not imagine it to be as cool and fresh as we are experiencing it this time of year —since the last heavy rain—especially in the evenings from

nine or ten o'clock to the next morning. The wind is blowing out
of the northwest. Heavy dew forms during the nights as though
it had rained. Some believe this combination of hot dew and cold
sun are the cause of the browning of the wheat, which is ruining
the wheat in the fields. At this time the rye is also suffering.

Among other news from the Lord Trustees we also heard that
our friend Mr. Habersham has become a member of the Council
in Savannah, from this we hope for good things. His intentions
are sincere and he has the best interests of our congregation at
heart. Mr. Habersham has not only great skill and experience
but also energy and courage. He will suppress his opinions to
neither his fellow councilmen nor the Lord Trustees regarding
the welfare of this country. Also it is good news to hear from the
Lord Trustees that they will not relinquish their governorship
over this colony. Instead, they were unanimous in renewing
their royal privileges. They are showing a great satisfaction at
our people's production of raw silk, and they promise to show us
all possible encouragement. What this will entail I do not know,
but I hope to find out in Savannah.

They have sent the decree to the Council that we should be
free to spin off the finished silk. This would save our residents a
lot of effort and expense, which they would have had in sending
their silk down river. If we only had allotted the diligent spinners of silk something for their efforts. I am also sad that they
did not give me the complete authority to cash enough bills of
exchange to pay for the silk already completed. The delinquent
payment is hindering their diligence.

Wednesday, the 10th of May. In Savannah I asked the President and his assistants about the boxes with the books and medical supplies, which we have been expecting for some time and
whose shipment Mr. Albinus mentions in his letter which arrived on the 27th of October. I asked the President and his assistants; but, they know nothing about it. Mr. Verelst did not ad-
dress this in the least in his letter to the Council; therefore I
assume it has been forgotten in the customs house in London,
for which we are sorry. I had them read to me what the Lord
Trustees had written to the gentlemen in Savannah. They attest

to their satisfaction at the Salzburgers' obedience to their decree concerning the production of silk.

They also desire the gentlemen of the Council not only to allow us to spin off the finished silk but also to give us support in every possible way. They would not like to limit the spin off of the silk only to Savannah or to one person; instead, they would like to make it equally beneficial to the colonists and England, as far as possible. Therefore, they would like it made known to the residents: whosoever wants to enjoy the favor of the Lord Trustees in the future should apply all possible diligence to the production of silk. There will be no lack of all possible encouragement and support.

Regarding the silk, they intend to send us in the next packet their thoughts and intentions which are along the lines that every family should have their cocoons spun here into silk by our skilled and experienced young women, which then should be sent to Savannah to be sold. Soon they would like to write to the Council the prices of the silk to the advantage of the colonists and thereby to absorb all expenses. Neither I nor the members of the Council understand this last point. We assume they would like to cover the expenses of spinning off the silk.

They agreed with my suggestion in one of my letters to Mr. Verelst, namely, that the wall on which the silk machine stands should have a chimney to lead the smoke out through the roof. Otherwise, the kitchen or place where the spinning off takes place will be full of impurities, which lowers the price of the silk on the reel. Because we noticed this mistake two years ago, last year we prepared to make arrangements to lead the smoke out a compendious chimney through the roof. And this is just the way we set up the second machine and wall this year, even though we were unable to set it up as we wished because of a lack of resources. It is the order of the Lord Trustees that such necessary things to enhance our silk production should be made at their expense both in Savannah and here.

The lack of skilled labor, especially carpenters, hinders us almost as much as a lack of cash payments. Therefore, many things must remain undone this summer, things which I wanted to have built near the mill and in the town for cash. For many reasons I do not let myself get involved with strangers. I hope it will improve in this regard when we receive servants. I forgot to mention one other thing in the letters from the Lord Trustees to the Council and to me. The most famous and most experienced silk merchant in London, Mr. Loyd had a piece of damask made from the silk prepared by us. It came out as well as could be desired in the opinion of the weavers and the merchants so that not only was our colony's silk not inferior to the Piedmont silk, which is deemed the best, but it was also judged to be preferable by a group of knowledgeable and impartial people. Because of this there is a lot of talk in London about the silk manufacture in Georgia. For the enjoyment of our friends in Germany, I would like to quote a passage from the last letter of Mr. Albinus, dated the 29th of December, last year. He writes:

> Especially in regard to Ebenezer, the Lord Trustees have given the Court Chaplain (who himself was present at one of their meetings) the solemn promise that they themselves will give special attention to this matter. The first thing they will concern themselves with is that indentured German men and women be sent. At their first meeting they will deliberate how they can be sent most cheaply and as early as possible. They shall also write Senior Urlsperger in Augsburg that in case Negroes must be imported, they will list all the conditions for Ebenezer, which you and my friends will suggest.

A very sick lying-in woman of our congregation in Savannah sent her husband to Ebenezer in a row boat, the same day I traveled to Savannah to baptize and administer a private communion. He missed me on the river, and I was in Savannah before he reached Ebenezer. God blessed my prayer and comfort of this otherwise ill-behaved woman the last time, and this time I have felt the same blessing. She herself has said that, in response to the prayer I made, our dear God blessed her in her difficult physical condition the previous time with the desired night's sleep, and now there is a noticeable remission of her sickness and an increase in her strength, for which we praised God's goodness.

Her husband is very ignorant and as a result insolent. Because I would not allow him to take Holy Communion and demanded he learn the first basic truths of the Christian Evangelical religion and offered to teach him myself in Ebenezer or Savannah and to give him the Small Catechism and Wirth's *Communion Book*.[3] But he did not come around. Instead, he helped himself through diligent reading and pitiful excuses, which his wife found not only unfounded but also vexing. I postponed the baptism until his return from Ebenezer, which happened last night. In his wife's presence, and along with the knowledgeable and evangelically minded sponsors, we talked to him sincerely and got a solemn promise from him to gradually learn the few passages in the Catechism which he had given up on, and to resign himself with heartfelt prayer to that order that is required for taking Communion in a worthy manner.

Friday, the 12th of May. The diligence of our dear inhabitants in their field work all year is so great it could not be greater. It appeared this spring as if they would be repaid with a good crop of European grains. However, it again pleased wondrous God to condemn our beautiful wheat fields with blight, through which almost our entire hope for a wheat harvest has been dashed. When one goes through the green wheat, which is still quite green, one's shoes become covered with rust as if it were scraped off old iron. In the rye one can see traces of mildew, but the harm here should be bearable. At our assemblies, our merciful God has granted us many blessings today and yesterday from the 65th Psalm, which was used last summer as the basis of the jubilee sermon in celebration of the Orphanage's jubilee day in Halle. We hope from God's goodness that He, in His time, will also visit our land graciously as expressed in this passage. His wealth and power are so great that no one is lacking.

Saturday, the 13th of May. During this evening's prayer meeting our dear God sent us a blessed preparation for the Whitsuntide, through the dear promise, Isaiah 44: 3–5 "for I will pour water on him that is thirsty." We were encouraged to new evangelical earnestness in desiring, accepting, and applying God's grace.

Sunday, Monday the 14th and 15th of May. We have celebrated Whitsuntide these last few days in physical quietude, Christian charity, and diligent use of the means of salvation; and a few people from Carolina and a young man from Abercorn turned up. The weather was very pleasant and this made the public church service all the more enjoyable for the adults and children who all like to come hither. We felt the assistance of the Holy Ghost noticeably during the preaching of God's word. We do not doubt that God will bless His Holy gospel abundantly in us as well as in our listeners and that He will hear the communal prayer in the name of Christ and for the sake of his intercession. May he continue to help us.

B. and S.[4] have written me again from Carolina and are happy that they should again be taken in as members of our congregation in our settlement. In order to further their physical and spiritual well-being, I will continue to do anything for them within my humble means. I also hope that everything is of more avail with them this time than in the past, after they learned first hand that Ebenezer has advantages over other settlements. The third man who moved with them to Carolina has already gone off further into the world and cannot be persuaded to turn back again by the pleading and remonstrance of his wife, who was raised in our orphanage.

Tuesday, the 16th of May. Today in the Zion Church there was a large assembly held by Mr. Meyer and me. At this meeting three elders and community leaders were elected to help Mr. Meyer take care of external business. First I made known to them the contents of the lovely letters from England concerning our external circumstances and their betterment, as is recorded on the 10th of this month in this daily register. I asked their opinion about the Trustees' intended new arrangements regarding the silk; namely, whether it is better for the Trustees to continue buying the cocoons for cash or to make the spinning off of silk general and to put a good price (called a bounty) on the spun silk for encouragement, and to pay a reasonable wage to the spinner. The government in Carolina pays thirty shillings Sterling for one pound of good spun off silk, upon which there is also a good bounty.

I was glad to see that the people realized it would be better to turn over the spun silk rather than the cocoons to the Trustees because in this manner a lot of loss is avoided in making the silk.

This is a way to encourage the children and women to be diligent in this endeavor and to let everyone spin off the silk. I
thought it preferable to write the Trustees soon about this before they make their intended new decree permanent and send
it to the members of the Council because then our humble re-
minders and desires might come too late. Therefore, I am asking the Lord Trustees in my current letters to give our congregation ten vats and as many machines for spinning off the silk.
Some neighbors want to team up and set up these machines in
their houses so that the women and girls can learn to spin. I also
pleaded with the Lord Trustees not to rescind or lessen the
bounty because that would depress their spirits and put an end
to the inchoate silk production, for which I also listed the causes.
Furthermore, I informed them in humble terms that three spinners have displayed uncommon diligence in their work by neglecting their own household chores and have incurred expenses with wood and by taking on help during the spinning.
They have achieved such skill in this activity that they are marveled at by knowledgeable people. Therefore, it is only equitable
that those who have broken the ice receive a just reward. I have
made them hopeful of this because the Lord Trustees promised
not to fail them in all possible encouragements.

A year ago, they granted each of the first silk spinners five
pounds Sterling; to this day the members of the Council still owe
it to them. A just compensation would make them willing to
teach other women and grown girls the art of spinning silk,
which the parents would like to see. I remember that the Lord
Trustees not only promised the deceased Italian woman[5] a respectable compensation (in addition to her yearly salary of one
hundred pounds Sterling) for her efforts in teaching other
women her art, but also fixed her salary so that she could live on
it in her old age. In this country, where the weather is hot, making silk is a hot and difficult job, by which one cannot drink just
water or eat the usual poor food. Since they have found a just
compensation for the Italian woman even though their goal was
not reached by this woman because of her amazing willfulness
and self-interest, I comfort myself and the others with the hope

that they will not leave those unrewarded by whom and through whom they have reached their goal.

II. The silk produced up until now is stored in a clean room next to my study and has been spun off on two machines in a spacious kitchen next to my house. Because my work is prevented through the commotion and because the house is often inconvenienced by the smell of the bakeovens or the smell of the dead worms in their cocoons in the heat of the sun as well as by foul water and worms discarded after the spinning off (not to mention other causes), I am asking them to have a separate house built for this purpose like the one in Savannah, which would not cost a lot. The ovens and chimneys to the vats, of which three should be set up, would cost the most, which they have already offered to give us.

III. The lack of good huts or houses which can be heated and cooled and aired out at the appropriate time has been a great hindrance to our poor people in the manufacture of silk. And, because some are not well enough off to build something special that is clear and warm and can be aired out, I have asked that the poor be given something for this, or that our congregation should be lent a sum without interest for a few years, which could be repaid year by year from the finished silk. Through this more than good advantage will be promoted in the silk manufacture in accordance with the wishes of the Lord Trustees. If our people had the resources to build with our cheap lumber houses with open rooms, many high windows and doors, and an attic of boards above and a clay floor below with an oven of tiles or clay, we could keep the delicate worms warm enough and the larger ones cool enough on hot days. This would protect them from sickness and death, save us a lot of mulch, and promote their growth.

I know from experience that people who are equipped with good rooms or chambers see their beautiful, well grown worms spinning themselves a cocoon within four weeks, which allows them to complete their work within five weeks. On the other hand, others spend about fourteen days longer. As a result, time is lost, mulch is lost , and silk is lost, which I cannot explain here.

The aforementioned houses also have the advantage of not letting the worms hatch too early as they do in fear of warm or hot weather, which penetrates the poorly built huts so easily. This way they can wait until enough leaves are on the trees. Because of the cold earth and the cold nights, the trees are not filled with leaves before the middle of April. If by this time the worms are so large that they eat in three or four days the amount they would normally consume in four weeks, then there are too few leaves, and not as much silk can be made as if they had delayed the hatching of the eggs until the middle or even past the middle of March.

It has already happened that the late frosts have frozen the young leaves on the mulberry trees. This caused the worms which hatched too early to die or else, to their harm, the worms had to be fed on salad or other unsuitable leaves. If we had a building like the one mentioned and made of our lumber, costing not more than three pounds Sterling, it would make the production of silk much easier; giving our people more and more encouragement. The worms not only reproduce at different times, depending also on age, warmth, and cold, but this is also dependent on cleanliness, which they do not have in houses where the people have their beds and take care of someone who is sick, keep their wet and dry provisions, and prepare their daily warm meals. I have gone into such detail in these matters because I want our patrons and friends to see that, if the silk production should come to a standstill, it should not be blamed on me or the poor members of the congregation.

IV. Cash money is the best and strongest inducement for the silk. They are poor and need the money immediately for their finished work just as is God's urgent decree for the good of the poor laborer. In accordance with the wish of the Lord Trustees, I have encouraged the production of silk by promising them cash payment. However, because I was unable to get this money from the Council in Savannah a year ago, I had to cash a bill of exchange, contrary to my intention, to pay the borrowed money on time. In the mean time I have let Mr. Meyer buy course linen in Savannah and other necessary things to make clothing. The

widows and other needy persons bought theirs by using an advance given for their silk. I will wait as long a I can.

Wednesday, the 17th of May. Yesterday we made new arrangements with the plantation school, which were approved by all. A
father brought his little son to me partially to request permission
to send him to school and partially to have me pray over him.
The boy repeated the verse which I assigned him recently: "The
child Samuel grew before the Lord and was pleasing to the Lord
and to men." I hope the parents on the plantations will also send
their little children to school because they do not have to give
more than six pence or a bushel of corn as a school fee every
quarter of a year. Previously they needed to contribute much
more to keep the last schoolmaster. The town schoolmaster is
paid a salary by the highly praiseworthy Society.[6]

Thursday, the 18th of May. I find it miraculous that only part
of the wheat in our fields is completely blighted whereas in other
fields the wheat is still fairly good. Indeed, in some fields
blighted and healthy wheat grow side by side. From this one can
conclude that neither the land nor the dew is to blame for the
blight, nor the fog. We have had no lack of rain this spring either. The Sicilian wheat and another variety which we got from
Purysburg are still unharmed, and from this I conclude that the
blight is caused somewhat by the mixing of the grains and the
early planting. They should sow their winter crops already in
the fall, but they usually do it just before or immediately after
Christmas. As long as they have no servants to help, they are unable to get to it earlier because of other matters. In Carolina they
have to change the rice seeds every third year; otherwise it becomes red and loses its value. Our herdsmen have lost their German crops completely out by the cowpen because a few weeks
ago they had quite a bit of extremely large hail stones, which
were as large as chicken eggs and crushed the crops and ruined
the pastures. A hen which was unable to get in quickly enough
was killed, and the cattle received bruises as large as eggs on
their hide. God has many ways and means to chasten mankind,
yet He still treats us with great mercy. With sadness I read in a
newspaper that God afflicted my hometown Forsta in Lower
Lusatia last summer with a terrible fire with which there were

miraculous circumstances which were of use to me and my congregation one evening during the evening prayer meeting. May God stand by the poor in this hardship, and also my siblings, as well as my in-laws and their children.

Friday, the 19th of May. After our dear God blessed me with time and strength to answer the last important letters of General Oglethorpe, the Lord Trustees, and other beloved benefactors in Europe, I sent the letters along yesterday with the daily register containing part of this month with a good opportunity to our friend Mr. Habersham in Savannah, to be forwarded from there. May God accompany them. May He let many good things be accomplished through the letters for the betterment of our congregation by the Lord Trustees and Mr. Vernon, to whom I wrote extensively about our situation. The detailed content of the letters is located at the end of the daily register we have just sent off.

In writing letters my thoughts are always so full of God's goodness, trials, the congregation's current state, and suggestions for the betterment of the congregation that I am unable to keep my letters to the Trustees brief, especially because I no longer keep a journal for them. I have no indication that my prolixity is displeasing; rather, they have attested many times to the contrary. He who accuses me as a minister of reporting about external, worldly matters too much in the daily register and the letters does not know about my instructions. Were someone else here, I would gladly be silent about such matters if it could be done without my neglecting my duties. I will most likely always be responsible during my lifetime for taking care of the congregation's external matters.

This morning, just as I wanted to travel to the plantation church and school, three large boats full of soldiers from Fort Augusta arrived to take our soldiers and their baggage to Frederica, where they must hurry to be discharged on July 1st. Their captain, Mr. Cadogan, visited me along with a cadet as is usually the case when people of importance come to our settlement. They always behave so that we cannot complain or be annoyed at their presence. For their needs and refreshment, we gladly give them what we have; and we allow ourselves to be drawn into a useful conversation with them. The soldiers were not harmful to us; they were useful, and we are sad that the regiment (with the exception of about seventy men) is leaving this colony. Their leaving worries me, not without reason; and I fear it may have bad consequences. At the end of last month I wrote about this not only to the commander in Frederica, Colonel Heron, but also in the previously mentioned letters to the Lord Trustees, General Oglethorpe, and especially to Mr. Vernon, with reference to the letters written to the Lord Trustees. I did not think it was necessary to report this in the daily registers we sent (namely concerning this point and another point about the Uchee land and in our vicinity).

Sunday, the 21st of May. For a long time now, we have had intense heat and a continuous dry spell. The mountains must be experiencing the same sort of weather because the water in the river is receding more and more. For harvesting the European crops (wheat, rye, and barely) now ready for harvest, this weather is very convenient. If the rain does not stay away too long, the Indian corn will not be harmed because it can withstand hot weather. I was amazed that one of our Salzburgers was able to distill a strong brandy from the stalks of the Indian corn, which has not yet reached a height of two feet, just like the brandy made in the West Indies of sugar cane. People are also using the yellow and the red plums in their stills for this purpose. They are able to produce this liquor cheaply (because they have their own plums, peaches, etc.), and it does them good when they work hard because drinking only water in this country can be very harmful.

Beer is brought from New York occasionally, but it is fairly expensive. They are not permitted by their poor earnings to buy wine and rum. On the old trees damaged by the late frost last winter, there are not many peaches; however, the younger trees are all the fuller. We do not have other trees because our residents have not had the time to spend on them. They are content to earn enough through their manual labor for the necessary food and clothing and to remain without debts.

A planter from Savannah Town (not far from Fort Augusta) sent me a letter through his son in which he wrote that he had a lot of wheat this year which he would like to grind at our mill and sell in Savannah. The aforementioned German man, who wants to build a ship mill for grinding and a sawmill near Purysburg at the expense of Mr. David Zübli, had built a mill near Augusta. However, a flood demolished the dam and caused the mill to overturn. As I spoke to our pious miller today, he said that our mill would not have fared any better if we had not prayed for it. Our mill has remained intact through prayer, and not through our skill or foresight. This Christian talk left a good impression on me.

Mr. David Zübli from St. Gall, who is still probably known to the Senior Urlsperger, had a lot of loss from the aforementioned building of the ship mill, for which he should be pitied.[7] We would have sold all the cut lumber if we had not used our better judgment.

Tuesday, the 23rd of May. Yesterday N.'s sister came crying to me and complaining about her husband's harshness against her. She also said she could not help but repay him in words with the same. Because I arrived this morning at her plantation, which lies furthest away, I found that she was more wicked than her husband about this angry dispute. She was so offensive that I was amazed at her husband's leniency. I reproached them with God's word for their sins, especially the offenses to their children and other people; and at the same time I told them of their duty and the manner in which their offenses and travail can be repented. Then I prayed with them. I hope this is helpful. Both of them are diligent workers and diligent churchgoers. However, they are not yet truly converted. From such a state can only come sin and vexation, which causes us no small sadness.

Thursday, the 25th of May. Today Mr. Meyer is traveling to Savannah to the Council. He and Mr. Vigera, whom he expects to meet here, want to acquire a good location for a plantation between our mill and Abercorn. Concerning this matter I wrote emphatically and in the best way to the President of the Council, Col. Stephens. At the same time I informed him that our silk has been reeled and is being safely stored with Mr. Meyer until it can be sent to the Lord Trustees along with the silk from Savannah. The cocoons weigh seven hundred and sixty-two pounds and five ounces all together. From this amount fifty-one pounds and five ounces are spun, of which the esteemed Mr. von M. /Münch/ will receive one and a half pounds of spun silk in accordance with his wishes along with the pertinent fleuret silk which Mr. Stephens promised to send to Mr. Verelst.

While the fine lovely spun silk was being weighed yesterday in the orphanage, a pious woman remembered the encouraging words of the esteemed Senior Urlsperger *plus ultra*, continue on! which he proclaimed in a fatherly letter upon completion of the first silk in Ebenezer, which weighed only a few pounds. If the Lord Trustees lend an ear to the reasonable suggestions I recently made, then the manufacture of silk could reach near perfection. After the boy servant ran away from the widow Granewetter, keeping up with the household chores became more difficult, which she especially feels during the wheat harvest.

Today she was happy and comforted as she did her field work. Sometimes, however, she gets anxious and fearful because she feels that God has burdened her too greatly and that she will not be able to endure much longer. The word of God is her comfort and refreshment, and she holds the Christian encouragement of a good friend for a precious blessing. She cited the story of the Syrian captain Naaman who received a great blessing from the friendly encouragement and advice of his servants to bathe in the Jordon according to the command of the prophet. We would like to help make her household chores easier, if only we were able to get her a servant or a maid. One cannot even get day laborers and other workers for cash this time of year. It is good that the final work in manufacturing the silk is ending just as the harvesting of the Indian corn, wheat, rye and barley is beginning so that one can take place after the other.

Friday, the 26th of May. Jesus is fulfilling His exquisite promise in Mrs. Riedelsberger daily and plentifully. I will love Him and reveal myself to Him. She especially enjoys the love and grace of her Savior. Through this her fear of death, which often plagued her, has disappeared completely. Today she would deem it a great blessing to be soon dissolved and together with Christ even though she is still young and happy beside her pious, diligent, and blessed husband. Her oldest daughter, a child of five years, is always sickly; yet, she loves her Savior, prays to Him, and yearns to die so as to be with Him soon in heaven. She is always so well behaved that she has never had to be disciplined to refrain from evil and be kept on the path of good.

Saturday, the 27th of May. For some weeks, we have had hot, dry weather. To be sure, this somewhat hindered the growth of some field and garden produce, yet it greatly promoted the wheat harvest and the other agricultural crops. Yesterday the wind came mostly from the north. As a result, it was cool and cloudy the whole day. In the evening a strong, cold wind arose, which brought us a cold but beneficial rain the entire night, during which a strong northwest wind blew. The air is very cool. We must keep ourselves warm during the night with good blankets and during the day with good clothing if one wants to avoid getting a fever or bodily pains

Sunday, the 28th of May. Mr. Meyer has only just arrived today because the strong northwest wind did not allow them to depart until late last night. He accomplished little because some members of the Council were absent and some had traveled to Frederica in order to receive in the name of the Lord Trustees the cashiered soldiers who are becoming colonists and want to receive fifty acres of land for planting. To benefit them in setting up their plantations, the following was done: each new colonist was given five pounds Sterling and a year's provisions or food. Mr. Meyer brought me a little letter from a German man in Savannah. He complained that his daughter wants to marry a young man in Abercorn against his will. She has already gone to him even though they are not married.

He asks me to marry them to avoid scandal. But I cannot do this until I have published their banns in Savannah where they are known. To do it here would only be a deception; this I will not do. I tried to persuade this young man to free himself of this scandal and meet with the parents of his bride in such a way that the marriage can receive their blessing. The third commandment is so important and so little known, and just that is a clear indication that God and His word are worth nothing to the blind and malicious.

Monday, the 29th of May. A while ago a pious and sickly

woman complained to me about the gravity of the temptation and blasphemous thoughts which fall like arrows into her soul, against her will and to her great sadness. Accordingly I instructed her from God's word and prayed with her. This condition lasted (as she told me) until Exaudi Sunday. Our merciful God had so blessed the verses of the exordium which we had contemplated, Romans 8, (the same spirit bears witness to our spirit) that all temptations[8] and sadness disappeared, and her heart was filled with peace and happiness. After this she went with blessing to Holy Communion. God is still keeping her under the chastening rod of the cross, and this she realizes to be healing and beneficial.

She praises God for all His wonderful and merciful guidance. When praying, I agree with her concerning the beautiful verse: "God is faithful who will not suffer you to be tempted above that ye are able," etc.; this strengthens one's belief many times. God will reveal Himself to be a true God also to the rest of the congregation because they now have recently become increasingly weaker of body and poorer of worldly goods. Many spirits have been cast down anew through the great damage to the wheat and rye. Flour in Savannah costs twenty-five shillings Sterling for one hundred pounds.

Wednesday, the 31st of May. Now we are starting to get more thunderstorms because we received so few during the spring. It must have rained more up near the source of the Savannah River than it did in our region before and after Whitsuntide because the Savannah has begun to rise noticeably by the last few days. The snow usually melts early in spring and causes the river to rise. This cannot be the cause of the river's rising now. In previous years at this time the river has been so low that our low lying mill was hardly able to turn. But now everything is working. It is only a shame that there has been so little to mill these last two months.

We are starting to get a little more now after the people have begun threshing their German grains. They are speeding up the threshing because the price of flour is so high in Savannah. God permitted them something extra of their wheat and rye, that was not ruined by the blight and mildew. This they are joyous about, and for this they praise dear God. A German orphan girl whose mother died at our settlement has served out her time in Savannah and is coming here in accordance with her mother's wishes to be taught God's word and be prepared for Holy Communion. Many young people of both sexes are being corrupted in this wild and liberal land. If they are in other people's service, especially the English and the French, they have no time to learn something of God's word and the catechism, and they are seldom permitted to go to church and listen to God's word. If they are left free and on their own, one notices little serious intention to catch up on that which was neglected. They consider themselves ready for Holy Communion when they have learned their catechism and a few biblical quotes. So they remain grossly ignorant and in conformity with the world.

If we present them in a pleading and friendly manner what is appropriate to a worthy use of Holy Communion and how they should not for His sake go with others but hasten with their diligent learning and conversion, then they keep away or turn to others. Some threaten to move away and think they will find a minister to give them Holy Communion. It is most dangerous for children: 1), if their parents die prematurely; 2), when the girls marry into other denominations because then many receive a Deist, an Arian, a Cynic, or an Epicurean.

JUNE

Thursday, the 1st of June. This afternoon we again had a severe thunderstorm with hail and rain; and towards evening, shortly before sunset, we saw a rather indistinct rainbow between east and south. For us it is no small wonder that there can be such large hail stones during this heat at this time of year. Perhaps to our friends in Europe who are familiar with our climate it is just as amazing as it is to us. We would really like to have an accurate thermometer and barometer to be able to eventually report the hot and cold temperatures to our in friends in Eu-

rope who have an interest in it. The sun rises now at one minute
before five o'clock and sets at one minute after seven o'clock.

Friday, the 2nd of June. Because I hold school at the plantations from 8:30 a.m. to 9:30, I have until 11 o'clock to relax a
little until people gather for the weekly sermon. If I am not
needed or do not visit someone in the neighborhood, I read the
blessed and edifying reports from East India concerning the
start and progress of the institutions there for converting the
heathens.[1] What today was, among other things, impressive and
edifying, which I think I will also use for the benefit of the children and adults, is the following report on the heathen school
children there:

> "We have a lot of hope for the children who are being raised by
> us in the Christian way. Even though they are heathen chil-
> dren, after being taught for a time, they are of a right fine
> spirit. They are diligent, hard-working, obedient, capable of
> learning, and content. In truth one does not see as much mis-
> chievousness, maliciousness, obstinacy, stubbornness, or irre-
> sponsibility as one must experience and see in most European
> children."

Today at 12 o'clock a thunderstorm arose out of the northwest, bringing a long, heavy rain. The wind came from the south
and before that from the southeast. After the rain it was cool
toward evening and during the night.

Saturday, the 3rd of June. This morning it was fearfully hot,
and there was a thunderstorm in the afternoon, which was gentle and lasted until evening without much rain. Many people
have left their European grains, especially wheat, in shocks or
standing in the fields. Therefore, they wish that God would bestow upon them some days of dry weather again to bring in that
which is unaffected by mildew and blight.

Sunday, the 4th of June. Today's Sunday has once again been
cheerful and blessed through the merciful reign of our faithful
God, and on it He has sent us much edification through the
reading of the Holy Scriptures, song, prayer, and the preaching
of His word. The young Mrs. N. gave birth to a baby boy, which,
because of its weakness, was given an emergency baptism. The

mother may be at fault for the great weakness of her child because she worked along with her husband more than was necessary, which did her little good, as this tends to be the way of the avaricious.

I think I will travel out there tomorrow, God willing, to pray over the child and to speak with the parents about what is necessary. She is usually very reasonable and follows a literal recognition of the Christian teachings: the love of worldly possessions is very strong in both her and her husband. This is a hindrance to the kingdom of heaven as is with the burdened in today's gospel. Oh, the misery. There it is said: "For what is a man profited, if he shall gain the whole world, and lose his own soul? or what shall a man give in exchange for his soul?" They know the saying well (Matthew 16:26).

Tuesday, the 6th of June. On Sunday I made it known publicly that I will begin the preparatory lessons again for the older children of both sexes toward a worthy use of Holy Communion. And my congregation have been asked to remember this pleasant work in prayer before the Lord so that it will not be lost on any child but be a blessing to each of them. There are now seven children, with one boy still expected, whose father has promised to send him in two weeks. In the first hour I enjoined upon them the word of the Lord Jesus: "Blessed are they that hear the word of God and keep it" and the three points of the catechism: 1), concerning the word of God; 2), the judicious proper use of God's word; 3), the great benefit arising from the judicious and proper use of His word. After this I will establish our dear and precious Catechism as the basis of the catechistic lectures which I also use on the plantation for young and old alike and from which our kindhearted God sends refreshment to the heart.

Wednesday, the 7th of June. Yesterday shortly before evening, a pious man was with me and told me with pleasure that God had revealed to his wife her previous sins and previous inability to repent and brought her to confess. Among the sins which oppressed her was her derision of good. This he had to endure from her and he endured this gladly. However, he is even happier now that God has led her to confess through the riches of His goodness, and forbearance and long-suffering. She sent for

me to come to her, which I did today. She had no little pangs of
conscience here and in Germany, both in and out of marriage.
Now, she bears witness in tears, gestures, and words to a great
fear, regret, and shame about her actions such as I have seen in
few instances. I presented her with sin as sin from God's word
and the suffering of Christ, and I warned her of comfort which
comes too quickly and premature as well as warning her of
Cain's disbelief: "My sins are greater than, etc."

All the time I said many things to comfort her that there is still
mercy for her and her weighty sins, and she has no reason to
despair. I led her to the 15th chapter of St. Luke, from which
next week's beautiful sermon is taken. The flour, fruit, and wood
she stole from her employer by persuading other women, she
would like to replace with crops if God would bless her. In the
meantime she will invoke God to replace everything with His
wisdom, omnipotence, and goodness. She also intends to exercise her Christian responsibility toward a certain person
among us, which can serve him as an opportunity to convert.

Friday, the 9th of June. The weather has begun now to become
dry after a period in which we had rain and thunderstorms almost daily. A scarce amount of European grain has been
gathered, and now the principal work is with the Indian corn
and rice, for which we have the most comfortable weather. Today I received a letter from Savannah in which not only Indian
cornmeal but also a large amount of boards for shipment are requested. It is only fortunate that we have enough water to run
the mill and send the lumber down river. Usually at this time
only the lowest water course is operative. There are many soldiers in Savannah who were discharged in Frederica and shall be
sent to England. Wheat flour is very expensive and one cannot
get enough of it. However, our cornmeal is cheap, even though it
is not as good to use as the European flour, especially in the sum-
mertime.

We have God to thank for not allowing our inhabitants to want
for income or food. Even though their work and lifestyle usually
involve great hardships because of the lack of servants. Since our
inexpensive boards—made from good lasting wood—have begun to become known, our sawmiller is unable to cut as much as

could be sold. We are lacking people, and the wages are too high. So the mill is unable to create the benefit to the congregation which we would expect if God were to change our situation. Yet the use we have from it for the good of our dear inhabitants is not to be underestimated.

Saturday, the 10th of June. The recently mentioned woman who was called upon to confess is treating the mercy she received for conversion faithfully. Now she uses the Hymns of penitence and of the Passion as well as the story of Christ's suffering and death to help her get to know the deep corruption in her heart more and more. She wants to have remorse and tears because she regards herself as a great sinner, who has long gone her way in security and disobedience. The beautiful sermon *The Heart of the Resurrected Jesus* unexpectedly fell into my hands the other day and from it I took something appropriate to her spiritual condition.[2] I read it in the presence of her husband and left it with her for further reference. With such souls I usually entreat them with the Lord Jesus's words: "He digged deep," to warn them of premature comfort, which is like mildew.

Sunday, the 11th of June. Yesterday afternoon we again had a strong thunderstorm with heavy downpours. This filled the paths, low-lying areas, and small rivers with water. It thundered late into the night. It may have rained heavily continuing into the evening almost through to midnight (this can be gathered from the dark rain clouds). Here, however, it did not rain much during the night. Today it was very hot; as hot as it usually is in summer. The wind blew from the south. Compared with the heat which the missionaries have experienced and reported in Trankebar the summer heat in this country is slight and bearable.[3] Also, it lasts no longer than two months, during which we still have a few cool and comfortable days and cool nights. It is a very good country; if only the inhabitants were better. Yesterday was the longest day of the year. May God help us from season to season until finally the day of judgment arrives.

Tuesday, the 13th of June. A little over three weeks ago a planter living near Savannah Town asked through his son whether he could have the nice and plentiful grain which he expected to harvest soon ground here. The son at that time was already seventeen days away from home, and he brought me this request on his return journey from Carolina. Therefore, he did not know, as I knew from our sad experience, that the father wrote to me through the same son that the wheat there did not turn out that well. As a result, he is sending nothing to the mill because he intended to send a lot (Haggai 2: 17–18). He expressed himself in the following manner:

> "Winter was cold, and the spring cold and dry, after which the weather became fruitful so that the wheat became better than it had appeared. In many places not much was produced because it became brown instead of yellow and consequently developed no grain. I myself had a half acre of the same blighted grain."

Our inhabitants are fairly convinced that the blight is caused by a late planting. Gschwandel always plants his wheat at Michaelmas, and his crops always turn out nicely. On the other hand, others do it just before Christmas and have sustained damage. There is so much work that they are almost unable to plant earlier. This would probably change if God would bestow us with servants.

Wednesday, the 14th of June. The widow Granewetter was married yesterday to a widower, one of the last German servants,[4] who appears to be a knowledgeable and well-intentioned man. She has a well-equipped plantation. She hopes her husband will have no cause to move to another settlement taking her and her two children from God's word and good care into the wilderness and danger. This is my concern and the reason why I could not deem this marriage well-advised.

Friday, the 16th of June. The soldiers who were here before the previous group came here and brought old and new uniforms to sell. The same clothing was sold to them in Savannah at a cheap price by the soldiers returning to England. All at once they have received three times as much clothing because this clothing was in arrears to them for three years. I hear that only a few have accepted land to colonize. The remaining, who were not placed in any of the three troops which marched to Carolina, are waiting in Savannah for two merchant ships to take them to London. Few of them have the desire to work; otherwise, they would not have become soldiers. As day laborers they would have enough work; but we cannot get anyone. I know of no other year in which the fieldwork became so difficult and burdensome to our overworked inhabitants as it did this summer.

We have received the request of a pious and faithful Salzburger, or Austrian, Schmidt, to let him build a house near the mill. He would like to give up his extremely laborious farming, move here, serve as a host to strangers coming to our mill and in our stead take care of all the things at the grain- and sawmill which until now have been time consuming for us. We sang today during the weekly sermon: *Warum sollt ich mich denn grämen.* For me and mine I let something be read from the living footsteps of God during the meal through which my belief was strengthened many times in a living God, capable of everything. Perhaps this help for Ebenezer is closer than we think. "Quicker than we can think, God can guide our hardship for the best. Soul, why art thou daunted? Dear Lord God is still living!"[5]

Sunday, the 18th of June. Today, the Fourth Sunday after Trinity, was blessed by the heartfelt mercy of our God. He has provided us with both strength of spirit and strength of body to preach His message to old and young, indigenous and foreign, who have come here from other neighboring regions. And He let some goodness be felt among our own congregation. Today seventy people attended the Communion, among whom six were strangers who usually support our community. At the time of the repetition hour, a few hours before evening, we performed a burial. Riedelsberger's oldest daughter, five years of age, died this morning at 2 a.m.

Because in the good effects of the Holy Ghost she was fairly similar to the eight year old daughter of Mr. Stöller in Cöthen whose edifying life was written about in one of the *Contributions to the Kingdom of God,*[6] I read the first part of this moving biography this morning with some remembrance of our children and adults through which our dear Savior sent both pious parents and all the mourners present a lot of comfort and rich edification. It also gave me the opportunity to make known the recognizable work of God in the soul of the deceased child. It was a truly pious and obedient child, who never caused her parents sadness but only made them joyous with her Christian behavior in both sickness and health.

She was not pleased by other children's lack of discipline. She liked to learn her biblical verses and pray; and during her long suffering she displayed great patience, letting her mother do with her as she pleased. She liked to hear about death. And she sincerely desired to be with her dear Savior. The last little saying which her mother tried to teach her by rote was : "My desire is to arise and dwell in heaven,"[7] etc. Yesterday morning she asked her mother several times to send for me so that I could pray with her, and this took place in the afternoon. Then I gave her the last rites in the name of God's Holy Trinity. God heard our prayer for a blessed and prompt dissolution and deliverance from her pains.

Tuesday, the 20th of June. The German man Straube, who came to us from Savannah, works very diligently because he gets little help with his work from his sick wife and six children, some of them small and some sickly. So he remains in very poor circumstances despite the help sent from us and others. He is a righteous man, and she has converted honestly to God too. Therefore, they know how to put up with their poverty and miserable circumstances, and they are displaying great patience. The oldest son is a good and pious child who brings us great joy in the school, the church, and the community.

Wednesday, the 21st of June. I see it as a special merciful providence of God that the merchant from Port Royal /Robert Williams/ was able to take the boards which he bought from us, to Savannah before the water level in the river dropped. Yesterday four men left the mill with the last eight rafts, which are carrying nearly ten thousand feet of lumber. With the water continually dropping, this would have been too late a few days later. Our Mill River is not yet cleared of the many fallen trees and old wood (we do not have the means to do this). Therefore, it is difficult for a loaded boat to get through at low water.[8]

Thursday, the 22nd of June. A pious woman rejoiced at the word which God spoke to his people; namely, He had given them good land. She applied this then to us and our land, and she knew how to state all the good which the Lord has done with and in this land. She also led me around her plantation and showed me her fruit-bearing trees and especially the fig trees that were filled with fruit and the beehives, and other physical blessings. It is indeed a blessed land. If only more pious people and honest workers were in it. This woman has been sick for a long time and is unsuited for field work. This year God has strengthened her body and mind so much that she is able to lighten her husband's very difficult profession, as she tells humbly with joy at God's wondrous goodness and with praise of His great name. She gave me the beautiful verse to take along for another pious soul: "Praised be God who," etc. "who according to his great mercy," etc. Peter 1:1 and placed the emphasis on the word "great."

Friday, the 23rd of June. The day after tomorrow the Germans of our confession are gathering again in Savannah to hear God's word and receive Holy Communion, which is why I am traveling there tomorrow under God's direction. May God be with my heart and tongue.

Tuesday, the 24th of June. Once again our merciful God blessed me in Savannah and on the trip down and back, for which His name should be praised and magnified. The weather was for the most part cool; and, as a result, carrying out my official duties was not in the least difficult, even though I preached twice, repeated the sermon once, and baptized a child. Yesterday four couples (some English, some German) were married, after which I departed from Savannah in God's name. For the marriage of the Germans I performed the ceremony as I do amidst our congregation: I make their banns public and sing and pray during the ceremony and give a sermon about a select passage from the Bible. This time it was the first Psalm.

During the English marriage ceremonies, which I do not perform differently from the so-called license issued by the authorities, I must do it according to the form set forth in their so-called *Prayerbook*. They all want to be distinguished people so they perform it like the people in England who let themselves be married in private without public notice after having received a license, and the regular minister makes no scruple of this. I do not let myself get involved with such licenses and marriages of the English and the French if there is a preacher in the country or in Savannah. Mr. Zuberbiller is still in England.[9]

Letters have arrived for us in Savannah from London and Germany, which contain pleasing news for the most part. May God be praised that our Fathers and benefactors are still alive, in passable health, and all blessed and that they have shown us great goodness through their blessed support. We received no letters from our esteemed Senior Urlsperger, Mr. D. F. and Mr. von M.[10] However, we read in the very pleasant letter of Mr. Albinus, and the same in the edifying letter from Mr. L., that they are well and kindly disposed towards us in a fatherly manner. The Lord Trustees let us feel many signs of their kindly disposition in the long letter written by their secretary, Mr. Martyn. With their new arrangement concerning the manufacture of silk, we hope it shall proceed better.

Thursday, the 29th of June. The Lutherans in Congrees, or Sachs-Gotha (a newly started settlement in South Carolina, one hundred and fifty miles northwest of Charleston), sent a joint letter to me in which they described to me movingly their need and their miserable condition, especially in regard to their spiritual life. They can never have an evangelical sermon, send their children to catechism, or partake in Holy Communion. This causes them great pain, and they have a great desire to obtain good evangelical books. They would deem it as a great benefit if one of us could come to them. It may be a desolate and inappropriate place to which many run from both Carolinas, Virginia, and Pennsylvania who do not like to remain in one place because of debts or are unable to remain for other evil causes.

Two German families from our settlement have moved there, who were well established here. Now they know what they had here and what they found there. The three pious German boys who ran away a few months ago at the bequest of their parents have settled there with their unscrupulous parents.[11] Previously their oldest brother had already run away there from his servitude. I have answered their letter: in it I gave them all the healing remembrances of God's word and advised them of the difficulties which prevent me from promising to travel to them. We will pray about it, and they should pray that God convince us whether one of us can go to them. In the meantime I am sending them good edifying books to be used at their meetings and in their homes. I do not have much trust in these people because I know from much experience that they talk a lot about religion and serving God; and then, when they have it, pay little attention to it.

Friday, the 30th of June. Today I was called from the plantation school unexpectedly to go to Mrs. Steiner, who has been seriously ill since yesterday evening and is no longer of sound mind. We kneeled down and brought her in the poverty of our prayer to the Lord Jesus, as I read this morning of the palsied man in Matthew 9. She has been sick for a long time and recently very near death. Afterward she recovered again through the use of medication so that she walked around the house and was able to do her household chores reasonably well. Because of the lack of servants, the women have to do a lot of hard labor sometime in dry weather and sometime in wet weather, which is not as sufferable in this hot climate as in the German climate. We regret greatly that it will be so difficult until we are able to get some servants. Still more we regret that we must burden our patrons and friends with such matters.

JULY

Monday, the 3rd of July. Last Friday (it was the 30th of last month) our boat came up from Savannah and brought me an invitation from Capt. Dunbar, an intimate friend of General Oglethorpe,[1] who wished to see me before returning to London. Shortness of time and necessary business prevented him from coming up to us. However, he would gladly have come up with some other officers if I had been unable to go down. I preferred to do that in order to avoid complications and expenses for our place.

On Sunday (it was the Sixth Sunday after Trinity) I preached
to the German people about the way to salvation through the
gospel; and in the exordium we contemplated the beautiful
words from Psalms 139:23–24. The sermon was repeated and
further explicated in the evening. I also had to baptize the child
of a German Reformed man and had to attend to some other
useful business.

Col. Heron, who is sending the cashiered soldiers to England
in two ships that have arrived, has promised me to look out the
best he can for our place if there is any danger from the Indians.

Mrs. /Maria/ Steiner died on the first of this month and was
buried the following Sunday. May God now care for the dear
feeble Steiner and his three still unreared children, two of whom
are also sickly! His housekeeping[2] is very difficult, which would
soon be lightened for him if he could only get a loyal servant or
maid; but this is not possible at present.

Friday, the 7th of July. It rained again yesterday and today;
but here with us it was not very much. Both by day and by night
the air is so cool that we must marvel.

We had to settle a coarse and vexing discord between two married people, in which God noticeably dignified us with His help.
The wife fears God with her heart but understands housekeeping too little; and this sometimes gives her husband the occasion
to sin no little against his wife and in other ways. No matter how
angry and mean he otherwise is, he still came in great sorrow
and bitter tears when I admonished him. The reconciliation of
the two married people followed very soon thereafter.

Sunday, the 8th of July. Two soldiers have petitioned to take
up and cultivate land at our place. They understand the German language and can therefore make use of our office, like the
others. One of the wives is from Wurttemberg and appears to
have a good disposition and love for God's word; and it is for this
reason hat she has actually chosen our place above others. Both
have a high regard for the late Mr. Driesler, who was godfather
to their only little son.[3]

Sunday, the 9th of July. Today during the afternoon service
the messenger from Savannah came here by horse and brought
me for my signature the petition from the Council and the most

prominent inhabitants of this colony to the Lord Trustees. It is
very well arranged; and they request that the Lord Trustees
might advance 1) the unification of our colony with Carolina,
and 2) the restoration of Oglethorpe's regiment. With this messenger I also sent our letter packet, which was addressed to the
Trustees' secretary, Mr. Martyn, to Capt. Dunbar for fowarding
to London. Early tomorrow morning the ship will set sail from
the Savannah River, and therefore I dispatched the messenger
quickly. We plan to write again as soon as the chests arrive here.

Wednesday, the 12th of July. The dog days are beginning today; and we must marvel that we have had such very cool
weather for some time. It has rained every day since the new
moon; and especially this morning we had a very heavy rain.
Therefore it has been a very wet summer. Up by Augusta and in
the mountains it must have rained very much, too; for the river
is rising again; and this is very good for our mills. There is now
much European grain to grind,[4] which does not last long either
in the straw or in sacks, but is soon hollowed out by worms.
Therefore, the people hurry with it to the mill as soon as possible.

For several years our inhabitants' cattle have increased considerably. They are a large part of their sustenance and they advance agriculture no little bit on land such as ours is. However,
because we lack herdsmen, they have not had the profit from
them that they should have been able to have with God's blessing. Rather, some of them have harmed their health by having to
seek their cattle daily themselves and to drive them home. Because servants have been lacking for so long, I have offered to
contribute a considerable amount of money from the physical
blessings which God has granted from Europe, if they wish to
make good arrangements for facilitating cattle-raising at the
cowpen and on the plantations and for that purpose to engage
loyal herdsmen from the community (for nothing can be accomplished with strange people) both at the cowpen and at home.
This will be a great relief especially for widows and weak people
who cannot seek their cattle themselves, and it will prevent great
loss of time. It appears that some men will be found willing to

plant less on their land and to serve the community as herdsmen until we can get servants.

Thursday, the 13th of July. A boy from among the town children, who is now in the preparation hour, has been sick with fever for several weeks; and during this time he has proved himself very Christian, as I heard today from his pious mother. He loves God and his Savior heartily; therefore he also loves His word and prayer. Consequently, he is especially distressed that he cannot come to the preparation hour with the other children. During his sickness he wished to know the Bible verses that I was accustomed to give to the children to take home for later reading and for memorizing. They are always the most important texts through which the articles of Christian dogma are clearly proved. Those children who have grown up and been trained with us already know all the basic and pithy verses by heart and have a great treasure in them. However, those who have come to us from other places are incited by their example to learn them gradually also. The above-mentioned child yearned for me for a long time and asked his parents to tell me of his longing. When I came today uncalled, it was very pleasing to him and to his parents, and they expressed more gratitude than one could wish for. They do not live in town but on a plantation in a somewhat remote corner. All sorts of obstacles keep us from visiting the good people.

Saturday, the 15th of July. This afternoon we had the pleasure of receiving and unpacking the gifts from Halle and Augsburg, consisting of books for us and the congregation and medications and various pieces of clothing and pertinent things. After the three chests had been opened, we knelt down before God, the Giver of all good and perfect gifts. We thanked Him communally for everything and called on Him to give us wisdom in applying these benefactions and to graciously reward all of our most worthy benefactors in Halle, Augsburg, Stuttgart, and wherever they are with spiritual and physical blessings in His mercy. A chest in which there were some quilts had broken and the beds and a piece of course linen were very much damaged and almost spoiled by the rain that may have entered on the journey from Charleston to Savannah. However, the books and the medicines from Halle and the books, Schauer's balm, linen, and woolen cloth from Augsburg in the large chest had not the least damage. Goods come easily as far as Charleston undamaged; but until they are brought to Savannah we always worry that they may be damaged through the negligence of the boatmen. We lost scarcely a moment in fetching them from Savannah after receiving news of their arrival.

Sunday, the 16th of July. On the Eighth Sunday after Trinity our host and constable /Bichler/ again suffered a great misfortune, through which he suffered worse than through all the tribulations that have previously occurred to him in physical matters. His only son, a well-behaved child of four and a half years was kicked so hard in the abdomen by his own horse in his father's presence that surely nothing but a premature temporal death can follow. The father trusted the horse too much and wished to give the little child the pleasure of giving the horse a basket of barley as fodder, but the horse got on top of the dear child, got it under its feet, and finally gave it a violent kick. So far our holy God has sent one misfortune after the other into this man's home. May God grant that he will humble himself under the hand of the Lord amidst such onerus events. With this horse he formerly sinned by conforming grievously to the world and thus saddened and vexed other people. And, afterwards, precisely this very useful horse was the cause of several serious accidents. May God bring him to contemplation and penitence! He has a very good understanding and other good talents so that he could become a very useful tool in the community if only he would let himself be drawn to God.

Monday, the 17th of July. A house has been built by the mill for Schmidt, the righteous Austrian. He moved into it last week, and today it was consecrated with the word of God and prayer. As a basis for the sermon I laid the salutary rules of life that were forwarded to us this time from Memmingen and which are of great importance and are very appropriate for my purpose in consecrating such a house. For this, Schmidt will not only be an overseer and worker in the mill-works but will also play host for the sake of strangers who have business there and shelter them and sell them necessary food and drink. For this purpose, at Mr.

Meyer's recommendation, he has received permission in Savannah. He will be a very useful man at the mills in various ways and greatly ease things for me and Mr. Lemke.

This afternoon, when I returned home from the consecration, I learned to my sorrow that Bichler's little boy had died from the horse's kick. I visited him this morning, prayed with him and others who were present, and blessed the child. The parents had not expected it to die so quickly. Since yesterday the child was more often unconscious than conscious and therefore perhaps felt little pain. What he spoke in his fantasy were things that he had learned such as short verses and from his ABC book. He was a very happy and well behaved child, in whom we had our joy. Now he is in a blessed place, to which his mother, a little brother, and a stepsister preceded him some years ago.

Wednesday, the 19th of July. A few days ago, during the regular gospel Matthew 7, we contemplated the great blessing of the discovery of the false teachers and the defense against their false teachings; and at the same time in the exordium I went through the words of St. Paul in Acts 20:29–31. When, on the following Monday, I looked through the many and useful books we had received from Halle, I also caught sight of a report of the Salzburgers from Prussia which, to be sure, was not pleasant; yet is very profitable for my use in the congregation. The report treats of the confusions that the Herrnhuters, according to their wont, have begun to stir up among the Salzburgers in matters of religion and faith.[5] Our wise and merciful God has not only revealed their impurities and poisonous intentions in time but has also put it into their (the Salzburgers') minds, in apprehension of further temptations from these sneaking people, to appeal in a humble narrative petition to the consistory at Königsberg and indirectly to their most gracious King, whose heart, we hope, our dear God will incline to the protection of his little flock against the spreading, dangerous seductions under the name of Christ.

This news in our worthy Pastor Frensen's reports of the Herrnhuter affairs seemed very apropos to me because of the previously mentioned material we had contemplated.[6] There-

fore at the next assembly I shall read aloud the letter to the con-
sistorium and to the King, which was undersigned by very many
Salzburgers. We must consider it a very noticeable disposition of
God, for which the trusting intercession of His servants and children can do much to protect us from this crew that likes so much
to get mixed up in things. While they were in the country they
made not the least attempt at our congregation. They were well
aware that I knew them. May our merciful God deign to continue to hold His hand above us, grant us trust in His word, and
so to steep all our parishioners in the recognition of the ways to
salvation that even the gates of hell cannot overcome us.

Sunday, the 23rd of July. This afternoon in a letter from Pastor /Johann Joachim/ Zübli[7] I received no good reports from
Congarees or Saxe-Gotha in South Carolina, where all sorts of
German people have settled who could not get along in other
provinces or who did not wish to do the right things. Those are
the people who recently wrote me a long letter in which they
earnestly requested me to come to them sometime and to supply
them with good books, which at last has taken place. The pastor
writes me that they live together swinishly, filthily, and disorderly and that their Reformed minister (who is also said to be a
very bad man) treats him worse than the worst in the congregation. They themselves wrote to me that there was great discord
among them all. Whenever I hear reports of other communities
in America where Germans have settled, my eyes again see the
great advantages that God has granted to our dear parishioners
and to other Germans around Savannah.

Tuesday, the 25th of July. Yesterday and today the President of
the Council and his Assistants have had a session, to which I, too,
had to go. I received from all the gentlemen the assurance that
Mr. Meyer may take up and use as he wishes the two hundred
acres of good land on the bank of Parker's collapsed saw mill between our plantations and Abercorn.[8] This land is not only one
of the most fertile but also better situated for trade with boards,
meal, and other things than almost any other in our whole district; and therefore we heartily hope that we will be able to
achieve the purpose that I actually have in entrusting it to Mr.

Meyer. Otherwise, according to the will of Lord Trustees and the opinion of the Council and authorities in Savannah, it should have been given to me as my own property.

In our own district, which is large enough, there is no more so-called good land left, rather all the good spots have been taken up and occupied by our people. To be sure, there is nothing but good land on the large low island across the Mill River; but our worn-out parishioners are now unable, and will remain unable as long as they have no servants, to develop this island, which is overgrown with very thick trees and with much brush and reeds. No one may venture on the so-called Uchee land because it has not yet been bought from these Indians.[9] Also, it is actually intended for a new transport; and therefore they do not wish to take from it the few plantation of the old inhabitants of our place.

Until now we ministers have always rightly granted our dear parishoners the preference and choice of settling that land on which they could first and best earn their livelihood under God's blessing. Although, except for the low land lying across the Mill River and the Uchee land, there is no more land now vacant and unoccupied in our entire region that is actually called good land, and really is, because of its natural and excellent fertility (for the entire pine forest is called infertile), there is no lack of right good fertile soil behind Abercorn and in the region of our cow-pen where our last German servants have settled.[10]

The Lord Trustees have allowed us ministers, like other ministers in the land, to take up a certain piece of land of three hundred acres, which, for the said reason, we have not yet done. Now I have submitted a petition to the assembled Council for a fertile piece of land between the said German people (who, as our co-religionists, use our office) and our very necessary and useful cowpen. In it I requested not only six hundred acres for myself and Mr. Lemke but also three hundred more to be saved for a future minister who might be requested and sent after our district and neighborhood have been occupied by German people. However, I myself must obtain the approbation of the Lord Trustees.

Our inhabitants, who have often walked or ridden through this region, assure us that there is very good land and the most beautiful pasture in the region in which we wish to take up the ministers' land, although it is rather remote from any navigable stream. To be sure, we do not need it at the present time because we have no servants. However, were we to postpone claiming it until the servants arrive, then it would be occupied by other, strange people to the great detriment of our cowpen or cattle ranch. It would also be to the harm of the German people of our confession who are now settled here and who in time will be able to enjoy the blessing of a ministry in their neighborhood. Around there (somewhat further in the direction of Savannah) lies still more good land; and a beautiful congregation could be settled there in little villages not far from each other, whom one minister and schoolmaster could serve. If God should grant us loyal servants and if through their industry we could cultivate a part of this beautiful land, it would serve greatly to alleviate our domestic situation. But we leave this, too, up to the Lord, who best knows what is good for us.

Wednesday, the 26th of July. Yesterday my dear colleague conducted the distribution of the charitable gifts of cloth, linen, and yarn, which our merciful God has recently granted from our dear Stuttgart, Biberach, Augsburg, and Memmingen. This was done in Jerusalem Church with contemplation of the divine word, song, and prayer. This time I could not be present because of my necessary departure for Savannah. At the conclusion of the preface of the 13th Continuation of the Ebenezer Reports,[11] our worthy father in Christ, Senior Urlsperger, called to us from an old and well known song the words, "Trust ye our Lord God, who hath created all things. He neither can nor will abandon you, He knoweth well what ye lack. Both heaven and earth are His, my Father and my Lord God, who stands by me in all need."[12] Written on the 15th Sunday after Trinity, 1747. There resounded publicly: "Fear not!" These beautiful words impressed not only me but also my dear colleague. Therefore, he laid them as a basis for the sermon he held at the distribution. May God strengthen us in our faith! Then we shall never lack

God's providence and comfort. And may He, for the sake of
Christ, abundantly and graciously reward our dearest known
and unknown benefactors for these and other charititable gifts
of goods and money, for which we have prayed to Him both publicly and privately up to now.

Yesterday in Savannah there was a great deal to do, for which
God graciously strengthened me. In addition to baptizing a German and an English child and edifying myself concerning the
Second Commandment at a meeting together with Lutheran
and Reformed German people, I had an opportunity to write a
few lines to the secretary of the Society /Vernon/ and some letters to our worthy brother Pastor Brunnholtz in Philadelphia
and to the former preacher in Savannah, Mr. Wesley, who has
had a congregation for some time in London. The latter has
commissioned a man in Savannah to send him a report about
the present status of this colony, and especially of Ebenezer,
which he still remmbers fondly. I thought I would be able to do it
better myself than an inhabitant of Savannah, who, because of
age and feebleness, cannot leave the city. For that reason I sent
him a rather long letter. At first he hung closely to the Herrnhuters; but he discovered their errors and left them already a long
time ago.

Thursday, the 27th of July. In this year the grapes on the wild
vines in the forests have turned out very well; and the blue
grapes can be gathered in great quantity in a short time, as I
myself have seen today. The blue grapes have sometimes a sweet
and pleasant, and sometimes a sour, taste; and they look like the
grapes in Europe. The vines run up to the top of both low and
tall trees; and one must marvel that, although they stand right in
between the tree leaves and other plants, they still bear so abundantly and have such good fruit that in many places in Germany
the grapes from the domestic vines do not taste as good. The low
areas, which bore crops a few years ago but are now grown wild,
have a multitude of such grapes and an unusual number of vines
of various kinds. Because there are so many of them everywhere, the birds cannot devour them so quickly, but some are
left for the people. This year our mulberry trees, peaches, and
corn have also had peace from the large birds, which usually do

great damage to the said fruit and other fruits. Now they have enough food from the wild grapes and other wild fruits.

Knowledgeable people rightfully draw this well based conclusion: that our colony is very convenient for viticulture, even if there are no mountains but only hills. Because the wild grapes like to grow in low areas and along the large and small rivers and climb up onto the highest trees, one should set out the vines according to their nature. This has not yet been done, and therefore nothing has come of it. All sorts of beautiful fruits grow in the country, especially apples; and one can enjoy fruit from the grafted apple trees already in the fourth year, and, indeed, gradually so abundantly and beautifully as one could wish for. It is the same with figs. People have claimed that pears will not prosper in this climate; but a month ago I saw beautiful pear trees with much fruit in a garden in Savannah, which were not yet ripe.

Friday, the 28th of July. Among the blessings that our dear God has shown us this summer we rightfully count His gracious protection against the Indians. Otherwise, when the fruit in the gardens and the watermelons and sugar melons in the fields are ripe, they are accustomed to come to our place and to the plantations and not only to eat what they wish (which we gladly allow them) but also to load their horses with them; and then they spare no trees. They know that the soldiers have left; yet they remain away, and this must needs be a sign of God's protective kindness. The former preacher in Frederica, Mr. Bosomworth, who married Musgrove's widow (a half Indian woman, i.e., a female person begotten by a white man and an Indian woman) and plays the part of a trader among the Indians, is a problem for this colony.[13]

Saturday, the 29th of July. While we were returning home late today from the confessional, Adam Straube's wife,[14] who has moved to us from Vernonburg with all her family through God's gracious miraculous dispensation, asked to speak with me. Some time ago after long struggle and imploring, God sent her grace to be rejoiced and comforted in Christ and His merits through faith. However, when she wishes to go to Holy Communion, she again has new and very great disquiet and anxiety, as she told me

with plaintive words and sighs. I spoke with her about the beautiful words of Jesus: "They that be whole need not a physician, . . ." also "Come unto me all ye that labour and are heavy
laden," and I suggested to her for devout reading later on the
Communion hymns *Jesus Christus, unser Heyland, der von uns* etc.

Also, some people from the neighborhood in Carolina came
to us in order, God willing, to attend divine services tomorrow or
to take Holy Communion with the congregation. We hear that
recently it not only rained unusually but that it was also so
stormy that the fences were torn down and that the Indian corn
was beaten to the ground. God has preserved us from such
storms and damage. Some days ago we had good weather for
hay, for which reason our people were very industrious in this
kind of work; but today at noon we again received a very strong
and cold rain with violent thunder, which lasted gently till evening. So far God has preserved us from lightning and fires.

Sunday, the 30th of July. After the thunder ceased yesterday
evening, it rained violently deep into the night; but today we
have had the kind of weather we have wished, as if it were autumn. Because various people from Carolina were with us and
we held Holy Communion with seventy-one people, we had a
very large attendance today, to whom the word of the Lord was
proclaimed in the morning and afternoon loyally and emphatically. We hear that in other places many people are lying
sick with fever, and very many German people in Acton and Vernonburg near Savannah. On the other hand, our dear God has
spared our people from such and other sicknesses this summer
or else has let them pass quickly, even though they have had
more work with their Indian corn in this summer than ever in
previous years because it has always been rainy and the
chopped-out grass has soon grown back again.

AUGUST

Tuesday, the 1st of August. For some weeks in the prayer
meetings and weekday sermons we have contemplated the important, edifying, and exemplary story of the Queen of Sheba in
1 Kings 10:1 ff., which Christ himself presented as a remarkable

story in Matthew 12. From it we got to know, and took to heart, the most important teachings that are hidden in it. Today in both churches, to awaken our hearts, I presented from this lovely story and other verses of Holy Scripture the great blessedness of those who come to Christ, who is more than Solomon. Then I explained to our dear parishioners from scripture and from our dear catechism the coming to Christ and also the great bliss of being with and in Him. Oh, what a blessing our merciful God shows us through His holy word, which we can treat in great tranquility, freedom, and Christian unity in the two weekday sermons on the plantations and every evening after work with song and prayer.

As we frequently hear from other places in Carolina and in this colony, a great many of our German compatriots must lack the good things that our kind God has shown us in spiritual and physical matters. There is surely no one among us, not even the weakest widow, who is as poor as most of the Germans in this country are. Some of them use our mills and complain pitiably of their poverty and are now happy to receive a little help from us; and they regret not having settled at our place with their families. Wicked Germans who have been in the land for a long time have filled up their minds with many ungrounded accusations against our land and its arrangements. To their harm they believed these more than the late Pastor Driesler, me, and other upright people.[1]

Thursday, the 3rd of August. For several months Mrs. Lechner has been much concerned with the salvation of her soul, and this has influenced her external life, such as her marriage and business affairs. She is now much more industrious, peaceful, and content with everything and more obedient than in former years to her upright and industrious, albeit simple, husband. Her former misbehavior and naughtiness are now causing her great pangs and often such unrest that she needs admonishment and comfort from God's word. She considers herself highly deserving of all God's chastisements, and she marvels that our just God has been able to put up with such a sinner for so long, to show her much good, and to offer her His inestimable grace.

She loves her two delicate children tenderly and is afraid God will punish them because of her, the mother's, wickedness, as it stands at the conclusion of the Ten Commandments. However, I guided her to the promise in it: "He will show mercy to the pious unto the thousandth generation," likewise, "The son shall not bear the iniquity of the father," etc. I also gave her instruction according to her present spiritual circumstance concerning some Bible verses such as "Give me, my son, thy heart and let," etc., "the Son of man is come to seek and save" and also about the story of the serpent lifted up in the desert and mentioned in John 3.[2] She was able to comprehend all this very well. Since he became pious, her husband has been a right useful and industrious man, whereas formerly, for various reasons, he did not have a good name. He came to a true conversion during a very dangerous sickness; and so far he has remained in it loyally and has increased in recognition and in other Christian matters. He was so consumed by his sickness and had become so miserable that I consider his recovery a miracle of God, as he and his wife also do.

Friday, the 4th of August. Among other beautiful books and tractates from Halle and Augsburg we were also sent the epicedia[3] of the old deceased Inspector Freyer, from which our dear God has granted me a new blessing. When I hear or read something about the departure of friends, Fathers, and patrons I know, it makes a deeper impression on my spirit than when I read and hear the same about other people. May my Savior, through His merits and the Holy Ghost, make me ready to follow them blessedly to the place where all pious people have been going for many thousands of years!

The good odor that the servants and the children of God leave behind them in the world after their departure does not only attest their faith but is also a great blessing for the friends left behind and others who like to edify themselves from other examples. Therefore it is a praiseworthy undertaking to print modest funeral orations and biographies, as well as epicedia, which also serve those who are absent. From the hymns printed with it I see that various servants of God whom I knew in the Orphanage in Halle[4] and greatly esteemed because of their

righteous nature are still alive. Some of them already belong
among the old disciples of Christ and might well take their departure soon. May the Lord anoint the younger workers with
the same spirit with which the old ones were anointed, and may
He never let His work there (for which the love in my heart is
growing more and more ardent) never lack righteous leaders
and workers.

Sunday, the 5th of August. Yesterday evening I received from
Abercorn a letter in which the surveyor announces that at the
command of the Council in Savannah he has surveyed a part of
the land for the Ebenezer ministers. He could not continue with
the remainder until he knew whether I was pleased with this and
what I further wished. This morning I went to see the entire
land together with a knowledgeable Salzburger, who had to be
with the surveyor from the beginning of the surveying until the
end; and I must admit that its likes are not to be found in the
entire district that has been surveyed for our Ebenezer, except
for the large island across the Mill River, where, however, no one
can actually settle because it is flooded from time time. This new
land, on which we wish to take up our long-since mentioned
glebe land, lies near Abercorn and the beautiful land that the
last German indentured servants have received as their property.[5] To be sure, it is somewhat remote from Ebenezer, but
therefore all the closer to our cowpen; and, since the surrounding land belongs to Ebenezer, it also serves it as a protection so
that no one will be able to disturb us in our possession of this so
necessary and useful cowpen. Three hundred acres have been
surveyed for each minister, and three hundred acres are reserved for a third minister, who will be necessary in time in this
area when the entire district is occupied, as is beginning to occur
now because of its great fertility.

Here there is not only the most beautiful land for all sorts of
crops but also very good wood for building and for trade with
barrel staves and such things; also there is such beautiful cattle
pasture in both winter and summer that I doubt that there are
many such areas in the country. There is also enough water
there for men and cattle at all times of the year so that nothing
else is lacking but people who can be settled there and who can

cultivate the beautiful soil. We do not know whether we will ever receive the means to begin anything there in order to improve our domestic situation, yet it is our duty also to provide for our successors in office and to take up land before it is taken up by others.

No one doubts any longer that the Lord Trustees will permit Negroes, and therefore the best land is being taken up here and there. We are still hoping for servants, since some of them could perform a very useful work here. We did not insist upon this land, rather, contrary to our thoughts and expectations, the providence of God has ordained for us to receive our glebe land in this region. The gentlemen of the Council say that they had no plenipotentiary power to give more than three hundred acres to any one town; yet they are leaving an entire stretch of nine hundred acres together for three ministers until they hear the opinion and will of the Lord Trustees.

Monday, the 7th of August. Just as God granted me a new awakening a few days ago from the biographies and epicidia of the late Inspector Freyer, He has now let me experience the same blessing from the two edifying curricula, namely, of the native preacher, Mr. Aaron, and of the missionary Obuchs (who is still well known to me) in the continuation we have just received of the East Indian Reports;[6] and for this I heartily praise His goodness. Just as I was partly shamed and partly awakened by the excellent example of the Queen of Sheba, which we contemplated in the prayer meetings and weekday sermons as a trusting soul and valuable tool from heathendom, I must also acknowledge that of the beautiful example of the late Pastor Aaron, whom I had never imagined as I recognize him now from this his curriculum as composed by the worthy missionary. God be praised for the blessing He has granted this blessed man and through him many of his compatriots, as also many Europeans!

Wednesday, the 9th of August. Some time ago I had given a little boy a small gift to encourage him to diligence in learning and to obedience toward his parents. Today I discovered that he had, to be sure, improved in learning but that his obstinacy and disobdience, especially toward his mother, was not yet broken.

The worst thing was that the two parents are not of one mind in raising children. Rather, the mother, who is actually a righteous woman, prevents rather than advances disciplining the child with the rod; and therefore a sinful exchange of words has taken place between the formerly contented and compatible parents. I was very well pleased with the husband's manner of drawing the self-willed boy from the bad and toward the good; whereas I let the wife recognize her mistakes and instructed her how to do better.

So far we have always had much rainy weather. This has, to be sure, done the crops no harm, but it has somewhat delayed the haymaking. Also, the many beautiful peaches like the rainy weather; but many have rotted on the tree before they could be used by drying and by being distilled into brandy. Now they are all past. The beautiful tasty watermelons are sweeter and more delectable in dry and hot summers than in wet and cool ones such as we have had so far. One must marvel how cool it has been this summer and in the preceding dog days not only at night but also by day. Today we have again received dry and warm, yet very bearable weather. It started out as if the water in the river would become as low as in other summers when something had to be repaired on the mills. However, it has begun to rise again and we will have to wait patiently with the intended repairs. There is agreat quantity of eels in our Mill River that bore large holes in the clay of the mill dam and thus make openings for the water that then eats further. We have no sand and stones here but must use earth and clay.

Thursday, the 10th of August. Last night a woman sent to me and said that she would like to complain of her spiritual sorrow to me but that she did not know whether she would live till the next day. Therefore, it would please her if I would come to her. I did so without delay and found her not physicaly, but spiritually, sick; and our dear God gave me wisdom and strength to speak to her from His word as required by her spiritual condition. For some time, especially since her sister's departure from this world, she has been earnestly concerned with her salvation. However, because she has suffered much weakness and because her conscience uses that as a reason for all sorts of reproaches and not only denies her the grace of God but even a new access to it, she has come into great disquiet and anxiety. It is good that she has not dragged that around with her long but revealed it to her ministers, and from this she has profited through divine mercy. During the prayer my dear Savior strengthened me noticeably so that I received a new awakening and encouragement from these nocturnally requested ministerial duties to perform my office and Christianity with renewed seriousness and loyalty through the grace of God. To be sure, there is a great responsibility in the evangelical ministry; but for various reasons it is also a valuable spiritual blessing for every righteous minister, which should encourage us to true loyalty.

Friday, the 11th of August. Our friend Mr. Habersham wrote me from Savannah that he had received a letter from Mr. Whitefield in which he has been given joyful news about the great blessing that God has granted him in his office from people of rank and ministers in London. In it he mentioned me, my colleague, and our congregation in a friendly manner. I was afraid, to be sure, that N.'s lack of caution and the calumny of another man in London might have turned the heart of this Mr. Whitefield from me. Mr. Habersham had written to him about my fear and thrown a better light on the evilly interpreted matter. Yet he explained himself so well in the letter that has just arrived that I can be very well satisfied.

Monday, the 14th of August. We hear from Savannah that very many Indians have come to Savannah under the guidance of an English minister, Bosomworth, to fetch their gifts.[7] On this occasion they are acting very defiantly and shamelessly and putting the inhabitants in worry and fear. They would have received their gifts at their own place, and the purpose of the gifts would have been better achieved if the said man had not caused this disturbance. Parliament has ordered three thousand pounds Sterling annually for gifts for the Indians in Georgia and South Carolina; but one has noticed that the kinder the English nation has shown itself to the Indians, the wilder and more spiteful they have become; and they claim from the inhabitants of this colony things that cannot be conceded to them. The said man has done great harm among these people, and he is blamed for all the misfortune that is feared.

Tuesday, the 15th of August. Yesterday evening my dear colleague brought me the sad news that Paul Müller's wife/Apollonia/ had been bitten by a poisonous snake, which people here call a rattlesnake, and that she has come into mortal danger. Her husband immediately opened the snake, which she herself had killed, and put its lung and liver on the wound, from which bright blood was running; and he also laid the posteriors of living chickens warm on the wound and gave the weak patient theriac with brandy. It appears that God blessed these means so that she seems to be out of danger provided she follows the advice she was given to keep herself in a gentle perspiration. To be sure, her foot and half of her leg are inflamed and swollen; but the pains in her breast, to which the poison had climbed, have subsided. Just as we prayed for her publicly and privately, we also praised our dear God, who doeth great things at all ends of the earth, for this new proof of His miraculous goodness. This I also did with her and her children in their house (for the father was not at home).

I also told her from God's word how she should properly apply this danger and her great rescue from it; and during this I told her the exemplary story in Numbers 21. She is an industrious and honest woman, and she suffered this unexpected incident while mowing grass. The bite of the rattlesnake is usually always fatal, and its poison is supposed to have the most violent and swift effect. It is even said that when a piece of of its exceptionally sharp teeth gets stuck in a shoe, boot, etc. and afterwards touches the limb of a man or animal, the limb will swell up and draw death after it. As the best remedy against the bite of this and other snakes it is recommended that the bitten person hold his foot up quickly because the poison does not descend but rises upwards. Also the leg must be bound tightly above the wound, and common kitchen salt must be placed on the wound.

Thursday, the 17th of August. The weather is continuing to be more wet and cool than dry and warm. If we had a thermometer to measure and determine the degree of cold or warmth, our friends in Europe would be amazed how cool it can be in this climate at this season. Here one must change clothes and blankets in summer as well as in winter and use now lighter ones and now cooler ones. Whoever keeps himself too cool in the evening, night, or morning will soon contract difficulties in his health. The sudden changes in weather, likewise the heating and chilling of the body, seem to me to be the chief cause of the many fevers and other bodily weaknesses.[8] Those who eat the local grapes very frequently complain of diarrhea and say that they are not as healthy as they are in Europe. Now the so-called fox grapes are becoming ripe which are large black grapes, the size of which we have never seen in Europe (as far as the individual grapes are concerned). They grow in large numbers on the banks of the rivers and in other low areas, some on low and some on very high vines; they have a thick skin and taste sweet and pleasant. There is also a very small grapevine in the dry forests, which only runs along the ground and bears similar grapes.

Sunday, the 19th of August. Yesterday evening I again received news in a letter about the great disturbance that the Indians are making at the instigation of N. and his wife.[9] She is a half Indian, and her brother is a wild and impudent chief among the Indians; and therefore she has a large following among them. If they are so wild and malicious at this time that such imposing gifts are being distributed to them, how much we will have to fear afterwards if God does not hold His hand over us and our land? As soon as I heard a few months ago that General Oglethorpe's regiment was going to be cashiered, I wrote to the commandant at Frederica, Col. Heron, and announced to him among other things that, with regard to the Indians, I feared that the gifts that had come for them from England would not accomplish as much among them as the presence of the regiment, and I have now been confirmed in this belief by a new example.

This evening one of our inhabitants told me that various Indians had passed by our cowpen on horseback, and one was also seen on horseback on the plantations. Therefore I hope they will finally be satisfied and be sent back to their homes. They should not have received their gifts in Savannah but rather at the place of their residence; but the frequently mentioned N. and his half-

Indian wife are to blame for this and similar disorders. They both wish to travel to England; perhaps they will not be allowed to return, which would be for the best.

Sunday, the 20th of August. This 13th Sunday after Trinity has been a pleasant and joyful day for us for various important reasons, but especially because it was the birthday of our dearest and highly esteemed Senior Urlsperger, the day on which he first saw the light of day sixty-four years ago. I already looked forward to this day several days ago to praise the Lord, our ever-lasting Savior, with our dear parishioners for the goodness He has shown to this our worthy father and benefactor and to peti-tion our heavenly Father to give him new strength of mind and body for this sixty-fifth year that he has entered. This I also did today in the public Sunday prayer meeting. Beforehand we sang from the little hymnal *Selected Hymns*[10] (which we have again been using temporarily for several weeks in the evening prayer meetings for repeating the newly learned hymns) the beautiful hymn *Auf, o Seele, preise deines Schöpfers Güte*, etc. and after the prayer, intercession, and thanksgiving the three last verses of the hymn *Lobe meine Seele! deines Jesu Thaten* , etc. But beforehand we announced to those who were singing and praying that today was the birthday of our dearest Senior, whom we, above all oth-ers, had reason to celebrate with praise, thanks, and prayer.

Tuesday, the 22nd of August. A young person from Purys-burg who has sojourned around our place for some time as a day laborer was bitten on his thumb yesterday by a rattlesnake, and from that his hand and arm are very swollen and the poison has penetrated a bit to his heart; yet with God's blessing he has been helped so far that he can go around again even if he cannot yet use his hand. Thanks be to God who can still always avert a mis-fortune. May He give grace so that the purpose of this chastise-ment will be achieved both in this person, who is not yet in a good condition, and also in others of the congregation.

When I was writing the former at four o'clock this afternoon I received the sad news that Mrs. /Elisabetha/ Meyer, the wife of our very useful surgeon and justiciar, had died. I had been with her shortly before and had had a very pleasant conversation with her and her husband from the gospel about Christ, the friend of sinners, and about the glory of eternal life, at which her mind was entirely aimed. Then, on our knees, we presented in prayer our and our patient's circumstances to our dear Savior. During this we profited especially from His noteworthy love for poor sinners according to the content of the 7th chapter of Luke and thus strengthened ourselves in our faith in His name. I had scarcely taken leave and had not yet reached my house before she had another hemorrhage as she did yesterday and in the previous night. When Mr. Meyer wished to hold her head and raise her up, she suddenly died. Now he is experiencing what I guided her to shortly before and also last night: "The lamb that is in the midst of the throne shall feed them, and shall lead them unto living fountains of water"[11]

Her entire life with us was a constant cross, during which she had not a single truly healthy day; and it is said that it was that way with her in Memmingen. Through the grace of God she bore her external and internal cross willingly and patiently; and, when it would sometimes seem too long or too hard in her very great pain, she greatly humbled herself before her Savior because of such disorderly emotions of impatience and implored Him for forgiveness. Her heart was always full of her Savior and of chosen Bible verses, and through them I was abundantly edified as often as I visited her. Yesterday she had me called unexpectedly to give her instruction, counsel, and comfort from the living word of God in her weakness; and this occurred through the grace of my Savior. Shortly before, my heart had been awakened through His spirit from reading Senior Heinold's little book *The Necessary Combination of the Law and the Gospel* and had been prepared for this ministerial duty of mine.[12]

Wednesday, the 23rd of August. Mrs. Meyer was buried this afternoon and God showed much good to my body and soul. For He armed me in my weakness with strength and joy to hold the funeral oration concerning the beautiful funeral text, which the deceased herself had chosen from Psalms 61:2–3 and written down along with some lovely hymns. Just as my dear Savior filled my heart then with peace and joy, I hope He will also have raised

up our dear Mr. Meyer through this dear word of the blessedness of true Christians in time and eternity and will have encouraged him to a new seriousness in his Christianity. In spiritual matters he owes many thanks to his pious wife, so
experienced in her Christianity, just as he praises the grace of
God that he was saved from conformity to the world by her
merits and was brought to the way of life.

Yesterday and today there was very violent weather, but at the
funeral it was quite bearable; therefore we thank God for letting
us hit the right time. Since Monday we have had constant rain
and very cool weather both day and night.

Friday, the 25th of August. Not only did it rain heavily off and
on last week, but the rain also continued this week from Monday
to Friday both day and night and filled all places with much water. At times we also had great storm winds from the northwest;
and, because the rain clouds were coming from there, we may
well fear that it has rained as much up there in the mountains as
down here; and therefore we can fear a great flood and inundation in the low areas along the river and therefore at our mills. If,
as it appears, the Savannah River should suddenly overflow at
this time and rise out of its banks, then not only many cattle will
perish but also much Indian corn and rice will spoil. The wheat
harvest was greatly damaged, and now if the hand of God were
also to destroy the corn, beans, squash, and rice, it would be hard
on the poor (since white flour and other breadstuffs are very expensive); yet it would not be more than a merited punishment
for our sins.

Saturday, the 26th of August. Someone wrote to me from Savannah that the disturbance from the Indians is completly over
and that nothing is to be feared from them now. They have
moved back to their homes.

Today the sky cleared again and it appears that we will again
have dry weather after the much rain because the wind has
shifted directly to the west. It rained in Savannah as violently as
here, the water in the rivers has risen so high in twenty-four
hours that all the mills have stopped. We still expect a great flood
from upstream.

Monday, the 28th of August. We are convinced more and more that the low rich land is, to be sure, very fertile, but not the best for that reason. Rather, those who have their plantations on high, even if somewhat poorer land, have the advantage, as can easily be seen now when there has been so much rain. On the said low rich soil everything is so saturated that the corn has fallen and is either being brought in half ripened or must spoil in the mud. On the other hand, on the high ground, even in the so-called pine woods, the corn, beans, squash, etc. are standing so beautifully that it could hardly be any more beautiful.

A man planted rice on a low wet spot right in the middle of the pine forest, which is now standing as abundantly as if it had been planted on the actually rich low riceland. It again seems to me that those who have bad land on their plantations have received the most corn, beans, and other crops. It depends more upon industry and the grace of God than on the soil; and I believe that, if the colonists here did not lack the two, they would have no reason to complain so much about the lack of good land. The land behind Abercorn, and not far from our cowpen, pleases us best; it is not too high and not too low, and it is uncommonly convenient for planting and cattle raising. Perhaps God will bless our efforts with the Council in Savannah so that, just as we have received the three imposing tracts of land of nine hundred acres in the neighborhood of Abercorn for our three preachers, we will also acquire a good district for the benefit of our cowpen and congregation.

Tuesday, the 29th of August. A young single woman has had to be kept from Holy Communion because of her wickedness and obstinacy, but she did not pay much attention to it, rather she continued in her frivolous and disobedient way, even though we worked on her in great love and with the word and by showing her physical benefactions. Finally it became unbearable for her master that she was making no effort to prepare herself worthily for the Lord's Table. He therefore announced to her that, if she would not conform to order, he would no longer suffer her in his house. She was, to be sure, defiant and looked around for another shelter; but, when I received news of this, I took her to task in the presence of her master and his wife and

told her, according to the introduction of Dr. Luther's small catechism, how miserable and perilous her spiritual condition was
and what punishment would be undertaken to break her de-
fiance and disobedience and, if possible, to save her soul. I also
told her of what great spiritual and physical blessings she would
rob herself if she did not accept good advice soon and conform
to Christian order. Since then I have noticed that she wishes to
turn over a new leaf. Today she came to me and announced that
God had awakened her heart to a new seriousness to save her
soul; and she asked me to admit her once again to the Lord's
Table.

Wednesday, the 30th of August. Since the last great rain we
have had right warm summer days, which is very good for ripening the grain and for making hay. The water in the river has
again fallen a few inches and our mills are all in full operation,
which is a great blessing for both the inhabitants and for
strangers. Perhaps it will fall so far that the necessary repairs we
recently mentioned can be made. For at high water the base of
the dam cannot be repaired.

Our worthy Mr. von M. /Münch/ has done us a very pleasant
favor by sending us Mr. Sturm's beautiful tractate on mill-con-
struction.[13] A correction has been made in one of the mill
courses according to its directions, and, to be sure, with very
good success and little expense. Now with low water twice as
much can be ground as previously with much water. If we let as
much water fall on it as we used to use, the mill would go too fast
and the meal would burn between the heated stones. Now we
can grind sixteen to twenty bushels in fourteen hours; and I find
it incomprehensible when it is said that as much, or almost the
same quantity, can be ground in one hour in some mills (even if
not in most) in Europe. The Salzburgers have not experienced
this in their country. If we let this one and the other low course
run as fast as they could according to the force of the water, especially after the new changes, many pieces would be broken by the
power of the water; and, as previously mentioned, the flour
would burn and become brown and bad-tasting. If the stones
have become hot from the continuous grinding, the miller must
stop the mill from time to time to cool them off.

We must acknowledge with thanks that on both mills we can grind thirty-two London bushels or more in a day and night or twenty-four hours. Every bushel is poured on and sent through three times, or four at the desire of some people. If we were to have a builder versed in mills for even a short time, much could be improved in our mills with little cost, as I now see from this example. My dear colleague has a good insight into mechanical things and is making Mr. Sturm's previously mentioned book useful to our mills, but we are lacking skillful and experienced carpenters among us. The two who possess good ability, namely Kogler and Rottenberger, have so much to do with their households, farming, cattle raising, and other things that we cannot get them for the necessary work. They cannot be persuaded to lay aside all other things and work only with their handicraft. They would have more work all year long than they could tend to; and they would become rich, if they were economical. Our other carpenters understand little or nothing and are not disposed to learn anything. Perhaps God will grant us some good carpenters from Germany, who would find work and rich support here.[14] We hoped to receive letters from Europe with the last opportunity from Charleston in order to learn whether or not we are to have servants; we received nothing, nor did the Councilmen.

Thursday, the 31st of August. The righteous and very skillful Brandner has been so weak for the past year that he has been entirely incapable of any work. He has the pale color of death on his face, he has no strength in his limbs, and he becomes tired from walking or doing the least work. A couple of other men seem to have his same sickness, which I consider a hectica. To be sure, they have used much medicine from Mr. Thilo and Mr. Meyer but have detected no good from it. A short time ago Brandner was told by Mr. David Zübli of Purysburg and some other people that a certain Swiss there knew of a good medication against this sickness and had already helped some people. To be sure, I could not advise him to use a medication that we did not know; however, since he cannot find any counsel here and the medicines he has taken have had no effect, I could not advise him against the trip to this otherwise very Christian and knowledgeable man. Today he had an opportunity to go down there; may God let it turn out well and may He, according to His gracious will, grant this pious Salzburger his health again, to the joy of his wife and three children. If it were my office and I could discover the *statum morbi*[15] of these and those unusual patients, I would gladly request counsel from the physicians in Germany, who are our patrons.

SEPTEMBER

Friday, the 1st of September. This afternoon Mr. Lemke traveled to Savannah in order to preach to the German people the day after tomorrow, the Fifteenth Sunday after Trinity, to hold Holy Communion with some of them, and to baptize some children. Mr. Meyer accompanied him because he had some business with the authorities. May God let both of them accomplish much good! Things are rather hard and difficult for the German people both in Savannah and in Abercorn, where at present very few families are settled on the new and very fertile land. However, we little note that they humble themselves before God and regret, among others, the sins that they have committed through all sorts of disloyalty in their short years of service in this country. Some, perhaps even most of them, secretly hate our place and its arrangements, even if they have received many kinds of spiritual and physical blessings from here. They begrudge our people the advantages that our merciful God has granted them in many ways over other inhabitants of this country. Many of these German indentured servants could have come to our place during their service if they had not let themselves be prejudiced against us by the other German people in and near Savannah and had not believed their lies and calumnies more than what was told them about us by our worthy Court Chaplain Ziegenhagen, Pastor Driesler, and others.[1]

Saturday, the 2nd of September. Riedelsperger's smallest child, four months old, died and was blessedly buried this afternoon. God granted both the adults and the children at the funeral a new awakening for an evangelical preparation for blessed eternity, as we could clearly perceive from their gestures and tears. At every burial we hold a funeral oration, during which we do not look to the praise of the deceased but to the edification of the living. In cases of death, people's minds are usually awakened and observant; and therefore the word that is preached surely makes a deeper impression. This child's parents are both heartily pious; and they praise God for the departure of this delicate and physically very miserable child, and I found this Christian attitude very impressive and pleasing when I visited them today after school (without knowing that it had already died).

Sunday, the 3rd of September. Since the last heavy rain we have had eight days of dry weather and a couple of days of right pleasant weather; and from Savannah we have received news that no flood or inundation is to be feared, since the river upstream was not raised more than three feet by the last rain. Praise be to God, who has graciously averted from our region that which we had feared. Toward Charleston it is said to have rained most unusually and the ricefields are under water. To be sure, rice can bear the water, but not over the tips of the ears; if it goes above them, then the rice spoils quickly. This crop is now very expensive and hardly to be had. The same is true of wheat flour, a hundred pounds of which costs twenty-five shillings Sterling.

Tuesday, the 5th of September. Today my dear colleague returned safe and sound from Savannah. He not only had to preach in Savannah and hold Holy Communion for some people of our confession, but also, at the request of the weak people of Acton and Abercorn, he had to preach at their place and baptize two children. On the way home to Ebenezer he was fetched from Abercorn to the few German people who have settled behind Abercorn in order to baptize a child. God strengthened him noticeably in all these activities; but during his absence God let me become sick with tertian fever. I have already begun to recover, for which I rightfully praise His goodness. On Sunday morning I preached here concerning the words of Job 10:12, "Thou hast granted me life and favor, and thy visitation hath preserved my spirit"; and from this our good God showed me much good. In the afternoon I treated, from the regular gospel

for the Fifteenth Sunday after Trinity, a part of the important
dogma of divine providence and care.

Thursday, the 7th of September. The younger /Martin/ Lackner and his wife are both sickly people, she is in childbed and
can spare herself little because she has no servant in the house
and there is much work with three small children. They are patient and content and gratefully accept help in physical things
and encouragement in spritual ones. The children are being
prepared in town for Holy Communion, and he told me that after the lesson he had found one of them kneeling under a tree
and praying heartily. This had both shamed and awakened him.
He had to admit that until now he had preferred to read and
hear than to pray and that he had therefore not progressed
properly in his Christianity. I heartily wished that he would
show more seriousness both in his Christianity and also in his
external business affairs.

Saturday, the 9th of September. After the heavy rain we had
about eight days of right desirable dry and warm weather, which
is much needed for making hay and harvesting the crops, also
for the ripening of some of them; but for the past two days wet
weather has begun again, and it also seems to cause the cold
fever of which we are again hearing now and then. The water in
the river has again become so low that we must marvel, but it will
probably not remain that way for long.

The German people in Congarees (a newly settled place in
South Carolina, a hundred and fifty miles upcountry from
Charleston) requested me some time ago in a letter to visit them
and put them aright. Now a good friend has written me from
Charleston that he is advising me to this trip because on it I
would see various useful kinds of agriculture in Carolina and at
the said place to the benefit of our inhabitants and also make
other good observations. At the same time I would have an opportunity to recover the three serving boys who ran away from
us and, along with their parents, ran to the said Congarees and
wish to settle there.[2] He said the governor would help me in this.
However well this friend means it and however useful the suggested things appear, I cannot resolve to undertake such a long,
expensive, and time-consuming trip, partly because of my weak

physical constitution, partly because of my actual professional duties at home, and partly because of the hardships of traveling in this country. The mentioned external matters actually belong to the office of our agent and justiciar, Mr. Meyer. How little might I accomplish with these people in spiritual matters I can learn from the example of their compatriots in and around Savannah. Congarees is a *Colluuies prauorum hominum*.[3]

Sunday, the 10th of September. On this Sixteenth Sunday after Trinity we held Holy Communion with seventy people, among them two from Purysburg and two who have just come to the congregation. May God let it redound to their salvation!

The locksmith /Schrempf/, who unnecessarily moved to Carolina some time ago, has a great desire to return here with his family; but returning will not be as easy as leaving because: 1) He sold his house and farm and what God had granted him here, and now he must first buy himself another house and build a forge. 2) Because there is very little money in Carolina, he had to do most of his work for credit, and now he will have much trouble and loss in collecting his debts. 3) He burned his feet in a charcoal heap, and his wife has become mortally sick, and their child has scarcely shown any improvement. He sent a messenger here today to fetch medicine.

Thursday, the 14th of September. I have been weakly for several days; and, because changes of air have been beneficial to my health at other times, I undertook a complete change four days ago and went down to Savannah with a good opportunity, from where, God be praised, I returned safe and sound today at midday. But I had more to do there than I had expected, for, in addition to having some business with the President and the other gentlemen ofthe Council, I had to baptize four children, partly of English and partly of German parents. A pious woman had some scruples about some expressions in the English baptismal formula, of which I freed her to her complete satisfaction; and afterwards the baptismal service was performed in the presence of her righteous husband and some Christian friends with mutual edification.

Some good news has reached Savannah: Parliament is said to have given the Lord Trustees 1500 pounds Sterling for the good of our colony. Two shiploads of German people are said to be underway to this colony either as free people or as indentured servants, likewise, in place of Oglethorpe's regiment another complete regiment is coming to protect this colony. To be sure, we have no written assurance of these new reports, since no letters have arrived, yet they are not doubted because the captain and several passengers, who arrived recently at Charleston in a ship, brought them. There is much dangerous fever in Carolina.

Friday, the 15th of September. Because of the plentiful rain we can well call this year a wet year, which, however, is a fruitful year through divine blessing. Even if the wheat and rye did not turn out well on all plantations, they still turned out all right on some of our plantations and at other places; and the Indian corn and beans, like the remaining crops, have a very nice appearance in the fields. Last night we had an unexpected severe thunderstorm with very heavy rain, and after that there arose wind and cool weather. In the past summer the storms have been few and not so violent as in other years.

Saturday, the 16th of September. For some time our dear God has been visiting the righteous Hans Flerl's righteous wife with many physical trials, especially with painful illnesses, in which she, as a Christian, has shown herself as a true Christian. Today she told me that it made a deep impression on her heart that the pious widow Zant, who is poor and has to support two children and a serving girl, had brought her some butter as a gift. She herself, she said, has a husband and a serving boy and has been able to do little or nothing for this pious widow. This Mrs. Flerl stands in great poverty of spirit, in which she considers the good works of other Christians better than her own.

Wednesday, the 20th of September. N.N. told me with joy that he now has hopes that his wife will truly devote her heart to the Lord Jesus. He said that, because of her love of the world, he had formerly doubted that she would ever be won. When I came to her on their plantation she told me that for some time she had had a strange feeling but did not know how to adapt herself to it. She still feels, she said, great joy in her dear Savior and has such a desire for His kind words that she would like to concern herself with them always. However, she said, she did not trust herself because she had formerly been full of hypocrisy and did not rightly regret her many sins that she has committed since childhood. Nevertheless, it pains her greatly to have insulted such a good Lord; also, she still feels very weak and is easily overwhelmed by frivolity and other spiritual enemies so that she is about to lose all comfort in Christ. And it seems to her that everything she feels in her heart about Christ and His word is nothing but her imagination. I recited for her the verse 1 Peter 12[4] "As newborn babes, desire the sincere milk of the word," . . ." If so be ye have tasted," etc.; and I gave her other instruction and admonition in keeping with her circumstances.

Sunday, the 23rd of September. Not very long ago N. from N. lived in great disunity with his wife, and they had to be heard by Mr. Meyer and me. When I heard not long ago that they were getting along well together and that the good admonitions they had received at the time from God's word had not remained fruitless, I gave her some money to use in her coming childbed, and thus I showed my pleasure in her Christian behavior. Today I heard the sad news that she had borne a dead child, which had died in the womb some days earlier, and was therefore in dangerous and distressing circumstances. We are asking God to let this severe and distressing event redound to the spiritual good of these people and graciously to avert such a thing from our other married couples. Perhaps another incident contributed to this present one, which recently happened to the pregnant woman. She had collected a kind of chestnut from a tree in the forest and inadvertently touched a certain worm, which was about one and a fifth inches long and as rough as a young hedgehog, which suddenly caused such pain as if she had been bitten by a poisonous snake. That has already occurred to several people among us in former years, including my wife, from which they were almost in mortal danger. The rough worm hangs very still on a leaf or twig; if a person just touches a hair with his limb, an almost unbearable pain starts immediately in the same limb and goes right to the heart and causes the person mortal fear just as a snakebite does. Today I let my children show me such a worm. It neither flies nor runs away but just pulls itself together like a hedgehog and is not easily killed because of its hairy skin.

Sunday, the 24th of September. In this autumn God has visited various of our dear inhabitants with fevers; therefore it has occurred that our assembly in the church this Sunday was not as large as it is usually accustomed to be. Our two schoolmasters are also sick, and things seem to be perilous for Köcher, the schoolmaster on the plantations.

Tuesday, the 26th of September. In the daytime we are now having right desirable dry and warm weather, which is very good for making hay and ripening the crops. On the other hand, it is severely cold. The water in the river has fallen so much that in some places the boat can hardly get across the sand. It has not been so low for a long time; but it serves us, too, since our mill dam can be repaired all the better without hindrance.

News has come to our place that five ships full of German people, among them also Salzburgers, are said to be underway, who are being sent here by the Lord Trustees.[5]

Thursday, the 28th of September. The locksmith N. /Schrempf/and his honest wife no longer wish to remain in Carolina. He has scarcely recovered from a dangerous sickness, and he came to us by land to make his removal to here certain. In his sickness God let him feel in his conscience the great sin of moving away from Ebenezer and the great spiritual and physical harm that he caused himself and his family. He wishes to thank God if he again has the good fortune to be a member of our congregation. He has bought a house here and will move here shortly. His example has made a deep impression on those of us who have desired to make a change. He is an industrious and skillful worker, and we can well use him.

The crops have turned out very well this year; and, because the birds are finding enough nourishment in the forest from grapes and other berries and also from little nuts and other plants, they are sparing the ricefields and cornfields. As soon as we have harvested the corn and beans and whatever else God has granted, we will hold our harvest and thanksgiving celebration, as is properly done each year. If our inhabitants had been able to plant more, they would have profited more abundantly during this fruitful year; but they were lacking strength and hired hands, still they are getting all they need.

OCTOBER

Sunday, the first of October. On this Sunday, the Nineteenth Sunday after Trinity, our merciful God has let us live a new month in rest, health, and blessing; and for this it is mete and right that we give Him humble praise. Last month He did, to be sure, send many kinds of fever and weakness among us after the many rains we had in the summer and the beginning of fall; yet in comparison with others in Carolina, it has still been quite bearable. We are now having a very dry period that is very good for the harvest. It must be the same way among the Indians up in the mountains because the Savannah River has become so low that the ebb and flood can be detected at our place and even up in Ebenezer Creek, and this has seldom happened.[1] The flood tide usually comes up to the milldam unless the water in the main river is so high and strong that it does not allow the flood to come up. The Mill River is very convenient for us for going between here to Savannah by boat, and it is a great blessing.[2]

None of the mills can operate now, but the water needs to rise only a little and then we will be able to use the lower course again. The mills are such a great blessing for us that no one who has a Christian spirit can think of them without praising God.

Monday, the 2nd of October. A friend communicated a couple of letters to me which Mr. Zouberbuhler (the Anglican preacher in Savannah) had sent from London to a friend in Savannah, and which give this reliable news: 1) that the Lord Trustees will send a transport of poor German people here to Georgia at their own humble request, with whom he himself (Mr. Zouberbuhler) will return to his former post after having achieved what he wished, a salary of fifty pounds Sterling annually. 2) that the Lord Trustees have received from Parliament for this colony not the £15,000 Sterling (as it was spread around here) but only £5304. This sum will hardly suffice to pay the many debts in this country, therefore we can hardly presume that they will send our inhabitants such loyal and industrious servants as we have requested. Furthermore, the secretary of the Lord Trustees has now written the same thing to the President and Council. When hearing such reports, my heart always says, "May He do with us and this land as it well pleases Him!"

Tuesday, the 10th of October. At the beginning of last week I had necessary business with the Council in Savannah; and, because our German servants also arrived there, I had to remain there for eight full days. I will summarize the main events that have occurred during my sojourn in Savannah and most concern our congregation in the following points: 1) God has so blessed my presentations, which were supported by Mr. Habersham (a member of the Council), that the gentlemen of the Council have granted our community all the good land behind Abercorn and up to our cowpen; and this will be surveyed for those who have have been provided with no land so far or only with very bad land. It is an excellent stretch of land, of which kind little is to be found. We have also had our glebe land surveyed in the same district, all told 600 acres, and an additional 300 acres for a minister who might come to a future congregation in this area.

Because Negroes or Moorish slaves are permitted now under certain conditions, good land will become scarce. Should the 300 acres for a third minister not be necessary, it can be used for the good of the young people among us when they come of age. On the other hand, the so-called Uchee land near us on the Savannah River will be reserved for some of our older inhabitants and workers, but especially for the loyal servants whom we are now getting and shall get in the future.

2) Sixty-three German people arrived fresh and sound in Savannah on the 3rd and 4th of this month, who were very well cared for by a good-natured captain named Peter Bogg. Only one single little boy died on the sea; on the other hand one was born at sea and still another soon after the arrival in Savannah. All of them were brought to a spacious house that belongs to our old friend in England, Mr. Jones,[3] and were maintained there at the cost of the Lord Trustees. Here I had an opportunity to preach the word of God to them in the evening prayer meetings and also in church on the Twentieth Sunday after Trinity, and in them I had right attentive and desirous hearers. For some time, whenever I have come to Savannah, I have been accustomed to

lay the Ten Commandments as a basis of my sermon; and for this I have made use of the very thorough and important examinations of the heart from the late Ambrosius Wirth's *Confession and Holy Communion Booklet*.[4] Now I was ordained to explain and inculcate into the hearts of the newcomers and others the content of the Fourth Commandment, which follows in the order of contemplation; and God granted me much help in this.

On Sunday I treated the regular gospel Matthew 22 concerning the wrath of our holy and just God at the scorners of His grace. In the exordium we contemplated the words from Psalms 90:11, "Who knoweth the power of thine anger?," etc. After one of the prayer meetings some young people came to me and said that, to be sure, it had not gone well with them on the sea voyage but rather some of them had behaved very badly, but the fault for that lay in that they had no word of God on the whole journey.

3) The authorities in Savannah and also other inhabitants there have, to be sure, attested enough that they would rather have Negroes than white people as servants, as the Lord Trustees well enough know. Nevertheless, they have selected twenty-one people from this transport, for some they have paid six pounds Sterling and some they have charged to the Trustees. These are mostly useful craftsmen like carpenters, wheelwrights, cabinetmakers, etc. and the most useful people. I have now brought to our place five families with children, two single little girls whose parents are serving one of the Councilmen, and fifteen single men who are mostly bakers, millers, tailors, and shoemakers. These were distributed in good order today by lot to our dear worn-out inhabitants as far as they would go, but the remainder got none.

Some servants from this transport have the promise from the gentlemen in Savannah that they will not have to serve more than one or two years; and it seems hard on those who were left for us to have to serve three years and five months. Because I was afraid of disorder and annoyance from this at our place, I had all our servants assembled and told them that I did not wish to take any to our place under compulsion. Therefore every man should tell me whether he would rather remain in Savannah and buy himself free in about three months (as the Trustees' permission reads) or go with me to Ebenezer where there were, to be sure, good foodstuffs but no work for them other than farming and cattle raising. They chose the latter and promised to follow their calling loyally. Otherwise I was resolved to follow the example of other people in Savannah and choose the best and to leave the others for the Lord Trustees and their agents in Savannah.

Two large families, who have very small children, could not be sheltered here by any householder; and therefore they fell through necessity to me and my dear colleague. We are engaging a pious Salzburger to instruct them in their work on a piece of land on the Mill River. I hope that the Lord Trustees will allow us something for their maintenance, as they are doing for the minister in Savannah with his big salary, who is receiving £24 Sterling annually to support his two servants. 5) The Lord Trustees have now allowed the introduction of Negroes, and the stipulations for that are not only fitting but pleasing. We will now see whether the colony will flourish from it.

Wednesday, the 11th of October. After the arrival of these servants a heavier burden has fallen on me than I have had in previous years. God, who has helped me numerous times in my whole life in miraculous ways, will mercifully help me further in everything and through everything that He lays on me so that I will be able to praise His name here and there.

Thursday, the 12th of October. One of our servants drawn by lots, a shoemaker by trade, was redeemed yesterday for £6 Sterling; and by this our honest and sickly Brandner was robbed of his servant, for which he had waited for several years. This anomaly can not be prevented because, according to their contract with the Lord Trustees, all these servants have three months grace to redeem themselves by anyone they wish and however they can. If this disadvantageous point were not in the contract, it would be better for us and for these servants.

Saturday, the 14th of October. During this dry autumn the Savannah River has become so small that the trees and trunks that have fallen into it stick up at many places or are covered with only a little water. That caused a boat that was coming down from Augusta loaded high with 1,200 pounds of deer hides to be capsized and the leather, that had to lie in the water for twelve days, to be totally spoiled. On both sides of the river stand a multitude of high and thick trees that sometimes fall into the river in heavy wind and rain, by which the earth is greatly softened. Indeed, many people who have their plantations along the river have the bad habit of felling the trees into the river and thus making the journey inconvenient and unsafe. In coming upstream, the boats must always keep close to shore where the current is weakest and the rowing easiest. The river has many bends; and therefore, when it comes around the corners, it rushes along with unusual violence. Because it is so crooked and has high trees on both sides, one can hardly use the wind and a sail as far as Purysburg.

When our servants arrived at Savannah, I sighed to God that, according to His gracious will, He might grant as much water as is needed for a mill course, because I well knew how necessary the use of the mill was at this time, when there is no flour or bread, rice, or anything else (with the exception of meat) in Savannah. On the same evening that I was planning to depart from Savannah with our newcomers, a small boat came from our place and brought me the joyful news that the lower mill course had unexpectedly received water again and that it could grind a rather large quantity by day and night. Thus God appears with His help at a time that we need it most. For a short time the low water has been a great blessing, because our milldam could be repaired as desired.

Monday, the 16th of October. Today I heard complaints from two householders about their servants, who acted restless because they had to serve longer than some in Savannah and threatened to run away. Their behavior moved me to call them all to me this afternoon with their masters so that I might speak with them about what was necessary for our and their good. First I let them show me the recommendations they had brought from Germany, from which Mr. Meyer wrote down their baptismal and family names, their homeland, and the place of their birth. Then I told them that an unpleasant report of unrest and evil intentions of some young people had caused me to hold this meeting. I told them that already for some years we had desired servants from Germany who had learned only farming and field work and who, we thought, would fit here best. We had also hoped to receive them. However, because they (our present servants) had offered themselves to the Lord Trustees to be sent to this colony as hired hands and serving girls, then the servants we had actually desired had had to remain behind. For the Lord Trustees had expressly written that Senior Urlsperger should not deal with any others, because it was not in the Trustees' means to do more for us than to send the present servants.

Now, before they were sent here, it had been told them often enough in London in the name of the Trustees that their tradesmen, such as bakers (which most in their transport are), millers, weavers, etc. had no value in this country, rather the most usual and frequent business was agriculture, and those who did not wish it should remain behind. In spite of that, they had chosen to come here. After many of these servants had been taken away from me in Savannah and I had noticed some unrest and disinclination to serve in Ebenezer, I had resolved to take with me only those who were willing to serve and to leave the unwilling ones there, but none of them who are here wished to remain behind, rather they promised to serve loyally. Now they should consider how improperly and unChristianly they were behaving when they were restless and glum about working or even wished to run away. For then they would disgracefully and irresponsibly break the contract that they had solemnly made with the Lord Trustees and now with the Council and of which they had a copy with them. In it they had promised with their mouths and with their signatures and their seals to serve for four years as serving men and women.

This breach of contract would bring them no blessing because it would be connected with a great loss on the part of our worn-out inhabitants. For, if they had not let themselves be sent here, then we would have received our real servants from Germany; and after their running away much time would pass before we could acquire the loyal servants we desired. This is not to mention that through the payment of the great sum for their passage the Lord Trustees were made unable to send servants for us now. Now, to deprive such prominent and beneficent gentlemen as the Lord Trustees of their money and our poor inhabitants such great loss in their support was surely no small sin and would bring them much dishonor if we should report their behavior to the Trustees and even to their fatherland. The Lord Trustees, I said, were prominent and very influential people who would report it to the King, who is also the Prince Elector of Hanover, so that such renegades and deceivers would be punished here in America or in their homeland if they returned home. Moreover, in the Empire, in Wurttemberg and other places, we had prominent benefactors who would easily find them out as cheats.

If their families knew to what place divine providence had led them, where they have the pure word of God and the Holy Sacraments and abundant opportunity for edification and godliness, then they would doubtless be much more satisfied by that than if they had come to Carolina, Cape Fear, Virginia, or Nova Scotia (where many Germans are now going), where Evangelical ministers and Christian order are wholly lacking. If they should prove themselves among us as Christian and industrious, then God would bless them and I would do my best to look out for their spiritual and physical welfare. Indeed, it might be so arranged that some of the loyal and industrious people would have their years of service somewhat shortened, for which the Lord Trustees would give their consent at my request. In conclusion I directed them to the words of Christ, "What I do thou knowest not now; but thou shalt know hereafter"[5] and to the story of Joseph and the little book of Tobias, which I recommended to them and their masters for later devout reading. I also promised to help them get good books; and right after the conclusion of the meeting I gave each of them a New Testament with the Psalter bound with it, which they were to bring along regularly to church for looking things up. Finally, the meeting was closed with prayer, and we parted from one another in good order and peace.

Wednesday, the 18th of October. The carpenter Krause worked hard while feverish and became dangerously sick as a result. He asked me to come to him to serve him with encouragement and prayer. He told me that it occurred to him, too, that hell is paved with good resolutions. The period of grace is a very noble thing; but, when it is past and has been evilly applied, it is a dreadful thing. I spoke with him according to his condition and recommended that he hasten and save his soul. Our locksmith, Brückner, appears to be in mortal danger. He has again contracted his old deeply-rooted malheure, namely, internal convulsions with vomiting and dysentary, with which he has been afflicted for some years. His soul has peace in and with God, and therefore he is certain of his salvation in Christ and is not afraid of death. The best medicines we have at our place are being used with trust in divine help. He is an honest and useful man whom we would gladly keep longer with us if it were the divine will. The medical student Mr. N. /Seelmann/, who came with the servants, lives in his house with him and also helps him out, even if I do not know whether he understands his art.

Friday, the 20th of October. A man who is seriously concerned with his salvation told me with tears that he had read, "Two will lie upon a bed"[6] . . . "Two shall be grinding at the mill, the one shall be taken, and the other left." He also cited with tears the words, "There will scarcely be a house, where none are damned."[7] He added that it always seemed to him that he belongs to those who will be forsaken and damned. However, from the nature of his penitent condition and from some verses such as "To this man I will look, even to him that is poor," etc., "Come unto me all ye that labor and are heavy laden," "The sacrifices of God are a broken spirit," "The Son of man is come to seek and to save,"[8] etc. I showed him that he was applying this to himself wrongly; Christ loved sinners such as he is and he should leave no room for a sorrowful spirit and the belief that he is damned because of his many former sins, rather he should hold to those verses and the words of Christ: "shall not perish but have eternal life."[9]

Today before the weekday sermon a pious inhabitant from here brought us the news that six of the servants in Savannah who have to serve, some one, some two, and some somewhat over three years had fled with two children and an unscrupulous instigator but had been found again. Among them are two brothers who had brought a good testimonial from the ship and had therefore been chosen by the minister /Zouberbuhler/ who had come over with them. This news distressed me for several reasons: 1) the bad name of the Germans here and in England will stink even more, 2) the people in the colony will be strengthened in their belief that nothing can be done with white servants, 3) the Lord Trustees are losing a large sum of money through the disloyalty of such people, since they have paid £6 Sterling per person in addition to other expenses they have already had with these people. 4) I have instructed them in Savannah daily and several times on Sunday from God's word and warned them loyally against disobedience against their parents and other superiors of all ranks according to the Fifth Commandment[10] and against scorn against the grace of God offered in the gospel for the Twentieth Sunday after Trinity. That is all in vain with such poor people and causes much blasphemy.

In the weekday sermon I had a good occasion to mention this disorder for the conversion and preservation of our servants, for I am now showing the reasons that our wise God has let be put in the Bible the sad story of Solomon's grave sinfullness in 1 Kings 2 and other similar incidents, which in themselves are just as edifying. This was not for their misuse, but for their right use as a mirror of the deep perdition of our hearts, for avoiding evil opportunities and bad company, and for recognizing from them that sin is the people's perdition, also that whoever stands there should well see that he not fall. I told them clearly that, if any of them let himself wish to follow in the footsteps of the renegades, he would commit the sin of the servant Onesimus, whose story I told them from the epistle of Philemon; and I showed how St. Paul not only sent him back to his place but also offered to pay the harm he had done. No servant who had betrayed the Lord Trustees so shamefully and had harmed their householders by running away could, according to Ezekiel 33:13, obtain forgiveness of sins but would drag a guilty conscience around with him, which, when once awakened by God's judgment, would be a true pergatory.

I also told them something about the locksmith from Wurttemberg who had passed through various grades of sin and had finally come to the gallows in Savannah a year ago. I added that, if my admonitions and promises did not have the desired results, this much would at least arise on my and their side, that I had performed my office on them and that they would have no justification on that day.[11] The Lord Trustees could not have been kinder to them as they were in accepting them at their request and sending them here and giving them a three-month period of grace to redeem or free themselves by repaying the £6 Sterling passage money. Also, I could not have treated them better or more cautiously then I did when I gave them a choice of whether they would prefer to remain in Savannah or to come with me to Ebenezer where, to be sure, there was plenty of work, but also, God be praised, enough foodstuffs. I did not wish to have any of them at our place against his will because I knew that compulsion only breeds anger and sullenness. Now, since all of them were willing to come along, it would distress me all the more if some were restless or even wished to run away because they lacked nothing and had to admit themselves that they had many advantages in spiritual and physical matters over those in Savannah.

I have heard from a couple of knowledgeable householders that the public admonition and warning given on Monday made a deep impression on the minds of these our servants, for which may God be praised! I hope the ones today will not be in vain. Last Sunday they all registered themselves among the communicants, but in the previously mentioned meeting on Monday I had said that I did not wish to repel anyone from Holy Communion by force but that for several cited reasons I would like for them to wait until the First Sunday of Advent, when we go to Communion again and hold a confirmation service with some children. They all accepted my advice and would rather wait than act too hastily. May God Himself prepare them and bless the law and the gospel for it.

Saturday, the 21st of October. Some of our young people as well as our present servants would be happy if we could distribute some Bibles and hymnals to them. I hesitate to trouble our dear Orphanage at Halle[12] with this especially because we have already received many of them and other good books and tractates from there. I would rather announce our lack of Canstein Bibles, extracts of the Freylinghausen hymnal,[13] and the catechismal books printed in Halle here rather than in a letter to one or the other of our worthy benefactors to get help in acquiring the said necessary books. There are still always requests for Arndt's books of *True Christianity*;[14] however, because there are already many in the congregation, we can do without them for a while longer if only we can get as quickly as possible the said books that we need in church and school. God will be Compensator for them.

Because in this country we must deal with people of all sorts of religions and sects, I would consider it a great benefaction if some dear well-to-do benefactors would donate to our church library Dr. Walch's *Introduction to the Religious Struggles in and outside of the Lutheran Church*.[15] These volumes would, to be sure, cost considerable money but also be of great use to us. With the last ship a great quantity of Latin and English, and a few Greek, books were sent to the library in Savannah, which a certain minister in London is said to have bequeathed.

Sunday, the 22nd of October. On this Twenty-second Sunday after Trinity fifty-seven people were at our Holy Communion. Our servants were all present; and therefore they were able to see and hear in what manner this holy sacrament is held among us, even though they did not commune with us. We pray with the congregation before and after the Communion, and during it we sing in a soft voice one or more devout hymns. Today I preached to them about the beautiful words of Psalms 37:37, "Remain pious and keep thee right, for such . . ."[16] and thereby led them to the important parable in the gospel. In the afternoon my dear colleague treated the keys to the kingdom from the catechism. There were some strangers here.

Monday, the 30th of October. I have again had to remain for a whole week in Savannah, partly to attend the deliberations concerning the safe introduction of Negro slaves into this colony and partly to preach to the German people there and to hold Holy Communion. I had, to be sure, business there every day, yet I yearned from one day to the next for my regular duties at home that are so pleasant for me. I particularly dislike missing

the blessed lessons that are held both in town and on the plantations for preparing some children for Holy Communion, especially since I am intending, with God, to admit some of the older
children to confirmation and Holy Communion on the First
Sunday of Advent.

I would like to have a copy of the now stipulated restrictions
under which the Negroes are to be brought to the country and
used here in order to send it by the next opportunity to our Fathers and friends. However, the time was too short and the councilmen were so busy that I could not realize my wish this time.
The restrictions are of such a nature that in this way the Negroes
could be not harmful for the land but useful because of the lack
of white servants, if only they are honored. When I reached
home I heard doubly distressing news: 1) that two of our new
servants had made their way secretly to Carolina in a canoe.
They had no lack of provisions with their householders, and
they had light work and therefore no justifiable right to run
away. Some servants in Savannah have very poor and not even
enough food, which they use as an excuse that six of them ran
away and have plunged themselves into mortal danger. 2) that
on his return from our mill a young man from Purysburg had
capsized in his boat, in which he had meal and butter, at a dangerous place and drowned. Many whole trees have floated there
together, whose branches are partly below and partly above the
water, and here the current is so strong that one can easily suffer
damage if one is not cautious. One could take another very safe
way; but, because it is rather roundabout, most large and small
boats choose this shorter, even though dangerous, way.

At this time a great cold has begun, which has not yet hurt my
health. The people are complaining here and there of cold
fever; but they do not seem to be in danger. Our locksmith,
Brückner, who was gravely sick before my trip to Savannah,
seems to be recovering again. He is one of those who have suffered loss through the runaway servants. Such running away is
very common in the English colonies here in America. The locksmith Schrempf, who moved to Carolina a couple of years ago
for worldly reasons, has now returned with wife and child. Now
that he has bought an expensive house he wishes to settle down

here again and guard himself from any changes. Our servants, too, are imagining pure splendor and good days in Carolina; but they would find it quite different if they had come there as servants.

Tuesday, the 31st of October. A medical student, thirty-four years old, also came to this country among our German servants, and he asked me in Savannah to bring him to our place and use him as a schoolmaster or however I could until he becomes known in the country and can serve his neighbor with his profession. He affected a good appearance and claimed to me that he had served the office of Pastor Struensee in Halle, which I later found to be entirely false. According to his own admission, he is inclined to Dippel's teachings and is therefore an enemy of the Lutheran religion and ministerial office.[17] In such a situation he could not be used among us, rather I took him back to Savannah last week,where he found an opportunity to travel via Purysburg to Charleston and presumably on to Pennsylvania.

The two men who chased after our two runaway servants learned in Purysburg that this medical student had asked about these servants and that, after he had gone on to Charleston, he had sent them orders to follow after him quickly. From that we could clearly see that he had incited these servants to run away and wishes to help them further on. He is, therefore, a hypocritical and ungrateful person; for not only has he received much good from Court Chaplain Albinus in London and from the Lord Trustees and from us here, but he is now seducing our servants. There is usually something basically bad about those who come to this country without being called; therefore I do not easily trust anyone now that I have been deceived several times. We are now applying all possible means to recover these two servants.

Among the servants who have remained in Savannah there is also a Salzburger woman who married a Catholic stocking weaver and worked as a canteen woman among the soldiers. She brought no good recommendation with her. She and her husband are now serving the minister /Zouberbuhler/ in Savannah. Those Salzburgers who have been scattered here and there in Germany might well have been led into much temptation; and therefore our people should thank God that they are so well led and cared for. We diligently remind them of the blessings of the Lord that they receive so excellently here both spiritually and physically.

We must wait to see how will it go with our servants. Some of them are still restless because they cannot practice their trades as apprentices and journeymen but must work as farm hands. I pity the Lord Trustees for having spent so much money for these people yet have not achieved their purpose. It is a great harm for us and the whole country that we have not received the kind of servants we described, those who have been nothing but farmers. We could then have convinced everyone that more could be accomplished with such servants than with Negroes. We would rather pay such servants than have the one we have received gratis.

NOVEMBER

Wednesday, the 1st of November. After my return from Savannah I began to impart something from the recently received letters for our communal edification. They gave very much material for recognizing humbly and with praise of God the good that God has shown us in this strange country and for praying right heartily for our worthy Fathers, benefactors, and friends who pray and care for us so lovingly, especially since it pleases the Lord to lay upon them so many kinds of internal and external tribulations for His and His kingdom's sake. These letters also give us a good opportunity to prepare ourselves before the Lord for the coming harvest and thanksgiving sermon.

Thursday, the 2nd of November. Today we held our annual harvest and thanksgiving sermon in town from the beautiful text Psalms 72: 18–19, and this is to be held tomorrow, God willing, in Zion Church on the plantations. We have very good reason to praise the Lord God with hearts, mouths, and Christian behavior for the miracles of His grace and goodness He has shown us so far in the realm of nature and grace. A year ago we had the thanksgiving sermon for the harvest and for peace at the same time; since then we have received a pleasant period of peace and, among other blessings, a good harvest and desirable weather for bringing in all the crops. May the Lord fulfil in us the beautiful promise: "Whoso offereth praise glorifieth me: and to him that ordereth his conversation aright will I shew the salvation of God."[1]

Sunday, the 5th of November. Because of our servants there is still much unrest, which falls mostly on me. They have all sorts of unfounded complaints; and those who are bakers, shoemakers, millers, etc. claim that they were promised in London to be able to work in this colony not as farmhands but in their trades. They also imagine that those Germans who recently arrived at Charleston in two ships are all treated as free men and will be settled directly on their own land and will receive a good support in cattle and provisions, all of which is a poem. Those among us who have received farmhands are best off, and all our inhabitants would like to have such servants. Still, we are not yet losing our courage, rather we hope that God will let this matter with the servants serve to our advantage.

Monday, the 6th of November. Even though it is the duty of the parishioners according to James 5:14 (which humble and grace-hungry little lambs of Christ consider a blessing) to call their ministers in their sickness, this duty is neglected by many among us; but they do not all have the same reason for this. Yesterday I learned that N.N. was dangerously sick: when I came to him I learned that he would not allow his wife to call me to him because his conscience told him that I would ask him about his previous domestic life and that there would be cause for much vexation. In this miserable man I have a good example of how firmly Satan holds his slaves and what strong and dangerous snares customary sins are. Physical anger, reviling, scolding, etc. have become second nature to him during his military life; therefore he commits great excesses at the least irritation; and his wife has a very hard life with him. I have shown him his danger but have not detected that he wishes to accept good advice. Yesterday a pious married woman was with me and complained with many tears against her husband's rough treatment of her and her children. Even though I do not know how to help her in this and directed her to prayer, patience, and Christian conduct toward her husband, it was still an alleviation for her that she had complained to me of her trouble and had received instruction from God's word. The children are from her first husband; and, because, among other things, this stepfather is restless about the small tuition, which for a quarter year per child is only six pence and, consequently, only a halfpenny per week, I paid the tuition for all three children.

Wednesday, the 8th of November. We have news that German people in Purysburg, even those who have received help from us, helped our runaway servants on their way to Charleston. If we did not have to fear evil consequences among our servants remaining in Ebenezer, then we would let these ungrateful and wicked people run off, who are, to be sure, doing harm to the Lord Trustees and to our inhabitants through this disorder, but above all to themselves. In order to do my duty and to avert more and greater disorders, I had a copy of their contract with the Lord Trustees made in Savannah, which I will send to a friend in Charleston, from which it can be clearly proved that these and other servants and maids had obligated themselves to four years of service by signing and putting their seals to the contract and are therefore punishable because of their breach of contract. I have written today to the governor in Charleston and also to our patron, Col. Heron, who stands high with the governor, and reported the loss that some of our housholders have suffered because of these runaway servants; and I asked them to help us extradite them. Approximately a year ago three German serving boys were also seduced, who are likewise residing in Carolina.[2] I hope we will recover them all again. If my letter has the desired effect with the said gentlemen, then others will lose their desire to follow the footsteps of such renegades.

Since Köcher gave up the school, I perform this pleasant work in the afternoons and have much pleasure in the diligence and good behavior of the children. In the last few days some very small children have joined us who were formerly frightened away from the school by the schoolmaster's severity and looked upon the school as a penal institution. I wish that my time and strength would allow me to continue this work every day. A capable schoolmaster is hard to find because he cannnot live on the small salary. In Savannah the Lord Trustees give 20 pounds Sterling; if we had such a sum we could almost employ two schoolmasters. For the said money they cannot find a schoolmaster in Savannah.

Friday, the 10th of November. So far the weather has, to be sure, been somewhat cold, especially at night, but also dry and pleasant, which I look upon as an especial blessing of God for me and my family. Because the buildings in this country, being made of wood, are quickly dilapidated, my house, too, needs a repair. Since the roof must be torn off and a new one prepared, we, our books, and our things would suffer if it rained. God be praised for having let us choose a good time to complete this necessary construction. The kind of weather we had last summer and autumn one can read in the following description of a very knowledgeable man in our neighborhood, who is accustomed to prepare a very useful calendar every year:[3]

> This summer has been one of the coolest and wettest that I have experienced in this country. Its likes are unknown to people who have already lived here for forty years. And, because the winter was cold along with the spring, the wheat has not turned out for the best. The cold winter made it thin; and in the spring toward summer the rust spoiled it greatly. Otherwise the summer crops have thriven rather well, provided the water did no damage. The month of August, which is mostly warm and dry, has been cold and wet this time so that the crops were almost as ripe at the beginning as at the end. And, if September had not had some fair and warm days at the very beginning, which lasted on into October, then the late planted rice and other crops would not have ripened. Because the weather has been so unusual, many, indeed, almost all people have become sick in September and October; yet very few of them have died. Generally the people are attacked by a fever, which changes from heat to chills. Such fevers are still lasting into November.

Sunday, the 12th of November. The locksmith Schrempf's wife was mortally sick in Carolina and came to our place very weak. Even before her husband had arranged their new household, she came to childbed; and in it she experienced a new and special help of the Lord. This young couple drew to themselves much disquiet and trouble by moving away to Carolina, which, however, has served them for much good through the grace of God. Their example also serves to let other inhabitants recognize better how much good the Lord shows here. What a great blessing it is among others that we have church and school and, in physical things, the mills, which double blessing many thousands of people, also many Germans in America, must do without.

Monday, the 13th of November. Old /Theobald/ Kiefer of Purysburg has sent his youngest boy to our place so that he can be instructed and prepared for a worthy participation in Holy Communion. Because of his great frivolity he is among the worst of the children in the preparation, even though he does not lack literal recognition. Nevertheless, his parents insist that I bring him soon to confirmation and Holy Communion. He has three well instructed and Christian-minded sisters and an honest brother here in our congregation, who are working on him with words, intercession, and example; and he is kept closely in school like the other children. May God save him from the dangerous snares of frivolity and change his heart! Otherwise I have some very fine children among the children being prepared, who uprightly love their Savior and His word.

For some time now Eigel has also sent his oldest son to the preparation hour on the plantations, but he was not consistent in this. He never let his children, including this boy, go to school; so now the boy can scarcely read a few words. Because he guards the parents' cattle, he seldom comes to church and he does not have a very retentive head. Therefore, he is greatly lacking in instruction and literal recognition. Nevertheless, the father has proclaimed that, if I do not soon allow him to Holy Communion, he will no longer send him to the preparation hour (which is held on the plantations only twice a week, namely, on Tuesday and Friday before the weekday sermon) because he cannot spare him from his work. Eigel and his wife take no care of their children's souls, just as they do not respect their own souls and neglect the means of salvation.

Wednesday, the 15th of November. We have news from Savannah that a rather large number of Indians have again gathered there to receive their gifts. I hope things will be more orderly this time than the last time. It surely comes from our dear God that we have been settled at a place that is quite remote and out of the way of the Indians and their vagrancies; and therefore we are somewhat spared from their visits. What a great blessing it is to have external quiet and good order at our divine services and official duties! Our dear God has continued the previously mentioned blessing of dry weather until now, even though it threatened rain on some days, therefore my house could be newly roofed and repaired while entirely dry. This repair will cost at least £12 Sterling. How happy I would be if the Lord Trustees paid it!

Thursday, the 16th of November. For some time, as far as business and my strength would allow, I have been reading in Dr. Antonius' *Collegium Antitheticum*[4] for my instruction and edification. In my previous years I have, to be sure, heard of this thorough and modest book, so necessary for a teacher; but I have had little opportunity to read in it. Now that the providence of God has brought me to and into it, I am finding so much of importance in it that I can hardly read enough; and I wish from my heart that others could be led to a reading and correct use of it sooner than I was. There is a greater treasure in it than one can so easily find in any polemical book of this nature. What astonishes me most is that some have had the heart to contradict such a thorough, experienced, wise, and cautious academic teacher in public writings. I consider it the happiest period of my life, when God brought me to Halle at the time that the three theologians were still living and teaching as the chosen tools of God; and therefore I have also heard our dear Paul Antonius, which greatly serves me while reading his writings.

Friday, the 17th of November. Among the servants who have arrived we have unexpectedly found a knowlegeable, skillful, and well-behaved young person, to whom we have given charge of the school on the plantations in God's name.[5] In his case it is too bad that he did not remain with his studies, for he went so far in school that he could soon have gone to the university. But he became a baker and miller and has completed four years as a journeyman and has forgotten much of his schooling. He has a quiet and docile spirit; and we are asking God to prepare him through His spirit to His glory and to the service of his neighbor and of our children. To be sure, he considered himself to be too young and incapable to direct the plantation school; yet he was willing to try it for a month. He not only saw and heard the method and order in which our children are informed but also received from me a written instruction and directions. I hold the catechismal lesson, this schoolmaster only has to instruct the children in reading and writing and to teach them the catechism and Bible verses and also to drill them, also to lead them to the right way. He instructs only three hours every day, and the rest of the time he tends to household and farming chores.

Saturday, the 18th of November. One of our inhabitants was in Savannah and had to see with his own eyes and hear with his own ears what godless goings on are there both day and night. A large party of Indians came down to receive their gifts. On this occasion the English, French, Germans, and Jews must stand in arms to arouse a fear in the Indians. Herewith they give out and pour out as much as anyone wants, and from such carousing arise the most dreadful sins and vexations, indeed, often danger and trouble for the neighbors. I plan to inquire carefully whether the Germans of our confession have also acted so sinfully and thereby vexed pious souls and annoyed heathens, Indians, and Negroes so that I can conduct myself accordingly in my future sermons and prayer hours and also holding Holy Communion. Things still look rather pitiable in this colony so that the inhabitants have more cause to weep than to laugh, more to fast and pray than to indulge themselves and to commit such disorder that vexes even the heathens and should not be heard among Christians. If Jerusalem does not improve, then the heart of God will turn fully from her; and He will make her into a desert in which no one dwells.

Monday, the 20th of November. Today a man coming from Carolina brought me the news that a ship with four hundred German people had gone aground on a dangerous sandbank and, after a strong wind arose, was entirely destroyed so that no

more than two sailors survived. One can see the flotsam of the
ship and its cargo floating around. Without doubt these people
wanted to go to Carolina, because the government and merchants there are now again concerning themselves with settling
their province with Europeans, especially with German people,
whom they let enjoy all sorts of advantages. Yet they also have
great difficulties, especially those who come as indentured servants. Generally they are not kept much better than the
Negroes.

Wednesday, the 22nd of November. The widow Graniwetter,
who recently married a German widower, told me that her former mistress in Augsburg, Mrs. Heinzelmann, had sent her an
edifying letter with a gift, by which she was again reminded, to a
new awakening, of the great spiritual good that she had enjoyed,
seen, and heard as a maid in her house. It is also a good odor for
me, indeed a strengthening of my heart, when something edifying is told about such people who are also our benefactors. With
their good example they are now working on our Salzburgers
who were perhaps once in their service or instructed by them in
some other way and have experienced what stands in the Epistle
of John 5:8. This Mrs. Graniwetter and her little children also
thank our dear God diligently for the good she had received
from Him through the service of her first husband, the pious
and very industrious Graniwetter. In addition to that is the orderly establishment of a good plantation, the construction of a
house and a warm chamber, which is exceedingly good for her
children in cold wintertime. His memory and example are a
blessing for her and for all who have known him, even though
he ended his daily work some years ago.

Thursday, the 23rd of November. For the last two days a severe cold has begun, which would have hindered the carpenters
on the construction if it had not been entirely completed yesterday. They assembled yesterday evening in my study and
thanked our merciful Father in heaven with me for all His blessings as well as for the successful renovation of my house, which is
more useful now in many ways than it was in the beginning. It is
also so well protected in the attic and elsewhere that it will need
little repair during my lifetime. The expenses were, to be sure,

quite high, namely, £25 Sterling, because construction is very expensive here since the workmen's wages run very high because of the high cost of merchandise. However, the greatest necessity demanded that the house be repaired; and therefore I trust the goodness of God that He will see in His good time to the payment of these expenses.[6]

Sunday, the 25th of November. It will soon be four years since God made the pious Mrs. Zant a widow and her two little children orphans, during which time He has always given her a Christianly contented spirit. If anyone knows how to praise divine providence, it is this widow. With His generous fatherly hand He has let so much good fall to her, even in physical things, that she has never suffered want and has not experienced the need that some families have sometimes suffered. Her neighbor, the righteous Glaner. shows her many Christian deeds of love, which our merciful God apparently repays. She has always hoped that her brother in Augsburg, Bacher, would let himself be persuaded by her frequent letters to come to her in Ebenezer. However, he wrote to her recently that he has married and that he will remain at his place, where God is also providing for him.

Sunday, the 26th of November. Our merciful God has now helped us so far that with this day we have survived this Twenty-seventh Sunday after Trinity and are spending it with blessing. In the evening prayer meeting we have communally praised a very undeserved kindness according to which He has averted during this entire church year all harm, serious commission of sin and vexation, also disquiet and obstacles to divine service and has turned His spiritual and physical blessings to us abundantly in many ways. May He also graciously hear our poor prayer for His blessings on the church year that is now beginning and to help us all to come through the effect of the Holy spirit to such a blessed condition as was presented to us today both from the image of the wise virgins as also from the beautiful verses of the exordium, 2 Peter 1:10–11.

On all Sundays and holy days of this almost-ended church year we have preached from gospel verses of Holy Writ as well as from the regular gospel the great blessings of God that Jesus so willingly and dearly merited for us and which He heartily wishes to grant us in the order of salvation (which is itself a very great blessing). Afterwards this was further inculcated catechismally; and, because an instructive verse has almost always been contemplated in the exordium, both the children and the adults have again garnered a fine treasure of chosen Bible verses in their minds and memories. There will be few of us who have not learned the exordium verses that have been so diligently inculcated and who will not have taught them to their little children. In school, in town, and on the plantations the verses of this and the previous church years are repeated along with the catechism; and that also occurs in the afternoons in the churches between the first and second hymns. Every verse is recited loudly and clearly three times for the sake of both children and adults.

What sometimes troubles me no little bit is that the catechism books in the Evangelical Lutheran Church do not exactly concur but have been produced in various places in Germany with additions and new explanations, since, according to my humble opinion, we should everywhere preserve exactly the words of Luther's Small Catechism as they are found in our symbolic books of our Evangelical Church. This would be of no little usefulness. I have sworn by the symbolic books, therefore by the catechism; and I hold it as a matter of conscience not to deviate in the least from the words as they stand in the said books of faith. Also, it is not necessary, because as much is written in the Biblical texts and in the short pithy explications concerning the articles of faith and the duties of life as is needed by simple and weak minds; and a minister has enough material in them to preach to his children and other listeners the articles of faith and rules of life of the Christian Evangelical Religion, as I, God be praised, have experienced so far in the preparation lessons with the older children. When young people come here from other places, our catechism generally seems strange to them because they have studied another, and it is sometimes difficult to convince them that ours is as good as theirs even if it seems that theirs has been enlarged and improved. Such dissimilarity causes much inconvenience.

Monday, the 27th of November. Now that the few frosty days

have again passed, we have had right pleasant spring weather since Saturday. The rain has been absent for a long time this fall; but it must have rained further upstream because the Savannah River has been rising for the last eight days, even if not very strongly. Just as God has abundantly blessed the fields and gardens this year with all sorts of crops, He has also let the acorns flourish very well, some kinds of them are of marvelous size.[7]

Jacob Mohr, a young man of Reformed parents in Purysburg, has resided at our place for some years and has also attended our preparation lesson from time to time, even if he has not learned much because of his inconstancy and disloyalty. He has also not let himself be brought into any correct external order; and, now that he is with orderly people, he is beginning to notice the spiritual and physical harm from it. He would like to come to Holy Communion, and I have given him hope for that if he will accept with hearty prayer the good advice that I and his householder give him. There are very many young people in this country who ask for neither instruction from God's word nor for Holy Communion, and Satan gets the best of them.

Tuesday, the 28th of November. A young Swiss, whose mother and sister live on a plantation lying in our area, had me marry him today in the Zion Church with a young French woman who was in school with us some years ago and afterwards moved away again with her mother. Because in the weekday sermon I had just preached from the story of Solomon some very important things about the deceit of sin and the causes of an unhappy married life, I see it as a divine dispensation that I had this young bridal couple and some other young German people, whom they brought here with them, as hearers. They will now have all the less excuse if they do not obey the words and the warnings and admonitions found in them. Generally I do not like to have anything to do with marrying strangers; but, when I must do so, I do not see it as if by chance, because such people, who otherwise live quite wildly from day to day, hear something from God's word and receive a spur in their conscience. This person published his banns three times in the English church in Savannah and brought me a written testimony and permission from the minister there that he could be married here with his people. Otherwise I would not have done it.

Wednesday, the 29th of November. It is no little harm to our inhabitants that, instead of farmhands and maids, they have received lads who do not understand farming and do not wish to learn it. The single fellows are finally adapting to work and order, but we are still having annoyance and trouble. Their work is poor, yet they demand much in clothing and provisions, so it is very hard for a poor householder to provide for a husband and wife and also for a small child. If they cannot get along with them or if they are afraid to get in debt because of them, then they push such married couples on me and I must provide for them and use them in any way I can. If we liberated them then they would either leave the country to beg or otherwise suffer great hardship; and it would have dire consequences among other servants among us, as one can easily guess.

Some of them are behaving well, which will be profitable to them; for we will try to give assistance to such honest people at the end of their years of service if they wish to remain at our place. Many seem to be keeping the attitude of journeymen and wish to return to Germany at the expiration of their service. If they do not convert, then they will become blasphemers of this country and perhaps of our congregation, even though they have received more spiritual and physical good than other servants in this and the neighboring colony of Carolina. As I hear, they have no pleasure, to be sure, from prayer and other edifying household exercises but remain with their customs, which, to a large extent, amount to the so-called *opus operatum*[8]. However, I am pleased that they diligently visit the public divine services in both churches, the weekday sermons, and the evening prayer hours with their masters. Who knows whether perhaps it was for the sake of their souls that they were sent into this quietude, which is too quiet for many of them.

Thursday, the 30th of November. The wheat flour that is brought here from New York and Pennsylvania is still excessively expensive and hardly to be had. Therefore our Indian cornmeal is still very acceptable in Savannah. Our inhabitants

have not planted as much corn as is required for sale as meal in
Savannah. Therefore Riedelsperger, who began a trade in meal
some years ago, journeyed yesterday to Carolina with some
other men to buy rice and corn. Because of the lack of servants
very little rice was planted here, even though it is the real crop of
this country. It was so cheap during the wartime that they preferred to devote their weak efforts to other things than planting
rice. However, in the past year it has become so expensive that
one has had to pay 12 shillings Sterling for 100 pounds, and it
was still hard to find, because during the war people in Carolina
applied themselves more to indigo than to rice. In this year it
has, to be sure, turned out very well; however, because it is being
exported heavily, it will not become much cheaper. This has now
moved our inhabitants to prepare rice fields, especially those
who have received servants.

By means of our very useful rice stamp our inhabitants can
prepare their rice and make it saleable much sooner than can be
done in Carolina with Negroes. For on our rice stamp's seven
mortars they can prepare a thousand pounds of rice in twenty-
four hours as beautifully as it is in Carolina. For fifty pounds of
rice a mill fee of about three pence is paid; and the owner has no
other trouble with it than to bring the rice to the mill and to fetch
it again after it has been stamped. There is still one difficulty
with rough rice, namely, that, before it is stamped, every householder must first shell it on his wooden handmill, which consists
of two wooden blocks instead of two stones. But even this difficulty could be alleviated if our people were really serious about
planting rice. For we have a beautiful opportunity to build a rice-
shelling mill on the grinding mill or rice-stamp at very small
cost, on which many thousands of bushels of rice could be
shelled in a short time with little effort.

If, however, such a mill were little used (as has been the case so
far with the rice-stamp), then there would be little income to
cover the building expenses and to maintain the machine itself.
For wood rots here very quickly, especially since the internal
millworks must sometimes remain under water in great inundations. Therefore we must have steady income to keep the works

in operation. For some time our mills have reached such perfection (God be praised!) that they are supporting themselves and, in addition, contributing something toward public expenses in the community. Therefore I was greatly disappointed in my hope that I would receive a skillful carpenter among the last servants. There was only one, to be sure, orderly and well intended carpenter (which is something rare because usually there are tipsters among them), who was taken from me by the minister in Savannah, who with other gentlemen there had the choice. Through a lack of capable carpenters little can be built among us properly and for a reasonable price.

DECEMBER

Friday, the 1st of December. Until now Paul Zittrauer's wife /Anna Maria/ has been visited with physical weaknesses and many other tribulations, and through them she has proved and strengthened her Christianity. Her heavenly outlook and her desire to be with Christ soon shine clearly from her gestures, words, and works; and her memories of her four tender children, who have gone ahead of her into blessed eternity, are a blessed help for her to hurry toward everlasting rest. Nine years ago she came into great uncertainty, superstition, and bad habits at our place with her sisters;[1] and, because God made it her spiritual birthplace, she hardly knows how to praise Him enough for His wise guidance and great mercy. She had not expected my visit; and, because she had yearned for it a long time in her present circumstances, it was all the more pleasant for her. Her serving girl, who had fallen to her from the transport of servants without her asking, is very well provided for by her and shows great desire for God's word, prayer, amd other practices; and she recognizes, with very beautiful expressions, the great spiritual advantages that our merciful God is showing to our children above many others.

Sunday, the 3rd of December. In these first Sundays of Advent we have had a good penetrating rain, for which we and our wheatfields have waited for a long time. Despite the rain we had a rather numerous assemblage in Jerusalem Church, and ninety-eight of them were at the Table of the Lord. Most of our servants were found among these communicants, who had wished to go to Holy Communion already six weeks ago. They had, however, accepted advice and waited until now for better preparation and have meanwhile heard from God's word in all sermons and prayer meetings what is required for godpleasing Christianity, a worthy participation in Holy Communion, and achieving salvation. Just yesterday, in the morning preparation hour at Jerusalem Church and in the afternoon in Zion Church, they were presented clearly and emphatically from Acts 2:17-18 the example of righteous and godpleasing parishioners to imitate so that, if some of them had come without penitence and faith, and therefore unworthily, they would have no one to blame but themselves.

So far God has blessed the late Ambrosius Wirth's little booklet on Confession and Holy Communion[2] in many of our parishioners, in which is given very clear instructions for true penitence and conversion, for sincere prayer and godly life. In it there are also right powerful prayers and hymns with the confession to be prayed and sung before and after the taking of Holy Communion. I have directed the servants in both the weekday sermon and in the confession service to this little book, which is in all hands among us; indeed, I laid it on the consciences of their masters to go through these beautiful directions with them gradually to prepare themselves worthily for Holy Communion.

I also announced that I am planning in the future in our confession service to lay this little book as the basis of the preparation service so that ignorant and weak people will be convinced that we are not preaching them a new dogma here, but rather precisely what is preached at other places of the Lutheran Church and in Nurnberg, where the said Communion booklet was printed, after being composed by the late Pastor Wirth from God's word and according to the content of our Evangelical articles of faith.[3] Today our merciful God has again granted us much good in the public divine service through the means of salvation. I preached from the gospel for the First Sunday of Advent concerning the mercy of our Lord Christ, for which dear material the comforting final words of the Bible in Revelations 22:21 gave me an opportunity.

My dear colleague, who in the previous church year had laid the Small Catechism of our blessed Luther as a basis for the afternoon catechisation, has resolved in God's name to contemplate in this church year those basic and pithy verses[4] that our children have memorized in the preceding period. This time it was the beautiful words from Philippians 3:7-11 concerning the priceless recognition of Jesus Christ our Lord. Yet, because our parishioners have the praiseworthy habit of reading the gospels or the epistles with their families before or on Sundays and holy days, this year they will not read them between the first and second hymn in the morning, rather they will apply them some minutes after the repetition of the verses learned and contemplated during the previous church year; and my dear colleague will probably do this every two weeks at Zion Church.

In the afternoon, year after year, we repeat between the first and second hymn either the catechism or Bible verses. Today I sincerely admonished our dear parishioners, among them our young servants, for the sake of the worthiness of the divine word and also for their own sakes, to become very familiar with the two Sunday verses contemplated each time by memorizing them. For this they have enough time at our place on Sundays and holidays, as also in the morning, at noon, and in the evening. Many mothers among us are right sincerely desirous of teaching their tender little children, as well as their somewhat larger ones, the exordium verses and the beautiful short texts and to repeat them. They often complain to me, however, that they gradually forget the verses if there are many of them. Because they can neither write nor read, they do not know what to do in reciting them, meanwhile their children forget some of the verses they have diligently learned. I underlined some of them with red ink, but this is rather inconvenient.

It would be best, easiest, and most useful if we had the opportunity and means to print on a couple of folios in octavo format all the verses we have contemplated publicly and have memorized in the last six or seven years. It would not cost much; yet it would be of great use among our young people, indeed, also

among the adults. Otherwise we do not martyr our children
with memorization but teach them Christian dogma catechismally, as is customary today in all well-run Christian schools.
For that reason the sermons and prayer meetings are carefully
repeated with the children at church school through questions.
In addition, we see to it that they diligently learn Luther's Small
Catechism and the Bible verses.

Because we sing a great deal, many beautiful hymns and
verses are learned and remembered by heart. I had planned and
also given the children hope that some of the older children who
have so far attended the preparation lesson diligently to their
noticeable growth and development in the Evangelical teachings
would be allowed to Holy Communion this Sunday with the congregation and that I would hold the confirmation service for
them beforehand. However, important reasons move me to
change my plans for the children's benefit and to postpone their
confirmation until after the new year (if God grants me health
and life). This I announced today to the congregation, and I
commended these children and their important intentions to
their intercession. I hope that the parents will be satisfied with
that. Old Kiefer of Purysburg and the ill-behaved N. insist on my
accepting the children for the sake of their work.[5]

Monday, the 4th of December. The rain lasted almost all last
night; but in the morning the sky cleared up again. It also belongs to the merciful providence of God over us that the rain
stopped for a couple of hours in the morning, even if it rained
heavily shortly thereafter and especially during the afternoon
divine service. Still, it let up completely after the end of church
and until evening so that our dear parishioners could come to
church dry and return to their plantations rather dry. Elsewhere
it is written, *Deus in minimis maximus est*; i.e., "God is greatest in
little things." Therefore it is meet and right to recognize the
footsteps of His providence in the so-called little things: otherwise one is an atheist, or like the heathens who know nothing of
God.

This morning private Communion was given to the very frail
orphan child Gertraut Kurtz, who is cared for in my house. She
has, to be sure, her weaknesses; and sometimes her obstinacy,

impatience, and even arrogance arise because of her natural simplicity, yet in truth she is a believer and lover of her Savior. She likes to pray and read and hear the word of God, and she learns the Bible verses diligently. She is so lame that she can neither stand nor lie but must sit day and night on her little bed. Because she cannot go to church to hear the word of God, for which she ardently yearns, I am holding for her a preparation lesson for Holy Communion with our larger children in the same room where she performs her light work of sewing. Our family prayer hours are also held here on Sundays after the morning service with those people who come to our house from their plantations so that she has opportunity enough to exercise herself in goodness and to prepare for a better life.

This afternoon I received an answer from Charleston concerning the two runaway servants,[6] of which I find it necessary to report the following: 1) Col. Heron, the former commandant at Frederica, who is now in Charleston with his company, has, together with our friend Mr. Dobel,[7] made much effort to persuade the governor to have the renegades arrested and sent back again. Also, the governor had proved willing to help in this even though he said that some Negroes had run from Carolina to Georgia and had not been extradited at his request. This success showed that it was better that we did not write the governor anything about the first or the last renegades or request his help in that, and this was also the opinion of our friends in Charleston. For it appears that people accomplish more directly through the use of English law than by seeking the governor's favor and authority. He is no friend of the Lord Trustees, General Oglethorpe, and this colony. He paid his compliments nicely and evinced great willingness to help us to our rights. But in reality he did nothing; indeed, he did not even wish to give back the first indenture or contract of the first servants of four years ago, which had been sent to him several months ago because of three runaway serving boys so that by means of it our friends in Charleston could proceed against them according to law. These boys are with their renegade brother at Congarees, 150 miles from Charleston, and our poor people have had to do without them for so long.

2) Col. Heron has finally obtained a warrant and plenipotentiary power for the judge and constable at Congarees, which Mr. Dart, a prominent merchant and good friend of this colony, gladly sent off with a letter to one of his friends; and we do not doubt that the two runaway servants, who have just traveled to the said Congarees, will be arrested, delivered to Charleston, and sent on to us here. But, as far as the three boys are concerned,[8] a copy of the indenture or contract must be made here in Savannah and attested as a true copy by the magistry in Savannah, for which reason I must travel without delay to Savannah with Mr. Meyer. Since we have had so much trouble and expense with the runaway servants, then we would like to get the other ones, too. For, if the last renegades succeed, then we must worry that others in this colony will follow in their footsteps and cause loss both to the Lord Trustees and to their masters.

This time I am sending to Court Chaplain Albinus the copies of my letters to the governor in Carolina and to Col. Heron, which I sent to Charleston through an express because of these runaway servants. I am relating this matter here in such detail so that our friends will know the status of our colony, the attitude of the rulers in Carolina towards it, and our difficulties with our servants and with foodstuffs. Thereby I am putting into the hand of our worthy Court Chaplain material to further our and the colony's good with the Lord Trustees.

The poor subjects in this colony are in a bind in more than one way. If this colony should remain under the government of the Trustees or receive a governor of its own or be incorporated under the government of the province of Carolina (which the people in Carolina would like most to see), then it will always remain the maxim of the Carolinians to prevent the flourishing of this colony as much as they can, as in the case of Port Royal. This is because the entry of ships into Port Royal and into our harbor is much easier and safer than into Charleston. Consequently, if this colony flourished, then the trade and navigation would in time turn from there to here. Yet, God is still the Lord on earth, He sitteth in the highest city. No matter how wisely they undertake it, God will go a different path, etc.[9] Among the human

means to bring this colony into good harmony with the neighboring one, one of the most important would be to place a governor in Carolina who is a friend of the Trustees and their
Georgia.

This afternoon a very strong wind arose that finally veered to
the west. Yesterday there was thunder in the distance, which is
customarily a sign of great cold or heavy rain; and it became very
cold during and after the wind.

Tuesday, the 5th of December. Our messenger, who returned
yesterday from Charleston, was in mortal danger on his way
there; yet God saved him from it in a miraculous way, even with
the loss of some of his little money. In Carolina there are many
runaway Negroes, who often remain in the woods for a long
time and go robbing. Two such black youths jumped out of the
bushes and gave him such a blow on his head that he fell to the
ground unconscious, whereupon they took his little money out
of his pocket and took his knapsack. However, because they saw
a gentleman on horseback coming with his servant on this road,
they ran again into the thick forest. There are more such high-
waymen in Carolina, therefore it is very unsafe to travel there on
foot and alone. Two such robbers are sitting in jail in Charleston,
who will probably have to pay for their crime with their lives. We,
thank God, know nothing yet about Negroes and therefore
nothing about lack of safety at home or on trips.

Wednesday, the 6th of December. Our long bridge has needed
repair for a long time; but because of a lack of workers we have
had to do with patchwork, which has caused vain expenses. Now
thick planks are being split in the woods near the bridge with
which to cover the bridge. For that they use thick poplar trees,
chop the soft outside wood away, and keep only the heart. The
soft wood around the heart amounts to about four or five
inches; on the other hand, the heart of trunks of the two trees
that I saw today are almost five feet in diameter. Such trees are of
marvelous length and useful almost to the top; they also split
easily and are of long duration. There are many of them on low
rich land.

Our new schoolmaster on the plantations /Wertsch/ fits well
into the position given him and is showing good diligence. If he

continues thus, then our children will be much better cared for by him than by the former one. Since the latter's resignation, the number of children has increased, and now the littlest come, too, who had a great anxious fear of the school and the severe schoolmaster or jailor. What a good thing a good fatherly school-master is. People should not let such a one suffer want but sharpen his industry in every possible way. This we would gladly do, if only we had the means.

With the present schoolmaster we have the following arrange-ment: he fell by lot as a servant to a pious Salzburger, whom he also helps with his work outside of school hours. For that he re-ceives food, drink, shelter, and care; but he must pay for his own clothes and laundry, for which purpose he receives L 4 Sterling annually from us. He does not use all this for clothing but can lay aside some for his future household. However, because his mas-ter must do without his servant in his work for three hours dur-ing the day, we give him L 2 Sterling as compensation for his loss. And, since he does not have to give his servant any clothes, he can keep him all the better in his other support. Through this arrangement both the master and the servant are benefitted. The former schoolmaster, Köcher, received somewhat more an-nually, which this teacher will enjoy after he has served for some years.

Friday, the 8th of December. After a long wait I have finally received a letter from our worthy Pastor Brunnholtz, which was already dated at the beginning of October. In it he refers to a previously written letter, which, however, has not yet arrived. This dear Brunnholtz has been sick again for several months and had just recovered from a hot fever and scarlet fever at the time that he wrote the letter, and he was still so weak that he could not yet preach. Because the two catechists, Mr. Schaum and Mr. Kurtz, have been ordained to the holy ministry, they give him some help in preaching, even though they already have their own congregations. Mr. Vigera has married and settled in Philadelphia, and therefore he will probably remain there. Mr. Meyer wrote concerning him and hoped that he could be per-suaded to come here again and let himself be used as a mer-chant. I have heard nothing about Pastor Muhlenberg even in this letter, but I hope to hear something pleasant from him shortly. The dear brothers are at an important post there, not only because it is a very free land but also because all sects have the same privileges there.

In my present letter I have warned Mr. Brunnholtz against a Dipplian[10] medical student /Seelmann/, and I have warned Mr. Vigera against a like-minded merchant's assistant from Strassburg, who both revealed themselves here and set their minds on going, presumably, via Charleston to Philadelphia. In this part of the world one must keep one's eyes open especially well and examine people carefully if one does not wish to be tricked and led to loss. The presently contemplated story of King Solomon's fall also gives us many salutary teachings and warnings in this matter. It is a Machiavellian maxim in these colonies that, if one wished to settle a country or a region with people, one usually writes a long letter, as stands in Zechariah 5.

In such new settled lands, anyone who has incurred debts or committed a crime is free in monetary matters if he merely swears a certain pro forma oath. In religious matters one may believe and confess anything one wishes everywhere in America; there is also dreadful de facto license in marriage matters. Such a place where all sorts of people flow together is Congarees in Carolina, which the governor wishes to occupy strongly against the Indians, and, to be sure, with German people. Therefore they have been given great license; and, because of this gentleman's all-too-great favor toward this new place, it is difficult for people to recover runaway servants. If it depended upon him alone, and if we could not make use of the English law for the recovery of renegade servants through good and influential friends in Charleston, we would be turned away with only empty words and compliments and would be held up in vain from one time to the next.

Sunday, the 10th of December. Among the last transport of servants[11] a couple have come who have been raised up to farm work and are used to it; and their masters are very pleased with them and have very good help from them in farming and housekeeping. And they are also so well content that they are now having a detailed letter written to their well-inclined governor in

Wurttemberg and to their families, in which they honestly report how they have fared so far on the journey through the care of the Lord Trustees and now in Ebenezer. Because it pleases them, they are not only requesting their families to follow them but are also attesting their desire for some skillful and industrious workers whom they know, who would find work and good earnings here. I plan to send this letter to Senior Urlsperger, because it will reach its right destination most safely through his hands.

If the workers named in this letter wish to come here voluntarily, we will be very pleased. We would advance their passage money until they could pay it back through their service, provided they wished to settle at our place. If they did not wish to agree to that, then it would be better for our friends in Europe not to get involved with them at all. If they had freedom to remain in Savannah or to move to Carolina, how would that help our efforts to get capable helpers? The kind that we want, such as carpenters, wheelwrights, coopers, sawmillers, and tanners, are very rare in the whole country and are easily persuaded to settle where it appears that they will earn the most money. If they would engage themselves in England as our servants in an indenture, or the kind of contract usual in this country, we would be most certain to get them. Here, if we found them to be orderly people, we could free them soon, to wit, under these conditions 1) that they settle at our place and help our community with their profession, and 2) that they repay in some years the money we have advanced. In this way both they and we can be helped. I wish that all our present servants were of such a kind as the two previously mentioned farmers are; yet some others are starting out well even if they have not learned farm work.

Tuesday, the 12th of December. For some days it has again been rather cold, yet the sun is shining and the air is temperate. Mr. Meyer and Mr. Lemke went to Savannah this morning to do some business, partly for themselves and partly for the community. For this purpose our Mill River is a great blessing, because with a moderate current we can go down to Savannah in seven hours and can come back to the mill in the same number of hours.[12] We like to keep our boat there to lighten the trip, which is otherwise rather difficult via Purysburg.

For already fourteen years the Lord Trustees have had an extensive and expensive cattle ranch and studfarm in Old Ebenezer; and it was then General Oglethorpe's intention to develop this place, which is lacking good land for cultivation, through this cattle ranch and also through the establishment of a sawmill; but both of them failed.

Wednesday, the 13th of December. The carpenter Zittrauer has built himself a new house, which was consecrated this afternoon at his and his pious wife's request in the presence of their neighbors, as has been customary among us since the beginning, with Christian simplicity and without circumstance or special ceremonies. An edifying hymn is sung, we pray, and something is preached from God's word; and at the end we pray on bended knee and conclude with a little verse from a hymn. Just as we recently began to lay the heart examinations according to the Ten Commandments from the late Ambrosius Wirth's *Confessional and Communion Booklet*[13], which is in the hands of all the parishioners, as a basis for the preparation sermon, we have made a beginning at this house consecration to acquaint the people with the beautiful rules of life along with the attached selected Bible verses, which stand at the end of this beautiful little book, and to explicate and instill in them. I plan, God willing, to continue with this in the future on such occasions. God let us feel His gracious presence keenly today.

Thursday, the 14th of December. I visited the servant of our pious miller, Zimmerebner, who has had cold fever for some time. Like many of the servants who have come here, he had many prejudices against true Christianity, which have, however, gradually fallen away. At first these young people were ashamed to bend their knees in prayer with their householders and housemates. However, because they have always seen that the entire community say their prayers in this humble way at public divine services both before and after the sermon, likewise in the evening prayer meeting, they have now begun to be ashamed of their obstinacy. I diligently admonish our people in private to show these strangers great patience in all things and to overlook secondary matters and weaknesses that come from ignorance and long habit. Once they have been better instructed from God's word and clear examples in Holy Scripture, much of their misbehavior will cease. The often-mentioned confessional and Communion booklet, which is read in pious families at my repeated recommendation, can be a good means to open their eyes through the grace of God.

The previously mentioned mill servant has become humble in his sickness, he is recognizing the grace of God in his master; and he greatly regrets that he cannot help him in the mill, since there is now very much to grind there. He arose from his prayer with weeping eyes. May our dear God keep our righteous and industrious miller, Zimmerebner, for many more years! He is known near and far as a just man, for whom not even wicked people betray the least suspicion that he will not give them what is theirs.[14] Where possible, he does not let the smallest grain go to waste. Physically, to be sure, he has an unimpressive appearance and speaks few words; but no one among the strangers has the heart to cause him worry or trouble or to cause any mischief at the mill. If one or the other of them wishes to misbehave, then he is chastised and corrected by his own comrades. That is another proof of the merciful and wise providence of God over us! On a board in the mill hang certain just rules in the English and German languages, according to which the local people and strangers must conduct themselves.

Saturday, the 16th of December. Yesterday, after the previous cold days, we had a rain, which became stronger last night. A strong wind arose, which again veered to the west; and therefore it again became bright, dry, and cold toward morning. This winter is dry and healthy.

This morning we buried Hessler's only little son, a child of two and a half years, who liked to pray in his short life and proved himself as patient and quiet in his very painful sickness. At almost the same time as this little boy died, Paul Zittrauer's little boy was born. Shortly before that his house had been consecrated with God's word, song, and prayer; and this brought his salvation-hungry wife a blessed preparation for her following childbed. For this she heartily rejoiced and praised God, who is dealing with her in pure mercy. For some time she has become very serious in her Christianity. To preserve and daily awaken this necessary and blessed seriousness in herself and family, she named her little child Ernst Christian in holy baptism. If all her children were still alive, she would have six sons together in ten years, but four of them are in eternal rest.

Monday, the 18th of December. The biting cold is still continuing; and, because with it the sky is sometimes overcast, it appears that further in the mountains there is snow, which is said to fall often at this time above Augusta. The water in the river has fallen just as fast as it rose. Because our inhabitants can bear the cold winter days in this country less than in their fatherland, they have arranged themselves according to their former local customs and put stoves in their chambers, whereby they and their children enjoy temperate warmth both day and night. This greatly helps those who, because of their poverty, cannot buy warm quilts. Other people in the country, such as Englishmen and Frenchmen, do not like stoves like the Germans, but make do with fireplaces, which, for various reasons, do not suit our people.

To be sure, wood is not lacking here, especially pine and fir; but good wood, such as oak and nut trees, is becoming rarer here and there because part of the good land on which such trees stand has been prepared already for several years for gardens and fields. As a result, the felled wood has been burned or has rotted. Also, every year more land of that kind is cleared of oak and other deciduous trees and made available for planting. If that continues for several years as the community increases, there will be nothing to find nearby but fir or pine trees. Of them there are large forests everywhere, which, however, are used only for lumber and boards. For a long time all the good firewood has been cut down around the town, and now it must be fetched with horse and wagon at considerable expense from far away. This costs us quite much every year, since we do not wish to burden our parishioners with chopping wood or any other work.

Tuesday, the 19th of December. It is surely not to be looked upon as if by chance, or to be ascribed to a person, that our pious widows are so well provided for physically and have it better here than many householders and their wives. Old Mrs. Schweighoffer sometimes experiences somewhat harder tribulations, for which she herself is to blame because of her all-too-great love for her children and her considerable obstinacy. Otherwise she could live better and more comfortably than anyone else in our place. She is already more than sixty years old. Fourteen years ago her right side was paralyzed by a stroke, and she has many other physical infirmities so that we must have much patience and put up with her. Her spiritual condition was better previously, as she herself recognizes; and she laments and deplores her fall. However, because she so clings to her children, who are not the best, she receives no little harm from that even though she is using the means of salvation diligently. She has been living for some time alone with her two children.

Wednesday, the 20th of December. Six German men from Vernonburg near Savannah have come to our mill. Because they have brought crops for almost all their neighbors to have it ground, they must wait for several days. This will serve them in that they will hear the word of God in Zion Church to prepare them for Holy Communion and for blessed eternity. They have little chance in Vernonburg to hear the counsel of God concerning their salvation, except for every two months, when one of us goes down to preach to the people of our confession and to adminster Holy Communion, during which some Reformed people from Vernonburg and Acton are accustomed to join us. From time to time God ordains for foreign German people who have secular business at the mill or elsewhere to hear a sermon in the evening prayer hour, even though they are often not lovers of God's word, the church, and the ministerial office. We also preach to them simply and seriously, as we do with all our parishioners, about God's counsel concerning their salvation, and we instill it in their hearts. But they will not accept the counsel of God concerning their salvation that is preached simply and sincerely and impressed on their hearts. Yet they should know that the kingdom of God with its treasures and order have been offered to them, and therefore they will have no excuse on that day.[15]

On the 26th Sunday after Trinity it was ordained that an old sinner who lives on General Oglethorpe's barony at Palachocolas came here with his boat and could hear a sermon on 2 Peter 1:10–11, "Brethren, give diligence to make . . ." He was very devout during it, and God granted me much joy during the sermon. When I saw this man across from me, I heartily wished that God would also seize his heart and bring him to the enjoyment of His grace. A few weeks later some of our people traveled to his plantation on business and heard that this man had presumably died, and therefore this was his last sermon. There is surely not a single sermon here among us that does not show the parishioners from God's word what God demands from them according to the content of the law and the gospel if they wish to escape future wrath and be restful here and blessed there.[16]

I had heard that young Lackner had had a stove placed in his previously cold dwelling in order to make the cold winter bearable for his weakly wife and three small children. For that reason I went to his plantation to praise God with him and his family and to pray to Him. However, I found the mother and the children at the fire in the kitchen, and I heard from her that she had enjoyed her heated chamber for only a few days. If at night God had not revealed a fire hidden in the boards and beams under the stove in time, they would have lost all their belongings in this conflagration, if not their life or health. Despite the fact that this Mrs. Lackner has had to suffer much sickness, poverty, and other kinds of tribulation, she still thanks our dear God heartily that she and her family are in quiet solitude and can prepare themselves unhindered for blessed eternity. Also, it is no small blessing that among us there is no noise before the holy days or misery in preparing for it physically, as is customary in both large and small cities. Those who have been in service with fashionable people know the difference especially.

After I had returned from Lackner's plantation, I called on Schoolmaster /Georg/ Meyer and his salvation-hungry wife /Magdalena/ at their request to consecrate their little living room, which they have only recently had prepared, with prayer and the word of God. I prepared myself according to the present time and laid as the basis of our awakening the basic and strength-giving verses[17], "This is a faithful saying; and worthy of all acceptation," etc. 1 Timothy 1;[18] and with it I made useful to me and them the beautiful examples that stand in the *Treasure Chest*[19], pp. 32 ff. along with the beautiful verse, "That is a dear word," etc. God let our hearts feel that He was present among us according to His promise. The poor people are so happy when God grants them a warm kitchen or chamber, while His Son, through whom He does everything, had to make do with a stable. When our miraculous God sends us young and wild lads, as our young Meyer used to be, I often think of the verse, "What I do thou knowest not now; but thou shalt know hereafter." I think the same thing with regard to our servants.

Thursday, the 21st of December. In our beautiful supply of books there are many edifying preparations for the holy Christmas celebration that have been held in Halle; and with them I have given pleasure to the dear children who come to me in the preparation lesson. I have given every boy and girl such a book to take home and also a brief instruction how to make their content profitable to themselves and their families before the holy celebration. We know that today, Thursday, is New Years Day in Germany according to the new calendar;[20] and this caused us already yesterday evening in the prayer meeting to praise our dear God for His goodness which He will have shown our dear German fatherland and our dear benefactors there and to invoke Him for mercy and blessing for them. On the occasion of the planned material concerning the means of grace and especially the word of God, I reminded my children in the preparation hour of the many spiritual and physical benefactions that have flowed to us from Europe so far in so many ways and how today many dear souls in Germany are doubtless praying for us to God in heaven and wishing us well and that it is much more our duty to do it for them. Thereupon we knelt down and prayed for us and our known and unknown benefactors. I also admonished them to continue doing the same at home.

Friday, the 22nd of December. After the last rain a most unusual cold began, yet without much wind. It seems to us that we have almost never felt the cold so cutting as at this time; and may

God avert all harm from our planted wheat, which previously experienced a heavy rain and now a very severe frost and still is not covered with snow as in Germany. A man who came from the region of Augusta in his boat told me that it had snowed heavily up there, from which we can expect much water in warm weather.

Saturday, the 23rd of December. The wind has shifted from the east to the north and then further to the northwest, and therefore very rough and stormy weather has arisen with much cold rain. Toward morning it thundered very violently and rained from time to time, yet the severe cold has broken a little. This is the pleasant period of preparation for the holy Christmas celebration, when we can allow ourselves less than at other times to be kept by the bad weather from visiting the hours devoted to it in the public assembly. Jerusalem Church is small and well protected so that the cold hurts us but little.

Sunday, the 24th of December. Yesterday after the evening prayer meeting a housewife had something to report to me so that I might not have unnecessary worry before and during the holy celebration because of an incorrectly understood matter. I happened to speak with her about her children, and I heard from her that her oldest boy had a better head for learning, but not such a good attitude or so many signs of God's grace living in him as her oldest girl had, even though she was only a child of something more than six years. She loves her Savior dearly, and through ardent love for Him she would rather die than live longer in the world. She also likes to pray, and she gives her mother much joy. She has such a pale color in her face and so many kinds of physical weakness that it well appears that she will not live long.

After the afternoon divine service another pious mother reported to me that her sick girl had already requested her several time to ask me to visit her. She, too, has a heavenly disposition and a true desire to die. She has much joy in two pious little girls who are already before the throne of the Lamb in heaven. She edifies herself in her patience in suffering and wishes to be with them and her dear Savior soon. In healthy days she had so willingly learned such a beautiful supply of Bible verses that we had contemplated in the exordiums of the sermons that she would not let her father rest, even in the midst of his work, until he had taught her the verse to be learned by reciting it for her. This child, of something more than six years like the previously mentioned one, serves her parents for much awakening with her marvelous and edifying speeches and Christian behavior. They would gladly give her to their dear Savior if He wished to take her through temporal death, since they are becoming aware of such clear signs of baptismal grace in her. She is a clever child by nature. She said to me to my comfort and awakening among other things the beautiful words, "The just shall live eternally, and the Lord is their reward and the Highest shall keep them."[21]

For that reason they shall receive a splendid kingdom and a beautiful crown from the hand of the Lord. These two pious girls have dear substantial parents with whom they are very well provided for physically; and, since they have a disgust in the world and a yearning for blessed death, their attitude seems all the purer to me.

Monday, the 25th of December. Yesterday evening God gave us grace to prepare ourselves before His countenance through communal prayer in church for the holy birthday festival of Christ our Savior; and to this our parishioners, both old and young, assembled in large numbers. Our dear Savior granted me time and strength before the holy days to be able to read with my family some edifying preparations for Christmas that had been held in Halle. Through His grace He so blessed these in me that the blessing from them flowed not only into the conduct of my Christianity but also into my important office. In many places in our German fatherland certain rousing preparation sermons are held before the holy feast days and other good exercises are practiced with song and prayer to encourage the people's spirits; and this is a very praiseworthy and necessary arrangement. Without it little blessing can be hoped for from the holy day sermons, especially among such people who, instead of preparing for the celebration, burden their hearts with worries about subsistence and good living in this world. Many people grow up in such blindness that they know little about the purpose and importance of the holy days; and they learn nothing about it if they are not guided to it by word and example in the preparations. In addition to what we contemplated for this purpose in the prayer meetings and the weekday sermons from God's word, the sermon of yesterday, the Fourth Sunday of Advent, was also aimed at it. Namely, with the gospel we treated the worthy preparation of our hearts for the advent of Christ our Savior, during which we contemplated the beautiful words from Psalms 68:5, "Sing unto God, sing praises to his name," etc.

On this first day of Christmas the entire congregation was together in the town church; and they were so numerous that it served us to no little joy and encouragement to sow the imperishable seed of the gospel into the hearts of so many devout listeners. In the morning, with the help of the Holy Ghost, I held a sermon about our dearest and most esteemed Immanuel, of which my heart was right full from reading in previous days Dr. Francke's exceedingly thorough and edifying preparation sermon concerning the words, "Here is Immanuel." In the afternoon my dear colleague preached and catechized on the beautiful text Zephania 3:14 ff., from which one can see what, in the time of the New Testament, should be the chief thing in the Christian Church according to the will of God, namely, that people should rightly enjoy the good of Christianity and find joy and comfort in their Savior. Our servants are causing us joy by visiting in an orderly and constant way the public divine service and the good opportunities for instruction, prayer, and edification and by being attentive from beginning to end. In external ways they have already changed greatly and put aside their fresh and impudent ways, and they are no longer ashamed to pray on their knees. They had an ugly, screeching, and very dragging way of singing that disturbed the sweetness, good harmony, and edification of our song; but now they are listening to advice.

Tuesday, the 26th of December. Our merciful God has also let us pass this second day of Christmas in health and blessing. However stormy it was before the celebration, God has granted us pleasant weather during the holy days and with it good rest, silence, and external good order. This evening a very stormy wind arose and there was also some lightning, even though we

did not hear any thunder. No strange German people appeared
this time at our place, except for a man and woman who came
today from Abercorn. Likewise, none of us went away, but we
had all of our parishioners together. Also, no one was kept away
from the public service by sickness (except " " ").[22] We know of
no patients now among our parishioners. A severe catarrh has
been around for several weeks; and some who did not guard
themselves against the great cold before the celebration have begun to cough.

We would have liked to hold a prayer meeting in the church
this evening, but the violent storm prevented us from doing so.
Singing and praying rightfully make up a major part of our divine service. We lack hymnals and also Bibles; all members of the
congregation are provided with New Testaments, even the children and servants. At the beginning and at the close of public
divine services on Sundays and holy days a chapter from Holy
Scripture is read loudly, slowly, and clearly; and every adult and
child reads along after it. However, because the servants and
some of the children have no Bibles, we cannot continue reading
the Old Testament, in which we now stand, so we began reading
the New Testament during the holy days in order that everyone
would be kept from vainly gazing around, which we consider to
be a sign of a frivolous and disorderly mind.

Friday, the 29th of December. A short time ago a fine youth
from Purysburg was drowned in the water, and no one had
thought that he has so many debts as has now been discovered
after his death.

Saturday, the 30th of December. Yesterday, while I was still
with the sick Sanftleben, I found him in a very bad physical condition. The sickness had suddenly become so severe that we
could not expect any good outcome. This morning I received
the news that he died yesterday evening; and therefore I had my
last prayer with him and his family. In it I called upon our dear
God in the name of His Son, our Immanuel, for the sake of
Christ's merits, not to blame this Sanftleben for having brought
upon himself this sickness itself and all the miserable conditions
in which he and his family found themselves, as he and his wife

well known. He was formerly an honest man who prayed diligently and loved God's word and good opportunity for edification. On the first day of Christmas he was in church, on the second he got side-stiches with unusual chills and fever. Because he
did not take any medicine soon and could not keep himself
warm in his miserable dwelling in this present cold weather, he
naturally suffered very evil attacks that ended with a quick
death. He is leaving a widow and two small children.

Sunday, the 31st of December. Sanftleben was brought from
the plantations to town yesterday before evening and buried
with the company of many people. Some time ago, for general
edification, I began in the funeral sermons at the burial of children to run through edifying examples of pious children who
died blessedly; and at this funeral I have begun to impart to the
pallbearers something from the edifying biography of the late
Pastor Mischke, who in my time was the meritorious inspector of
the schools at the Orphanage at Halle, I had formerly laid another beautiful example of a pious shoemaker in Naumberg
in the funeral sermons of grown people as a basis of edification.
Although such a type of funeral sermon might not be approved
of by everyone who does not know our arrangements, it is
enough for me that I know that God is granting me and my dear
listeners much blessing through it for their edification and preparation for a blessed death. Such curricula or accounts of the last
hours of the servants and children of God are not just read as
they happen to be written, but I have an opportunity to lead the
listeners into God's word and to instill in them very important
dogma and duties of life.

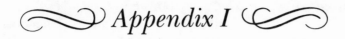

Appendix I

SONGS SUNG BY
THE SALZBURGERS
IN THE YEAR 1749

Hymns followed by F-T and volume and song (not page!) number are reproduced in Albert Friedrich Fischer—W. Tumpel, *Das deutsche evangelische Kirchenlied des 17. Jahrhunderts* (Gutersloh, 1916, reprinted Hildesheim 1964). Authors of all identified hymns are listed in (AF) Albert Friedrich Fischer, *Kirchenlieder-Lexikon* (Gotha, 1878, reprint Hildesheim 1967).

Ach, möchte ich meinen Jesum sehen . . . (Alas, if only I could see my Jesus), by Maria Magdalena Böhmer. DR 13, p. 1

Auf, Ebenezer! werde heut zu Gottes Lob erwecket . . . (Up, Ebenezer. Be awakened to the praise of God), unidentified. DR 13, p. 25

Auf, O Seele, preise deines Schöpfers Güte . . . (Up, oh soul, praise thy Creator's goodness), unidentified. DR 13, p. 97.

Jesus Christus, unser Heiland . . . (Jesus Christ, our Savior), by Martin Luther. DR 10, 13, p. 88

Liebster Jesu in den Tagen dieser Niedrigkeit . . . (Dearest Jesus in the days of this humiliation), anonymous, in Halle Hymnal. DR 13, p. 21

Lobe meine Seele! deines Jesu Thaten . . . (Praise, my soul, the deeds of thy Jesus), unidentified. DR 13, p. 97

Warum sollt ich mich denn grämen . . . (Why then should I grieve), by Paul Gerhardt. DR 13, p. 73

APPENDIX II
Cumulative Index to Volumes I through XII

Salz = Salzburger, Pal = Palatine
Some of the following words and names do not
appear alphabetically in the various indexes but,
as indicated below, are subsumed under entries such
as Crops, Disease, and Fruit.

Aaron, convert in India, 11, 12
Abercorn, village near juncture of
  Abercorn Creek and Savannah
  River 1–12
Abercorn Creek (Mill River), branch
  of Savannah River 1–12
Abercorn Island, between Savannah
  River and Abercorn Creek, 5
Aboab, Davis, author, 11
Absolutum Decretum 8, 12
Acton, German and Swiss settle-
  ment, 11
Acorns 4, 5, 6, 11, see Fruit.
Adde, Friedrich, s Salomo, 8
Adde, (Johann) Heinrich, s Salomo,
  5–8
Adde (Ade), Margaretha, w Salomo,
  5, 6, 8, 9
Ade (Adde), (Hieronymus) Salomo,
  Swabian 5–9
Adult education, 9
Agriculture, see Crops.
Albinus, Johann Georg, hymnist, 11,
  12
Albinus, Mr., Court Chaplain, 11, 12
Alligator, 2, 4, 9
Alther, Johann, Swiss butcher 7
Altamaha River, river in central
  Georgia 1, 2
Anabaptists 8, 11
Anton, Leopold, Count of Firmian,
  Archbishop of Salzburg, 1
Anton, Paul, Pietist writer, 1–3, 5, 9

Appenzell, Appenzellers, 4, 5, 11
Apples, 11, see Fruit.
Arians, religious sect, 11
Arndt, Johann, Pietist writer, 1–12
Arnensee, Pastor, treatise by, 4
Arnold, Mrs., letter to, 3
Arnsdorf (Ernstdorf), Andreas
  Lorentz, Pal, 3, 4, 7, 8
Arnsdorf, Catharina Dorothea, Pal,
  w Andreas Lorentz 3–5, 8, 11
Arnsdorff, Catherina Dorothea, Pal,
  d Andreas Lorentz, 5, 6, 8
Arnsdorf, Magdalena, Pal, d. An-
  dreas, 7, 8
Arnsdorff, (Johann) Peter, Pal, s An-
  dreas Lorentz, 6, 7, 8–10
Arnsdorf, Sophia (Catharina), Pal, d
  Andreas Lorentz, 5, 8
Avery, Joseph, English surveyor,
  8–12
Augsburg, city in Swabia, 1, 2, 3,
  8–12
Augusta, city up the Savannah River,
  5, 10, 11
Augustine, Mr., English settler, 1
Ausführliche Nachrichten, 5, 7, 8,11,
  see Ebenezer Reports.

Bach, Gabriel, Salz 1–8
Bach, Margaretha, nee Staud, Pal,, w
  Gabriel, 7
Bacher, Anna Maria, Salz, w Bal-
  thasar, 8, 9, 11, 12

Bacher, Apollonia, Pal, d Matthias, 8
Bacher, Balthasar, Salz, 8, 9, 11, 12
Bacher, Christina, Salz, w Matthias, 9, 10
Bacher, Maria, nee Schweiger, Salz, w Thomas, 6–10, 12
Bacher, Matthias, Salz, 8, 9
Bacher, Thomas, Salz, 2–4, 6–10, 12
Baptisms, see Births and Baptisms.
Balsamus cephalicus, 2
Barber, Mr. Jonathan, chaplain at Bethesda, 7, 8
Baptisms, see Births and Baptisms.
Barker, Joseph, keeper of cowpen, 5, 8
Barley 5, 8, 11, 12. See Crops.
Barn, 4
Barley stamp, 12
Bauer, Andreas, Austrian, 3
Baumgarten, Siegmund Jacob, professor at Halle, 1, 3, 4
Bavaria, province in Germany, 3
Baynton, Peter, merchant in Philadelphia, 1
B*ck, German drifter, 11
Beans 2–5, 7, 8–12. See Crops.
Bears, 3, 4, 9, 10, 12
Beaufain, Hector Bellinger de, merchant, 7
Beer, making of, 1, 3
Bees, 3, 5–7
Beginning of Christian Life, see Dogma...
Behm, Martin, hymnist, 11
Beiträge zum Bau des Reiches Gottes, 8, see Contribution.
Belcher, Jonathan, gov. of Massachusetts, 1–3
Bell for church, 7, 11
Benefactions, 1–12. See also Charities and Gifts.
Beque (Becu), Gilbert, French baker, 1, 3, 11
Beque, w above, 3
Berein, German chaplain in London, 6–8.
Berenberger, Margaretha, Salz, 6, 8
Berlin fever powder, 8, 10
Bernstein, C.A., composer, 5

Bethesda, Whitefield's orphanage near Savannah, 7–9, 11
Beyer, pastor in Zezeno, 2
Bichler, see Pichler.
Bilfinger, Georg Bernhard, theologian at Tübingen, 3
Birds, cause damage, 4, 5
Births, 2, 4–6, 8–12
Bischoff, Anna Maria, Pal, 6, 7
Bischoff, Heinrich, see Bishop.
Bishop, Friederica, Pal, nee Unselt, w Henry, 8–10
Bishop (Bischoff), Henry, former servant to Boltzius 2–9, 12
Blacksmiths, see Smiths.
Bloodletting 4, 7, 12
Blumengärtlein, religious tract, 11
Bogatzky, Carl Heinrich, Pietist author, 2–12
Böhler, Peter, Moravian missionary, 5, 6, 8
Böhme, Anton Wilhelm, Pietist theologian, 2, 3, 5
Böhmer, J. H., hymnist, 5
Bohemian pastors in Berlin, 7
Bohner, Magdalena, hymnist, 8
Boltzius, Christina Elisabetha, d Johann Martin, 8
Boltzius, Gertraut, w Johann Martin, 2, 5, 6, 11
Boltzius, Gotthilf Israel Johann Martin, 6–8
Boltzius, Johann Martin, pastor at Ebenezer, 1–12
Boltzius, Samuel Leberecht, s Johann Martin, 8
Boltzius, Mrs., mother of Johann Martin, 1, 2, 3
Bonin, Ulrich Bogsilaus von, hymnist, 11
Book of Gifts and Benefactions, 8
Book of Universal Mercy, 12
Booklet of the Blessings of God, 8
Books, donation of, 12
Bosomworth, Thomas, Anglican minister, 12
Boston, Mass, von Reck in, 1
Bötticher, inspector, 3
Bounty, 8, see Corn-shilling.

Bourquin, Jean, Swiss surgeon, 8
Bourgeois respectability, 3
Boynd, Dr. of Rotterdam, 3
Bozoardic powder, medicine, 5
Brandner, Maria, nee Hierl, w Matthias, 2, 3, 5, 6, 8
Brandner, Maria, d Matthias, 8
Brandner, Matthias, Salz 2–6, 8, 11. 12
Brands, cattle, 5
Brandy, 3, 8, 11, 12
Braunberger, Matthias, Salz 1–3
Breithaupt, Abbot Joachim Justus, Pietist author, 1, 3, 4, 7
Brent, Pietist theologian, 1
Breuer, Pastor in East Prussia, 5, 10
Brickl, see Brückl.
Bricks 6, 9, 10
Bridges, 2, 4, 9
Brückl, Barbara, Salz, 9
Brückner, Georg, Salz, 3–12
Brückner, (Anna) Margaretha, nee Muller, Pal, w Georg, 6, 7, 9
Brunnholz, Johann Peter, pastor in Philadelphia, 11, 12
Bryan, Hugh, South Carolina planter, 2, 6, 8
Bryan, Jonathan, South Carolina planter, 2, 8–10
Buchfelder, E. W. hymn by, 3
Bücher vom wahren Christentum, 6, see True Christianity.
Buckwheat, 5
Bugenhagen, Johann, Pietist theologian, 1
Bühler, Peter, error for Böhler, Peter, 8
Building of the Kingdom of God 6, 7
Burgsdorff, Landeshauptmann von, benefactor, 3, 9
Burgsteiner, Agatha, Salz, w Matthias, 2–4, 6, 8, 9
Burgsteiner, Johannes, s Matthias, 8
Burgsteiner, Matthias, Salz, 1–8
Burgsteiner, Ruprecht, Salz, 8, 9
Burgsteiner, ———, d Ruprecht, 9
Busk, Indian ceremony, 3
Butienter (Butjenter), Heinrich Alard, court chaplain, 1–8
Butter, 3, 4

Cabbages, used as fodder, 12
Cadzand, place in Holland, 1, 9, 10, 11
Callenberg, Dr. Johannes Heinrich, missionary to the Jews, 1–3
Calves 2–8
Calvinists, see Reformed.
Camuso, Maria, Italian silkworker, 8, 9
Canstadt, port of embarcation on Neckar, 7–9
Canstein Bibles, 7
Cardobenedictin, 3
Carl, Dr. Johann Samuel, physician, 3, 9
Carl Rudolf, Prince of Wurttemberg, imposter, 9
Carolina, see South Carolina, North Carolina.
Carp, 8
Carpenter, Nicholas, English boy at Ebenezer, 2, 3, 6, 8
Carpenters, 2, 5, 6, 10, 11, 12. See Georg Kogler, Fr. Müller, Stephan Rottenberger, Schubdrein brothers.
Carts, 8
Catholics, slip in, 5, 11
Catholic soldier, converted, 10, 11
Cattle, 1–12
Cattle disease, 9, 10
Causton, Thomas, keeper of the stores, 1–8, 10
Causton, Mrs., wife of above, 3
Cedar wood, 10
Census in Ebenezer, 10
Charleston, city in South Carolina, 1–12
Cherokees, 3, 5, 8, 9, 11, 12
Chicasaws, 5
Chiffelle, Henri François, Swiss minister, 4–6, 8
China de china, 4
Chinkapins, 2, 3, 6, see Fruit.
Christ, (Johann) Gottfried, converted Jew, 3–11
Christ, nee Metzger, w Gottfried, 9, 11
Christ–Bescherung (Christ's Gifts), devotional work, 5, 7

Christ the Core of Holy Writ, by A. H. Francke, 3

Christ the Sun and Substance of the Holy Scripture, same as above.

Christ's Christmas Gifts, religious treatise, 1, 3

Christliche Anweisung, religious tract, 11

Churches, 6, 7, 8, 12, see Jerusalem and Zion.

Churching, 2, 3, 5, 6

Church penance, 3, 7

Clapboards, used for building, 3

Clauder, Mr., pastor in Halberstadt, 1, 5

Clausewitz, Prof. Benedikt Gottlieb, Pietist author, 7

Clausnitzer, Tobias, hymn by, 3

Clay for chimneys, 2

Clay eating (pica), 7

Coins, currency, and copper money, 3, 11, 12

Collin, Friedrich Eberhard, Pietist writer, 3–5, 7

Columella, Roman writer, 11

Commandments, Ten, 3

Commentary, work by Johannes Arndt, 1

Communal labor, 2, 3, 10

Communion, 1–10, see Holy, see Holy Communion.

Compendium der ganzen christlichen Lehre, religious tract 11

Compendium Theologicum, by J. A. Freylinghausen 3, 4, 7–9, 11

Confirmation 10, 11. See Holy Communion.

Consecration, see House consecration.

Consilia Latina, religious tract, 6

Consilium medicum, medical treatise, 2

Construction, see Church, Mill.

Contemplation of Solitude, devotional treatise, 8

Continuations, the continuations of the *Ausführliche Nachrichten*, 8–11

Contribution to the Building of the Kingdom of God, religious tract, 1, 3, 6–8. See *Beiträge*....

Cooing Dove, devotional work, 3, 4

Coram, Capt. Thomas, Trustee, 1–5

Corn, 2–11. See under crops.

Cornberger, Gertraut, w. Johann, 4–8

Cornberger, Johann, Salz, 3, 4, 7, 8

Corn–shilling, subsidy on crops, 4, 8–10. See Subsidies.

Corpus Evangelicorum, Protestant Body at Regensburg, 3, 6, 11

Costerus (Kosterus), friend in Holland, 1–3

Cotterall, Clement, 1

Cotton, 5, 11

Council in Savannah, 11, 12

Counterfit money, 2

Cowherds, 8, see Herdsmen and Friedrich Nett, Jacob Schartner, Michael Schneider.

Cowie, Capt., captured by Spaniards, 12

Cowpen (Old Ebenezer), 8, 11

Cows, see Cattle 1–12

Crabgrass, 11, 12

Cranwetter, see Graniwetter.

Crasselius, B., hymnist, 5

Crause, see Krause.

Crause, Barbara, nee Einecker, 4, 6

Crause, Leonard, 5, 6

Crecelius, pastor at Reicheltheim, 8

Creeks 1–9, 12. See Indians.

Crell, Walburga, Salz, 9

Crocodile, see Alligator.

Crops, 1–12. See barley, beans, corn, oats, peanuts, peas, rice, rye, spelt, sweet potatoes, wheat, German crops, crop reports, fruit, vegetables.

Crows, destroy corn, 3

Cudulur (Cudalore), mission at, 7, 11, 12

Cugel, see Gugel.

Currency, see Coins.

Curtius, see Kurtz, Jac. Fr.

Custobader, Catherina, Pal, 8

Cypress trees, a durable wood 10

Damius, O. C., hymnist, 4

Darien, Scots Settlement 5, 6, 8, 12

Das gewaltige Eindringen in das Reich Gottes, religious tract, 7

Dasher (Täscher), Martin, Swiss, 8

Daubaz, Capt., 5

Deaths, 1–12

Deer, 3–8, 12

Deer horn, 8

Decretum Absolutum (Absolutum Decretum), 8

Degmair, Matthäus Friedrich, chaplain with first Salz. transport 1, 3

Deists, sectarians, 11

Delamotte, Charles, schoolmaster, 4, 5

Depp, Anna Elisabeth, Pal, 7

Depp, ..., bro Anna Elisabetha Kieffer, 10

Depp, Valentin, Swiss, 8

Depp, Mrs., mother Valentin, 8

Diamond, Capt., 4

Diarrhea (usually dysentary), 4

Die Auferstehung Christi, religious tract, 7

Dietzius, Andreas Gottfried, passenger with Salz, 2, 3

Diseases, 1–12. See "Clay eating," Diarrhea, Dysentary, "Epilepsy," Fever clot, Malaria, Scurvy.

Doctrine of Atonement, religious tract, 12

Dogma of the Beginning of Christian Life, by A. H. Francke, 4, 5, 7, 8, 10, 11

Dover, English port, 1, 3

Drese, A., hymnist, 5

Dresler, Catharina, w Johann Georg, 9

Dresler (Dressler), Johann Georg, Pal, 8, 9

Dressler, W. C., hymnist, 5

Driessler, Ulrich, minister at Frederica, 8, 11, 12

Driessler, w of above, 11

Drought, 5, 10, 11

Duché, Andrew, potter, 6–8

Ducks, wild, 2

Dunbar, Capt. George, master of *Prince of Wales,* 1, 2

Durninger, Mr., benefactor of Salzburgers, 9

Dürrenberg, province adjacent to Salzburg, 12

Dürrenbergers (Tirnbergers), religious exiles in Cadzant, 1, 3

Dysentary, 3, 4, 12

East India, site of Lutheran missions, 3, 4, 8, 11, 12

East Prussia, see Prussia.

Ebenezer, Salz settlement, 1–12

Ebenezer Creek, unnavigable waterway from Old to New Ebenezer 1–12

Ebenezer Reports, see *Ausführliche Nachrichten.*

Egger, Margaretha, Salz, 6

Egmont, John Percival, Earl of, 3, 7

Eigel, Georg, Salz, 8, 9, 11

Eigel, Ursula, Salz, w Georg 9

Eigel children, five in number 9

Einecker, Barbara, Salz, 7

Einecker, Gertraut, Salz, 3, 5, 6

Eischberger, Anna Maria, Salz, w David 8, 9

Eischberger, Catherina, Salz, d Ruprecht, 8, 11

Eischberger, David, Salz, miller, 9

Eischberger, Johann, Salz, s Ruprecht, 8

Eischberger, Maria, Salz, w Ruprecht, Salz, 2, 3, 5–7, 9

Eischberger, Ruprecht, Salz, 2–9, 11, 12

Elers, founder of Halle bookstore, 5, 6

Emigrant Fund, fund for Salz exiles at Regensburg, 1

Empire (Holy Roman Empire), 8

End of a Righteous Person, religious tract, 1

Ende, Baron von, benefactor, 8

Engelbrecht, Martin, Augsburg engraver, 7

English lady, refugee at Ebenezer, 9

English language, study of, 2, 11

"Epilepsy" (any paroxysm), 10, 11

Epistle Prayers, by A. H. Francke, 5

Erbauliche Betrachtungen vom Ursprung und Adel der Seelen, 6

Erfurt, German city, 4
Erfurt Bible, inexspensive scripture, 11
Ernst, Heinrich, hymnist, 12
Ernst, Johannes, s Josef, 8
Ernst, Josef, h of Anna Maria, 3–9
Ernst, (Anna) Maria, wid Josef, 3, 4, 7–9
Ernst, Sabina, d Josef, 8, 11
Ernst, Susanna, d Josef, 8
Essentia amara, medicine, 3
Essentia dulcis, medicine, 2–4, 8
Europa, ship bring Swiss transport, 8
European crops, see German crops.
Evangelische Lehre, religious tract, 12
Eveleigh, Samuel, merchant in Charleston, 4, 5

Fabric of God's Kingdom, Pietist treatise, 3
Falck, Gabriel, questionable Swedish preacher, 5, 6
Fallowfield, John, English official, 6
"Fathers," patrons of Georgia Salzburgers, 5, 7, 8, 10–12. See G. A. Francke, Samuel Urlsperger, Friedrich Michael Ziegenhagen.
Feesen, a kind of spelt, 11
Felser, Georg, Salz, 3
Felss, Pastor, minister in Lindau, 9
Fences, 4, 8–12
Fever, 3–6, 8–10, 12. See Disease.
Fever clot, 7, 9
Figs, 11, see Fruit.
Fire, for clearing woods, 3, 4
Fireplaces, 2, 3
Fish at Ebenezer, 2, 3, 5, 8 (under carp)
Fish otter, 2
Fischer, Rev. J. G., pastor at Cadzant, 1, 3
Flax, 5, 11, 12
Fleiss, Balthasar, Salz, 1, 3
Flerl, Anna Maria, Salz, w Hans, 5–9, 11, 12
Flerl, Carl, Salz, 3, 5, 8–10
Flerl, Hans, Salz, bro Carl, 3, 5–12
Flerl, Maria, Salz, w Carl, 5, 6, 10
Flörl, see Flerl.

Flour and meal from mill, 3–5, 8, 10
Flower Garden (Blumengärtlein), religious tract, 11
Forceful Entry into the Kingdom of God, devotional tract, 4
Fort Argyle, fort on Ogeechee River, 2, 7–9, 11
Fort St. George, in Georgia, 3
Fort St. George in India, 11
Fort Venture, fort on Savannah River, 11
Fourth Salz transport, 8
Francis, English captain at Fort Venture, 9
Francis, Mrs., Palatine wife of captain, 9
Francke, August Hermann, founder of Francke Foundation in Halle, 1–12
Francke, Gotthilf August, s A. G. Francke, 1–12
Francke Foundation, charitable institute in Halle, 1–3,5, 7, 8, 11
Francke, Paul, Pal from Purysburg, 4, 7
Frankfurt on the Main, German city, 3
Frankfurt on the Oder, German city, 3
Frederica, town on St. Simons, 3–12
Frederick William, King of Prussia, 7, 8
Freihaupt, Abbot, professor at Halle, 3
Freylinghausen, Johann Anastasius, professor at Halle, author, 2–12
Freylinghausen hymnbook, 2–4, 7, 10–12
Frisch, Johann Friedrich, 6
Fruit, 6, 11. See Apples, Grapes, Peaches, Pears, Plums, Quinces, Olives.
Fry, Capt. Tobias, master of the *Purrysburg*, 1–3

Gamekeeper, refused by Boltzius, 5
Garden of Paradise, devotional work by Johannes Arndt, 1
Gebhart, Elisabetha, d Philip, 8

Gebhart, Eva, d Philip, 8
Gebhart, Magdalena, d Philip, 6, 8
Gebhart, Martha, w Philip, 7
Gebhart, Philip, Pal, 6, 7, 12
Gedicke, L., hymnist, 5
Geese, reference to goose eggs, 9
Geistreiches Gesangbuch, hymnal,
    11, 12
Gemig, merchant in Hamburg, 2
Georgii, Privy Counselor, benefactor,
    8, 9
Gerdes (Guerdes), Heinrich Walther,
    pastor of Swedish church in
    London 1, 3–5
Gerhard, Paul, hymnist, 3–5, 8, 11
Gerlach, shoemaker in Naum-
    burg, 12
German Chapel in London, 2, 8, 11
German crops (wheat, rye, barley,
    oats), 11, 12. See Crops.
German Indian trader, 5
German servants (Palatines), 5, 6, 8,
    10–12
Germans at Charleston, 4
Germans at Purysburg, 2–5
Germans at Savannah, 4, 5, 7–9,
    11, 12
Germantown, town in Pennsylvania,
    1, 11, 12
Gersdorf, Henriette Catherine,
    hymnist, 12
Gertrude Book, (Gertrudenbuch), Cath-
    olic devotional book, 3
Gewaltige Eindringen in das Reich
    Gottes, das, religious text, 7
Gichtel, Johann Georg, religious
    zealot, 4
Giessendanner, Johann, nephew of
    Johann Ulrich, 8
Giessendanner, Johann Ulrich, Swiss
    minister in S.C., 4, 5, 8
Gift of Christ, 5, see Christ-Bescherung.
Glaner, Georg, Salz, 8, 10, 11
Glaner, Gertraut, Salz, nee Lem-
    menhoffer, w Georg, 9, 11, 12
Glanz, Sebastian, Salz, 2, 3, 8
Glass windows, 5, 6, 10
Glaucha, town near Halle, 4
Glaucha Home Liturgy (Glauchische

Haus-Kirch Ordnung), religious
    tract, 7, 11
Glockengiesser, Mr., manufacturer
    of Berlin fever powder, 9
Glocker, Bernhard, Salz, 8
The Glory and Dogma A.C., religious
    tract, 10
God's Sacred Heart, religious treatise,
    11
Göbel, Johann, Prussian deputy, 2, 3
Göcking, Pastor G. G. G., author,
    1, 7
Goldeck, place in Salzburg, 12
Golden A.B.C. Book, devotional tract,
    5, 6
Gotter, Ludwig Andreas, hymnist, 8
Graham, Dr., neighbor of Salzbur-
    gers, 10, 12
Graniwetter, Anna Catharina, Salz,
    w Caspar, 9, 10–12
Graniwetter, Caspar, Salz, 8, 9, 11
Grapes, 2, 6, 8, 9, 10, 12, see Fruit
    and Vines.
Grass, burned each winter, 10
Grimmiger, Andreas, Austrian, 3,
    5–9
Grimmiger, Anna Maria, wid
    Bischoff, w Andreas, 8, 9
Grimmiger, Catharina, d Andreas,
    3, 5, 8, 9
Grimmiger, Sabina, first w An-
    dreas, 3
Gronau, Catharina, nee Kröher,
    Salz, w Israel Chr., 5, 6
Gronau, Friederica, d Israel Chris-
    tian, 10
Gronau, Hanna Maria, d Israel
    Chr., 8
Gronau, Israel Christian, assistant
    minister in Ebenezer, 1–12
Gronau, Israel Christian, Jr., son of
    above, 8, 9
Grossgebauer, Theophilus,
    author, 11
Gruber, Hans, Salz 1–3
Gruber, Johann, Salz, s Peter, 8
Gruber, Maria, Salz, nee Kröhr, wid
    Mosshamer, wid Peter Gruber,
    5–9

Gruber, Peter, Salz, 2–8
Gruber, Schönmann, see
    Schönmannsguber.
Grünig (Grüning, Griening), Abra-
    ham, Swiss, 3–5, 8, 11
Gschwandl, Margaretha, nee Hofer,
    first w Thomas, 2, 8
Gschwandl, Sybilla, Salz, second w
    Thomas, 6, 8, 9
Gschwandl, Thomas, Salz 1–11
Gschwandl, ... , child of Thomas, 2
Guard, mounted at Ebenezer, 3
Güldenes A.B.C., see Golden A.B.C..
Güldenes Messbüchlein, Catholic devo-
    tional, 7, 8
Güldenes Schatz-Kästlein, devotional
    work, 6–8
Guerdes, see Gerdes.
Gugel (Cugel, Kugel), Matthias, 4th
    Salz transport, 9
Gullman, Mr., British resident at
    Frankfurt, 1

Haberer, Anna Barbara, Salz, w Mi-
    chael, 9
Haberer, Michael, Salz, 9
Haberfehner, Franz, Austrian, 3
Haberfehner, Magdalena, d Franz,
    3–8, 10
Haberfehner, Maria, w Franz, 3
Haberfehner, Susanna, d Franz, 5, 8
Habermann, Johann, 6
Habersham, James, merchant, 5–12
Haeremond, captain of the Charles, 6
Hagen, Josef, Moravian in Sa-
    vanah, 8
Hahn, German in London, 3
Halle, city in East Germany, home of
    Francke Foundation, 1–12
Halle hymnbook, 7, 11, 12, same as
    Freylinghausen's hymnbook.
Halle orphange, 4, 5, 11
Halle Pietism, influence of, 1
Hamilton, Henry, English wig-
    maker, 8
Hamilton, Regina Charlotte, w.
    Henry, 8
Handel, Friedrich, arias by, 12

Handschuh, Mr., minister in Phila-
    delphia, 11
Hanover, city in Germany, 2, 12
Hardt, Hermann von der, German
    scholar, 3
Hares, 8
Harness, donated by Whitefield, 11
Harper, Simon, English boy, 8
Harrington, James, English sociolo-
    gist, 11
Harris, Francis, partner of
    Habersham, 6, 7, 11, 12
Hartmann, Johann Ludwig, 6
Hässler, see Hessler.
Hässlin (Hesslin), Frau von, bene-
    factress, 4–8
Häussler, Christina, unmarried
    Salz, 9
Haus–Tafel, book by Martin Luther,
    6–8
Hawks, 12
Hay, 3, 10, 12
Heavenly Kiss of Love, religious
    tract, 9
Heinrich, Anna Magdalena, Pal, d
    Peter, 10
Heinrich, Anna Maria, Pal,
    d Peter, 6
Heinrich, Catharina, Pal, d Peter, 8
Heinrich, (Johann) Georg, Pal, con-
    firmed, 11
Heinrich, Juliana, Pal, w Peter, 8
Heinrich, (Anna) Margaretha, Pal, d
    Peter, 8
Heinrich, Peter, deceased, Boltzius'
    Palatine servant, 6, 8–10
Held, Conrad, Pal, 7, 8
Held, Elisabetha, Pal, w. Conrad,
    6, 8
Held, Elisabetha, w Conrad, 6
Held, (Johann) Georg, Pal, s Con-
    rad, 6, 8, 9, 11
Held, Maria, Pal, w Georg, 11
Held, (Hans) Michael, Pal, s Conrad,
    7, 8
Helfenstein, Christian, s Dorothea, 8
Helfenstein, (Anna) Dorothea, Pal-
    atine, w Joh. Jac., 3–9

Helfenstein, (Johann) Friedrich, s
    Dorothea, 4–6, 8
Helfenstein, (Johann) Jacob, Swiss
    tanner, 3
Helfenstein, (Johann) Jacob, s of
    above, 5, 8
Helfenstein, Jeremias, s Dorothea,
    5, 8
Helfenstein, Johannes, s Dorothea, 8
Helfenstein, Maria Christina, d Dor-
    othea, 6
Helfenstein, Maria Frederica, d Dor-
    othea, 4–6
Helmstedt, university town, 3
Hemp, being raised 11
Henkel, Count von, author, 11
Herdsmen, 2, 4–7, see Cowherds.
Hermann, J., hymnist, 5
Hermann, bleacher in Kempten, 8
Hermsdorf, Capt. Adolf von, Ger-
    man officer, 3
Hernberger, Anna Justina, w Franz,
    6, 7
Hernberger, Franz Sigismund, tailor,
    3–8
Heron, Col., commandant at
    Frederica, 122
Herrnhut, estate of Count Zinzen-
    dorf, 8
Herrnhuters, 5, 8, 11, see Moravians.
Hertzog, Martin, Salz, servant at or-
    phanage, 3–10
Hesslin, see Hässlin.
Hessler (Hässler, Hössler), Christian,
    Salz, 3–9
Hessler, Elisabetha Christina,
    Salz, 11
Hesslin, see Hässlin.
Hewitt, Mrs., Indian interpreter, 8
Hierl, Maria, Salz, 1
Hildebrand, Deacon, pastor in
    Augsburg, 1, 5–8
Hirte, theology student at Halle, 5
Hoe, inferior to plow, 10, 11
Hofer, Anna, Salz, 1
Hogs, 4–6. See Pigs, Swine.
Hohleise, benefactor in Augsburg, 8
Holtzendorff, Johann, judge at

Purysburg, 1, 4, 7
Holtzer, Catharina, d Susanna, 5–8
Holtzer, Susanna, Austrian widow,
    3, 4
Holy communion, 1–12
Holtzer, ..., d Susannah, 4
Holy Roman Empire, 8
Homann, map maker, 10
Honey, 3, 5, 11
Hopewell, ship, 12
Hopton, ..., Charleston merchant,
    8, 9
Horbius, Johann Heinrich, Pietist
    writer, 8
Horses, 1, 5–11
Horse collars, 10
Horse harness, 10
Horton, Major, commandant at
    Frederica, 11, 12
Hossenecker, see Ossenecker.
Hössler, see Hessler.
House consecrations, 5, 8–11
Household Conversations, devotional
    work by Paul Anton, 1, 5
Huber, Lorentz, Salz, 1, 3
Huber, Margaretha, Austrian or-
    phan, 5, 8
Huber, Maria, wife of Lorentz 1
Huber. Maria, w Lorentz, 1, 3
Huber children, 2
Huber, Mrs., German benefac-
    tress, 8
Hunter, Patrick, physician at
    Bethesda, 7–9
Hymns, 4–7, see Appendices to
    Vols. 7 ff.

Ihler, Maria, wid from Purysburg, 5
Indentured servants, 12, see Ger-
    man servants.
India, missions in, 7, 11, 12
Indian Hut, area near Ebenezer,
    2–5
Indian trader, 2, 8
Indians, 1–12. See Cherokees,
    Chickasaws, Creeks, Uchees.
Indigo, 12

Informatorum biblicum, devotional work by Johannes Arndt, 1
Ingham, Benjamin, English missionary, 3, 4
Ironstones (lumps of clay), used for building, 10
Inspirationists, sect in Germany, 5
Introduction to the Study of the Passion Story, religious treatise by Freylinghausen, 3, 7

Jenys, Paul, Speaker of house in S.C., 1
Jerusalem Church in Ebenezer, 10–12
Jews in Savannah, 1, 2, 6, 8, 12
Joch, Dr. , biographer, 4
Johnson, Robert, gov. of S.C., 1, 2
Jones, Noble, surveyor, 1–5, 8
Jones, Thomas, keeper of the stores in Savannah, 5–10
Joseph's Town, settlement near Savannah, 1, 4
Jubel-Predigten, devotional tract, 8
Judith, ship, 11
Juncker, Johann, professor at Halle, 2, 5, 8, 12

Kalcher, Margaretha, Salz, w. Ruprecht, 2–11
Kalcher, Maria, d Ruprecht, 8, 10
Kalcher, Maria Magdalena, d Ruprecht, 8
Kalcher, Ruprecht, Salz, manager of orphanage, 2–8, 11, 12
Kalcher, Ursula, d Ruprecht, 8
Kaltschmidt, benefactor, 7
Käsemeyer, Catharina, Pal, w Johann Martin, 8
Käsemeyer, Clemens, Pal, s Martin, 8
Käsemeyer, Dorothea, Pal, d Clemens, 8
Käsemeyer, (Johann) Martin, Pal, 7, 8, 9
Kehlius, G., hymnist, 5
Kendal, Duchess of, benefactor 160
Kendal, Duchess of, benefactress, 10

Kent, Lt. Richard, commandant at Augusta, 5
Keymann, Christian, hymnist, 12
Kieffer, Anna Elisabetha, nee Depp, Pal, w Jacob, 8, 10
Kieffer, Elisabetha Catharina, Pal, d Theo, Sr., 8
Kieffer, (Johann) Jacob, Pal, s Theo, Sr., 6–8, 10, 11
Kieffer, (Anna) Margaretha, Pal, w Theo, Sr., 8, 10
Kieffer, Margaretha, Pal, d Theo, Sr., 8
Kieffer, Maria, nee Bacher, wid Meyer, w Theo, Jr., 10, 11
Kieffer, Theobald, Sr., Pal from Purysburg, 2–11
Kieffer, Theobald, Jr., s Theobald, Sr., 5–11
Kikar, ..., Ranger, tailor apprentice from Hamburg, 5, 9
Kinder-Bibel, juvenile scriptures by Abraham Kyburg, 11
Kitching, Capt, master of *Hopewell*, 12
Klein, pastor in Cleves, 3
Kleinknecht, pastor in Leipheim, 8
Kleinschmitt, Johann Jacob, engraver at Augsburg, 1
Klocker, Bernhard, Salz, 9, 10
Klocker, Elisabetha, Salz, w Bernhard, 9
Klocker, Eva, Salz, d Paul, confirmed, 11
Klocker, Gertraut, Salz, d Paul, confirmed, 11
Klocker, Paul, Salz, deceased, 11
Klosterberg, author 11
Kocher, (Johann) Georg, Salz, 9, 11
Kocher, Georg, s Georg, confirmed, 11
Kogler, Barbara, nee Rossbacher, wid Riedelsperger, w Georg, 5, 6, 8, 9, 11, 12
Kogler, Georg, Salz carpenter, 1, 3–12
Kohleisen, Angelika, Salz, d Peter, 11
Kohleisen, Maria, Salz, w of Peter, 9, 11

Kohleisen, Peter, Salz, 9, 12
Koitsch, C. T., hymnist, 4
Koller, Engel, Swiss, niece of Hans
    Krüsy, 8, 9
Koller, Maria, Swiss, d Engel, 8
Der Königlichen Dänischen Mis-
    sionarien aus Ost-Indien eingesandte
    Berichte, missionary reports, 7
Kornberger, Gertraut, nee Einecker,
    Salz, 9
Kornberger (Cornberger), Johann,
    Salz, 4, 8, 9
Kornberger, Maria, Salz, d Johann, 8
Korthold, Dr. Christian, Pietist
    writer, 9
Kosterus, see Costerus.
Krämer, Anna Maria, Pal, 8
Krämer, Johann Christoph, Pal, con-
    firmed 11
Kranwetter, see Graniwetter.
Krause, Barbara, Salz, w Leonhard,
    4, 5, 6, 9
Krause, Leonhard, Salz, 5, 6, 8, 9
Krausendorf, town in East
    Prussia, 11
Kreder (Kröder), Catharina Ap-
    ollonia, Salz, 9
Kröher (Kräher, Kräuer), Barbara,
    Salz, 1, 2, 8
Kröher, Gertraut, see Boltzius,
    Gertraut.
Kröher (Kräher), Maria, Salz, 5, 6,
    7, see Gruber, Maria.
Krüsy, Adrian, s Hans, 9, 9, 11, 12
Krüsy, Hans, Swiss from Purysburg,
    5–10, 12
Künlin, Conrad, Salz, 8
Künlin, Maria, Salz, wid Conrad,
    8, 9
Kurtz, Anna, Salz, w Matthias, 11, 12
Kurtz, Eleanora, Salz, d Matthias,
    11, 12
Kurtz, Gertraut, Salz, d Matthias,
    11, 12
Kurtz, Matthaus, Salz from Cadzant,
    9–12
Kurtze Anweisung zur wahren, lautern
    und apostolischen Erkäntnis Jesu

Christi, devotional work, 7
Kusen, Henning, pastor in Ger-
    many, 4
Kustobader, Catharina, Pal, 5, 9
Kyburg, Abraham, author, 11

Labhart, Johann Heinrich, mer-
    chant in St. Gall, 3
Lacey, Capt. Roger, 5
Lackmann, P,, hymnist, 5
Lackner, Catharina Barbara, Salz,
    nee Ulmer, w Martin II, 9–11
Lackner, Elisabetha, Salz, sister Mar-
    tin, 6
Lackner, Gertraut, Salz, 8
Lackner, Hanna, Salz, d Martin, 8
Lackner, Margaretha, Salz, w
    Martin I, 6, 9–11
Lackner, Martin I, Salz of 3rd trans-
    port, 3, 5, 7, 9, 10
Lackner, Martin II, Salz of 4th
    transport, 9–11
Lackner (Lechner), Veit, Salz, 10
Lackner, Tobias, Salz, 1, 3
Lampton, Richard, Charleston mer-
    chant, 5–7
Lancaster, English boatman, 3
Landfelder, Agatha, Salz, d Veit,
    8, 11
Landfelder, Ursula, nee Wasser-
    mann, Salz, w Veit, 3, 5, 6, 8, 9
Landfelder, Veit, Salz, 2–6, 8, 9, 11
Lange, Dr. Joachim, author, 9, 12
Lange, Johann, theologian in
    Bautzen, 1
Lapis infernalis, medical stone, 8
Laue, Samuel, pastor in Wer-
    nigerode, 1, 3, 5, 6
Laurentii, Laurentius, hymnist, 11
Lautereck, German city, 4
Lechner, Elisabetha, Salz, 9
Lechner, Magdalena, Salz, w Veit, 9
Lechner, Veit, Salz, see Lackner,
    Veit.
Legacies, 9, 10.
Lehre vom Anfang christlichen
    Glaubens, 8, 9, see Dogma.
Leihofer, Anna, Austrian, 3, 5, 6

Leimberger (Lemberger), Christian, Salz, 3, 5–10, 12
Leimberger, Margaretha, Palatine, nee Staude, w Christian, 6–9
Leinebacher, Georg, Pal, 12
Leinebacher, Salma, Pal, 12
Leitner, Dorothea, Salz, w Josef, 9
Leitner, Josef, Salz, 3–9, 12
Lemberger, see Leimberger.
Lemke, Hermann, assistant pastor, 11, 12
Lemmenhofer, Maria, Salz, w Veit, 3–6, 8, 9, 11, 12
Lemmenhofer, Maria, Salz, d Veit, 8
Lemmenhofer, Paul, Salz, 3–5
Lemmenhofer, Veit, Salz, 3–7, 8, 9, 11, 12
Lewenberger, Christian, Pal, 6, 7
Lewenberger, Margaretha, Pal, 6, 7
Lindau, city in southern Germany, 3, 4, 8
Linder (Lindner), Johann, captain from Purysburg, 5, 6, 8, 9
Little Garden of Paradise, 7, see Arndt.
Little Treasure Chest (Güldenes Schatzkästlein der Kinder Gottes), devotional book by Carl Heinrich Bogatzky, 9–12
Livestock, see calves, cattle, horses, oxen.
Lochner, probably same as Lackner, Lechner.
Locksmiths: see Brückner, Lackner, Schrempf.
Lodenstein, Jodocus von, hymnist, 11
London German Chapel, 11
Long lots, found at Ebenezer and Vernonburg, 18
Lord Trustees, see Trustees.
Lotter, Tobias Conrad, Augsburg engraver, 6, 7
Löwenberger (Lewenberger), Christian, Pal, 5, 10
Löwenberger, Margarethe, Pal, w Christian, 5, 10
Lowther, Rev. Richard, 3

Ludwig (Ludowick), Christian, author, 3
Lumber, 5, 10, 11
Luther, Martin, reformer 1–8, 10–12
Luther's catechism, 2, 5
Luther's Postille, 10
Lutherans in Purysburg, 2, 4, 12
Lutherans in Savannah, 4, 11, 12
Lutz, Samuel, theologian, 8

Mackay, Capt. Hugh, officer, 4
Mackintosh, see McIntosh.
Macpherson, captain of Rangers, 1–3
Madeira wine, 2, 4
Madereiter, Hanna, Salz, w Hans, 1–3, 8
Madereiter (Madreuter), Hans, Salz, 2, 3, 8
Mäderjan, Daniel Gottlieb, pastor in Thommendorf, 2, 5, 6, 7
Madleitner, Salz in Augsburg, 11
Madras, city in India, 5, 11, 12
Maggizer, see Muggitzer.
Majer, Johann August, deacon in Halle, 1, 5, 6
Malabar, Lutheran missions at, 3, 4, 8
Malaria, 4, 5, 9, 10. See Disease.
Malcontents, disaffected element in Savannah, 5, 6, 7
Manitius, pastor, missionary to Jews, 5, 6
Map of Georgia, inaccurate, 9
Marriages, 2, 5–10
Martialia, 2, see Medicines.
Martini, Pastor, 4
Martyn, Benjamin, secretary of SPCK, 3, 5, 12
Masig, see Mazzique.
Matthews, Jacob, trader, 4
Matthiesen, Junner, German wigmaker at Dover, 1, 3, 4
Maulshagen, Carl, historian, 3
Maurer, Barbara, Salz, 4, 5
Maurer, Apollonia, Salz, 6, 7
Maurer, Barbara, Salz, 3, 4, 8, 9, 11

Maurer, Catharina, Salz, 5, 6, 8
Maurer, Elisabetha, Salz, w Gabriel,
   8, 9
Maurer, Elisabetha, Salz, d Ga-
   briel, 8
Maurer, Gabriel, Salz 1, 5–9
Maurer, Georg, Salz, 9
Maurer, Hanna Margaretha, Salz, w
   Hans, 12
Maurer, Hans, Salz, 3, 5–9
Maurer, Johannes, Salz, s Hans, 8
Maurer, Maria, Salz, w Hans, 9
Mayer, see Meyer.
Mayer, pastor in Halle, 6, 8
Mazzique, Joseph Anthony, spy, 6, 7
McIntosh, Aeneas, captain at Pal-
   achocolas, 3, 9
McLeod, John, pastor at Darien,
   5–8
Medicines, 1–12, See balsamus ce-
   phalicus, Berlin fever powder,
   bozoardic powder, carbobenedicti,
   china de china, cortex Peruvianus,
   essentia amara, essentia dulcis,
   fever potions, ipecacuona, lapis in-
   fernalis, martialia, polychrest pills,
   pulvis antispasmodicus, saltpeter,
   Schauer Balm, snakeroot, spirits
   of vitriol, theriac, Venetian
   theriac.
Meditations, devotional work by Abbot Breithaupt, 1, 11
Meier, pastor, 3
Melons, 4, 8
Memmingen, Swabian city, 2–8,
   10, 11
Memorial and Thanksgiving fest, 11
Mengden, Gustav von, hymnist, 8
Metzger, ... , d Jacob, marries Gott-
   fried Christ, 9
Metzger (Metscher), Jacob, Pal from
   Purysburg, father of Mrs. Christ,
   5, 6, 10, 11
Metzger, Johann Jacob, son of above,
   2, 5
Meyer, Elisabeth, w Johann Ludwig,
   9, 12
Meyer, Elisabeth, w Johann Georg, 11

Meyer, (Johann) Georg, bro Johann
   Ludwig, 8, 9, 11
Meyer, (Johann) Ludwig, physician
   with 4th Salz trans, 8, 9, 11, 12
Meyer, Magdalena, Swiss, d Ursula,
   8, 9
Meyer, Maria, wid, d Matthäus
   Bacher, 9
Meyer, Ursula, Swiss widow, 8, 9
Mice, destroy crops, 5
Midwives, 3, 6, 8, 9, 10. See Land-
   felder, Bischoff, Rheinländer,
   Maria Bacher.
Mildew, harms wheat, 12
Mill River, 11, 12, see Abercorn Creek.
Mills, 3–12
Millers, see Pichler, Eischberger.
Millstones, 3, 4
Minnet, Isaac, French merchant at
   Dover, 1
Mischke, inspector at Halle, 1–3, 5,
   6, 8, 12
Mittensteiner, Matthaus, Salz, 3
Mohr, Jacob, Pal from Purysburg, 12
Moller, Martin, author of sermons, 2
Money, see Coins.
Montaigut (Montaigue), Samuel?,
   Purysburg merchant, 2–7, 10
Montaigut, Mrs., w above, 7, 10
Moore, Francis, recorder at Fre-
   derica, 5, 6, 8
Moors, see Negroes.
Moravians, sect, 3–6, 8, 11
Morell, Johann Georg, mayor of
   Protestant Augsburg, 1, 3
Mosshammer, Johannes, Salz, 1, 2, 4
Mosshammer, Maria, Salz, w
   Johannes, 2, 3
Mossheim, Johann Lorentz, Abbot
   of Marienthal, 1, 3
Mount Pleasant, fort on Savannah
   River, 11, 12
Muggitzer, Hans Michael, Salz, 3–7
Muhlenberg, Heinrich Melchior,
   pastor from Halle, 3, 9–12
Mühl Fluss, see Abercorn Creek.
Mulberry trees, planted for silk-
   worms, 3, 5, 6, 8, 9, 11, 12

Müller, (Johanna) Agatha Elis-
abetha, d Friedrich, 4, 6, 8
Müller, Anna Maria, nee Krämer,
w Paul, 6, 9
Müller, (Anna) Christina, w Fried-
rich Wilhelm, 4, 5, 8, 9, 11
Müller, (Anna) Christina, d Fried-
rich, 5, 6, 9
Müller, Friedrich Wilhelm, from
Frankfurt, 3–9
Müller, (Johanna) Margaretha, d.
Friedrich, 4, 5, 7
Müller, Maria Magdalena, d. Fried-
rich, 8, 11
Müller, (Johann) Paul, s Friedrich, 5,
7–9
Müller, (Johann) Simon, s. Fried-
rich, 4
Müller, Dr., author of *Heavenly Kiss
of Love,* 9
Müllern, Johann Gottfried von, con-
ductor of 4th Salz trans, 8
Münch, Chretian von, banker in
Augsburg, 1, 8, 11, 12
Munden, Senior of Lutheran minis-
try at Frankfurt, 1
Munich, Bavarian city, 10
Musgrove, John, Indian trader, 1, 2
Musgrove, Mary, halfbreed wife of
John, 1, 2, 4
Musgrove's cowpen, 3, 5, 7, 8
Muskmellons, 3
Mutzen, Lutheran minister at Rot-
terdam, 3

Neander, Joachim, hymnist, 3, 4, 8
Necessary Self-Examinations, The, re-
ligious treatise, 5–8
Negroes, 1–12
Nett, Friedrich (Ludwig), Palatine
cowherd, 5–9
Nett, (Elisabetha) Magdalena, Pal-
atine, w Friedrich, 8, 9
Neu klingende Harfe David's, song-
book, 5, 6
Neumarkt, Georg, hymnist, 2, 3
Neuss, Heinrich Ludwig, hymnist, 8
New Ebenezer, early name of new
site, 2 , 3

Newman, Henry, secretary of SPCK,
1, 2, 3, 5, 6, 8, 10
New Windsor, Swiss settlement on
Savannah River, 4, 5, 7, 8
Nitschmann, David, Moravian, 3
Norris, Rev. William, Anglican min-
ister, 5, 6, 8
Nuts, wild, 8, see Chinkapins.

Oats, 5, 11, see Crops.
Obuch, Mr., missionary in India, 8
Ockstead, Causton's estate, 5, 8
Ogeechee River, blackwater river
parallel lower reaches of Savannah
River, 1, 2, 7, 9–12
Oglethorpe, James Edward, founder
of Georgia, 1–12
Old Ebenezer, first location of Salz-
burgers, later the Trustees' cow-
pen, 3–5, 7–12
Olives, 9
Orangeburg, German settlement in
South Carolina, 4, 5, 7, 8, 10
Orange trees, die, 12
Orchards, 11
Ordination Speeches, by Abbot
Breithaupt, 1
Ordnung des Heils (Order of Salvation),
religious treatise, 5, 6, 8
Orphanage at Ebenezer, 3–9, 12
Orphanage, at Halle, 1, 2, 5, 6, 8
Ortmann, Christoph, schoolmaster,
1–10
Ortmann, Juliana, w Christoph, 2–9
Orton, Christopher, Anglican minis-
ter in Savannah, 6, 8–11
Ossenecker, Thomas, Salz, 3
Ossenecker, Anna Catharina, Salz, w
Thomas, 3
Ott, Carl Sigismund, Salz, 2, 5, 6, 9,
10,
Ott, Catharina, Salz, w Carl, 9
Ottolenghe, Joseph, convert, 12
Ovens, 8
Overseers, 11
Oxen, 4, 5, 6, 8

Paedigogium, school for gentry in
Halle, 7

Paint for church, 11, 12
Painting, sent to Vigera, 10
Palachacolas, a small fort up the Sa-
vannah River from Ebenezer, 1–6,
8, 9, 10, 12
Palatinate, 4, 7
Palatines, 4–10, see Germans.
*Paradis-Gärtlein (Little Garden of Para-
dise)*, devotional book, 5, 6–9, 12
Parker, Henry, Savannah magis-
trate, 9
Passion and Easter Sermons, devo-
tional work, 8, 9, 11
Pastorale Evangelicum, devotional
work, 5, 6
Peaches, 2–12, see Brandy, Fruit.
Peanuts, 8
Peas, 3, 11, 12, see Crops.
Perceval, John, see Egmont.
Penner, Elisabeth, Pal at Frederica, 8
Persimmons, 5, 6
Philipps, Sir John, benefactor of
Salz, 1
Pica (clay eating), 7, 11, 12
Pichler, Johann Gottfried, s
Thomas, 8
Pichler, Margaretha, nee Kieffer
Salz, w Thomas, 5, 6, 8, 9, 10
Pichler, Maria, first w Thomas, 3–6
Pichler, Thomas, Salz, 2–11
Piederl, Catharina, Salz, 1, 5, 6
Pietism, 2, 4
Pietistic vocabulary, 2, 5, 11
Pigs, 2–5, 11. See Hogs.
Piltz, Andreas, Salz, 8, 9
Piltz, Sybilla, Salz, w Andreas, 9
Pine forests, praise of, 10
Pitch, 2
Plasching, pastor at St. Petersburg,
4, 5, 8
Pletter, Elisabetha, Austrian, w
Johann, 5–7, 9
Pletter, Elisabetha, Austrian, d
Johann, 9, 10
Pletter, Johann, Austrian, 5–9
Ploss, Dr. Octaviano, physician at
Augsburg, 1, 7, 8
Ploto, Baron Christof von, 4
Plows, 7, 8, 10–12

Plums, 7, 8, see Fruit.
Polychrest pills, 4
Poor–box, 3, 4
Poor Man's Apothecary, medical
treatise, = Dr. Carl, *Armen Apoth-
eka*, 9
Porst, Provost, Pietist author, 1, 5, 9
Port Royal, small port in South Car-
olina, 1, 4, 7–12
Postille, by Arndt, 3
Postille, by Spangenberg, 3
Postills on Redemption, by Paul An-
ton, 1
Potatoes, see Sweet potatoes.
Poultry, 2, 4, 5, 8, 9
Prätorius, Benjamin, hymnist, 11
Prayer books, 4
Predestination, 8, 12
President (of Council in Savannah),
10–12
Preu, pastor in Oettingen, 3, 7
Prieber, Christian, Saxon vision-
ary, 11
Prince of Wales, Capt. Dunbar's
ship, 1
Protestant Body (Corpus Evan-
gelicorum), caucus in Regensburg,
3, 11
Prussia, refuge of Salzburger exiles,
1, 2, 3, 7, 8, 10–12
Pulvis antispasmodicus, 2, 3, 4, see
Medicines.
Pure Milk of the Gospel, devotion work
by Spener, 9
Purker (Parker), builder of mill, 5,
8, 9
Purrysburg, ship that brought ist Salz
trans, 1, 3
Pury, Charles, son of Jean, 4–8
Pury, Jean, founder of Purysburg,
1–5, 7
Purysburg, Swiss settlement across
and down river from Ebenezer,
1–12

Quinces, 11, see Fruit.
Quincy, Samuel, Anglican minister,
1, 2, 4

Raccoons, 4–6, 8
Radishes, 10
Rangers, mounted scouts, 8, 9, 11
Rattlesnakes, 1, 2. See Snakes and
    Snakebite.
Rauner, Leonhard, Swabian, 2–8
Rauner, Maria, d Leonhard, 2, 5,
    7, 8
Rauner, Maria Magdalena, Pal, w
    Leonhard, 2, 3, 5, 7, 8
Rauner, Matthias, s Leonhard, 8
Rauschgott, Simon, Salz, 2
Reck, Ernst Ludwig von, bro Philip,
    2, 3
Reck, Jacob, Purysburg cobbler, 2–9
Reck, ..., w of above, 8
Reck, Baron Philip Georg Friedrich
    von, commissioner of 1st Salz
    trans, 1–5, 8, 11
Red Bluff, site of New Ebenezer, 2,
    3, 6–9, 11
Reformed, German and Swiss Calvi-
    nists, 3–5, 8, 11, 12
Regensburg, seat of German Diet, 1,
    2, 3, 5, 8, 11
Regnier, Jean, physician with Mora-
    vians, 5, 8
Reicheltheim, town near Frank-
    furt, 8
Reissner, Adam, hymnist, 3
Reiter, Gertraut, Salz, w Peter, 8, 9
Reiter, Magdalena, w Simon, 7, 8
Reiter, (Maria) Magdalena, nee
    Gebhart, w Simon, 7, 8, 9
Reiter, Peter, Salz, 3–6, 8, 9
Reiter (Reuter), Simon, Salz, 2, 3,
    5–8
Reiter, wid, 11, 12
Rende, inspector of Augsburg poor-
    house, 8
Resch, Andreas, Salz, 2, 3
Resch, Sybille, w Andreas, 2–5
Reuter, Maria, Salz, 1, 3
Reverend Fathers, 7, see A.G. Fran-
    cke, Samuel Urlsperger, Friedrich
    Michael Ziegenhagen.
Rheinländer, Christian Colemann, s
    Friedrich, 8

Rheinländer, Friedrich, Palatine, 1–
    5, 8
Rheinländer, Maria (Anna), Pal, w
    Friedrich, 2–10
Rheinländer, Maria (Anna), d
    Friedrich, 8
Rheinländer, ... s Friedrich, 3, 4
Rhenish Palatinate, 7, see Palatinate.
Rice 2–8, 11. See Crops.
Rice birds, 7
Rice press, rice stamp, 7, 8
Rice, wild, 6
Richard, Jacques, Swiss officer, 7, 8
Richter, Christian Friedrich, physi-
    cian in Halle, 2–8
Riedelsperger, Adam, Salz, 1–5, 7
Riedelsperger, Barbara, Salz, w
    Adam 2, 3, 4
Riedelsperger, Catharina, nee Valen-
    tin, w Stephan, 3, 5
Riedelsperger, Christian, Salz 3, 5–9
Riedelsperger, Maria, Salz, w Chris-
    tian 1, 6, 9
Riedelsperger, Nikolaus, Salz, 2, 3
Riedelsperger, Stephan, Salz, 3–7
Riedelsperger, Mrs., ill, 11
Rieger, Pastor, sermons of, 9
Riesch, Rev. Bonaventura, clergy-
    man in Lindau 1, 2, 4, 5–12
Rieser, Anna Margaretha, wid Ihler,
    2nd w Michael, 8
Rieser, Anna Maria, 1st w Michael, 5
Rieser, Anna Maria, d Michael, 8
Rieser, Balthasar, Salz, 3, 4, 6, 8
Rieser, Bartholomäus, Salz, s Bal-
    thasar, 1, 2, 4, 5–12
Rieser, (Johann) Georg, s Bar-
    tholmäus, 3, 5, 6, 8, 9
Rieser, Gottlieb, s Michael, 8
Rieser, Magdalena, Salz, w Simon, 9
Rieser Maria, nee Zugeisen, Salz, w
    Bartholomäus, 2–6, 8, 9
Rieser, (Johann) Michael, Salz, oldest
    son of Bartholomäus, 3–6, 8–10
Rieser, Simon, Salz, invalid, 8–10
Rieser, s Bartholomäus, has planta-
    tion, 11
Rinka, Martin, hymnist, 8

Riser, see Rieser.
Rist, Johann, hymnist, 4
Road construction, 10
Robinson, English boy with Gronau, 3, 5, 6, 7
Rodigast, Samuel, hymnist, 4
Rogall, Georg Friedrich, author, 8, 9
Rohrmoser, Barbara, see Kröher, Barbara.
Roman Catholics, 1, 8
Roner, Magdalena, Salz, 9
Rose, Peter Rudolf, game-keeper with Moravians, 5
Ross, Hugh, surveyor fr Purysburg, 4–6, 8
Roth (Rott), Georg Bartholomäus, Bavarian, 2–5, 7
Roth, Maria Barbara, w Georg Bartholomäus, 2, 3
Rothenberger, see Rottenberger.
Rottenberger, Catharina, nee Piedler, Salz, w Stephan, 2, 3, 5, 6, 8, 9, 11, 12
Rottenberger, Christoph, Salz, 8–10
Rottenberger, David, Salz, s Stephan, 8
Rottenberger, Stephan, Salz, 1–5, 7, 8, 11, 12
Rottenberger, Susanna, Salz, d Stephan, 12

Sabbath, violated, 10
Sachs-Gotha, German settlement in South Carolina, 8
St. Anne's Church in Augsburg, 1
St. Augustine, city in Florida 4, 7, 8, 12
St. Gall (Sankt Gallen), Swiss Canton, 3, 4
St. Johns River, Florida border, 12
St. Simons Island, on coast of Georgia, 3, 4
St. Ulrich's Church in Augsburg, 1
Salfeld, city in Germany, 11
Sale, William, English merchant at Dover, 1
Salt of the Earth, devotional work, 1, 3
Salzburg, German province, 1

Sammlung auserlesener Materien zum Bau des Reiches Gottes, devotional work, 6, 7
Sanftleben, Elisabetha, sister Georg, 6
Sanftleben, Georg, Silesian carpenter, 2–10
Sanftleben, Magdalena, nee Arnsdorff, Pal, w Georg, 7, 8, 10
Sassafras trees, 3, 8
Savannah, chief city in Georgia, 1–12
Savannah River, river flowing past Ebenezer, 1–12
Savannah Town, trading post in South Carolina opposite Augusta, 3–6, 8, 9, 11, 12
Sawmill, 2, 3, 5, 7, 8, 11, 12
Sawyers, need of, 10
Saxe–Gotha, German settlement in South Carolina, 9
Schade, Conrad Caspar, theologian, 3
Schade, Johann Caspar, author-hymnist, 3, 5, 7
Schäffler, see Scheffler.
Schaitberger, Josef, Salz exile in Nurnberg, 1–5, 7, 8, 12
Schamalto, chief pastor in Leipzig, 12
Schartner, Jacob, Salz, Pal 5–9
Schartner, Maria, Salz, w Jacob, 8, 9
Schatz-Kästlein, devotional work by Bogatzky 3–12
Schauer, Johann Caspar, manufacturer of Schauer's Balm 1–7, 10
Schauer's balm 2–11
Scheffler, Catharina, nee Kraher, Salz, w Johann, 9
Scheffler, Johann, 5, see Silesius, Angelus.
Scheraus, Johann, Salz, 9, 11
Scheraus, Maria Helena, 9
Schindler, J., hymnist, 3
Schinmeyer, author of Schatz-Kästlein, 11
Schlatter (Schlotter), merchant in St. Gall 4–8

Schlechtermann, Johann Peter, Pal, 6
Schlechtermann, Josef Michael, bro Johann Peter, 6
Schlopfer, Gabriel, Swiss detractor, 8
Schmid, Pastor, author of *Biblisches Medicum*, 10
Schmidt, Barbara, d Hans, 8
Schmidt, Catharina, nee Zehetner, w Hans, 3–6, 8
Schmidt, Johann (Hans), Austrian, 3–10
Schmidt, J.F., hymnist, 4, 5
Schmidt, Johann Eusebius, hymnist, 12
Schmidt, Maria, w Hans, 9
Schmolck, Benjamin, theologian, 3
Schneider, Abraham, 6
Schneider, Anna, Pal, 1st w Michael, 8
Schneider, Elisabetha, 2nd w Michael, 8
Schneider, Johann Georg, s Michael, 8, 11
Schneider, (Hans) Michael, Pal herdsman, 5, 7, 9
Schonfeld, Baron von, benefactor, 2, 3
Schönmannsgruber, schoolmaster at Purysburg, 2–4
Schönmannsgruber, w of above, 4, 7
Scholl at Ebenezer, 2, 5
Schools: on plantations 8, 10–12
Schoolmasters: Christoph Ortmann, Hans Flerl, Ruprecht Steiner, Bernhard Klocker, Georg Kocher.
Schoppacher, Gertraut, 6, see Steiner, Gertraut.
Schoppacher, Margaretha, Salz, d Ruprecht, 1
Schoppacher, Maria, Salz, w Ruprecht, 1, 2, 3
Schoppacher, Maria, d Ruprecht, 8
Schoppacher, Ruprecht, Salz, 2, 3, 7, 8
Schrempf, Ruprecht, Salz 9–12
Schröder, J. H., hymnist, 5
Schubert, Heinrich, author, 7

Schulius, Georg, Moravian missionary, 5, 6, 8
Schultz, Dr., director of schools in East Prussia, 10
Schultze, questionable preacher in Charleston, 3
Schumacher, chaplain with 1st Salz trans, 1, 3
Schumann, Pastor, chaplain to the Salzburgers in East Prussia, 8–12
Schütz, Johann Jacob, hymnist, 3, 5, 12
Schutt, J. P., hymnist, 5
Schwab, Sibille, Salz, 2, 6
Schwaiger, see Schweiger.
Schwaighofer, see Schweighoffer.
Schwartzburg, Aemiliana Juliana, Countess of, hymnist, 3, 7
Schwartzwälder, Anna Maria, Pal, w Johann, 9
Schwarzwälder, Johann, Pal from Old Ebenezer, 6, 8, 10
Schweiger, Anna, nee Hofer, 1st w Georg, 2
Schweiger, Catharina, d Georg, 8
Schweiger, Eva Regina, Pal, nee Unselt, 2nd w Georg 2–6, 8, 9
Schweiger, Georg (Jerg), Salz 1–6, 8, 9, 12
Schweiger, Maria, see Bacher, Maria, 6
Schweighoffer, Margaretha, nee Pindlinger, Salz, w Paul, 1–10
Schweighoffer, Maria, d Margaretha, 5–8
Schweighoffer, Paul, Salz, 1, 2, 3
Schweighoffer, Thomas, s Margaretha, 5, 8
Schweighoffer, Ursula, d Margaretha, 5, 8
Schweikert, Christian, servant to von Reck, 1, 2, 3
Schwenkfelders, sect, 3
Scrip issued in Ebenezer, 9, 11
Scriptural Instructions, by Urlsperger, 11
Scriver, Christian, hymnist, 11, 12. See *Soul Treasure*.

Scurvy 2, 3
Scythes, purchase of, 12
Secret Diary by Boltzius, 3
Seckendorf, Field Marshall von, 12
Seeds, 2, 3, 8
Seelen-Schatz, religious tract, 11
Seinler, inventer in Halle, 11
Send-Briefe, work by Schaitberger, 8, 12
Sericulture, 3, 8–12
Seuter, Matthäus, printer in
  Augsburg, 7
Shannon, William, Irish murderer, 7
Sharecropping, 7, 10
Sheftall, Benjamin, Jew in Savan-
  nah, 1, 5, 6, 8
Shingles, 3
Shoemakers, 5, 6, see Adde; Reck,
  Jacob; Ulich; Zettler.
*Short Description of the Present Status of
  South Carolina,* propaganda pam-
  phlet by Jean Pury, 1
Sicilian wheat, 12
Sickness, see Disease.
Silesia, German province, 2, 5
Silesius, Angelus, German mystic
  and hymnist, 3–5, 8
Silkgrass, 11
Silk culture, see Sericulture.
Silkworms, 3, 8, see Sericulture.
Simon(nds), Peter, owner of *Purrys-
  burg,* 3, 6–8
Siron, German gentleman in Phila-
  delphia, 1–4
Skunks, 10
Slavery, 1, 6–8, 11, 12
Slaves, see Negroes.
Smallpox, 5
Smalwood, merchant in Purysburg, 3
Smiths, 5, 11. See Lechner, Leitner.
Smithy, bought by Salzburger, 5
Snakes and snakebite, 1–3, 5,
  7–10, 12
Snakeroot, 9
Socinians, sectarians, 8, 11
Society, see SPCK.
Sola bills, bills of exchange issued by
  Trustees, 8, 9, 11, 12
Sommer, Rev., Pietist theologian in

Cöthen, 5, 6, 8
Songs and singing: instruction, 10
Soul Treasure, devotional tract by
  Scriver, 5, 11
Spangenberg, Johann, religious
  writer, 2, 3
Spangenberg, August Gottlieb,
  leader of Moravians in Savannah,
  3, 4, 8
Spaniards in Florida 1–7, 12
Spanish invasion of 1742, 10
Spanish mulberry trees, 12
Spanish spy 8, 9
SPCK (Society for the Promotion of
  Christian Knowledge), missionary
  society in London, 1–9, 11–12
Spelt, 9, 10, 11, see Crops.
Spener, Philip Jacob, Pietist leader
  1–3, 5, 6, 9, 12
Spengler, Lazarus, hymnist, 3, 4
Spielbiegler, Johann, Salz, 3, 5–8
Spielbiegler, Rosina, mother Johann,
  3–8
Spinning wheels, 5
Squash, 2, 4, 5, 12, see Crops.
Squirrels, 3, 4, 6, 12
Starck, Pastor Christoph, author, 11
Statius, Martin, author, 8
Staude, Margaretha, Pal, later w
  Gabriel Bach, 7
Steinbacher, Barbara, Salz, 9
Steiner, Agatha, d Ruprecht, 2
Steiner, Christian, Salz, 2
Steiner, Christian, Jr., 8
Steiner, David, s Christian, 8
Steiner, Gertraut, nee Schoppacher,
  w Simon, 3, 5, 6
Steiner, Maria, nee Winter, Salz, w
  Ruprecht, 2–4, 6–10, 12
Steiner, Ruprecht, Salz, 1–12
Steiner, Sara, d Simon, 7, 8
Steiner, Simon, Salz, 1, 3, 5, 6–8
Steinmetz, Abbot, German the-
  ologian, 7
Stephens, Thomas, s Col. Stephens,
  leader of Malcontents, 7, 8, 9
Stephens, Col. Wm., Trustees' secre-
  tary in Georgia 5–12

Stills, for peach brandy, 10, 11
Stollberg, Countess of, Pietist
   author, 9
Storehouse in Ebeneser, 3
Storehouse in Savannah 2–6
Stoves, iron, 7, 11
Strassburg, German city, 8
Straube, Adam, Pal from Vernon-
   burg, 12
Straube, Pieta Clara, w Adam, 12
Sturmer, Georg, bro wid Graniwet-
   ter, 12
Stuttgart, German city, 8
Subsidy on grain, 4, see Corn-shill-
   ing.
Sugar melons, 3, 11, 12, see Crops.
Surgery, 8
Surinam, colony in South America,
   mentioned, 10
Swallows, 12
Sweet potatoes, 2–6, 10–12
Swine, 5, see Hogs.
Swiss boy, 9
Swiss servants, 2, 4, 8
Swiss settlers, 4–6, 8
Sympathetic cure, 9
Syrup, 3

Tabula economica, treatise by Martin
   Luther, 6, 8
Tail–mail, objection to, 3, 7
Tailors, 5, see Herrnberger, Christ,
   Helfenstein boy, Kikar, Metzger.
Tannenberger, David, Moravian
   shoemaker, 5
Tar, 2
Ten Commandments, numbering
   of, 5
Tennhardt, Johannes, Pietist, 3
Terry, John (Jean Thierry), recorder
   at Frederica, 8, 9
Theologia mystica, religious tract, 8
Theologia Pastoralis, see Klosterberg.
Theologia Viatorum, see Porst, Prior, 9
Therapy and cures, see Bloodlet-
   ting, Sympathetic cure, Snakebite.
Theus, Christian, Swiss minister, 8

Theus, Jeremias, Swiss painter in
   Charleston, 9, 10
Thilo, Christian Ernst, physician,
   3–12
Thilo, Friederica, nee Helfenstein, w
   Christian Ernst, 8, 9, 11
Third Salz trans, 3, 4, 5
Thomasius, Christian, philoso-
   pher, 3
Thommendorf, town in Silesia, 7
Thomson, Capt. William, importer
   of Germans, 2–12
Thompson, Mr., righteous man in
   Philadelphia, 11
Thunderbolt, place near Savan-
   nah, 1
Timber, 5, see Lumber.
Timothäus, printer in Charleston,
   1, 3
Tirnbergers, 3, see Dürrenbergers.
Tobler, Johann, Swiss settler, 4, 7,
   8, 12
Tomochichi, Indian chief, 2, 3, 4, 6
Tranquebar (Trankebar), site of
   Lutheran missions in India, 4, 8,
   12
Treasure Chest, 3, 4, 6, 8, 12, see
   Schatz-Kästlein.
Treutlen, Johann Adam, Pal, 11, 12
Trostquelle fur Betrübte, etc., religious
   tract, 11
Trout, 5
True Christianity (Wahres Christentum),
   devotional book by Johannes
   Arndt, 1–12
Trustees for Establishing a Colony in
   Georgia, 1–12
Tübingen Response, decision con-
   cerning Moravians, 3
Tullius, German mason in Purys-
   burg, 2, 3
Tumblers, religious sect, 12
Turkeys, 2, 3, 5
Turnips 2, 4, 10, 12
Turpentine, 4, 12
Two Brothers, ship of Capt. Thom-
   son, 1
Tybee Island, at mouth of Savan-
   nah, 8

Ueberschwengliche Erkenntnis Jesu Christi, Die, religous tract by J. L. Zimmermann, 7
Uchee Indians, 4, 5, 8
Uchee land, 12
Ulich, Johann Caspar, shoemaker, 6, 7, 8
Ulm, South German city, 7
Unselt, German schoolmaster in Purysburg, 4
Unselt, Anna Justina, d Unselt, 5, 6
Unselt, Eva Regina, see Schweiger, Eva Regina.
Unselt, Sybille Friederica, d Unselt, 5, 7, 8
Unterricht für Kranke, ec., religious tract, 11
Urlsperger, Johann August, s Samuel, 1
Urlsperger, Samuel, Senior of Lutheran ministry in Augsburg, 1–12

Valentin, Catharina, 3, 5, see Riedelsperger, Catharina.
Vat, Jean, Swiss, commissioner with 2nd Salz trans, 1–5, 8
Veesen, see *Feesen.*
Vegetables, see Head Cabbage, Chards, Radishes, Raven, Turnips.
Venice, merchants send donation, 10
Verelst, Harman, Trustees' accountant, 3–9, 11–12
Vernon, James, Trustee 1–4, 5, 8, 9
Vernon, Admiral, 8
Vernonburg, Swiss and German town on Vernon River, 9, 11, 12
Verzeichnis der vornehmsten Gaben, devotional work, 7
Vigera, Johann, citizen of Strassburg, conductor of 4th trans, 8–10
Vines, see Grapes, Viticulture.
Viticulture, 6–11. See Grapes, Vines.
Volmar, Michael, German carpenter, 3, 5, 8
Vom rechten Wesen des Christentums, devotional tract, 6

Wachsmann, Boltzius' cousin in Berlin, 3, 4
Wächter-Stimme, religious tract, 11
Wahres Christentum, 11, 12, see *True Christianity.*
Walbaum, Counselor, benefactor 3–6, 8, 9
Waldhauer, Barbara, 8
Wallpurger, Mrs., Purysburg wid, 7
Wallpurger, ..., s of above, 7
Walther, Johannes, hymnist, 11
Walther, Rev., pastor at Frankfurt, 1
Walther, Mr., printer, 12
Walthers, Mr., English agent at Rotterdam, 3
War of Jenkins' Ear, 4, 5
Wassermann, Elisabeth, Salz, 6
Wassermann, Ursula, see Landfelder, Ursula.
Watch-house (guard house) at Ebenezer, 2, 3, 5
Watchman's Voice, see Wächterstimme.
Watermelons, 2, 3, 11. See Fruit.
Watkins, Mr. ..., officer, 9, 11
Watson, Joseph, alderman in Savannah, 9, 11
Waysenhaus = Halle Orphanage
Weaving, 6, 7, 11
Weekly History, London paper mentions Ebenezer, 9
Weidner, Rev., pastor at St. Ulrich, 1
Weisiger, Daniel, passenger to Pennsylvania, 1–4, 11
Weiss, M., hymnist, 5
Weissenbacher, Jacob, Pal, 11
Wells, 5, 9, 10
Wernigerode, German city, 2, 3, 11, 12
Wesley, Charles, bro John, 3
Wesley, John, religious leader, 3–5, 8, 11
Wheat, 5, 6–9, 10, 11. See Crops.
White Bluff, site of Vernonburg, 10, 11
Whitefield, George, English evangelist, 3, 5–12
Whooping cough, 11
Wild cats (term includes raccoons), 4

Williams, Capt. Robert, leader of the Malcontents 6, 8–10
Winckler, J.J., hymnist, 3, 5
Window panes in church, 9
Winde, Hermann, dissertation by, 3
Windhausen, home of von Reck, 4
Winter, Maria, see Steiner, Maria, nee Winter.
Wine, 3
Wirth, Ambrosius, author, 11
Wistar, Caspar, resident at Philadelphia, 1
Wolf. G. G. hymnist, 5
Wolves, 2–5, 9–11
Wooden shoes, 2, 4
Woodpeckers, 12
Woodruffe, Mr., merchant, captured, 12
Wool, 5, 11
Worms, in corn, 4, 8, 11, 12
Wragg, Samuel, Charleston merchant, 6
Wudrian, Valentin, author of *Scola Crucis*, 2
Wurttemberg, duchy in southern Germany, 8–10
Wurttemberg, Prince of, see Carl Rudolf, 9
Wurttembergers among indentured servants, 5

Yiddish books, 2
Yokely, Capt. John, master of *James*, 3

Zant (Zent)
Zant, Bartholomäus, Swiss 2–10
Zant, Sibille, w Bartholomäus, 11, 12
Zehetner, Catharina, see Schmidt, Catharina
Zeltner, Dr., 1
Zettler, Elisabetha Catharina, nee Kieffer, w Matthias, 8, 9, 11
Zettler (Zedler, Zetler), Matthias, Salz, 3–6, 8–12
Ziegenhagen, Friedrich Michael,

royal chaplain, "Reverend Father" of the Georgia Salzburgers, 1–12
Zimmerebner, Margaretha, nee Berenberger, Salz, 6–9, 11
Zimmerebner, Ruprecht, Salz, 3–11
Zimmermann, error for Zimmerebner
Zimmermann, Prof. Johann Liborius, author, 7
Zinzendorff, Count Nikolaus Ludwig von, leader of Moravians, 3–5, 8, 9
Zion Church, church on Plantations 10–12
Zittrauer, Anna, nee Leihofer, w Ruprecht, 5–8, 11
Zittrauer, Jacob, Salz, 8
Zittrauer, Johannes, 8
Zittrauer, Johann Georg, 8
Zittrauer, (Anna) Margaretha, Salz, w Paul, 6, 8, 9
Zittrauer, Maria, Salz, w Ruprecht, 6, 9
Zittrauer, Maria Magdalena, 8
Zittrauer, Paulus, Salz, 3, 5, 6, 8, 9, 11
Zittrauer, Ruprecht, Salz, 2, 3, 5, 6–9, 11, 12
Zittrauer, Samuel, s Paul, 9
Zouberbuhler (Zoberbiller), Bartholomaus, Swiss clergyman, 3–6, 8, 11, 12
Zübli, Ambrosius, Swiss, 3, 5–10
Zübli, Jacob, resident in Philadelphia, 12
Zübli, Johann Joachim, Swiss clergyman, 3, 8, 11
Zübli, David, bro of Ambrosius, father of Johann Joachim, 4–10
Zübli, Johann Jacob, bro of Ambrosius and David 4, 6, 7, 9, 10, 12
Zugeisen, Maria, 6, 8, see Rieser, Maria, nee Zugeisen.
Zurich, Swiss city, 8
Zwiffler, Andreas, apothecary with first transport, 1–5, 7, 9, 10
Zwiffler, Mrs., w Andreas, 2, 3

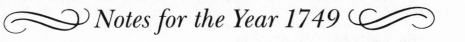

Notes for the Year 1749

JANUARY

1. John 1:16.

2. Ebenezer Creek, a sluggish and unnavigable creek, ran from Old Ebenezer, the original Salzburger settlement and now the Trustees' cowpen, to the Red Bluff, the site of New Ebenezer. Recently several German families had settled along it.

3. The Great Ogeechee, a blackwater stream, ran parallel to the lower reaches of the Savannah. Although slavery was not yet officially legal in Georgia, South Carolina slave-owners were already taking out large grants and would soon drive out the yeoman farmers, as Boltzius had predicted.

4. Ruprecht Schrempff, Henry Bishop, and Georg Held. See entry for 22 March.

5. Boltzius frequently preached to "legalists," those who feared the law of the Old Testament more than they trusted the grace of the New Testament.

6. Boltzius' memory must have failed him here. Both Luther and the King James Bible say that two shall be in the field. Matthew 24:40–41.

7. Isaiah 59:2; 1 John 3:15.

8. Karl Heinrich Bogatzky, *Güldenes-Schatzkästlein der Kinder Gottes*, Halle, many printings.

9. Thomas Bosomworth, the new Anglican minister, married a half-breed named Mary Musgrove and took over her trading post, thereby neglecting his ministerial duties.

10. Boltzius, who had already lost some parishioners to Pennsylvania, constantly belittled that province to dissuade others from going there.

FEBRUARY

1. With land free for the asking, no capable worker wished to work for anyone else, since status depended upon ownership of land. Adjusted to a labor-rich European economy, Boltzius complained of the un-Christian wages demanded by the greedy laborers in Georgia.

2. This name appears as Lechner, Lochner, and Lackner, the last form being the one that survived.

3. "Temptation" (*Anfechtungen*) meant the temptation to doubt that grace could overcome law. See Jan., note 5.

4. It is to be remembered that "Reformed" meant not "Protestant" or "born again," but a follower of Calvin or Zwingli, in this case Johann Tobler, a Swiss

of New Windsor. The book was *des sel. D. Johann Schmids, aus Strassburg, Buspredigten.*

5. This was Maria, the "youngest" of two daughters. She married Josef Schubdrein and her sister, Hanna Elisabetha, married Johann Flerl.

6. Adam Straube, who arrived in 1738, married the widow Pieta Clara Häfner and adopted her six children.

7. It is doubtful that melting snow had much effect on the height of the Savannah River.

8. At this time "the last Germans" were those who arrived in 1746 on the *Judith.*

9. The silk interests in Savannah conspired to prevent the Salzburgers from spinning out their cocoons in order to monopolize this profitable task themselves and thus earn the greater profits.

M A R C H

1. Romans 8:34

2. The various German states had already introduced the new, or Gregorian, calendar in place of the Julian. Boltzius, as an English subject, used the old calendar until the British adopted the new one three years later.

3. The "them" surely refers only to the hares. There is no evidence that the Salzburgers ever trapped deer, even though *Netzjagd* (chasing deer into nets) was popular in their mountainous homeland.

4. *Glauchische Hauss-Kirch Ordnung, oder christlicher Unterricht* Halle 1699.

5. The Salzburgers celebrated a Remembrance and Thanksgiving service every year at the anniversary of their arrival in Georgia.

6. St. Patrick's Day is still the most extended drinking bout of the year in Savannah.

7. Psalms 73:1.

A P R I L

1. From *quasi modo geniti infantes,* "as newborn babes," words of the introit for Low Sunday.

2. *die Erklärung des hohenpriesterlichen Gebeths Christi, welche den sel. Herrn Past. Freylinghausen zum Autore hat.* Johann Anastasius Freylinghausen, one of Boltzius' professors at Halle, was the editor of the hymnbook used at Ebenezer. See Oct., note 9.

3. *des seligen Prof. Franken Buspredigten, oder des Herren Past. Freylinghausen Epistelpredigten.* August Hermann Francke, the founder of the Francke Foundation in Halle, was a prolific writer. The borrower was Tobler. See note Feb. 4.

4. *des strassburgischen Theologi, D. Johann Schmidts, Busspredigten.*

5. There were four renegade brothers: Iscariot, Lorentz, Michael, and Peter Richard, three of whom absconded from Ebenezer and one from Savannah. The original name may have been Ritschard.

6. Boltzius, or his editor or type-setter, has made an error. It should read "Augustine."

7. See Feb., note 6.

8. It was costly because it contained gold dust.

9. The "masonry" refers to the brick or tile surface built to protect the wooden walls from the fires under the boiling pots. See entry for May 10.

10. Tobler again. See Feb., note 4.

11. The word *Hauswesen*, like *Haushalt*, included the entire domestic economy of the household and farm.

12. This well composed letter appears in *The Colonial Records of the State of Georgia*, ed. Allen D. Candler, Atlanta 1904 ff., Vol. 24, pp. 433–444.

13. A "justiciar" or "justiciary" was the manager of an ecclesiastical or secular estate. Johann Ludwig Mayer (later spelled Meyer) consented to assume this heavy burden despite ill health.

14. East Prussia was adjacent to Lithuania, which was Catholic.

15. *wo Negers überhand nehmen*. This means where slave-labor prevails, that is, where the slave-owners are in power.

16. *das schöne in Wernigeroda gedruckte Büchlein, die Lehre von der Buse und Vergebung der Sünden genannt*. The city of publication is now spelled Wernigerode.

MAY

1. To the Reformed (see Feb., note 4.) and the Lutherans, the latter being "our co-religionists."

2. Johann Arndt, *Vier Bücher vom Wahren Christenthum*, Halle, many printings, was a best-seller among the colonial Germans.

3. The "Small Catechism" was by Luther. The second work was Ambrosius Wirth, *Christliche Anweisung*. See Oct., note 4.

4. Bishop and Held. See Jan., note 4.

5. Maria Camuse (Camuso).

6. The "praiseworthy Society" was the Society for Promoting Christian Knowledge, a missionary society in London that had been the chief agent in bringing the Salzburger exiles to Georgia. It paid the salaries of both pastors and the schoolmaster and also collected many donations for them.

7. Ship mills, which were common on the Danube, had a large paddle like that of a paddle steamer. The current of the river turned the paddle, which turned the millstones. The advantage was that the ship rose and fell with the level of the river and was never idle, as the Ebenezer mills so often were, when the river was too high or too low. It is not known why Zübli's ship mill failed.

8. See Feb., note 3.

JUNE

1. The Francke Foundation was then supplying missionaries for Danish Lutheran missions in East India.

2. *das Herz des auferstandenen Jesu*, unidentified.

3. See note 1, above.

4. Until the fall of 1749, the "last German servants" were those aboard the JUDITH, which arrived on 22 January 1746. This new husband was Johann Caspar Walthauer.

5. *Gott kann eher/ als wir denken/ unsere Noth zum Besten lenken. Seele! was verzagst du doch? lebt doch unser HErr Gott noch*, from a hymn.

6. The individual contributions (*Beiträge*) to a large compendium of re-

ligious writings titled *Sammlung auserlesener Materien zum Bau des Reiches Gottes.*

7. *Im Himmel ist gut wohnen/ hinauf steht mein Begier, etc.*, from a hymn.

8. The Mill River, or Abercorn Creek, was a branch of the Savannah River, which was almost shut off at the northern or upstream end and therefore very sluggish. That made rowing easier than on the often swift main channel despite the danger of fallen trees.

9. Bartholomew Zouberbuhler, as he called himself in Georgia, was a Swiss from Appenzell dwelling in Purysburg. Finding no living as a Reformed minister, he converted to the Anglican Church and was ordained in London. He returned to Georgia on the *Judith* but returned to London to fight for a better wage.

10. Dr. Gotthilf August Francke, son of August Hermann Francke, and Chrétien von Münch, an Augsburg banker and benefactor of the Georgia Salzburgers.

11. See April, note 4.

JULY

1. Capt. George Dunbar, who brought the second Salzburger transport to Georgia.

2. See April, note 11.

3. Ulrich Driesler, a pastor from Wurttemberg, was much loved during his short tenure in Frederica.

4. "European" or "German" grains were wheat, barley, rye, and oats, as opposed to Indian corn and rice.

5. The Herrnhuters, known in America as Moravians, claimed to be a movement in the Lutheran Church. Boltzius, like other orthodox Lutheran ministers, considered them dangerous innovators. Although a party of them resided in Savannah fom 1736 to 1738, they made no efforts to proselytize any Salzburgers.

6. Frensen was a pastor ministering to the Salzburger exiles in East Prussia.

7. Joachim Zübli, later Zubly, was the son of David Züblin of Purysburg. He became a Reformed pastor in South Carolina and later in Georgia, which he represented at the Second Continental Congress.

8. A man named Parker had built a mill but abandoned it when he was not allowed to use slave labor. Boltzius says that he was actually a native Swede mamed Purker.

9. The Uchee land across Ebenezer Creek belonged to a small tribe, then reduced to some thirty braves and soon extinct.

10. See June, note 4. As the "last German servants" worked off their indentures, Col. Stephens directed the Reformed to Acton and Vernonburg and the Lutherans to Abercorn and Goshen.

11. The *Ausführliche Nachrichten*, the original of the *Detailed Reports*, were issued in a series of continuations.

12. *Vertrau du deinem Herre Gott, der alle Ding erschaffen hat. Er kann und will dich lassen nicht; Er weiss gar wohl, was dir gebricht. Himmel und Erd ist sein; mein Vater und mein Herre Gott, der mir beisteht in aller Noth!.* From a hymn.

13. See Jan., note 6. To acquire some sea islands as private property of his wife, the "Empress," he incited the Indians to cause trouble.

14. Pieta Clara, the widow of Paul Häfner of Vernonburg. See Feb., note 6.

AUGUST

1. See July, note 3. Because many Germans were leaving German Village at Frederica, Driesler was advising them to go to Ebenezer, where they would find a Lutheran ministry.

2. ......; Ezekiel 18:20; Proverbs 23:26; Luke 19:10; the story of the brazen serpent is told in Numbers 21.

3. Epicedium, funeral oration. Inspector Freyer, unidentified.

4. Boltzius had taught at the Halle Orphanage while studying in Halle.

5. See June, note 4.

6. Aaron was a native Indian convert, who converted many of his compatriots to the Christian church. A picture of him, wearing a turban and beak-shoes, appears in a pictorial history of Georgia with the amazing caption, "A Salzburger Colonist." *The People of Georgia*, ed. Mills B. Lane. Savannah, Ga.: Beehive Press, 1975, p.26.

7. The authorities in Savannah, having been warned of possible violence, honored the Indian guests with an armed honor guard consisting of most of the able-bodied inhabitants of the city.

8. Most fevers, including malaria, were blamed on changes in the weather.

9. See Jan, note 9. It was inconsistent of Urlsperger to suppress the name here but not elsewhere.

10. *auserlesene Lieder*, unidentified.

11. Revelations 7:17

12. *Herrn Sen. Heinolds nöthige Verbindungen des Gesetzes und Evangelii.*

13. *des Herrn Sturms schönen Tractat vom Mühlenbau.* See June, note 10.

14. God soon did so, in the persons of the Schubdrein brothers.

15. The condition of the sickness.

SEPTEMBER

1. Court Chaplain Ziegenhagen was instrumental in having many German immigrants in London sent to Georgia. For Driesler, see Aug., note 1.

2. See April, note 5

3. A cesspool of wicked men.

4. This is 1 Peter 2:2.

5. As will appear, this was a considerable exaggeration.

OCTOBER

1. Ordinarily, the tides reached up only as far as Purysburg, a reason why the town was placed there. Except when the Savannah was unusually high, people could row, or even drift, that far up with the flood.

2. See June, note 8.

3. Mr. Thomas Jones, who succeeded Thomas Causton as keeper of the stores in Savannah.

4. *des sel. Ambr. Wirths Beicht- und Abendmahlbüchlein.*

5. John 13:7.

6. Boltzius' memory must have failed him here. Both Luther and the King James Bible say that two shall be in the field. Matthew 24:40–41.

7. Exodus 12:30. The King James version says there will not be a house without "one dead."

8. Isaiah 66:2; Matthew 11:28; Psalms 51:17; Luke 19:10.

9. John 3:16.

10. Boltzius calls this the Fourth Commandment, numbering according to the Roman and Lutheran system. The command to honor one's father and mother was extended to include all spiritual and secular superiors.

11. The Day of Judgment.

12. See Aug., note 4.

13. The Canstein Bibles were inexpensive Bibles published by Karl Hildebrand, Baron von Canstein. Johann Anastasius Freylinghausen's *Geistreiches Gesangbuch* was the hymnal used at Ebenezer.

14. See May, note 2.

15. *des Herrn D. Walchs Einleitungen in die Religionsstreitigkeiten in und ausser der lutherischen Kirche.*

16. The King James Bible has an entirely different rendition.

17. *der Lehre des Dippels zugethan.*Dippel was an innovative theologian within the Lutheran Church who was opposed by the orthodox.

NOVEMBER

1. Psalms 50:23

2. See April, note 5.

3. Johann Tobler of New Windsor was a noted mathematician and calendar maker.

4. *in des seligen D. Antonii Collegio Antithetico.* This was Paul Anton, Boltzius' mentor at Halle. See the end of this entry.

5. This was Johann Caspar Wirtsch, later Wertsch, a baker's apprentice, who subsequently became one of the two most influential members of the Ebenezer community.

6. God did so, through the Lord Trustees.

7. Acorns were an important feed for swine. The Red Bluff, the site of New Ebenezer, had been discovered by Salzburgers gathering acorns for their swine.

8. "The work performed," the divine service itself, rather than its symbolic meaning.

DECEMBER

1. She had been brutalized while serving an Indian trader near Augusta before coming to Ebenezer.

2. See Oct., note 4.

3. Ambrosius wirth, *Das Nürnbergische Kinder-Lehr-Büchlein, Nurnberg 1729.*

4. *Kern- und Kraftsprüche.* English has no exact equivalent.

5. Urlsperger was sometimes inconsistent with his deletions. He named Eigel in this connection in his entry for 13 Nov.

6. These were adult runaways, in contrast to the Richard boys.

7. John Dobel, a Savannah schoolmaster and friend of Boltzius who had to

flee the wrath of the Malcontents in Savannah because of his opposition to introducing slaves.

8. The three Richard boys. See April, note 5.

9. *Gott ist doch Herr auf Erden: er sitzet an der höchsten Städt. Wenn sies auf klügste greifen an, so geht doch Gott ain andre Bahn, etc.*, from a hymn.

10. See Oct., note 17.

11. "The last transport" are now those who came with Capt. Peter Bogg on 2 October 1749. See June, note 4.

12. See June, note 8.

13. See Oct., note 4.

14. Like Chaucer's millers, those in Germany were often accused of cheating their customers. As the Swiss used to say, "The miller has the fattest swine" (because he spills his customers' grain for them.)

15. The Day of Judgment.

16. Boltzius is again contrasting the law and grace. See Jan, note 3.

17. *Kern- und Machtsprüche.* See note 4 above.

18. Verse 15.

19. See Jan., note 8.

20. England had not yet introduced the Julian calendar, which it did three years later.

21. *Die Gerechten werden ewiglich leben, und der Herr ist ihr Lohn, und der Höchste sorget für sie.* Wisdom 5:16.

22. Boltzius failed to insert these names.

Index

Aaron, convert in India 92; Aug., note 6

Abercorn, village near juncture of Abercorn Creek and Savannah River, mentioned 17, 91, 104, 155, a great blessing 145

Abercorn Creek (Mill River), branch of Savannah River, not yet cleared 74, has many eels 93, a great blessing 110

Acorns; Nov., note 7

Acton, German and Swiss settlement, many sick 88, mentioned 104, 149

Agriculture, see Crops.

Albinus, ..., court chaplain in London, letters from, 50, 52, letter quoted 54, 76, showed kindness 122, 141

Anton, Dr. Paul, theologian, 128; Nov., note 4

Arndt, Johann, Pietist author, 49; May, note 2

Augsburg, city in Swabia, source of gifts, 21, 80, 81, 85

Augusta, city up the Savannah River, mentioned 2, 3, 18, 51

Ausführliche Nachhrichten, Ebenezer reports; July, note 11

Bacher, Balthasar, ill 4

Bacher, Mrs. Thomas, ill 19, 21, recovers 25

Baptisms, 55, 75, see Births and Baptisms.

Barley, ripe in May 47, harvest beginning 64, see Crops.

Beer brought from New York, 62

Benefactions, see Gifts.

Bichler, Thomas, Salz, suffers misfortune 80, his son dies 82

Bieberach, German city, source of gifts 85

Birds, less destructive this year 109

Births and baptisms, Balthasar Bacher's child 31, two English children 31, children in Savannah 86, 106, Paul Zittrauer's boy 147

Bishop (Bischoff), Henry, Englishman, former servant to Boltzius, gone to S.C. 2, wishes to return 28; Jan., note 4

Bogatzky, Carl Heinrich, Pietist, author of *Schatz-Kästlein der Kinder Gottes* 27, 151; Jan., note 8

Bogg, Peter, master of *Charles Town Galley* 111

Böhmer, Maria Magdalena, hymnist 157

Boltzius, Johann Martin, pastor at Ebenezer *passim*

Bosomworth, Thomas, Anglican minister and Indian trader, agitating among Indians, 87, 94, 96; Jan., note 9

Brandner, Matthias, Salz, opposes slavery 44, mentioned 102, loses servant 113

Brandner, daughter of Matthias 14

Brandy, being distilled 47, made from peaches 62, 93, from plums 62, from corn 62

Brückner, Georg, Salz, ill 41, 117, recovers 121

Brunnholtz, Johann Peter, pastor in Pennsylvania, letter to 86, letter from 143, is warned 144

Cadogan, Capt. George, officer under Oglethorpe, visits Ebenezer 3, 61

Calendars, new and old; March, note 2

Camuse (Camuso), Maria, Piedmontese silkworker in Savannah; May, note 5

Canstein Bibles, inexpensive scriptures 120; Oct., note 13

Cattle, calves sold in Savannah 13, wild cattle 17, 28, cattle brands 28, cowpen 40, 79, 146, cattle have increased 79, herdsmen to be engaged 79

Charleston, port in South Carolina, *passim*

Cherokees, see Indians.

Churches, see Jerusalem Church and Zion Church.

Collegium Antitheticum, religious tract 128.

Communion Book, by Wirth, 55. See next entry.

Confession and Holy Communion Booklet, religious tract 118, 146

Congarees, Congrees, settlement in South Carolina 76, 83, 105, 140, 144

Construction, see Mill, Jerusalem and Zion church.

Continuations, issues of the Ausfüehrliche Nachrichten 85

Contributions to the Kingdom of God, religious tract 73 Cotton, being woven 26

Corn, harvest beginning 64, cornmeal expensive 134

Cöthen, city in Germany, mentioned 73

Council, governing body in Savannah, consisting of a President and five Assistants, convokes assembly 17, gives permission 23, 51 mentioned 52, 83, 91

Cows, Cowpen, see Cattle.

Creeks, see Indians.

Crops, good this year 109: barley, flourishing 16, ripe in fall 47, harvest beginning 64; beans, ripe in fall 47, a good crop 100; corn, ripe in fall 47, harvest beginning 64, flourishing 16, a good crop 100, cornmeal, expensive 7, 134; rice, planted on high ground 100; rye, damaged by mildew 55, harvest beginning 64; squash, a good crop 100; watermelons 93: wheat, expensive 7, flourishing 14, 40, suffers from rust 42, from blight 55, 60, from rain 99; Sicilian wheat 60

Council, governing body in Savannah, petition from 78, mentioned 111

Darien, Scots village, mentioned 7

Dart, Mr., merchant 141

Deaths: Riedelsperger's child 103, Hessler's child 147

Deer, destructive 23

Dippel, deviant Lutheran minister in Germany 122, 144; Oct., note 17

Dobel, John, English friend 140; Dec., note 7

Dogma of Penitence and the Forgiveness of Sins, religious tract, 46

Driesler (Driessler), Johann Ulrich, minister at Frederica, highly regarded 78, mentioned 88, 103; July, note 3

Dunbar, Capt. George, English seaman 77, 79; July, note 1

East India, scene of missionary activity 68, 92

East India Reports, missionary reports 92

East Prussia, see Prussia.

Ebenezer, Salzburger settlement near Savannah *passim*

Ebenezer Creek, unnavigable waterway from Old to New Ebenezer, inhabitants along 2, mentioned 110; Jan., note 2

Eels, damage dams 93
Eigel, Georg, Salz, keeps children
    from school 127
Epistle Sermons, by Freylinghausen 36
Englishmen, visit Ebenezer 2, 8, 31
Essentia dulcis ad oculos, eye lotion 39
European crops (wheat, rye, barley,
    oats), 16, 23, 32, 55, 62, 68, 70.
    See Crops.

"Fathers," Salzburger patrons, 45,
    49, 76. See G. A. Francke,
    Urlsperger, Ziegenhagen.
Fever (malaria), 108, 109
Flax, being woven 26
Flerl, Anna Maria, nee Hopflinger,
    w Hans, serious Christian 107
Flerl, Hans, Salz, marries; Feb., note
    5
Flour, price of 66, expensive 70
Forst, town in Lower Lusatia,
    Boltzius' birthplace 60
Francke, August Hermann, founder
    of Francke Foundation in Halle,
    author mentioned 12, 36; April,
    note 3, June, note 1
Francke, Gotthilf August, s A. G.
    Francke, 76; June, note 10
Frederica, British outpost near Flor-
    ida, mentioned 3, 7, 18, 38, 51
French, danger from 45
Frensen, Pastor, reports on
    Herrnhuters in Prussia 82; July,
    note 6
Freyer, Inspector, writes epicedia 90
Freylinghausen, Johann Anastasius,
    professor at Halle, author of
    Geistreiches Gesangbuch, (*Compen-
    dium Theologicum*, and sermons 12,
    36; April, note 2
Freylinghausen Hymnbook
    (*Geistreiches Gesangbuch*), favorite
    hymnal at Ebenezer, printed at
    Halle in many editions 120
Fruit, 87: apples 87, figs 87, grapes,
    wild, very abundant 47, 86, be-
    coming ripe 96; peaches, in bloom
    16, for brandy, pears 87

Gerhard, Paul, hymnist 157
Geistreiches Gesangbuch, see
    Freylinghausen.
German crops (= European crops),
    48, 60, 66. See wheat, rye, oats,
    barley.
German servants, 84, 91, 103, arrive
    in Savannah 111, distributed to
    Salzburgers 112, six abscond 117,
    unhappy 124
German Village, at St Simons; Aug.,
    note 1
Germans in Savannah 2, 19, 27, 47,
    75, 78, 103, 120
Germans, perish in shipwreck 129
German Reformed, see Reformed.
Glaner, Gertraut, pious Salz 23
Glaner, Matthias, pious Salz, ill 4, 5,
    8, 131
Glaucha House-church Order, Pietist
    tract 24
Glebe land 84, 91
Graniwetter, Anna Catharina, nee
    Sturmer, Salz, wid Caspar, de-
    clines marriage 26, depressed 37,
    loses servant 44, 64, marries 72,
    receives gift 130
Grapes, wild, 87, 96
Gristmills, very profitable 13, 22
Gronau, Christian Israel, deceased
    colleague of Boltzius, mentioned
    38
Gschwandl, Thomas, Salz, opposes
    slavery 44, plants early 72

Habersham, James, merchant, mem-
    ber of Council, mentioned 6, 12,
    13, 61, obtains wharf 34, member
    of the Council 51, sends letter 94,
    supports Salzburgers 111
Hailstones, 60
Halle, East German city, home of
    Francke Foundation, source of
    gifts 21, 80, medicines from 8, Or-
    phanage at 12, 90, 119
Halle Hymnal, see Freylinghausen.
Handschuh, Mr., catechist in Phila-
    delphia, mentioned 5, ordained
    33
Hardwick, lost town of Georgia;

Jan., note 6
Hares, destructive 23
Harris, Mr. John, partner of
    Habersham 34
Haymaking 93, 101
The Heart of the Resurrected Jesus, re-
    ligious tract 71
Heinold, Senior, author 98; Aug.,
    note 12
Heinzelmann, Mrs., lady in
    Augsburg, mentioned 130
Held, Hans Michael, Pal herdsman,
    gone to S.C., wishes to return 28;
    Jan., note 4
Herdsmen, see Cattle.
Heron, Col., former commandant at
    Frederica, letter to 62, 96, sending
    soldiers to England 78, mentioned
    125, 139, 141
Herrnhuters (Moravians), religious
    sect, in Pennsylvania 33, in Prussia
    82; July, note 5
Hessler, Christian, Salz, his son dies
    147
Holy Communion, refused, 54, held
    69, 137, held in Savannah 75, 104,
    120, a woman repelled 100
Horton, Major, commandant at Fre-
    derica, ill in Savannah 3, dies 6, 7,
    exhumed 13, had planned restric-
    tions on slavery 20, supporter of
    slavery 38
House consecrations: Rieser 1,
    Schmidt 81
Hymns, see Appendix I.

Indians, danger from 45, have not
    molested Salzburgers 87, come to
    Savannah 94, 96, 128, 129
*Introduction to the Religious Strug-
    gles...*, religious tract 120

Jerusalem Church, town church in
    Ebenezer 85, 136, 152
Jones, Thomas, former keeper of
    stores in Savannah 43, 111; Oct., 3
Judith, ship; June, notes 4, 9

Kalcher, Mrs. Margaretha, w

Ruprecht, sick 3
Kieffer, Theobald, Sr., Pal from
    Purysburg, mentioned 127
Köcher, Georg, schoolmaster on the
    plantations, sick 109, gives up
    school 125, 143
Kogler, Georg, Salz, chief carpenter
    and sawmiller, mentioned 102
Königsberg, city in Prussia, men-
    tioned 82
Kornberg (Cornberger), Mrs.
    Gertraut, Salz, has miscarriage 4
Krause, Leonhard, Salz, sick 116
Kurtz, Gertraut, daughter of Mat-
    thias 139
Kurtz, Matthias, Salzburger from
    Cadzand 17
Kurtz, Mr., minister in Philadelphia
    5, ordained 33

Lackner, Martin, Salz, sick 105, in-
    stalls stove 150
Lackner, Mrs. Martin, Salz, sick 105,
    150
Lange, Dr. Joachim, author 5, 32;
    Jan., note 6
Law of Old Testament 3
Lechner (Lackner), Veit, Salz, lock-
    smith, converts 10
Lechner, Mrs., w of above, con-
    cerned with salvation 89
Leimberger, Christian, Salz, opposes
    slavery 44
Lemke, Hermann Heinrich, assistant
    minister in Ebenezer, preaches in
    Savannah 1, 27, 103, 104, 145,
    teaches catechism 46, receives land
    84
Lemmenhofer, Maria, Salz, wid Veit,
    still lives in house 22
Little Treasure Chest, see Carl
    Heinrich Bogatzky.
Lloyd, Mr., silk expert in London 54
Locksmiths, locksmith from Wurt-
    temberg hanged 118, see
    Brückner, Schrempff, Lechner.
Lord Trustees, see Trustees.
Lumber industry: in demand 13, 14,
    16, 19, 70, 74

Luther Martin, Small Catechism
132, 138, 139, hymn by 157
Lutherans, at Saxe Gotha 76
Lutherans in Savannah 1. See Germans in Savannah.

Marriages 75
Martyn, Benjamin, Trustees' secretary, letter from, 50, 51, 76, petition to 78
Mayer, see Meyer
Medicines: *essentia dulcis* 21, 39,
Schauer's Balm 80. See Halle.
Memmingen, German city, source of
gifts 85, mentioned 98
Meyer, Elisabeth, w Johann Ludwig,
glad to remain in Ebenezer 36
Meyer, Johann Georg, teacher,
brother Ludwig 150
Meyer (Mayer), (Johann) Ludwig,
physician with 4th Salz trans,
mentioned 11, to be justice of the
peace 12, 108, deputy 17, goes to
Charleston 21, returns 29, serves
as justiciary 43, 46, 82, 83, weighs
silk 46, goes to Savannah 51, 63,
103, 145, returns 65, holds assembly 56
Meyer, Elisabetha, daughter Ursula,
moves to Ebenezer 9, 10, ill 36,
dies 97–98
Meyer, Ursula, Swiss wid, moves to
Ebenezer 9, 10, ill 36
Mildew, harms rye 55, 64
Mill River, see Abercorn Creek.
Mills, 101–102, see Gristmills, Sawmills.
Mischke, Inspector, inspector of
schools in Halle 156
Mohr, Jacob, youth from Purysburg
133
Mount Pleasant, fortress on Savannah River above Ebenezer, mentioned 17
Mühlenberg, Heinrich Melchior,
pastor from Halle, mentioned 5,
143
Mulberry trees (for silkworms),
recover from frost, 46, see Silk

culture.
Müller, Apollonia (Mrs. Paul), 25, 95
Münch, Chretien de, Augsburg
banker, mentioned 63, 101; June,
note 10
Musgrove, half-breed woman 87

Necessary Combination, etc., religious
tract 98
Negroes: being introduced 3, rebellion feared in S.C. 20, slavery
championed by Whitefield 42, opposed by Salzburgers 44, restrictions on 7, 20, 121, danger from
45, 46, 142, prepare their own
grain 48, will be permitted 92, are
permitted 111, 120
New Windsor, settlement in S.C.;
Feb., note 4
Nurnberg, German city, mentioned
137

Obuchs, Mr., missionary 92
Ogeechee River, blackwater stream
parallel lower reaches of Savannah
River, mentioned 3, 17, 18, 31,
area being settled 2; Jan., note 3
Oglethorpe, James Edward, founder
of Georgia, mentioned 25, 32, his
regiment disbanded 43, 47, 79,
letter from 47, 61
Old Ebenezer, first location of Salzburgers, now the Trustees' cowpen, mentioned 2, 24
Orphanage in Halle, mentioned 12,
55

Palachacolas, fort on Savannah
River, mentioned 17, 34, 150
Parker's (Purcker's) mill 83; July,
note 8
Parliament, grants money 110
Peaches and peach trees, great quan-
tities of 47, see Fruit.
Peas, ripen in fall 47
Penitential Prayers, tract by Johann
Schmidt 12
Penitential Sermons, tract by
A. Francke 36

Petition against slavery 46
Pine forests, recommended by
    Boltzius 32, 51, 100
Port Royal, small port in South Car-
    olina, mentioned 45, 74, 141 Presi-
    dent, 52, 63, 83, see Council.
Prussia and Lithuania, refuge of
    Salzburger exiles 82–83
Purysburg, Swiss settlement across
    and down river from Ebenezer,
    mentioned 7

Reformed, followers of Calvin and
    Zwingli 12, 78, 83, 86, 149; Feb.,
    note 4
Reuter (Reiter), Simon, Salz, op-
    poses slavery 44
Rheinländer, Johann Martin, or-
    phan 14
Rice, ripens in fall 47
Rice stamp 135
Richard, Laurentz, Pal servant, runs
    away 44; April, note 5
Riedelsperger, begins trade 135
Riedelsperger, Mrs., fulfilled by
    Jesus 64
Riedelsperger, daughter dies 73
Rust on wheat 42, 55
Rottenberger, Stephan, Salz carpen-
    ter, mentioned 102
Rye, damaged by mildew 55, 64,
    harvest beginning 64, see Crops.

Sachs-Gotha (Saxe-Gotha), settle-
    ment in South Carolina 76, 83
St. David's Day, celebrated 44
St. George's Day, celebrated 44
St. Michael's Lutheran Church in
    Philadelphia, mentioned 5
St. Patrick's Day, celebrated 25, 44
Salzburger woman in Savannah 122
Sanftleben, Georg, Silesian carpen-
    ter 155
Savannah, chief city in Georgia pas-
    sim
Savannah River, river fronting Au-
    gusta, Ebenezer, and Savannah 66
    et passim
Savannah Town, trading station

near Augusta, mentioned 62
Sawmill, has started earning money
    49
Schauer's balm, a medication 80
Schaum, Mr., minister in Phila-
    delphia, ordained 33
Schmidt, Pastor Johann of
    Strassburg, theologian 18, 37;
    Feb., note 4, April, note 4
Schmidt, Johann, Austrian, wishes
    to build house 73, it is consecrated
    81
Schatz-Kästlein, see Bogatzky.
School on the plantations, arrange-
    ments for 60
Schoolmaster in town 49
Schrempff, Ruprecht, moved to
    S.C., wishes to return 28, 106, 109,
    121; Jan., note 4
Schrempf, Mrs., w above, very weak
    126
Schubart, Heinrich, author, men-
    tioned 12
Schubdrein, Josef, Pal carpenter;
    Feb., note 5
Schweighoffer, Margaretha, old Salz
    wid 15
Seelmann, Johann Christian, medi-
    cal student 117, 122, 144
Selected Hymns), hymnal 97
Servants, run away 37, greatly
    needed 54
Ship mill, built for David Zï, 63;
    May, note 7
Sicilian wheat, withstands blight 60
Silk culture 18, 21, 26, 35, 37, 39;
    silkworms hatching 21; reeling is
    restricted 18; white mulberries in
    leaf 21, recover from frost, 46, silk
    being weighed, 46, 64, production
    ends for season 47, Salzburgers
    may spin off silk 52, Ebenezer to
    have filature 53, support from
    Trustees 53, discussion about 56,
    63–64, spinning off silk 57, de-
    scription of silk industry 57–60
Small Catechism, by Luther, used 55
Snakes and snakebite 95, 97
Society, see SPCK.

Soldier, settles at Ebenezer 51, 78
Soldiers, visit Ebenezer 61–62, 72, cashiered 70
Spaniards, danger from 45
SPCK (Society for the Promotion of Christian Knowledge), missionary society in London, supports town schoomaster 60; May, note 6
Squash, ripe 47
Steiner, Maria, nee Winter, w Ruprecht, ill 23, 77, dies 78
Steiner, Ruprecht, opposes slavery 44, feeble 78
Stephens, Thomas, s Col. Stephens, Malcontent 45
Stephens, Col. Wm., Trustees' secretary in Georgia, President of the Council, mentioned 6, letter to 37, mentioned 63
Stöller, Mr, daughter deceased 73
Straube, Adam, Lutheran from Vernonburg, moves to Ebenezer 15 , works diligently 74; Feb., note 6
Straube, Pieta Clara, wid. Häfner, w Adam, moved to Ebenezer 38, 87; Feb., note 6, July, note 14
Sturm's book on mill building 101, 102
Stuttgart, city in Wurttemberg, source of gifts 80, 85

Thilo, Christian Ernst, physician, mentioned 11, 102
Tobler, Johann, Swiss mathematician; Feb., note 4, April, note 10, Nov., note 3
Trade: in butter, flour, calves, lumber 13, 22, 37
Trankebar, city in India, mentioned 71
Treasure Chest, 151, see Bogatzky.
True Christianity, mentioned 49
Trustees for Establishing a Colony in Georgia, mentioned 45, 49, 51, will not give up rule 52, support Ebenezer silk industry 53, letter from 76, petition to 78, permit slavery 112
Turnips, ripe 47

Uchee Indians, neighboring natives 18; July, note 9
Uchee land, tract across Ebenezer Creek 18, 62, 84, 111
Urlsperger, Samuel, Senior of Lutheran ministry in Augsburg, mentioned 45, 64, quoted 85, his birthday 97

Verelst, Harman, Trustees' accountant, letter from, 52, letter to 53
Vernon, James, Trustees' secretary 86
Vernonburg, Swiss and German town on Vernon River, mentioned 15, 16, 87, many sick 88, men come to mill 149
Vigera, Johann, of Strassburg, leader of fourth Salz transport, now in Philadelpha 33, desires plantation, 63, has married 143, is warned 144
Vines, vineyards planted 47, see Viticulture.

Wages, excessive 10
Walch, Dr., author 120; Oct., note 15
Walthauer, Johann Caspar, Pal; June, note 4
Watermelons 93
Wertsch, Johann Caspar, teacher 142; Nov., note 5
Wesley, John, English clergyman 86
Wheat, suffers from rust 42, ripens after May 47, 60, harvest beginning 64, aided by dry weather 65, damaged by rain 99
Whitefield, George, English evangelist, his wife ill 12, letter from 42, 94
Williams, Robert, merchant, mentioned 45, 74, 146
Wirth, Ambrosius, author 55, 112, 137; Oct., note 4, Dec., note 3
Worms, eat crops 32, 39
Worm, hairy, poisonous, 108

Zant, Sibille, nee Bacher, wid. Piltz,

wid Bartholomäus, has fever 16, gives butter 107, content 131

Ziegenhagen, Friedrich Michael, Court Chaplain, Reverend Father of Georgia Salzburgers, mentioned 7, 23, 50, 103, letter to 21, 46; Sept., note 1

Zimmerebener, Ruprecht, Salz, 146

Zion Church, church on plantations, mentioned 41, 56, 123, 137, 149

Zittrauer, Anna Maria, Salz, w Paul 136

Zittrauer, Paul, Salz, house consecrated 146

Zittrauer, Ernst Christian, s Paul, born 148

Zouberbuhler (Zuberbiller), Bartholomäus, Swiss, Anglican minister in Savannah, 78, sends letter 110, chooses servants 118, 122; June, note 9

Zuberbiller, see Zouberbuhler.

Zübli, David, Swiss at Purysburg, 63, built mill 102

Zübli, Johann Joachim, Reformed minister 83; July, note 7 is wife ill 12, letter from 42, 94

Detailed Reports on the
Salzburger Emigrants
Who Settled in America . . .
Edited by Samuel Urlsperger

VOLUME FOURTEEN, 1750

Contents

Introduction
by George Fenwick Jones

v

Daily Reports of the Year 1750

1

Hymns Sung by the
Georgia Salzburgers in 1750

222

Notes
for the Year 1750

225

Index
for the Year 1750

237

# INTRODUCTION

Because this volume is being bound together with Volume XIII, which outlines the story of the Georgia Salzburgers, it is unnecessary to repeat the story here. Therefore we will put the reader *in medias res,* into the year 1750, while life in Ebenezer was proceeding smoothly. Agriculture was flourishing, and cattle raising was increasing as a result of the purchase of the Trustees' cowpen and cattle at Old Ebenezer. Silk manufacture was also advancing and was surpassed only by the lumber business, which was calling for yet another sawmill. The Salzburgers' boards, shingles, and barrel staves had won a good name and were being exported to the West Indies in great numbers.

The most tragic event in the year 1750 was the epidemic of a disease diagnosed as *Friesel,* or *das rote Friesel,* which has been identified as "the purples," and "military disease," as well as scarlet fever and measles. The symptoms as described do not let us identify the disease with any precision. It attacked both adults and children, mostly the latter, and was often fatal. Among its victims were two of Boltzius' children. After having often persuaded his parishioners that they should praise the Lord for having taken their children while they were still without sin, he now had to convince himself twice in one week of this Pietistic principle.

Because of the high infant mortality, the Salzburgers were without help on their farms. Many of the Palatine servants who had come the previous October on the *Charles Town Galley* had proved unsatisfactory: some had absconded and others were lazy and refractory. Because the aging and often childless Salzburgers could not find hired hands, many of them were convinced by their English neighbors that they should acquire slaves. Boltzius and most of his flock still opposed the introduction of slavery on moral, social, and economic grounds; but the authorities in Savannah had put such pressure on Boltzius that he no longer openly resisted it; and several of his parishioners, including previous opponents like Christian Leimberger, were beginning to buy slaves. These were mostly bought on credit from the Salzburgers' friend and patron, James Habersham, who was now a successful merchant and the secretary of the Council in Savannah.

Aware that the Salzburgers were in such dire need of labor, and hoping to prevent the use of slaves, Urlsperger determined to recruit more Protestant German immigrants. The Duke of Wurttemberg being opposed to emigration from his realm, Urlsperger sought his emigrants in the territory of the Imperial Free City of Ulm, a thriving city-state on the Danube, especially in the area of Leipheim. Since many people were going from there to America anyway, Urlsperger argued that it would be better for them to go to Ebenezer, where they would find spiritual guidance, rather than to areas without Lutheran clergy. To stimulate interest, Urlsperger's son and successor, Johann August, composed a promotional pamphlet praising Georgia as the foremost American colony. This pamphlet was in Latin, and this indicated that it was aimed at the clergy, who were to approve all applicants.

To judge by the results, the ministers appear to have chosen their emigrants well. Many of them paid all or much of their passage money and were mostly substantial people and well above the usual run of immigrants. They proved a valuable addition to the Salzburgers, to whom they conformed and with whom they soon intermarried. After they were followed by two more Swabian transports in the next two years, the Swabian dialect seems to have replaced the Salzburgers' Bavarian dialect as the dominant one in Ebenezer.

Daily Reports
∾ Of the Year 1750 ⌐⌐

JANUARY

Monday, the 1st of January. Yesterday, Sunday, the last day of
the year, our dear God granted us much good from His word;
and today He has again begun to let the streams of His love and
kindness flow out over us through the contemplation of His dear
and sweet gospel. I not only noticed this in my own heart but also
experienced it in several of my dear listeners to the praise of His
glorious grace. May He graciously hear our common prayers
which were sent off to Him several times on bended knees in the
name of the Lord Jesus for us and our establishment in spiritual
and physical matters, and for our authorities, benefactors, and
German Fatherland;[1] and may He be pleased with our weak of-
ferings of praise for all the spiritual and physical blessings He
has shown us for the sake of the blood of Christ that speaks for
us. The weather has been delightful and pleasant yesterday and
today; and our parishioners, both large and small, have assembled in such numbers at the public divine service and communal
prayers and have also shown themselves so orderly and devout
that it could not have been anything other than joyful for us.

Wednesday, the 3rd of January. After General Oglethorpe's
regiment was disbanded,[2] two soldiers settled at our place. They
behave themselves very well and visit the public divine service
diligently and devoutly like the others. A short time ago they
bought a plantation on Ebenezer Creek and built a hut there. I
have been asked to visit them, which I did yesterday afternoon.
For the first time I bent my knees with them in their new house,
which was very enjoyable for me and them.

Wednesday, the 10th of January. All sorts of necessary official
business and a trip to Savannah from the 5th to the 10th of this
month have prevented me from continuing this diary in the past
days. Therefore, I wish to catch up with the most important
things and briefly summarize the following points: 1) On the 3rd

of this month in the evening I unexpectedly received a packet of
letters from our worthy Fathers,[3] benefactors, and friends in
Europe, which again contained nothing but joyful and edifying
news that awakened us to the praise of God: e. g., that our merciful God has graciously heard our and other believers' prayers in
that He has again mightily strengthened the health of His servants, our worthy Fathers in London, Augsburg, and Halle. and
has kept them until now for the good of His church and of us.
We are still enjoying their fatherly love and intercession un-
abated. Through their service and otherwise through His wise
providence our dear God has preserved our old benefactors in
their affection for our congregation and has applied a considerable new blessing to our institutions through a legacy.

Moreover, the Lord Trustees have lent a gracious ear to my
humble suggestions for the advancement of silk manufacture.
Mr. Verelst's letter of September informs me that they were very
pleased with the forty-nine pounds and thirteen ounces of silk
spun off by our people which was sent off to them last summer
and that, at my request, ten families among us will receive two
pounds Sterling each for building a convenient hut for preparing the cocoons. They also gave orders and plenipotentiary
powers for one of our skilled carpenters to make machines for
spinnning off the silk,[4] one for each of the ten copper kettles
which they wish to send us with the next ship, each costing thirty
pounds Sterling, and that for each of them two neighbors will
join together and learn to spin off the silk through mutual help.
Every girl who wishes to learn it thoroughly is promised two
pounds as encouragement.

Because, according to that, the Lord Trustees are making
such good arrangements for advancing silk manufacture and
have actually put a part of my imperfect suggestions into their
fiat, I have been strengthened in my hope that they will also be
pleased by the other and more important part of my petition
and suggestions: namely, to arrange the price of the spun-off
silk like the government in Carolina (at least as an encouragement for a few years) in such a way that good pay will be given
both to the producer of the cocoons and to the person who spins
it off as a good reward for their industry and thereby put them

in a position to participate correctly in this business that is so pleasing and profitable for the English nation.[5]

Mr. Verelst promises me to report in his next letter the remainder of the Lord Trustees' desires in answer to my letters, and I am awaiting this eagerly. Meanwhile, I heartily rejoice at this good news, especially since it came early enought in this year to encourage our inhabitants to continue their industry in planting and caring for the white mulberry trees. Their feelings about this had been much cast down by an unpleasant report that the Lord Trustees wished to give a low price for the silk from now on. They had not heard this from me or from Mr. Lemke, but from Savannah and other places.

2) On the 4th of this month we had a general assembly of all our inhabitants, who elected new leaders from their midst for taking care of some external business[6] and otherwise for the advancement of good order. On this occasion I advised them of some of the content of the letters we had received, with the promise to make the main and most important points useful to me and to them after my journey, God willing. I found very dear and impressive the beautiful verse that our dear Senior Urlsperger called out to our entire congregation at the close of his letter from Psalms 52:10: "But I am like a green olive tree in the house of God: I trust in the mercy of God for ever and ever."[7] My God, grant me also this firm faith and blessed hope!

3) On the 4th of this month I journeyed to Savannah for official reasons: to preach the word of God to the German people of our confession there and other nearby areas and to administer Holy Communion. Since Christmas we have had rather pleasant weather; but toward Sunday (it was the 7th of this month) it changed, and it has become a cold and hard winter, which especially the cattle and other beasts in the forest will feel, not only because of the great and almost unusual cold but particularly because of the smooth frozen snow that has lasted for several days. It rained and snowed alternately and then froze again so that the grass, the trees, and the bushes are hanging full of frozen snow and icicles. The branches have been bent entirely crooked, and many of them have been broken down here and there. Otherwise there are very few crooked branches in this

country. Therefore, some workers who need such a thing for making something consider a usable bent branch or piece of wood to be a rarity. If we were to see such frozen clumps of ice on the trees every year, then we would probably also see more bent wood.

In such cold weather, poor people who have become accustomed to this warm country suffer very much with their children in their very poorly protected huts because of their lack of warm clothes and quilts; and I wonder why (if they do not have the means to build warm dwellings) they do not build little heated rooms of clay like poor peasant folk in many places in Germany and like some Indians in this country, since such material is to be had here in superabundance, near at hand, and free of charge. Unfortunately, the attendance at divine services also suffers greatly in such cold winter days, as I have now experienced in Savannah also. Yet I was pleased that a fine little flock of hungry souls not only assembled in the morning and afternoon to hear the divine word but also asked me to hold a prayer meeting for them in my quarters, which I did with heartfelt pleasure. I had only twenty-four communicants. I received a letter from the area of Charleston that informed me that the last German indentured servants to arrive have been sold in all parts of Carolina and that the children must serve many years after their parents are redeemed. To the contrary, the children of the servants in this country are freed along with their parents. It is a great trial for our inhabitants that, instead of the servants they had described and desired from proper places in Germany, they have received all sorts of wild artisans who are unfitted for agriculture and that the best artisans among them, such as carpenters, wheelwrights, cabinet makers, etc. have been held back by Mr. Z. /Zouberbuhler/ and other gentlemen.[8]

Thursday, the 11th of January. After I had returned safely from my trip, which was rather difficult because of the cold weather, and had caught up with my work that I had neglected meanwhile, I have had time to read again with devotion the lovely, newly received English and German letters, which I had read with only a fleeting eye because of the intended necessary trip; and I praise God for the blessing, encouragement, and strengthening of my faith that He granted me from them. May He repay our worthy friends and Fathers with manifold grace and blessing for the time and effort that they spent in writing such blessed letters and may they find a blessed fruit from that in heaven.[9]

It also seems great in my eyes that our loyal God has inclined various benefactors of all classes to a very special love for us and that they have continued so richly to lay their generous gifts into the hands of the Reverend Dr. Francke and Senior Urlsperger.[10] These gifts, which were for the continuance of our institutions and for the better subsistance of us two and for the education of my two boys[11] have been forwarded here safely through the untiring efforts of our worthy Court Chaplain Albinus. In the account from our dear Halle and in the letter of our dear Senior I find such beautiful details of it that we marvel, rejoice, and praise our merciful God. If I could recite details here and name the worthy benefactors, it would, to be sure, be very edifying; but I fear that it might annoy our benefactors, who would rather have their good works hidden. Some of them are now in the Church Triumphant and will be followed by their good works. May the Lord in His mercy preserve those who are still alive and refresh them in life, suffering, and death!

Sunday, the 13th of January. The very cold weather has again let up completely, and it has almost become summer. Because the snow melted quickly, a lot of water is running together; and the low river is beginning to rise. Today toward evening we again received another heavy rain.

In the confession service today we also had a confirmation service with an orphan girl and six boys. One is from Purysburg, one is a Reformed young man of twenty-seven years who has already held to our congregation for several years and wishes to remain with it.[12] Another boy moved to our place with his parents two years ago and is learning a good handicraft from our town schoolmaster. His mother is Reformed, but she keeps herself as a righteous member of our congregation. The remaining boys have already been at our place for a long time with their parents. The girl, who is an orphan with neither father nor mother, has been in service in Savannah; and, after completing her period of service, she would have remained in false freedom with wicked compatriots and in ignorance if I had not insisted, according to my guardian rights with which her dying mother had entrusted me, that she move here and be instructed. Our dear God has accomplished much in her with His word, and she has become a completely different person so that she has caused us much joy through her love for God's word and her Christian behavior.

A righteous nature is also revealed in one boy, others have many good emotions and good resolutions and have changed themselves noticeably in external ways. One of them, the son of E., has a love for God's word and for prayer but has a great obstacle in his wicked and worldly parents so that he has not increased more in recognition and is better grounded in practical Christianity.[13] The twenty-seven year old servant from Carolina is the worst of them all both in recognition and in change of life, for which some ill-behaved people among us are probably to blame, whom he wrongly considers to be his friends. He promises much good and is now receiving a better testimony from his employer than in past times. Because he insisted so assiduously, both through himself and through others, upon being admitted to confirmation and Holy Communion and because I had been told that further exclusion would turn him away from our place and into some sinful place, I no longer refused to let him go along with these children.

Before the confirmation I repeated what I had preached in the last preparation sermon from Acts 2:37-38 about righteous parishioners; and I also instilled in those then being confirmed and then confessing the important words of admonition and warning in Hebrews 10:22-31: "Let us draw near with a true heart," etc., which words of God I had previously laid on their hearts with great diligence in the last preparation and prayer meetings. This holy act has again made a good new impression not only on the children but also on the other people present; and I ask God (and I am helped in this by the congregation) that a fruit will remain from it.

Sunday, the 14th of January. On this Second Sunday after Epiphany we held Holy Communion with seventy-five persons. Among them was a righteous man from Purysburg, whose son is found among the children who went to the Lord's Table for the first time today. I baptized this boy more than fifteen years ago, not long after my arrival in this country; and of the children we have baptized he is now the first to be confirmed. Until now they have been only such as were born already in Germany or Salzburg and have come to Ebenezer in four transports or from other places in this land.[14] If God continues to grant his blessing on the preparation, then the next candidates for confirmation will consist mostly of children who were born here and have been raised in the fear and admonition of the Lord and who, for the most part, give me good hope.

Both yesterday before the confirmation and also today before the act of Holy Communion, I told the congregation something about the spiritual condition of these seven children with regard to their Christianity, which they should apply partly for their awakening, partly for their intercession, and partly for avoiding unpleasant judgments. These children, as well as other young people, who have now enjoyed for almost sixteen years the bene-faction of instruction for confirmation and Holy Communion, were encouraged again in the sermon about the friends of Christ and after the sermon by the previously mentioned words of Hebrews 10 to be aware of their salvation during their period of grace. May God lay a rich blessing on all this for the sake of Christ!

Monday, the 15th of January. In the afternoon of the day be-fore yesterday we had a heavy rain during the confession ser-vice. Then a very strong wind arose that lasted all night, drove the clouds away, and veered to the west. To be sure, yesterday and today it became very cold at night but very pleasant in the day. We consider this a great blessing, especially yesterday be-cause of the public divine service. We are accustomed to enter into the church record the name, the fatherland, and the days of birth and baptism of those children who are admitted to Holy Communion for the first time.[15]

When I was asking a mother today for these facts about her son, I found very beautiful subject matter for joy and for the praise of God. She told me among other things that until now she has had to shed many tears because of her husband's poor observance of Christianity; but yesterday she again received hope that he had picked himself up again through God's grace and wished to be more serious. God had pulled at his heart mightily through His word. When, after the sermon, he let him-self be persuaded to attend the prayers in the orphanage with the honest Kalcher, he received much profit from it, according to his own admission. He had, she said, also begun to pray again at home with her and the children. He is, to be sure, sickly; but she also promised God that she would gladly have a sick husband, if only he were pious at heart.

She further told me that she looked upon it as a gracious disposition of God that her son was an apprentice with Christian people and at the same time so near to the church. He should have gone to another master, whose trade he would have liked to learn; but he saw that the man had little fear of the Lord, and, therefore, he chose a different work with a pious master. Another person had told her that she had recently felt unexpectedly a cordial love for this youth and, to be sure, as noticeably as if it had flowed down into her heart from heaven, and this on the occasion of his sincere prayer in silent solitude, when he himself did not know that anyone was hearing him. Afterwards she called him to herself and asked him to pray with her that way, whereupon God placed a beautiful blessing on this person.

Tuesday, the 16th of January. Yesterday was chosen for putting the long bridge between the town and the plantations into a safe and durable condition; and for this purpose all the men of the community have lent a hand to complete the work in one day. All the foundation is good: only the planks and the split crossbeams were rotten. I had some business with the leaders of the community before evening and I reached the bridge just as the work was over and everyone wished to go home. I was asked to pray with them first, which I did with pleasure. At the same time I thanked God for having mercifully averted all harm from man and beast, although some people and their horses were sometimes near great misfortune.

This morning the sawmiller Kogler showed me the place where the shoemaker N. barely escaped an evident misfortune. He is given to drink; and, therefore, I had sincerely warned him several times with the example of the shoemaker Arnsdorf, who was also given to drink and who drowned while drunk. When this miserable man, whom no admonition or threatening had helped so far, was crossing the mill bridge while a bit under the influence, he missed his step and fell into the millrace some nine feet from the millwheel. Through the counsel and an advance payment of dear Mr. N. a very advantageous improvement had been made on the first course, which saved this man's life. And, therefore, we are doubly pleased that we spent some money on this arrangement. May God let this incident and this miraculous rescue serve this poor man as an occasion for true conversion!

Friday, the 19th of January. The content of Mr. Verlest's last letter has served to encourage our inhabitants greatly to devote themselves seriously once again to planting mulberry trees for the manufacture of silk. It is an especially great benefaction for our poor people that every poor family will be given two pounds Sterling for building a hut for processing the silk more conveniently. We will probably find more than ten families who need this benefaction, yet God will look out for these even if the money ordered by the Lord Trustees will not extend to everyone. Because their generous ordinance will give our young women a much desired opportunity to learn thoroughly the spinning off of silk, there are now more apprentices than can be accepted this year by our three spinners. Each of them will accept two: indeed, girls who are daughters of parents with many mulberry trees and who have already had practice in silkmaking. The others can then practice it and raise a good number of trees (which here takes from three to four years on good soil) before they need to spin off silk.

Sunday, the 20th of January. During this week, both in town and on the plantations, I have informed the congregation of the edifying contents of the lovely letters from our worthy Fathers and friends in Europe that we recently received. God be praised, it was to my and other people's rich edification. I hope that our Fathers and benefactors will find a beautiful fruit in heaven from the writing of these letters, which have given us so much profit through the blessing of God. We remember them diligently before the Lord.

The old woman N.N. /Granewetter/ who married N.N. /Caspar Walthauer/ has only one daughter still at home; and the latter has suddenly been seized by a very severe epilepsy and brought into a very dangerous condition. Since yesterday she has regained consciousness a single time; and her first and last words since the attack of sickness were "Something is pressing on my heart, and that is my sins." Her mother and father show no seriousness in their Christianity and allow much useless gossip in their house, which greatly annoyed this otherwise well-natured girl, especially since the mother did her no little harm with untimely thoughts of marriage.[16] In this girl's plight and apparent mortal danger the consciences of her parents and siblings are becoming active again; I only hope that their good resolutions will be realized. Even though I could not speak with the girl, I could still say what was necessary with her relatives, who were present, and pray with them for the patient.

I visited the lying-in woman, Mrs. Hessler; and, since she needed assistance because of her husband's poverty, I brought her some money, which the couple accepted with very humble and sincere thanks to God and the benefactors. I was told many edifying things about her recently buried two and a half year old son; his memory serves the parents for their awakening and strengthening of their heavenly mind. For example, the said child had often said before his last sickness: "Tomorrow I will come to heaven." When the two older brothers told him that he was not yet in heaven but still with them, he kept on saying, "I am coming to heaven tomorrow. Only pious children come there, the naughty ones do not come there." His mother had to give him two books; one of them he considered his Bible and the other his hymnal. He whiled away his time with them, and he often had a certain verse sung to him from the song, *Sieh hier bin ieh Ehrenkönig*, etc. He did not want to sleep until his mother had prayed with him, then he fell asleep quite satisfied, with his hands folded.

Sunday, the 21st of January. Concerning another sickly girl who had a great desire for her dear Savior and for death, I was told that she had said that her dear Savior must not love her because He did not take her to Himself but let her get well again.

On this Third Sunday after Epiphany I received a letter from the surveyor in Abercorn in which he informs me that finally, at my representation, he had received instructions from the President and Assistants of the Council to survey the fertile land behind Abercorn for our inhabitants.[17] It is a new sign of divine providence over us that we are receiving the said highly fertile land, which is very convenient for agriculture and cattle raising. Until the very end this was fraught with all sorts of difficulties. To be sure, this evening wet weather has begun that is inconvenient for surveying, yet the eleven men (mostly young unmar-

ried people) who wish to take up their plantations in that region
went out to be present at the surveying.

Tuesday, the 23rd of January. N.'s /Granewetter's/ sick daughter has recovered from her dangerous epileptic illness that continued most violently for almost two days. Since one could give
her little or no medicine, only the famous Schauer balm was
used diligently externally on the arteries of her hands and head,
and this was of great use.[18] Partly the wet weather and partly
other things kept me from being able to travel to her plantation
to present the girl from God's word her obligation to this new
goodness of God. Since Christmas God has knocked rather re-
soundingly in three ways at the home of this family to awaken
them from their sleep of security:[19] for 1) one of their sons-in-
law died; another son-in-law was attacked by side-stitches and
fever at a burial; and 3) the youngest daughter was visited with
epilepsy. I caused the husband to think about this remarkable
threefold visitation of God and asked him to safeguard his salvation. He was again mightily touched and made many good resolutions. God also granted him and others much good from His
word in today's weekday sermon.

Wednesday, the 24th of January. This morning I held up to
the said father and his whole family God's merciful conduct towards them and their poor conduct towards Him, and I warned
them from God's word against further disobedience and ingratitude and also against persistence in customary sins.[20] They have
all resolved upon much good, and they prayed with me willingly
and sincerely. The widow N.N. is now living here, too. Her two
little boys are so weak that we can hardly hope for them to survive. We also prayed for her, and our dear Savior showed us
much good. We also asked Him, for the sake of His merits, not to
hold the mother to account that she, too, was to blame to a large
extent for this sickness and the premature death that we feared
for these children, for she has moved around several times with
her husband and changed their habitation. At their last plantation they suffered much for lack of a dwelling.

Thursday, the 25th of January. I learned by chance that Mrs.
Granewetter's little son, a child very weak from its birth, was
bedridden. This moved me yesterday to visit the mother and
child and to pray over them and also to impart comfort from the

word of God to the mother in her suffering, comfort that she greatly needed and of which she is capable. This morning she sent a man in from her plantation and informed me of the death of her child, about which everyone who loves her and her child rejoiced more than grieved. In her widowhood she was healthy, contented, and calm; but, after marrying an old widower /Walthauer/, who came to this country four years ago as a servant just to better her domestic situation,[21] she has fallen into much disquiet. I think that God has taken responsibility for this frail little boy for her own good, because it moves something out of the way of the stepfather that was making him restless.

It is the law in this country that, when a dying father leaves a son behind, his land falls to him and the mother can not convey it to anyone else or sell it.[22] This usually hinders a widow in a second marriage, or else she suffers trouble from her husband, who will not move onto, or willingly remain on, the land that does not belong to her but to his stepchildren. And that is the case with this Mrs. Granewetter's second husband, who went to Purysburg a week ago for one day but has not yet returned.

Saturday, the 27th of January. The surveyor returned to Savannah several days ago without finishing his business. A few weeks ago a great planter with many Negroes took up a large piece of land in the area where our young people wish to take up their land; and now that the surveyor wishes to survey our people's land, there is almost nothing usable left over. As soon as I heard that, I immediately wrote to Mr. Habersham and made the suggestion that we get at least six plantations of fifty acres in the same good region. Now he informs me that the surveyor has new orders to accommodate our people the best he can. He is still using many persuasive arguments that our people should acquire Negroes and that I should use them at the mill for (in his opinion) the great profit of the community. Otherwise, he did not see how our poor people would be able to exist very long. I more or less shudder at Negroes and such complications, nor do I believe that our Salzburgers know how to use them correctly; yet, I shall commend the matter to our Lord, who knows our needs.

Sunday, the 28th of January. For two days and two nights there have again been very strong and cold storm winds, and between them it also rained heavily yesterday afternoon. Old Gschwandl[23] and his daughter had to go out into the forest in the rain to come to the aid of a suffering cow; today they both have the dangerous sore throat with high fever, and the daughter has caught the purples at the same time.[24] I do not doubt that this bodily tribulation will serve the spiritual good of them both. He is a diligent man in God's word and prayer; the daughter does not lack literal recognition and good resolutions but she does lack sufficient loyalty. Our dear Savior, our loyal Shepherd, surely follows all the souls among us right untiringly and powerfully; and He seeks in all ways to bring them to His grace or to keep them in it or to strengthen them in it. Oh, if only He could achieve His purpose in all of them!

Thomas Bichler, who has a consumptive fever in a high degree, seems to be going nearer and nearer to his end. Today he said that he was not afraid of death; for he keeps his faith in Him who says, "I am the way, the truth, and the life: no man cometh to the Father but through me".[25] He was crying as he said this, and he fell asleep again from his great exhaustion. We presented the condition of his soul and body to God in prayer most humbly and sincerely and asked Him, as the expert on hearts, to reveal to him clearly his spiritual leprosy, his original sin and disbelief, and all other sins committed in his life, and to grant him true remorse and true faith in Christ, who, in today's gospel Matthew 8: 1 ff., especially revealed His loving Jesus-heart to all suffering people, and to prepare him in this order better and better for his end. His wife, the pious Mrs. Bacher's daughter /Maria/, is expecting her confinement at any time.

Monday, the 29th of January. Like the deceased Sanftleben some time ago, our honest Hans Schmidt has changed his plantation and way of living several times. He is an upright lover of the divine word, he prays diligently, and is a serious Christian; and God gives him the grace to keep free of unbelieving and heart-gnawing worries about making a living and to hold firmly to His promises. Today I brought him the dear words of our divine Savior, "The mountains shall depart and the hills be removed," etc.;[26] and after that we prayed. His little son from his first marriage was recently violently sick with the purples and epilepsy so that human eyes saw no hope for his recovery; yet, he did recover, and in him our Savior proved Himself to be a mighty and kind Lord, as He was presented to us last Sunday from the Book of Wisdom 16:12-13 and from the gospel on the Third Sunday after Epiphany.

Today I found the senior Gschwandl already out of bed and well on his way to a good recovery. We prayed and thanked God together. On Sunday the news came to our place that Mr. Habersham and Mr. Harris fear that their ship that sailed away at the beginning of last August may have suffered misfortune at sea. At that time I had written very much to the Lord Trustees about silk culture in Ebenezer and how it might be better advanced. Copies were retained, which I packed together yesterday and sent with a brief little letter to Court Chaplain Albinus. Peter Schubdrein is still in Savannah and is taking this little packet with him.[27] Our inhabitants are now very busy planting young mulberry trees, as we are also doing on the mill plantation, where there is a desirable opportunity for making silk.

Tuesday, the 30th of January. When I came to the sick Bichler today, I found him a little stronger. He is well applying his period of grace for a penitent and trusting preparation for blessed eternity. He complained of his previously unrecognized great and inordinate self-love and pride with tears, and he asked me to speak right out to him and tell everything that I recognized wrong in him. He would not hold it against me now as he used to do. He is not satisfied with himself because, in examining the course of his life as far back as he can remember, he has not felt the great divine sorrow and remorse for his many and great sins as he wishes or considers necessary; whereas, his heart and eyes wish to flow away with tears. He cannot speak for crying when he considers the great love of God in Christ for him as a great sinner; and it grieves him heartily that he has so often insulted such a good God and great Benefactor with so many sins. I told him that this was the right sorrow towards God, which is joined with a general hate for sin and with a sincere love to, and yearning for, the Savior so that one would rather die than intentionally insult Him further. If God found it necessary to grant him a greater measure of sorrow at his sins, then it would soon come to him.

I recommended to him the Passion story and the beautiful Passion hymns. Another good sign of the sincerity of his penitence I find in his poverty of spirit: he does not think himself worthy of the least of God's gifts, rather, when good people bring him something for his need and refreshment, he cannot marvel and humble himself enough at the clear proofs of the providence of God, who knows his needs, that he lets so much good fall to such a great sinner. Not only because he is very poor, but also because he is much in debt in the community and especially to a merchant in Savannah, he has had many worries;[28] but now his heart has been freed by God, whom he can now trust to provide for his family. While I am writing this, the word comes that this Bichler's pious helpmate has borne a healthy little girl. We prayed this morning for her at her sick husband's house.

A young person who was instructed and confirmed here some time ago requested the late Pastor Freylinghausen's *Compendium of Theology*[29] in order to repeat from it what was formerly preached to him and others. He was one of my dearest and most diligent pupils, who thoroughly understood everything that was preached about this compendium from God's word, and he also led a pious and Christian life. Afterwards he got into very troubled spiritual circumstances in which he remained for a considerable time and did nothing but complain, and he refrained from Holy Communion for a long time. However, he has found himself again; and I hope he will someday become a useful person, provided that he becomes and remains right loyal. In his external service with a pious family he practices writing; perhaps we can use him here some day as a schoolmaster. He has very good natural gifts.

Another master told me today that his apprentice is behaving very christianly and righteously and that he had no complaint whatever against him. He has especially great love for the word of God; and no greater pleasure could be given him than to be allowed to attend the sermons and prayer meetings all the time. Yesterday N.'s oldest little son, a child of three years, was buried, who was surely ruined by his parents' badly run household.[30] At his burial we completed the very edifying life story of the pious and richly blessed, little daughter of the late Dr. Stöller in

Köthen; and from it our dear God granted my soul and my parishioners indescribably much good. May he let a fruit from it last into heaven!

Together with Mr. Meyer I held a conference with the leaders of the congregation, which was very useful to me in many matters. I would like so much (and my dear colleague is of similar mind) to help advance not only the salvation of our dear parishioners but also the physical improvement of their plantations with regard to farming, dwellings, cattle raising, and a trade in all sorts of lumber products; and we find all sorts of real obstacles. After having heard the opinion of the community through these leaders, I am traveling at the suggestion of Mr. Habersham and in the name of Jesus to Savannah in order to see whether something can be arranged through the counsel and aid of this friend of ours for the improvement of our external circumstances, since my last suggestions are no longer valid.

Wednesday, the 31st of January. Yesterday evening our boat came back from Savannah and brought us letters that had been sent to us on a ship that arrived in Charleston. We have reason to praise God that all our worthy Fathers and benefactors in London and Germany are still alive and are still faring well, also that Messrs. Habersham and Harris's ship, on which were our chests with the spun-off silk, arrived safely in London last October, about which it was announced a few days ago that it had been lost at sea. Mr. Verelst and the Secretary of the Society for Promoting Christian Knowledge, Mr. Broughton, have written to me in a very friendly way.

I have now been charged by a prominent gentleman in Germany with a commission which, to be sure, I will gladly carry out, but which will take a considerable bit of my time.[31] For I must not only confer with experienced people here and in Savannah about the points that have been given to me to answer, the correct answers to which have the spiritual and physical welfare of certain persons as its aim, but I must also write many folios with much reflection.[32] I like to work when granted divine grace, and it is truly a heartfelt joy to serve God and my neighbor in my humble way; but, because I must let myself be used for all sorts of things, I must suffer all kinds of judgments, especially if I can not do it to the satisfaction of this or that person.

A woman who arrived with the last people[33] came to me with her little child that was born on the ship and was baptized by the young Matthew Neidlinger; and she asked me to enter this child in our baptismal and church register. From her confession and tears I recognized with joy that our dear God had not only touched and awakened her heart through His word, to which she listens diligently, but has also brought her to a true feeling of her sins, which she formerly either did not know or did not recognize as such. She considers it a gracious dispensation of God that she has come into this tranquility and to the acquaintance of a pious Salzburger woman. God is also working mightily on her husband, and His word is penetrating to his heart.

FEBRUARY

Thursday, the 1st of February. There were several reasons for my trip to Savannah that I finished today, safe and sound, God be praised, which concerned my health and the physical welfare of the congregation; and with God's help I was able to accomplish one thing and another, even if not everything, as desired. The last suggestions that I made (by which to be sure, my aim was the improvement of the subsistence of the entire community, but especially of the poor among us) were not approved by the members of the community. They would gladly have inexpensive goods from England and the West Indies, but they do not wish to work cheaply enough for us to achieve our purpose. In order that I might have fewer public expenses they have offered to do some communal works, with which I shall be satisfied until they themselves see the difficulties of communal work or of a contribution for paying off some public expenditures.

Now at the present time I know of no other means to raise and advance the members of our community than for them to undertake all sorts of wood working, such as splitting barrel staves and shingles and dressing lumber for houses in the West Indies and for us to procure for them a fairer merchant to take such woodwork from them at a fair price.[1]

I found the last to be impracticable and harmful for us; on the other hand we would fare much better if we sold our boards and other woodwork at a fair price and bought from the very same merchant as much West Indian goods, such a sugar, rum, and syrup, as we need, instead of payment. We must avoid complications in merchandizing, since we do not have the people for it. A single unfortunate incident of importance could give such a blow to our small undertaking that everyone would lose courage. In the meanwhile I have found three merchants who will gladly take our inhabitants' barrel staves, shingles, hoops, and dressed lumber at a very good price, since they are assured that they will be provided with better work from them than from the slaveholders in Carolina. They now have enough work throughout the whole year and good and certain payment, as every reasonable person must admit.

The second reason for my trip this time was to discuss this and that with our friend Mr. Habersham concerning the content of his last letter to me. He advised that those among us who have money should buy Negroes and move to larger plantations and thus give their neighbors room for farming and cattle raising. As far as the poor are concerned, one must remember that one might help them get some Negroes. He himself offered to procure some such Negroes for them on credit. These suggestions were, to be sure, announced to our inhabitants; but I have heard that they do not wish to be confused with this matter, and in this they are doing the right thing, for another upright merchant in Carolina, who would also like to trade with our inhabitants, told me that, if poor people borrowed Negroes, they would become slaves of their slaves and of the merchants, and also lazy people. If they had the money to buy one, there is less danger; but they should not buy one newly brought from Africa, but rather one that was born in Carolina or at least has learned the English language and how to work, because nothing can be accomplished with the new ones without the encouragement and example of the old Negroes.

To be sure, I shall not in the least way prevent the use of Negroes at our place since I have already had to suffer for a long time the reproach in this country of having stood in the way of the inhabitants' desire for Negroes. If our inhabitants can get good farmhands for money and work with them in the wood business, they will proceed more surely and can do without the Negroes. The Lord Trustees would just have to make better arrangements, perhaps with a jail or workhouse, to punish runaways or disobedient servants. If they planted less and worked more in the wood business, the work in the shade would be easier than with corn and rice, etc., in the heat of the sun; and it is much more profitable. To be sure, this work will at first get off to a slow start because they have had no practice in it, but everything would become easier with time. This could also be a means of bringing more servants and other useful German workers to this colony and to our place.

How well the poor German people would be advised if they would let the Lord Trustees send them here instead of going to Carolina, Pennsylvania, etc., for they care for the people in a fatherly way both in the contract and on the voyage; and God has always granted grace for the colonists and servants to come here safe and sound.[2] On the other hand, in Savannah I heard the sad news that some Swiss and many Germans have arrived before Charleston in a ship in a right pitiful condition. Many died on the way; and now that the ship must remain at a certain distance, four or five must be buried in the sea every day. The minister Zübli wished to go with another man to these compatriots of his; but, while he was still rather far from the ship, he smelt an almost unbearable stench of death, which apparently kept him away.

The third reason for my trip was to ask the President and his Assistants to pay me the money ordered by the Lord Trustees for advancing silk manufacture, or at least to assure me that I will receive it from them at the proper time.

In the evening prayer meeting I had the opportunity to tell the German people many good things about the seventh commandment, which followed in the order of contemplation.[3]

Sunday, the 3rd of February. Dear Mrs. Kalcher in the orphanage has had bodily weaknesses for some years, which have sometimes attacked her unexpectedly in church, at which time it always appeared that she was very near death, or rather near a blessed dissolution. She has lived until now, contrary to her and other people's expectation; and our dear God doubtless granted this for the good of her righteous husband, her children, and our community. Like the prophetess Hannah in the Bible, she is in prayer almost day and night and lets neither work nor physical weakness keep her from it. The dear word of God and the sacraments are greater in her eyes than anything else in the world, and she feels their power abundantly in her soul and in the entire conduct of her Christianity. Yet it pleases our wise God to humble her both inwardly and outwardly so much that she feels little comfort in her soul. Rather, she must fight much with disbelief, doubts, anxieties, and other powers of darkness, so that one could also say in her case, "Without feeling I will trust".[4] Yet our Savior is so true to her that He aways reaches His merciful hand to her hardest spiritual suffering and temptations[5] and lets fall into her heart this or that powerful or comforting gospel verse with great emphasis during prayer or tears. She has no lack of external suffering either, which, however, appears minor and easy in her eyes. Her husband is just like her in his righteous thoughts and seriousness in his Christianity.

This morning a pious Salzburger sent me a letter by his son in which the following was written:

> I cannot help but inform your grace in what a dilemma I have been in this week because of the incorrect report about the Negroes; for we are told that you now see the matter entirely differently and that we will not be able to get along without Negroes, which I cannot comprehend and which is entirely against the faith that I feel very powerfully through the grace of God. I was greatly strengthened in this faith when, after the edification hour, I heard your steadfast thoughts; and I cannot see it as anything but a hearing of our poor supplication, which[6] has strengthened your heart among all kinds of ideas that may be false. Oh, may you continue untiring in the power of God; full of hope and faith I see a glorious crown of reward over you and your descendants. May the Lord awaken our hearts to a right great trust in Him!, for He is a Lord over all things.

I must marvel how one can spread such untruths about me in the community during my absence, as if I had changed my mind about the Negroes and their introduction and as if I were now convinced that our inhabitants could not get along without them.

Monday, the 5th of February. Through the merciful providence of God we have reached a point that the very fertile and well situated land behind Abercorn has been surveyed for some

people, mostly young ones, and just as I requested. Not long ago
I wrote to Mr. Habersham, who is a member of the Council, that
it would be to the harm of the Lord Trustees and to the poor
people if the surveyor surveyed the plantations according to his
previous custom. He makes only one main line, and he directs
himself according to it in surveying the plantations, one after
the other. Thus it occurs that many turn out almost entirely un-
usable; and it could have been different if he had used reason
and fairness and had excluded the entirely worthless and unus-
able land from the plantation. A person receives only forty acres,
and all or most of it should be good, but this seldom happens.
This time it has been surveyed as our people wish. There are ten
of these small plantations: namely, four for four families who
have been settled until now around the town on small and somewhat poor plots of ground, and six for six young people, some of
whom are still apprentices.

I would have liked to see some of our householders abandon
their very unproductive land and settle on this new land; and for
this I would gladly have given them some assistance. However,
they found moving away very undesirable for several reasons: 1)
They are already worn out and can no longer do heavy work like
felling trees. 2) For some years they have so built up their dwellings and spent so much on houses, kitchens, stalls, and barns
which they would have to leave behind for small payment while
establishing themselves again with new expenses on another
piece of land. They would not be able to make use of the sawmill
at all, and they could use the gristmill only with great difficulty.
3) They would thereby distance themselves greatly from divine
services and the schools; and they could bring their hearts to this
last less than to anything else.

Some of them are beginning to make use of the very fertile
land on the island on the Mill River, which reaches for several
miles in length and breadth. If they could continue in this and if
others would aid them, we would have here the most beautiful
cattle pasture and fruit orchards. Only much work is required
here because of the reeds and thick trees and bushes; and at
times it is flooded by the Savannah River, especially at some
places, which makes the soil very rich and fruitful. This island is
a great blessing for our inhabitants if only because of the quan-

tity of useful wood. Grass grows here so rapidly and abundantly that one must marvel. It lacks only good workers.

Good Mrs. Granewetter has borne a great cross after she married a widower /Caspar Walthauer/, who came to this country four years ago with the German servants.[7] He is no lover of the divine word and of prayer, as she is, but prone to greed and worldly cares. At the same time he considers himself much cleverer than other people, and he makes very coarse judgments over good books and good people. A certain book, called *Cabinet Preacher*,[8] is his best book, with which he passes his time and drives away his melancholy and is sometimes moved to merriment and laughter. I would have liked to speak with him, but I did not find him on his plantation. From Mrs. Granewetter's words I realized that she had adjusted herself well to this cross and knows how to speak lovingly to him and to answer. She also prays diligently for God to open his eyes and save his soul, even if his body should perish.

Tuesday, the 6th of February. For some days we have had very warm weather both day and night, as a result of which the plum and peach trees have budded and blossomed. We do not notice the same thing in the mulberry trees; also, it would not be good if the leaves and blossoms came out so early, because they cannot bear any frost. Yesterday and today the wind has veered to the cold evening and midnight regions[9] and it is as cold as if it would snow again. The water in the river has been steadily rising for several weeks and is now so high that it has stopped all our mills.

A good friend in Charleston[10] has made every possible effort so far to recover our two servants and three boys who ran away to Congarees in Carolina. However, he appears to be hindered in that by the government itself, which gives protection and safety to all sorts of people who have flowed together at this newly settled place and thereby deprives people of their property. It now appears that our poor people will not recover their servants and that I will also lose the money spent in searching for them. I fear that this matter will be of evil consequence with other single servants, especially when the dry spring and summer come, since it is easier to travel then than in winter. At our place they are kept very well in work, food, and in other things; but anyone who knows the mind of frivolous tradesmen apprentices, who love bodily freedom and visiting cities, cannot expect much good from such people who do not convert to God, especially since they know that there is no possibility of getting them back from Carolina and that it is easy to get there from Georgia.

Thursday, the 8th of February. Yesterday evening a German man arrived here by boat from Savannah Town in South Carolina and asked me to marry him to an English widow, which was done today in our church with Christian witnesses.[11] He speaks good German although he has already lived for many years in America among the English; but the widow cannot speak a word of German, and therefore the marriage had to be conducted in the English language for her sake. They were both moved by God's word, and they showed in a noticeable and praiseworthy way their joy at the marriage that is customary here. The husband has been in our Sunday services and evening prayer meetings a few times when he has come down here or gone back up, and he told others that he was edified. He is attached to our Evangelical Lutheran religion and is a sincere lover of it. Some time ago there was a German man, a mill builder by profession, in our neighborhood, who, to be sure, also called himself a Lutheran but did not have even the appearance of any religion. He was very devoted to drink; and now I hear that he was drunk near Augusta and froze to death in the last snow and great cold. Thus God seizes people!

I have learned from what this and that person have told me that up there where Augusta is situated there is very good land that hardly has its likes in fertility. However, such people have gathered there who cannot get along elsewhere; and therefore it is said that things go on there in a godless way, and it is more scandalous than heathen, just as in Congarees, which is only a day and a half journey from Augusta and Savannah Town. If our place had the advantage of fertile land that other areas have, all sorts of nations and sects would already be living among us. But God's providence has allotted us a land with which we can be very well satisfied, but at the same time He has granted us, according to His wisdom and benevolent goodness, advantages which we should rightly consider among the most important in the world. These are the following: His word, the holy sacraments, the ministry, freedom of religion, churches, schools, sawmills, gristmills, and rice stamping mills. We are also situated between the main river and some tributary rivers, called creeks, so that we have the most beautiful opportunity for trade and travel. The people do not live only from farming, but from many other things that the Creator has given them in their land. Ours has also been ordained for us, which will be revealed in due time.

Friday, the 9th of February. A good friend in Savannah gave me a German calendar that was composed and printed in Philadelphia for the current year. Since many calendars in this country contain many foolish and merry things, this one is, to the contrary, arranged seriously, usefully, and even edifyingly. In addition to the lovely verses that appear between all the changes in the moon, it also contains a truthfully composed narrative of the nature of this colony and of colonists in Africa. While reading them, I marveled that the author gave our Ebenezer such a good testimony. It reads as follows:

> How do our (the German) people live in Georgia? Answer: The soil is not good for German crops; and, even though they sow and plant according to German ways, their crops do not have half the weight or quality of those further north. Viticulture should prosper better in the future, as also cotton, rice, Indian corn, etc. This land may be very good for making tiles and bricks, earthenware, glass, etc. The forests are said to offer tar, cypress shingles, boards, barrel staves, etc. Some of the people live very poorly, because no trade and merchandizing flourish. But, despite the poor soil, one colony of those who have been sent there, Salzburgers who had been expelled from their fatherland for Christ's sake, have built up a fine city, plantations, and mills with uninterrupted prayer and almost superhuman work, so that they eat their bread by the sweat of their brow and can support themselves honestly and in a Christian way. In their need they are so calm and content that they could serve as the most beautiful model for all Germans in America.

Later it also says that the Salzburgers have two Evangelical Ministers, whom the Society for Promoting Christian Knowledge called upon and sent.

To be sure, it is true that the soil of this colony, at least from the sea up to the area of Palachocolas (which is a good day's trip above us on the Savannah River) is not especially good for raising German grains such as wheat, rye, and barley; but it is all the more convenient for trade in all sorts of wood products, preparation of pitch and tar, and producing cotton, wine, and mulberry trees for developing silk manufacture, if only there were enough people and pertinent arrangements there.

Good and useful oak, cypress, pine, and black nut trees, etc. have become very scarce in the previously occupied colonies because of irresponsible misuse, so that one now already pays, e.g. for a thousand staves for rum barrels three to four pounds Sterling, which until a short time ago were worth two pounds Sterling or less. Since N.'s deceit[12] we have not been able to move our inhabitants to prepare the said wood products for export to the West Indies, even though we have given them all sorts of suggestions. I hope that the very good price that is now being given will incite them to it. To be sure, in our area there are not many white oaks, which alone are used for staves for rum barrels, but there are all the more of them on the very rich land behind Abercorn, which have now been surveyed for ten families who belong to our community.

Likewise, there are very many white oaks standing on the Uchee land near our town,[13] which is ours, even if not yet occupied. There is a great quantity of water oaks and cypresses in our district, the former are used for syrup barrels and the latter for roof shingles in the West Indies. Cotton grows easily and abundantly here, but it has this inconvenience that the seeds stick very firmly in the lint and it takes a man or a woman a whole day if one wishes to free a quarter of a pound from the seeds and prepare it for spinning. Now we know of a little machine that costs a couple of shillings, through the help of which a single person, even a child of six years, can prepare from four to six pounds and not get even the least bit tired.[14]

Saturday, the 10th of February. Today at noon a very violent storm with rain, hail, and thunderbolts arose in the south. It struck in a pine forest across from us; and, along with the downpour, the wind was so strong that it threw down not only many roofs but also the strongest fences. The wind drove the rain with such force through the roofs and walls and windows that we and other people had little that was dry in our living rooms, chambers, attics, or kitchens. This unusual storm lasted for only a few minutes, otherwise it would surely have caused more damage. It is said to have been less violent on our plantation. God be praised for having averted greater danger.

Monday, the 12th of February. Saturday night N. suddenly became dangerously sick and did not expect to live until morning. He contracted the dangerous side-stitches, from which God soon freed him again. He has a sincerely pious wife, who accomplished more through prayer than through work, even though she is also industrious in her work. Her desire for God's word is very great, and she regrets no time or effort spent in hearing it and in repeating it with other pious people and in praying. She lives in great poverty with her husband and children, but is sincerely content.

Tuesday, the 13th of February. Our servants have brought some very bad habits into this country, which they sometimes do not even consider to be sins: the misuse of the holy name of God, cursing, swearing, and unnecessary asseverations are very common among them, and some of them are amazed that we consider such things to be sins in Ebenezer. Now, because such things in themselves are not serious sins, but rather are very vexing, I do not let an opportunity pass easily publicly or privately to present to them from God's word both the ugliness of this sin and the great harm they are doing to others by it, especially the children. This was done again just yesterday in the prayer meeting. I also warned the other listeners sincerely to not to participate in foreign sins,[15] report evil customs and practices, as can be clearly seen from the two remarkable verses Leviticus 5:1 and Proverbs 29:24.

These poor, mostly unwitting, tradesmen-apprentices have still more un-Christian habits, sayings, etc., which I hope God will free them from. With them and others I am excellently served by the late Wirth's *Confession and Communion Booklet*[16] and in it the heart examinations and duties of life according to the Ten Commandments. On this and that occasion I can prove and convince them that what they hear here is not our own dogma but the Evangelical dogma of the entire Lutheran Church that is based on God's word. I wish I were in a position to give this booklet even to these strangers, as it is now in the hands of all our householders. Some of them have already requested one from me, but they will have to make do with borrowing until I have several dozen sent. They could be very simply bound. They are showing a great desire for hymnals and Bibles, but I cannot serve them in this now.

In the meanwhile I have given each of them a New Testament with an attached Psalter, which they bring to church diligently in order to read the chapters with us and to look up the chief verses that must be looked up by the congregation during the sermon. Then they can see with their own eyes and almost grasp with their hands that we are teaching not according to men but according to God's word and that no more or less can be demanded of people than what stands in the holy scriptures of the Old and the New Testaments. Still, we are happy that they visit these good opportunities gladly and diligently.

Thursday, the 15th of February. This morning the widow N. reported to me that her youngest remaining little boy had followed his father and his little brother, who was buried recently, into heaven through a temporal death. In their nine years of marriage they had five children, but all of them died at a tender age. I hope that this procedure of God will serve to their true conversion and righteous Christianity. She has a naturally good disposition and also loves God's word. However, because her heart has not changed, some of her inborn bad habits sometimes show forth. She is now living with her parents-in-law, and therefore in a large family, where it is sometimes right turbulent. Perhaps God will soon ordain that she will have her own plantation and therefore more quiet for her own good.

On judgment day we will know clearly and with certainty the reason why our dear God has let most of our children who were born here die already at a very tender age, and whether it is the nature of this climate and whether the mistakes of their parents have contributed something to their premature deaths.

Last night it thundered and rained heavily; and, because it was as warm as spring at the time, not only the peach and plum trees but even the mulberry trees are putting out seeds and leaves. Our inhabitants are devoting themselves seriously to silk manufacture, for which they are getting more and larger trees every year. This is a very convenient land for this, and I marvel that so few in this country apply themselves to it. When we moved to this so-called Red Bluff fourteen years ago, if our inhabitants had wished to follow the advice given them and had planted many mulberry trees, how useful it would be for them now! The reason that almost no one in this country wishes to devote himself to this light, pleasant, and useful business is simply the all-too-great wages that are customary here that the least worker can demand and get.

It is said that, after the Lord Trustees stop giving encouragement, silk making will scarcely bring one shilling per day. On the other hand, in daily wages, if they work for other people, they get from eighteen pence to two shillings, and even more in other places in this country. And, therefore, they leave off silk manufacture as, in their opinion, a poorly paying matter. However, they do not remember that 1) they are disobeying the authorities, our dear Lord Trustees (who are truly a right gracious authority) and are doing their part in preventing them from achieving their intended purpose in establishing this colony. 2) They do not consider that, once there are enough trees on hand and nearby, it will be very easy work for weak people of all ages; 3) that the work with the silkworms takes place at a time when one is not kept from other business of agriculture and husbandry, for it starts very early in the spring after the fields have already been prepared for planting and, indeed, after they have been long cultivated with European crops.

To be sure, the planting of Indian corn takes place already in March and April, but then it proceeds rapidly. On the other hand, chopping out the grass is the most difficult and tedious work, which occurs when the silkworms have spun themselves in their cocoons and this business has been completed. In five weeks all the work with the silk making is completely past, except for the spinning-off, provided one understands it well and has a warm dwelling. It is indeed a great blessing for poor people if they can earn something according to their strength not only now and then but throughout the whole year, even if it does not occur at one time. Now they can earn something in the spring with silk making, in the summer and fall with planting and making butter, and in the winter with spinning, knitting, etc.

4) Silkmaking is something that will bring everyone steady earnings. On the other hand, not everyone, e.g. widows, old

people, children, and frail people, can earn something with day wages or in the field. Also, there is not and will not be work for day laborers all the time. What will such people who have not planted any mulberry trees or have not learned silk making do after this? With such high wages every gentleman or man of means must gradually fail. For the work of the best day laborer in the field or in housework or in rowing a boat, etc., is hardly worth six pence (according to local comparison of things), yet he must give the day laborer eighteen pence or two shillings or more for light or heavy work in winter or in summer. Thus, every time he uses a day laborer he will become poorer by one or two or more shillings. How much does that amount to all together? Now that Negroes are being introduced into this colony, for which the unfair day laborers, servants, and other workers are to blame, there will be little for poor people to earn in daily wages, as is already evident in and around Savannah.

5) If the principle were right that, "if I cannot get the usual wages on my own land, then I would rather not work at all," then all agriculture in this country would be stopped. For everyone agrees that the most industrious workers in the field, when they compare the work and the harvest, do not bring more than four pence per day. But what a great difference there is between work in the field in the hottest summer and work with the silkworms in the shade in the spring? And the profit is even greater: namely, once things have been properly arranged with trees, adequate dwellings for keeping the worms warm at first and cool and airy at the end of the fourth week and once we have gained more experience.

I know from experience in my house that my wife, who has entered the business through obedience to the Lord Trustees and as an example for our inhabitants, can make over a hundred pounds of cocoons with the help of only one other vigorous woman whom she needed only in the last three weeks and that she had more pleasure than effort with it.[17] Let us suppose that one pound of silk cocoons costs nine pence, then a hundred pounds would make seventy-five shillings Sterling, which a woman can earn in five weeks with a maid who helps her in the last period in picking leaves and other domestic chores. Further, let us suppose that she must spend some fifteen shillings every year on her forty mulberry trees, which are required for a hundred pounds of silk, until they have grown up and need no more special attention, then the profit still amounts to three pounds Sterling. The more silk that is made, the greater the profit, if one just knows how to manage it.

If God should let me live, or my dear colleague (who is entirely of my mind in all matters), then we would like to make a test near the mill where we have a great number of beautiful trees on good soil, in order to convince both inclined and disinclined people in a few years and show them what an easy and profitable matter silk making is, even if we cannot expect that the Lord Trustees will give a bounty or encouragement forever. I will add only one reason why I consider silk making such a useful thing: namely, one can make it to one's advantage in this country no matter where one wishes to live.

Mulberry trees grow everywhere, if one just does not let them strangle in the grass. In addition, one finds convenience for silk-making everywhere, whether one lives on the river or deep in the country, near or far from the capital and mercantile city. On the other hand, with rice, corn, beans, sweet potatoes, barrel staves, shingles, and other heavy things it is a very difficult matter if one does not live on a river and near the place where he can bring his crops and things to market. Also, if one had fifty pounds of spun-off silk, which is no longer a secret among us,[18] then it could be sent at small cost not only to Savannah but even to England; and its value would amount to fifty pounds Sterling. But I must also add that, if the Lord Trustees were to withdraw their hand and their encouragement before this useful matter were properly established and matured, many would lose their courage; and I would be disgraced before many of them, for whom I have made every possible effort near and far in order to achieve the Lord Trustees' purpose.

Our people see no example of industry in silk making in the whole country among either prominent or simple people. Indeed, there are always people who predict for them that with time it will not be worth the effort; and it would be no wonder that everything fell in ruin again if the Lord Trustees withdrew their hand. As mentioned, the high daily wages stick in everyone's head. Nothing can be done in this by compulsion, rather one must await the help of God at the time and in the manner that pleases Him. Meanwhile, as a superior, I must not become tired or cross in achieving His purpose by accomplishing the common good in some other way with God's guidance and prosperity.

Saturday, the 17th of February. Our people who had taken something for sale in Savannah brought back an unpleasant report: namely, that two more servants had run away; but on their way to Augusta they had been delivered into the hands of the English by the Indians in a cunning way. Now they will surely be punished as an example to the others. It is now raining a great deal; therefore, we can well expect high river water and the flooding of low areas around the river. There is now, to be sure, much to grind and to saw at our mills, and an inundation would cause great hindrance in this. But it will be the Lord who does it, if it happens. Why should His servants not be pleased by it? "He can, better than we think, turn all bad into good."[19]

As soon as people hear about the boards from our mill, none of them will remain lying here even if we could saw such beautiful durable boards on ten mills. They are also exported to the Spaniards and French in the West Indies; and a merchant told me not long ago that he is to bring many boards that he ordered here to a French place, etc. Provided God's grace continues to protect and bless them, they will continue to prosper as they have begun, to the great advantage of our place. If we had capable builders, we could undertake many useful things.

Monday, the 19th of February. We have unexpectedly received right hard and biting winter weather again. For several days the wind has come from the north and has brought us cold rain, snow, and ice. The trees are hanging full of icicles that are breaking the branches. The plum and peach trees were in full blossom, and the sap was rising in the mulberry trees and they were beginning to sprout seeds and leaves so that we must worry that they will suffer great damage as they did two years ago. The right hand of the Highest can change all things. This very cold weather kept many weak people and children from visiting the public divine service yesterday, Sexagesima Sunday, both in town and on the plantations; for, when it is cold here, then it is much more painful for the inhabitants than in the northern colonies because they are used to warmth.

The day before yesterday I had an opportunity to send to Savannah our current packet of letters and the diary from January of this year to the 17th of this month, which Mr. Habersham is, if possible, to put it into the hand of Capt. Gill, who is standing by in Port Royal ready to sail. However, the very wet and uncomfortable weather that has come has prevented the man from his trip so that this packet will be sent off only in a few days.

Among the servants of the last transport were some tradesmen who are useful and necessary here, such as carpenters, wainwrights, cabinet makers, etc., who, however, were picked out in Savannah. Now it has come about that two fine people, who, with their brother at our place, were the best in the whole transport, were redeemed from the Savannah minister by payment of twelve pounds after some prescribed heavy work was finished.[20] At the beginning of last week they moved to our place and are working for me as carpenters for a very low wage out of gratitude to me for advancing them the money. We need them very much both for building the town school and also for other dwellings that our people need, God be praised! for the impending happy silkmaking. I see this also as a sign of divine providence over us that we have received these skillful and industrious brothers, who live a Christian life, for which I formerly had no hope. Skillful and well behaved tradesmen are a rarity in this country, mostly they are bunglers or cursers and drunkards who come from Germany into the New World. If one gets them as servants, they are restless and seldom do well because they know that their trade has value here and that they can quickly earn their passage money. If God has resolved to occupy this land with white people, then everything that appears impossible must be made possible. For important reasons I cannot at present believe that it is according to the will of God that this land, in itself fertile and well situated, will be filled with Negroes or Moorish slaves.

Wednesday, the 21st of February. Yesterday the rainy weather let up, but it got all the colder in the night. We will soon see how much the former and present cold have damaged the crops and trees. Many large and small branches have been broken off by the heavy icicles, and they almost cover the driveways and foot-paths from the town to the plantations and to the mill. It is, therefore, a new testimony of divine providence over mankind and cattle that no damage has been done through the falling of the branches since we have always been walking, driving, and riding. Also, there are many horses and cows in the forest both by day and by night.

Thursday, the 22nd of February. The worldly minded N. has brought herself and her daughter into need and debts. When I was talking to the mother and daughter about it today and pray-ing with them, they both became very moved, and I only wish it would blossom into a true conversion.

A soldier's wife who has settled at our place with her husband loves God's word sincerely and is showing a fine sincerity in her Christianity; in my house she remembered certain sins for which she has often apologized to God, and she believes that He has forgiven them for the sake of Christ. When she fled during the Spanish invasion from Frederica to Carolina, all of her chil-dren died, one after the other, so that of nine only a single one was left to her. At the time she took these sad circumstances so to heart that she lost her mind and gnawed the flesh on both of her arms from her hands to her elbows, from which one can still see the marks. She is a native German and wishes to support herself honestly, even though she and her husband cannot bear such hard work as farming demands.

I wish that all of our weak and worn-out workers would plant only as many crops as they need for their family's use; most of their time they should and could apply to easier and more prof-itable work, which they could do according to their strength and mostly in the shade. It is a blessing worthy of thanks that there is more work and opportunity to earn some cash at our place than there are people who wish to work and earn.

Year after year a great quantity of staves for barrels, cypress shingles, and dressed lumber of pine and cypress are demanded for export to the West Indies, for which a good price is paid. Similarly, much money would be earned by those willing to bring the sawed cypress logs to the mill by water. This is no difficult work, since the cypress trees stand in a great quantity around Abercorn Creek and the Savannah River.

Sunday, the 25th of February. Today, Esto Mihi Sunday, eighty-six people were at Holy Communion, among them a mother and her son from the area of Purysburg. It will soon be revealed how much our dear God blessed in their souls His word, which was preached to them yesterday in the preparation and confession services in both churches and today in the sermon. In any case, all of them listened diligently and hungrily. The weather was good, even if very windy.

Monday, the 26th of February. Today I was, by request, on the new land by Abercorn, where several German people have settled, to baptize a child there. The whole day was spent on this trip, for not only did I baptize his child, but also the people gathered to hear God's word and to pray with me. I read to them the beautiful 25th Psalm, repeated from it the summary of my sermon yesterday concerning its eighth and ninth verses, and instilled in them the main truths of this beautiful psalm. The people showed me great love, insisted that I enter their homes, and asked that I or my dear colleague would sometimes come to them and preach the word of God to them and, if possible, to hold Holy Communion. When I gave them hope of that, provided they would improve the road, their joy was very great. They are all Evangelical Lutherans.[21] One of them served for three years at our place and, after completing his service, lived here for a year; and here he converted righteously to God and is now a light among his compatriots. In my presence he praised God sincerely for having ordained so wonderously according to His wisdom and goodness for him to come to our place and instruction despite all the dissuasion of the wicked German people around Savannah, by which God has illuminated and given a new birth to his soul.

Through God's providence the German people have received a very good, fertile, and well situated land, than which they could not have wished for anything better. For that reason they wish to call it Goshen. Some of our young people have also taken up their land in this neighborhood; therefore, a community of the Evangelical Lutheran religion will gradually assemble here.

They are all very poor yet (as it appears to me) contented. They are working industriously and hope to be saved somewhat from their poverty by a good harvest. We must always preach to them of love and Christian tolerance, as I did today. They diligently hold their meetings on Sundays and Holy Days and have for it the late Dr. Spener's *Gospel and Epistle Sermons.*[22]

A very fine married couple bear the cross that the husband has gradually lost all his strength and is incapable of work; his face is as pale as a white cloth and his blood is as thin as water and nut colored. Such patients do not complain of any pain, but only of great fatigue. This condition afflicts mainly industrious field workers in hot weather and may well be a form of hectica. Several men among us are afflicted that way and know of no medication against it. None of Mr. Thilo's or Mr. Meyer's medicines have done any good.

Tuesday, the 27th of February. N.N. has been excluded from Holy Communion and other privileges of Christians because of his vexing life (he is very given to drink); but last week he came to me and asked me to accept him again and let him go to Holy Communion with his wife and other members of the congregation. I admonished him sincerely to a true repentance and conversion of his life and let him go this time. He hears God's word regularly and also has a good literal recognition;[23] indeed, he would be a useful man in many ways and prosper well in his household if only he wished to desist from his vice of drunkeness. His wife, who is honest,[24] would like to see me announce to the congregation that he is being allowed to Holy Communion again at a new promise of improvement and to admonish him publicly of his duty. However, I considered it advisable to be lenient with him this time, too, and to reserve severity for the future (if it becomes necessary with this man, who already has already become skilled in boozing).

I guard myself from the highest and most extreme grade of punishing vexations, just as from excesses in them; and God has always helped to keep them from being necessary. It appears that God has mightily seized this N. in his conscience again, for eight days ago he was in extreme danger of crushing his head in the millwheel. Recently he heard the sad example of one of his drinking buddies, who moved from Purysburg to Savannah

Town and drank himself full, as was his custom, and died in the snow during a cold night. Today I stopped of at Kohleisen's house. I reminded him of the promise he made before and during the confession service, warned him against lying and disloyalty and also against a relapse into his old sins, whereby he would distress God, His servants, and His children and would draw God's judgments on his neck. I also showed him from God's word which means he should use and in what order, if the last should not be worse for him than the first. Then I prayed with him and his family. This afternoon I visited some other families on the plantations, where our dear God granted us much for our common edification. It gives me an especially great pleasure whenever I recognize the grace of God in our little school children, which puts many of the bigger children and adults to shame. The pious parents, especially the mothers, not only teach them Bible verses but also lead them in prayer, intercession, praise, and thanks. They love me and my dear colleague and pray for us, which redounds to my very great comfort.

Wednesday, the 28th of February. We hear from Savannah the sad news that a merchant and planter in the region of Purysburg, who has only recently returned from New York in his vessel, capsized in his boat not far from Savannah and almost lost his life. Two Negroes died in the water, but he and a Negro saved their lives with difficulty. They would both have lost, if not their lives, then at least their health, on a wet and swampy land in the cold night if a man passing by had not heard their cries and brought them back to Savannah. The greatest loss, according to this gentleman's estimate, consists of important letters that were in a trunk and could not be found, even though a considerable reward was promised to seekers and finders. With his Negroes he had caught a swimming deer and let them cut its throat, but the deer struck out with all four feet in such a way that the boat turned over. This merchant is now having many boards cut at our mill in order to take them to the French West Indies. Now at the end of this month I am again thinking with humble and grateful heart of the divine goodness, which has so far averted all harm from us and has granted us much spiritual and physical good. Hallelujah!

MARCH

Thursday, the 1st of March. Last night after the prayer hour I was told something about a servant and his wife that has caused my conscience no little disquiet today. He was formerly a soldier and absorbed some disgraceful superstitions and forbidden arts;[1] and he has started practicing them in the house of N.N. The circumstances are partly silly and tasteless and partly annoying; and I was amazed that the old widow would tolerate such godless things, which caused a great vexation. Today I did not find the servant at home; meanwhile I examined his wife and mistress, who at first pretended ignorance; but afterwards they confessed the wicked deed, at which the son of N. was also present but tried to extenuate the circumstances as much as possible.

By directing them to the spiritual examination concerning and from our duties according to the the First Commandment, I showed them what a curse they had brought upon their house through this heathen, yea gypsy-like, behavior of their servant, of which they were aware. This would strike their souls, I said, if they did not show real repentance. Hereby God made it known that their hearts are still unchanged despite all their good practices. Formerly I could not convince them of this, but now it can be done better.

Friday, the 2nd of March. German people who come into this country uncalled have generally not amounted to much in the fatherland; and, unfortunately, I now know from much experience that they will continue here what they began there.

Saturday, the 10th of March. Contrary to my expectations I had to delay eight whole days in Savannah, where, to be sure, I was not idle but was able to spend my time partly in preaching, holding Communion, and conducting prayer meetings and partly in visiting and encouraging the German people and writing letters to Carolina and London, but particularly in attending the meetings of the Council. Still, it was painful for me to have to be away so long from my regular official duties. It was the gen-

tlemen of the Council who kept me away so long. They are tired
of the all-too-great expenses of the Lord Trustees' cowpen at
Old Ebenezer and have again offered to sell it to our congregation and it took a long time for them to come to a proper decision and contract.[2] A large part of our people's and inhabitants'
welfare demands that this cowpen not come into strange hands
because they would not only carry off a large part of our cattle,
which are scattered here and there, but also spoil and very much
reduce the pasturage. Praise be to God, who has now helped us
in this matter!

God has also granted the benefaction that the gentlemen of
the Council have willingly ceded us the ironwork for a new sawmill that is to be built here, for otherwise it would have gradually
spoiled in the storehouse in Savannah. It weighs more than a
thousand pounds. The gentlemen of the Council have also approved the help they promised for completing the ten machines
for spinning off the silk, the building of ten huts for poor people, and the L 2 Sterling for every young female who will learn
silk spinning in this year. However, I shall not need any money
from them now because our congregation will owe them a great
sum for the said Trustees' cowpen. This will all be paid off gradually partly by the just mentioned encouragements from the
Lord Trustees, partly with our expected silk, partly with boards
for the public buildings in Savannah, and partly with beef,
which is readily bought in Savannah.

It is not by chance that our miraculous God has let these blessings I have reported of the cowpen, the iron work for a new sawmill, and the encouragements for silkmaking, come to us at this
time, since it is the anniversary of our arrival in this country, after we suffered many trials for two years in Old Ebenezer and
were removed to this spot on our pilgrimage. I am coming home
with the words of Hebrews 11:5-6, which are to be my text at our
Memorial and Thanksgiving Festival, and with the words of the
exordium, Psalms 116:7-9. How much good we can still hope
for!

Sunday, the 11th of March. Our servants at the mill (two industrious and Christian young married people) almost lost their
lives a few days ago, as I was told after my return. After finishing
their work, they wished to eat a soup for supper, which the wife

herself had prepared. Because it was too hot for the husband, she put it in the window. We do not know whether something poisonous fell into it or whether it had previously been in the water or in the food; but they must have eaten something poisonous, because both of them had such a terrible attack of vomiting all night long that they saw almost nothing before them but death. However, God blessed the medications and soon gave the husband his health and strength back again. The wife's recovery, however, was slower, but she is now out of danger. In Savannah a friend told me that I should warn our inhabitants against the wild honey that is found in hollow trees in the forest. Recently a Negro brought some to his master's plantation not far from Savannah, and all the occupants of the house became sick from it. A child that had eaten rather much of it swelled up and died before the doctor could arrive from nearby.

Monday, the 12th of March. Sixteen years ago today we who belong to the first Salzburger transport came ashore in Savannah after withstanding the sea voyage; and we began to live in huts like the patriarchs and the folk whom the Lord redeemed from Egypt and from oppression with His mighty arm. Already a week ago yesterday, on Invocavit Sunday, I announced to the congregation that our Memorial and Thanksgiving Festival was to be held this Monday. Yesterday after the morning sermon I not only announced this festival we were to celebrate once but also told our parishioners how fitting and useful it would be if both the townsfolk as well as those who dwell on the plantations would attend our public prayer hour, which is to be held again by day for the first time now that the days are getting longer. This occurred, and many people prayed and sang with us this time.

Because various newcomers have come to our place since the last Memorial and Thanksgiving Festival, I briefly explained to them before the prayer the occasion and purpose, as well as its proper and God-pleasing celebration; and I encouraged them to prayer and the praise of God. God granted us His word abundantly both this morning and this afternoon; and the parishioners gathered in a large number to hear it. My heart was afflicted and somewhat disquieted and depressed by an unpleaant report that I had to hear yesterday evening and in more detail this morning; but, during the preaching of His word from Psalms 116:7-9 and Hebrews 13:5-6, God so roused my spirits that I must praise His kindness for it. Yesterday during the afternoon divine service two of our unmarried servants ran away and traveled to Purysburg in a stolen boat with the purpose of going further into the land. They are, like the former renegades, two baker assistants, who had it good with their householders and whom no one would have expected to run away. Two other servants helped them in this; indeed, had there been room in the little boat, one of them would have run away, too.

Tuesday, the 13th of March. Yesterday evening after the repetition hour news came here that the runaway servants had been caught in Purysburg and brought back here. I thank God that Mr. Meyer is still holding the office of judge at our place. If we must proceed with the punishment of wickedness, this does not harmonize with my evangelical office, indeed, it would draw much criticism. He has sent these two renegades, along with their instigator, to the authorities in Savannah, who will proceed with them according to the laws of the country (which are rather lenient in this regard).

Other German people in this country are so wicked that they can't easily stand the punishment of a German, even if they can stand seeing an Englishman punished. In their work, intercourse with their neighbors, and dissolute life, their behavior is of such a kind that they have a bad odor among the Englishmen, who are their benefactors; and they have made themselves unworthy of the great affection of the Lord Trustees. I, too, have little love for them; therefore, I will hardly make any more effort to further the coming of redemptioners or other Germans into this country. To be sure, I will still serve them with my office, but I will be careful not to let myself be used for their worldly purposes and intentions. For I know from much experience that we are subject to unkind judgments and calumny if we do not approve of their wicked obstinacy and cannot agree with their wicked nature. The Court Chaplain /Ziegenhagen/ does much good for them in London, but (as I have learned here) it is not well applied.

Some people have learned hypocrisy and smooth words here, but this is often revealed here. Much good in spiritual and physical matters has been done for our indentured servants not only in London and on the sea voyage, but also since they have been with us; yet we find little gratitude in them. To be sure, they are moderating their juvenile pranks and behavior; yet, I still know no one who has accepted the word of God for his conversion and improvement. I have had the salvation of their souls as the purpose of my association with them and attitude towards them from the first hour that they arrive in Savannah; and for this reason I have overlooked much and have assigned them to Christian-minded and substantial householders, but I have had little joy from them.

Wednesday, the 14th of March. After the misery I had during the past two days, our dear God has again comforted me and raised me up. Our schoolchildren, especially the little ones, have given me much pleasure by the things I have seen and what I have heard of them; and I have been planning to give them a pleasure in return and to give them and their mothers an occasion to praise the Lord. For that reason a short time ago I bought some neckerchief cloth in Savannah at a moderate price, which I and my dear colleague would have gladly distributed to them directly after the Memorial and Thanksgiving Celebration, that is, yesterday; but my own business and also the disquiet with the servants did not allow it. It took place today with blessing and joy both in town and on the plantations.

First they recited the verses we had contemplated on Sunday and at our festival, and I recited to them the beautiful words from 2 John 4[3] with the application that so far the girls had pleased me more with their good behavior than the boys had and that I, therefore, wished now to make them a pleasure in return by giving them a neckcloth. We would also think of the boys if we saw improvement in them at school, in church, and on their way home. With the gift, every little girl also received a lesson and an admonition. We have thirty-two girls in the two schools; and all of these received a gift, which amounted to thirty-three shillings Sterling. After this pleasure with the children, I had another at the consecration of a new house below the mill where various neighbors and other Christian people had gathered.

Friday, the 16th of March. Yesterday morning I was called to

Abercorn to baptize a German child. I let the German people living in the neighborhood know that I wished to preach the word of God to them and to sing and pray with them if they could assemble at a designated place between our glebe land, Abercorn, and the German people's plantations; and this they gladly did. The sermon was about the words "Let your conversation be without covetousness; and be content with . . . " etc. "What should a man do . . . ?"[4] In this hut there was also a sick Catholic man, who considered it a great blessing of God to hear the word of God. He thanked me for my visit and encouragement with weeping eyes; and he acknowledged that this physical sickness was redounding to the health of his soul. I notice no popish dogma in him even though he does not declare himself for us publicly.

Sunday, the 18th of March. We are having a very pleasant and at the same time fruitful spring. Even though the rain seems to have been lacking so far, we still see no lack in the trees and other plants. This may be the result of the snow, by which the earth was saturated several times. To judge by appearances, provided God gives His blessing to our work, much silk will be made this year because the mulberry trees are now in fuller leaf than we have ever observed before. The industry that nearly all of our inhabitants are showing in the useful and easy work is admirable. It is a pity that I have not yet received from the Lord Trustees an answer to my letter concerning the price of silk, as Mr. Verelst promised in his last letter. Also, cauldrons for the spinning off should have been sent, but our people are still waiting for them.[5]

Monday, the 19th of March. Young Mrs. N. fears that she will soon be a widow and that her three little children will be orphans; because her husband has contracted an apparently dangerous sickness through immoderate work. Both marriage partners are so keen about work more through avarice than through necessity, and they have raised so many crops that their health could not possibly have held out in the long run. I hope that God will let this chastisement redound to the salvation of their souls.

The pious widower, Steiner, has ceded the plantation he has had so far to his neighbor; and with the money he received he has bought another, which he considers better and more fertile.

He has already settled himself nicely on it, and this morning he had his house consecrated with God's word and prayer. His physical strength has greatly decreased, and his three boys are still small and weak. As a result, they cannot yet help him much in the field and in his housekeeping and husbandry.[6] He is patient and content with God's guidance.

Wednesday, the 21st of March. One of the most prominent inhabitants of Purysburg informed me in a letter that the governor of Carolina is withdrawing the subsidy on silk manufacture. Therefore, an Italian is selling his cocoons at a very low price and will even move away. Since no one now understands how to spin off the silk, I have been asked to recommend a skillful and practiced woman from our place. However much I would like to help my neighbor, I am in no hurry to let myself be used for such things by strange people. Yet, it is always the custom of both prominent and simple people of this and the neighboring colony to write to me in all sorts of secular matters, since there is no one else present who is willing to take on common things for the good of the congregation. To be sure, in answering letters and in other such matters I make great haste, yet it still takes a lot of time because of their complexity. I beg God, and hope in His mercy in Christ, that He will not let my actual spiritual office be harmed by such numerous external matters that are piled up on me.

N.N. has allowed her servant (a rather dissolute person) to carry on all sorts of superstitions with disgraceful misuse of the name of God in order to free her cattle from the evil that other wicked people are supposed to have done to them; and in the whole domestic economy.

This her son has helped loyally both with her and his own cattle. Indeed, they are so blinded that they firmly believe that their cows have been helped by this miserable man and his superstitious amulets and ceremonies, which are almost like magic. And now they think they are enjoying the profit from it in their milk and butter. Indeed, they say that their stalls have been made so safe that no wicked person or witch can come in and harm the cattle as long as they stand on that place. Today I investigated and described this godless carrying-on, by which the entire congregation has been vexed; and I made a beginning toward punishing it by withdrawing certain benefactions which the mother and son have enjoyed and should continue to enjoy. This will soon be proclaimed in the community and will somewhat avert the vexation.

At present they do not recognize the wrong but deem their proceedings to be innocent and ascribe the improvement of their cattle to this sinful art and to the blessing of God, which He has placed on it.[7] In this I look on them with great pity, but also with great disgust. As long as they will not bring the fruit of repentance, I do not look on them as members of the Christian community. The godless servant is a good friend of a very wicked and shameless young hunter, who wished to settle in our region but moved to Purysburg. He is said to be full of such wicked arts. What miserable people come into this land!

Thursday, the 22nd of March. Some of the women on the plantations have requested me to hold a singing lesson twice every week and to teach them the melodies in our hymnal that they do not know, just as was done a few years ago in town. The beginning of this so useful and for me pleasant practice was made this morning on the plantation of the pious widow /Maria/ Bacher. To be sure, we are actually holding a singing lesson; but we pray and praise God at the beginning and the end of the lesson. Some errors have gradually been sneaking into the melodies we have formerly learned; and, if we did not prevent them in such private singing lessons, they would finally become general and habitual. May God be pleased with this practice for the sake of Christ!

The orphanage[8] is now being repaired from the ground up, or rather rebuilt; and meanwhile Kalcher and his family have had to move into an adjacent building. She told me that, in her first prayer outside of the orphanage, God had forcefully reminded her of all the major benefactions that had occurred to her and many other living and now deceased people in it and that this had aroused her to His hearty praise. Among the special blessings of the Lord she counts the special merciful assistance of the Lord in her threefold very dangerous births, the frequent public contemplations of the divine word conducted in the orphanage, the communal prayer, the safe birth of several children, and the blessed departure of some believing people from this world, etc. Because of the many spiritual and physical blessings she has received she has a great love for this house so that she often implores our dear God to let her live there until she is carried from there to the churchyard.

This new building will be a third shorter and narrower than the previous one was; but it will also be all the higher, namely, with two stories. Therefore, it will also be more impressive and spacious that the old orphanage was. A part of it is destined for holding school; and a parlor and chamber along with the attached kitchen will be used by Kalcher for his family. The remaining room will be at the service of the widows and orphans, and also of the sick, who will consider it a blessing to live, work, and enjoy necessary care in it. Unless the greatest necessity drives them to it, they do not respect the orphanage and prefer to get along miserably in their own homes. Until now the widows and orphans outside of the orphanage have cost me £9 Sterling.

Friday, the 23rd of March. N. must often feel bitter pangs of conscience for having been disobedient and unkind towards her father even in his last sickness ten years ago. Some time ago she converted righteously to God, and we notice in all her actions that it is her earnest purpose to be saved. She does not think it by chance, but a just chastisement of God, that nearly all her children have been taken away from her by temporal death. In the case of her brother, she used God as a tool to bring him out of his wild and disorderly life and to our place. My conversation and prayer with her was very pleasant and blessed for me. N.N.'s wife is being visited rather severely by our dear God with external and internal sufferings; yet she has had no harm, but only profit, from it, as we can now recognize from her confessions and Christian behavior. She has been so purified in this furnace of misery and has so increased in her recognition and experience of Christianity, and, to be sure, in a short time, that I marveled and rejoiced at it when I spent a short time in conversation and prayer with her before the countenance of the Lord.

Sunday, the 25th of March. In this month we have had very dry and partially hot weather, and the parched soil has greatly needed a penetrating rain. Yesterday toward evening it thundered a little; and some black clouds came from the west, which brought us rain and hailstones on two occasions. Since then it has again become as cool as autumn air is accustomed to be. Even though there was little rain, it was still a blessing for which we thanked God. Some of the hailstones were the size of a walnut; however, because not many of them fell, they probably did no damage to the green rye and wheat in the fields.

Monday, the 26th of March. My dear colleague and I have often been told that there is a good and convenient opportunity at the lower part of our plantations to build a new sawmill. We consider this very important because we look upon such establishments as a means by which we can provide our inhabitants with a good service. Therefore, several weeks ago, my dear colleague inspected the place with our two best builders. Today I traveled there with him and the two said men, and, to be sure, not without profit and joy at God's gracious care, which is gradually being revealed to us in external matters. Thus providence has settled our dear Salzburgers at a place that has a noticeable advantage over the most fertile areas of this country, even if it is not recognized by everyone. At this place there is right desirable opportunity to build a durable sawmill, which in this country is a rare, useful, and productive work and which must not be judged according to the circumstances in Germany.

The following are the reasons that our sawmill, which is now in a very good condition, has not contributed much more than the support of all the mills: All of our mills, consequently also the sawmill, stand on an arm of the Savannah River and have had to be fortified at great expense against the tearing of the current and because of the frequent dangerous inundations. The repairs, which are very considerable, require extensive expense every year, even if not as much now as in the early years. Only one gristmill runs almost all year. On the other hand, the other gristmill, as also the sawmill and barley-stamp, must stand still for several months in summer when the water in the river is too low. Indeed, even if they always ran, the grain that is brought to the mill from here and other places would not suffice to give the miller steady work, because even under present conditions it must often stand idle for many days and nights. Nevertheless, these works must be kept in shape even if they do not run constantly and earn something.

If there were more people in the country and if more of them would plant European crops, then the income from the gristmills, as from the rice-stamp, would be considerably increased. For a little more than a year we have noticed a remarkable increase in the income from the sawmill, which we wish to apply to the building of a new sawmill, since God himself is ordaining it and leading us to it. We can promise ourselves more advantages and stronger returns here than from the one we now have. For, 1) the gentleman of the Council will cede us the iron work gratis; provided the Lord Trustees are willing; and the Lord Trustees will more likely be pleased than to oppose having their sawmill, which is lying idle here, be of use to the colony. A few weeks ago I wrote to Mr. Verelst about it.

2) This sawmill will not be built on an arm of the Savannah River, where great expenses are required to strengthen it against danger. Rather it will be built on a little river that comes out of the country and flows into the Mill River, where we fear no tearing current and no inundation. We can now have it built by our own people and, indeed, much more cheaply than then when we had to send for a strange builder, to whom I had to pay £ 10 Sterling per month and thus £ 30 all at once in a quarter year. This is to say nothing of what was paid to the mathemetician and engineer Mr. Avery, who had laid a durable foundation. An unexpected death ended the mill construction he had begun.

3) There is a countless number of mature pine trees in the area of the mill that is to be constructed, and they can be brought to the mill easily from all directions, because the empty wagons ride uphill from the mill and return downhill loaded with wood. The boards can be brought a short way by land carriage and, at high water, in little rafts to and on the Mill River, and afterwards in larger rafts to Savannah and to the ships (as has been done so far). This place is situated about a half an hour from our present mills; consequently, our inhabitants will have an opportunity to earn something to facilitate their economy both from constructing the mill and from chopping and from bringing in the logs, and later with rafting the boards. This has always been one of our purposes in undertaking such public works. We hope, however, that at the same time it will bring in so much to the congregation that the communal expenses for it will be, if not entirely covered, at least greatly decreased. We are not the least bit

worried about the sale of our boards, not even if we had ten saw-mills (as a merchant from Port Royal said to me recently) that ran day and night. So far, we have been unable to saw as many boards as there are hands reaching for them. Not only the wood, but also the very accurate cut give the boards from our place an ad-vantage over all others. The merchants who transport them to the English and French in the West Indies, admit this themselves.

From the following I think our friends in Europe will be able to see the difference between here and in Europe in regard to the sawmill. The following price is paid gladly and for cash money for the boards we bring down, either on the water or on the landing there: hundred feet

1	inch	5 shilling	pence
1 and 1/4	"	5	"	6
1 and 1/2	"	6	"	–
2	"	7	"	–

Those men who take them down in rafts receive six shillings for a thousand feet; and, because they take 10,000 feet or more each time, two men with two helpers (since 10,000 board feet require four men) earn sixty shillings or three pounds in four days, and they must spend two nights on the water. They travel with the ebb and remain still during the flood.[9] The money other people earn at the mill is such a sum every year that one must marvel. If he wishes to be industrious, the sawmiller alone can earn £2 Sterling every week (that is, in six days, since he does not saw at night). For this reason industrious and knowledgeable people are looking forward to the mill we are planning. In other places in Europe sawmills are sometimes harmful for a country be-cause they consume much wood and spoil the forest, but we do not have to worry about that here. The sawmill we are to build will be set in a region where our plantations end and where nothing can be seen far and wide but dry sandy pine forests. Consequently, no plantations can be set here, so the plentious, beautiful wood would be of no use to anybody, unless it were made useful for the entire community, as previously mentioned, through the help of a sawmill.

Wednesday, the 28th of March. The hailstones of a few days ago did more damage than we expected, but we must ascribe it to divine goodness that it was not even greater. In the middle part of our plantation they fell in great quantity, and some were as large as chicken eggs. The peas, and the rye that had formed ears too soon, were beaten almost down to the ground, and a great many leaves were knocked from the mulberry and other trees. After that the air became very cold, windy, and dry both by day and by night. We greatly need rain, for which we are humbly invoking God, the Source of all gifts. The people who live in town are now showing a great new desire to learn the new melodies and hymns from our hymnbook. This pleases me greatly and is encouraging me to equal diligence. Neither the time nor my strength would allow me to assign an hour in the day or night for it; and therefore for this practice I will apply the two hours on Tuesdays and Fridays that were formerly dedicated to the public prayer hours. A beginning of this was made yesterday evening (Praise be to God, to our edification and enjoyment).

Friday, the 30th of March. I see it as a testimony of divine paternal care for us that we have received at our place the three Schubdrein brothers who came to this country with the last servants and redeemed themselves in Savannah with our help.[10] They have already given several proofs of their industry and honesty among us; they are lovers of the divine word, live quiet and Christian lives, are domestic and contented, and show a very tender love to one another. They are now building the school and orphanage under one roof; and, as soon as they are through here, various other jobs are waiting for them. No one can be found for work from our own carpenters (most of whom do not understand very much); they all have their own homesteads and are without servants. Three of them are among those who bought the cowpen or cattle ranch from the Lord Trustees for the congregation and are therefore involved in much business.

It is no little harm that we do not have enough capable carpenters at our place. We do not wish to have any of them sent expressly from Germany; for such people are too proud of their profession and make great pretensions. For some time now I have promised our young people £2 Sterling, if they would take up a trade and settle amongst us.

After our congregation has me buy the said cowpen or cattle ranch of the Lord Trustees, it will furnish many small and large hides, some of which will spoil and some of which will be sent to Savannah if no one amongst us learns how to tan. A shoemaker here practices this work, but he understands it too little. I have no love for his bungling because he sins through it. If such a craftsman well understood his craft and showed proper industry, he could do a lot of good here for himself and his neighbor. The fresh or raw hides here are exceptionally cheap, also the chalk; there is a quantity of bark from red oaks here in the neighborhood gratis. There would be no lack of market for the leather, because it is sent to other colonies. Fish oil in some quantity is also inexpensive. Boards for vats and whatever else is demanded for establishing a tannery can be had amongst us easily and cheaply. Also, my practical help will not be lacking. The only thing lacking is a skillful and willing man who would and should learn tanning from a Frenchman in Purysburg, who is willing to come here for a certain amount of money.

APRIL

Sunday, the 1st of April. May God be heartily and humbly praised for having again let us end another month happily and begin a new one with health and blessing! Not only we ministers and teachers in the churches and schools, but also our parishioners, both grownups and children (with very few exceptions), have been hale and hearty for the past three months of this year; and our arrangements, institutions, and occupations have proceeded without hindrance to the noticeable advantage of the community. I especially rejoiced when my dear colleague told me that God had right noticeably blessed the income from our gristmills and sawmills and thereby given many people in our community a good chance to earn money and also enabled us to set some money aside for constructing a new sawmill.

The excellent fir trees, with which large districts are filled, would stand there entirely useless if they could not be made into boards. Few places in Germany have any that are so beautiful and long right to their tops. They also have tender veins or yearly growths (as our people call them) and are very durable, as far as the heartwood is concerned.[1]

After completing her years of service, the daughter of a de-

ceased widow has come to our place at the request of her dying
mother to have herself educated here. This she now recognizes
not as a burden but as a blessing. She has good reason for this,
for much spiritual and physical good has been done for her here
in the house of my dear colleague (in which her mother died).
She has been instructed as loyally as possible both by him and by
me and prepared for Holy Communion. Because she previously
served the President,[2] she is now being requested by another
person in authority, whose wife would take good care of her. I
am pleased that she does not wish to change her place without
God and her superiors. Provided she remains loyal to the grace
she has received, she can still become a useful tool for the glory
of God. To be sure, I would prefer it if only our dear God would
enable her to remain at our place; but meanwhile we must move
cautiously.

Monday, the 2nd of April. Yesterday our dear God began to
fulfill our desire for a fruiful rain; today it rained more and even
more penetratingly. God be praised for this blessing! Because of
the great heat of the sun and the dry wind, the gardens and
fields have been very parched and dry; and the growth of the
leaves for fodder for the silkworms has also been held up. I was
summoned to Savannah for today with the seven men who have
bought the Lord Trustees' cattle for themselves and the community in order to discuss this important matter thoroughly and to
sign a contract. God blessed this journey to the strengthening of
my health, even though the rain drenched us.

Friday, the 6th of April. Both the extensive business with the
President and his Assistants and the weather were to blame that I
could not return home before this morning. The gentlemen of
the Council showed me and our people every conceivable kindness and cleared away everything that could possibly have been
harmful or a hindrance to them in the right use of the cowpen
they had bought, and they were as kind as we could have hoped
for in every way. God very clearly revealed the footsteps of His
fatherly care in that, and I would be very disappointed if the
members of the community were blind or ungrateful for it. I
plan to report the details in letters. The German people behind
Abercorn who were in Savannah also had some spiritual and
physical profit from my humble services.

Saturday, the 7th of April. A German man behind Abercorn has been dangerously sick for a long time; and (as it seemed to me when I visited him a few weeks ago) he had some very good emotions. Now word has been brought to me that he has died. His wife requested me to come and hold a burial sermon for him. Unfortunately, I could not grant her wish because he died in his popish religion that he brought into the country with him. To be sure, he read and loved the Bible and also made use of Protestant books and public divine service; yet, he would not come over to the truth. After all, as I told the messenger, it is written, "For with the heart man believeth unto righteousness; and with the mouth confession is made unto salvation."[3] We cannot even agree to go such a long way to our co-religionists' funerals, which demands some expense and an entire day. It is enough for us to preach God's word occasionally on their own plantations and hold Holy Communion every three or four months and try to serve them here and in Savannah in their physical needs. I gave the messenger a beautiful book to take with him, namely, Senior Urlsperger's *Instruction for the Sick and Dying*, which they should use for their sick and at their funerals.[4]

Tuesday, the 10th of April. This morning a young Swiss called on me, who had come to our place yesterday from Congarees in Carolina. He told me that there was enough work at the said place but that there was no money and the workers had to accept goods, meat, cattle, or crops as pay. The soil is very good but does not lie on any convenient river and is a hundred and fifty English miles from Charleston. Since they cannot bring their crops to market in Charleston except by land, the profit is very small because of the transportation costs. The people there live far apart and are therefore well dispersed, almost each in his own wilderness. Things are said to look rather bad among them spiritually, but it seems that most of them are concerned more for good land and physical freedom than for the one thing that is necessary.

Friday, the 13th of April. Yesterday morning (as occurs on Maunday Thursday every year) we commemorated the establishment of Holy Communion in both churches and preached to the congregation the dogma of Holy Communion from 1 Corinthians 11:23 ff. Today we celebrated the memory of the life,

death, and burial of our dearest Savior in both the morning and
the afternoon; and we held Holy Communion with eighty-four
persons. In this nearly ended period of the Passion we have contemplated the story of the suffering and death of Christ from
evangelist Luke. May God grant us a lasting blessing from it!

Monday, the 16th of April. Yesterday and today Holy Easter
was celebrated according to the old calendar,[5] during which we
preached abundantly from God's word. Our dear Lord granted
us much strength in body and mind; and we hope that He, in
His goodness, will not let the sown seed of His word be in vain
and remain without fruit, since we have invoked Him for this
both publicly and privately. The wife of our schoolmaster
/Georg/ Meyer had to hold her Easter celebration on her sick-
bed. She is a true disciple of the Lord Jesus and very well acquainted with His cross and guidance. She attended Holy Communion on Good Friday with the congregation and did not let
her physical weakness prevent her. Our dear Savior so blessed its
trusting enjoyment in her soul that she was once again assured
of the gracious forgiveness of sins and of being a child of God
and of having hope of everlasting life. To be sure, she is very
weak in her body and at times full of pain; but she is strong of
mind and well content. She considers it a great blessing and a
gracious guidance of God that He has led her into the wilderness
of solitude and the cross, where He speaks to her in such a
friendly manner after He has brought her to a recognition of
and feeling for her sins and to a trust in her Savior.

Wednesday, the 18th of April. Yesterday morning I traveled to
the German people behind Abercorn at their request and
preached the word of God to them in the morning and afternoon, held Holy Communion, and married a couple. The bridegroom is a sincerely pious person, who was converted righteously to God during his years of service at our place and who,
through God's gracious providence, received a very fruitful and
very well situated plantation in the said area behind Abercorn.
He married an orphan from our community, the late Klocker's
oldest daughter /Gertraut/, who is well provided for with this
young person. The inhabitants of Abercorn and of this only now
settled beautiful region that they call Goshen have shown great
joy that they can be served with the word of God, holy baptism,

and Holy Communion at their place, since we are not far away. They follow, and I hope that God will gather a little flock here that will serve Him in spirit and in truth and give a good example to other co-religionists.

Their industry in building huts and in cultivating, and also in cattle raising, is, to be sure, very great; but I am afraid they will not keep it up long. Therefore, I admonish them to the *festina lente*[6] according to the example of our inhabitants. During the first years the work in the great summer heat, the extraordinary sweating and the drinking of much water do not appear to hurt them especially; but gradually their blood becomes so thin and weak that one can see in their faces the harm they have done to themselves.[7] In a few years some of them have lost all their strength and are now incapable of hard work. These new colonists are poorer than our people and are bad off when first establishing themselves. What the Lord Trustees allow them does not go very far.

Thursday, the 19th of April. Yesterday I received a letter from Col. Stephens, in which he advised me that two more German people had absconded, one from him and the other from another magistrate. Someone was sent after them, but it seldom happens that such renegades are found because among the German people in this colony and in Carolina they have people nearby who support and hide them. Once they are there, there are a thousand difficulties in getting them back again. Of the servants of the last transport[8] who remained in and near Savannah, all have run away but two, who were on their way but were caught and brought back. Those who have wives and children can not get away so easily, otherwise they would probably go away, too. If I did not know how well our and other servants are kept in this colony and how much more care they enjoy than those in Carolina, this wickedness and ingratitude would not trouble me so much. Our single servants are not to be trusted either, even though they have been outwardly quiet and withdrawn since the punishment of the last three renegades, who were arrested in Purysburg.

There has fallen to me a large family of nine persons, namely, four adults and five small children,[9] all of whom will be freed with their parents.[10] Now I know from experience what a burden and loss it is to have such people in service. There is almost as great a difference between their service and work and that of the Salzburgers as between day and night. Therefore, a weak Salzburger hired-hand or maid is better and more useful than two strong ones of the kind that have come to us.

For some time our inhabitants have put their faith in silkmaking and have therefore made every possible effort, and they are still doing it with amazing industry. It appears, however, that the Lord Trustees have no means to encourage this useful matter further; and, consequently, I fear that this activity will fail. God still liveth: "Soul, why art thou daunted?"[11]

It is no wonder if our dear inhabitants let themselves be persuaded in their difficult circumstances to acquire Negroes, if only their means will allow it. A good Negro costs at least 30 £ Sterling, who among us could raise such a sum? No one would easily let himself borrow. I recently revealed my scruples to the Council in Savannah regarding the purchase and holding of Negro slaves; and I was assured that they were eternal slaves in their own land and that they lived under great tyranny and difficult circumstances and were legally bought and sold. Therefore Christians should feel no more scruples in buying them or possessing them than the Patriarchs and even Philemon himself in the New Testament, to whom St. Paul sent back the servant Onesimus and demanded not his emancipation but just good treatment. They also have an opportunity to come to a recognition of Christ.

Sunday, the 22nd of April. There is now a very great and almost unbearable heat. It may have rained a couple of times at our place in the past week, but few drops fell on our plantations. Therefore, things look pretty bad for the European grains,[12] which have had almost no penetrating rain for more than two months. Yesterday evening a very strong wind arose from the west that rushed up as if it would bring a strong rain with it, and at the same time it was pitch-black dark. But it left without any rain.

Wednesday, the 25th of April. Several months ago the Evangelical Lutheran people at Congarees in South Carolina (which newly settled place they also call Saxe Gotha) asked me to come to them and serve them with the holy word and with Holy Communion. I have sent them books for adults and children, and at the same time I have written that my circumstances did not allow such a long journey. Now again I have received a letter in which they repeat the same request, and they add that I should help them get a church and minister. They now make up a congregation of two hundred and eighty souls[13] who could all go to a church if it were built in the middle of their surrounding plantations. The Reformed had received 500 £ Carolina money (which amounts to somewhat more than 500 guilders) from the government for building a church, but no one wished to help the Lutherans if I would not do it.

A couple of families have moved from here to there, who could have supported themselves well here; afterwards three grown boys were seduced from their service and two servants ran away, all of whom are being sheltered in Congarees. The inhabitants there (as a minister from Carolina once wrote me) live together in a brutish way and respect their Reformed minister very little. I have no heart for these people. If they were really concerned about God's word, then those who went away from here would have remained with us, and others would not have settled on such gathering places of evil people, since there is also good land and nourishment at other places. Their bellies are their God, as one must imagine of most German people in these regions. In this self-same letter I find that they have built and are building a gristmill and sawmill. Why should they not be able to build a meeting house if they are serious?

Friday, the 27th of April. A couple of years ago unknown Christian friends and benefactors of our community gave us a chest full of bound volumes of the late Ambrosius Wirth's *Confession and Communion Booklet*,[14] which has been reprinted in Nurnberg and of which every family has received a copy. We rightfully treasure this little booklet because of of its thorough examination of the heart according to the holy Ten Commandments and because of the scriptural duties of life and the accompanying Bible verses. Some young people, and some who came to our place after the distribution, have a great longing for this little book. Also, a favor would be done to other German people in this country with them, and perhaps through divine kindness they would be used as a means to bring them to a better recognition of themselves and of the way to salvation. Therefore, we would be very happy if some twenty-five of the said booklet could be sent here. They do not have to be donated, for one can well pay a couple of shillings for such a lovely book. Hymnals from Halle, Bibles, and Arndt's *Book of True Christianity* can not long be requested gratis. May our loving God repay our known and unknown benefactors for all the good they have done for us so far!

MAY

Tuesday, the 1st of May. At the end of last month, after a prolonged period of severe drought, God gave us several long-lasting rainstorms, one after another, for which we owe Him our most heartfelt praise and thanksgiving. Our barley and European peas shot up high and fast in this heat; they turned completely white and some have been harvested already. It remains to be seen what the wheat and rye harvests will yield. What God does is indeed well done![1]

N.N. and Mrs. Schweighoffer are the oldest people in our community; both are past sixty now and they have experienced a great many things. Mrs. Schweighoffer is a true disciple of our Lord Jesus, although taking care of her is probably not an easy task for her family; she is beset by many sinful weaknesses, which are due not only to her age and her many infirmities but are also rooted in her excessive love for her children.

N.N. has always been a mean and ill-tempered man; and even now, when he is practically facing death, he is giving no sign of genuine repentance. I talked to him sincerely and showed him from God's word the right path which he could take in order to escape impending damnation. I also admonished his family and encouraged them to read to him aloud, to pray with him, and to converse with him particularly on those spiritual matters which would prepare him for a blessed death.

Wednesday, the 2nd of May. Today Mr. Meyer resigned his office as judge, and I could not very well refuse to accept this obligation once again.[2] God will not fail me, nor forsake me. The office of judge is made especially difficult by the fact that those people in the community with whom one cannot agree become angry and embittered, to the detriment of the ministerial office. I believe God will guide me in this also! He will grant me understanding in all things, just as He has given me strength of body and mind so far, as well as a cheerful disposition, so that neither work, nor travel, nor other obligations have turned into a burden for me.

I well see that it is God's will that I shall manage our community in secular matters also; and I am, therefore, ready to accept this responsibility willingly and await His fatherly assistance and blessing. Our benefactors here in this country realize that appointing a judge in Europe to act as an agent for Ebenezer could be damaging to our community and not at all in its best interests.

Saturday, the 5th of May. I had to go to Savannah for a few days on private as well as communal business, and I returned safely yesterday evening. God be thanked! Various improvements have been made since Mr. Habersham joined the Council, and several ineffectual and tedious people have been dismissed from their public offices. I notified the Council of Mr. Meyer's resignation, and I was assured of the members' complete support and their willingness to advise me in public matters; and I have no reason to doubt their future assistance.

It pleases me in Savannah that the Germans living there are eager to hear God's word and that, when they learn that one of us preachers is in town, they arrange to come together for a meeting in a suitable house in the evenings after their work is done. This time I preached to them on the subject of Christ's dear words: "Blessed are the pure in heart".[3] Last Sunday, the second after Easter, my dear colleague, Mr. Lemke, was down there; and he preached God's word to them and held Holy Communion.

Tuesday, the 8th of May. Our schoolmaster on the plantations[4] is not only held in high esteem by his pious mistress; but at school he conducts himself also with so much eagerness and good faith that we are very satisfied with his services. I hope this young man will, in time, turn into a useful tool for God's glory. This afternoon a man who lives here asked me to give him permission to allow two Negroes or black slaves, whom he wished to hire, to work on his land on Sundays. He thought it was an emergency since he could get neither these Negroes nor white laborers to work in his fields on weekdays. I would have thought neither this man nor his wife capable of such an un-Christian request; it was encouraged by the bad practices of others who allow their Negroes to work for themselves and earn money on Sundays. Two other men, each of whom keeps a Negro, may also conform thus to the world.

This example makes it quite clear how some of our people here succumb to temptation as far as Negroes are concerned and how poorly some of the colonists follow the guidelines and the restrictions regarding Negroes as set down by the Lord Trustees. It is expressly stated that no one should permit his Negroes to work on Sundays; rather, they should be given the opportunity both in their masters' house as well as in their neighborhood to educate themselves towards an understanding of Christian religion.

Wednesday, the 9th of May. Today, at noon, a German arrived in our settlement and visited my home; he has been living in Pennsylvania for the past twenty years. He, his wife, and nine children traveled to Augusta, taking the longer route over land. He would like to settle there and build a sawmill; according to him, he has received permission in Savannah to do so. I asked him what his religion was and received the unexpected answer that his father had been a Lutheran schoolmaster in the Palatinate and that he himself adhered to no particular religion, but considered himself to be a Christian. Holy baptism, in his view, is not a sacrament but merely an empty ceremony. His children had not been baptized, he said, and he did not celebrate Sundays, but rather the Seventh Day. He was, however, unlike the English Seventh Day Adventists.

From what he told me I was able to convince him that he did indeed not adhere to a formal religion but that he was nevertheless a member of a sect. He behaved in quite an overbearing manner and, although in error, quoted a jumble of sources in order to prove himself correct; he believed our church to be confused and lacking in understanding. He could not stay long, and I was glad to see him depart. Judging from his view of religion, shared by others no doubt, Pennsylvania must be in a pitiful state indeed! May God help His servants![5]

Thursday, the 10th of May. An old Reformed widow has been visiting our settlement regularly and has attended the preaching of the divine word frequently and piously. Once again, she has arrived from Purysburg; and she assured me that her soul benefitted greatly from God's word in our sermons and prayer hours. I visited her, and she told me that she had resolved to talk to me regarding her soul's condition but was afraid she would be too ignorant for such a conversation because she was Reformed. I tried to put her at ease and asked her to come and see me frequently and to talk to me freely. For the past few years she has found herself troubled by frightening thoughts regarding her fate after death.

God has been sending us very good weather for some time now. Many praise God and point out that the European crops have turned out better than one could have expected or hoped for after the long and hard drought. Hail has done severe damage on some of the plantations; otherwise, the wheat and rye crop will be better and larger than in previous years, and there is no sign of mildew or rust.

Saturday, the 12th of May. The old widow I mentioned earlier visited me this morning in order to tell me of her spiritual problem, especially since she has to leave for home and be with her son on Monday. She has been raised in great ignorance; God, however, has led her to the realization of her sins and the recognition of her Savior since she suffered from various tribulations in her old age, and since she came into the home of a good and pious man who adheres to our religion.[6] Since that time she has, to be sure, worried rather badly about her soul's condition, but she also experienced some inspiration and consolation by the Holy Ghost.

She has a solid foundation in Christian matters and offers astonishing proof that her prayers are certainly being well received. I was quite impressed and edified by the naive manner in which she mentioned the blessings which my office has wrought in her soul and the simple way in which she told me of the good things which God had sent to her since her last husband's death. People like her are always amazed to see the abundant advantages, both spiritual and physical, which God sends us when they come to visit us and to witness our children's skill at answering questions when they take part in our preaching of the divine word and our prayer hours and when they learn that all of our efforts are intended for the best of our community.

Monday, the 14th of May. For the past twenty-four hours we have had heavy rains, but without thunderstorms. Afterwards, yesterday, it was warm and dry again; and the weather was quite suitable for harvesting the European crops.

N.'s family[7] is one of the most disorderly among us; it seems these people may come to a bad end and be a proper warning for the rest of us. The old man has been sick for some time now, but he still clings to his habitual worldly concerns. I visit him frequently, instruct him in the order of salvation, and explain it to him clearly, using God's word. At the same time I try to impress upon his mind the most obvious lessons contained in God's word in order to inspire him and to awaken his soul; yet I notice very little improvement. Approximately half a year ago he married a sickly, but very pious woman, who is more than willing to aid in saving his soul. However, he has but little esteem for her and does not pay much attention to what she has to say. His oldest daughter used to live in our settlement and was widowed here; she left, after receiving a great deal of assistance and support from us, and moved to S. in order to get married again; she did not prosper.

The oldest son still lives here, a miserable creature both spiritually and physically. One of his younger brothers suffers from dropsy, and the next younger brother is also a useless and corrupt man, who will probably not amount to anything. One of the daughters is still unmarried; and, of all of them, she is least ignorant of God, of His counsel, and of human salvation. She is not without any talent either, but her mind is turned towards wordly matters and, in this, she follows the steps of her parents and siblings. I pity them all. The best I can say of them is that, so far, all are attending faithfully our preaching of the divine word; and they still continue to read it and to listen to it. Perhaps our miraculous Lord will work a change of heart in one or more of them, either in health or sickness.

Wednesday, the 16th of May. The German settlers of Goshen (a rather fertile and easily accessible area near Abercorn) like me to visit now and then and to preach God's word to them. Today the fine weather made it convenient for me to go there; in God's name I made the trip and preached to them on last Sunday's gospel, Dominica Cantate, dealing with God's fine spirit and its effects on grace. Most Christians, unfortunately, are blind and ignorant of this most important teaching, and this is very much to their disadvantage; a fact I was able to demonstrate by quoting Bible verses and passages from the catechism. If our dear God continues to dignify me by letting me preach His word to these German people, to which I am sincerely inclined but from which I am often hindered by the remoteness of the place and by my many tasks in our congregation, then I intend to choose our little church catechism as the text on which to base our contemplation, about which I am fond of preaching.

Some people are prejudiced against accepting both the truth and an honest Christianity. I believe, however, they can be convinced, by quoting from the catechism, that more than lip-service, pretense, or meaningless conformity, such as just going to church or practicing religion superficially, is necessary for being a true Christian. A young couple, to the annoyance of their neighbors, had been quarreling a great deal. After my sermon I asked them to come to the glebe land at Goshen and tried to reconcile them. Our merciful God saved me from great danger on my trip back, just as He had done already several times during my stay in this country in the past. O soul, never forget this!

Thursday, the 17th of May. I got news that Mrs. Waldhauer, the former widow Graniwetter, and her only little daughter are dangerously ill, so I went to visit them this morning on their plantation. I found them both recovered but unhappy and in distress. No doubt her old, stingy, ill-mannered husband is the reason for this. I spoke to both of them, but I do not know how much it will help. She herself is not entirely without blame either, although her husband's conduct encourages her transgressions. Oh, how rare is a true Christian unity between so-called Christian married couples! Our listeners often have an opportunity in the past to find confirmed by God's word the damage done by such marital discord as well as the resulting distress.

Sunday, the 20th of May. Several Englishmen arrived by boat today, this Rogate Sunday; I expected trouble and uproar, but nothing happened after all. It is a considerable blessing that English law protects the sanctity of Sundays so strictly and severely punishes misconduct on these days. Although in this country (and this may be true of other colonies, too) people generally do not observe these well-meant laws too closely, I can, however, point to the legal facts when dealing with disorderly people and, in case they persist in their troublemaking, I am empowered to enforce the law as a justice of the peace. So far, thank God, this has not been necessary.

Since Mr. Meyer resigned his office as Justice of the Peace and passed it off on me, I have re-read the English civil code, which is contained in the very thorough book *The Office and Authority of a Justice of Peace* by W. Welson. I translated the laws which pertain to our people into German and plan to read them aloud in our next community meeting. Whenever impudent people have to be kept in order, they like to refer to English freedom. However, in the future they will be confronted with the actual laws and will be forced to concede that English laws do not encourage undue licence and libertinism.

Monday, the 21st of May. Among the previously mentioned Englishmen were a man and his wife who asked me to baptize their child, which they had brought along. I did so today in Jerusalem Church. They chose three witnesses for the baptism from among our congregation; and, since the mother of the child knew German (several years ago she spent some time here with us and also with other German-speaking settlers), I held the baptismal service in German. The child was already eight months old because its parents had been unable to find a preacher at the place where they lived until now.

Tuesday, the 22nd of May. Recently, the official in charge of building churches in Savannah asked for a larger number of boards from our mill. These boards have to be of a certain length, thickness, and width; and we did not have in stock what was needed. Normally, the mill can not be operated around this time of the year because of the low level of the river water. We were worried that the building of the church might be delayed because of the lack of needed boards. God, however, brought it about that the water rose and the needed boards could be cut to specification within a few weeks and be sent to Savannah on five rafts today. Our community benefits greatly from both the gristmill and the sawmill, especially since the mill-dam was re-built so well and our costs for repeated repairs have gone down. For this we humbly praise God's mercy. We cannot cut as many boards as there are customers for them; therefore, we decided to build another sawmill along a little stream which is fed by a natural spring and thus does not depend on water from rainfall alone.

Wednesday, the 23rd of May. Young N. contracted a violent fever from too much labor and excessive heat. He paid no attention to his condition and continued to work hard unnecessarily despite a paroxism; and, as a consequence he is now so ill that he is unable to do any work at all. He still refuses to spare himself and will probably start to waste away and die before his time. As the saying goes: "Avarice is the root of all evil." He is obsessed with greed although he has considerable means. His wife, the former G. from B., cried and told me, in his presence, that it was her dearest wish that, as the result of a divine merciful plan, her husband would be restored to health and be transformed into a better man. Indeed, it seems that there is beginning to be a growth in the good he has received, heard, and perceived here from God's word and from his pious father-in-law, Mr. G. and also from Master Z., who loyally looked out for his soul. His wife also has a fine talent to urge the divine truth upon him in a plain and firm manner.

She considers this present misery, as well as other things in her marriage which did not turn out as well as expected, a well-deserved punishment for her sins. She regrets especially that she did not follow the advice of her old, pious father, but rather conformed to the world in a crude manner and ignored all his warnings. I also visited the widow Sanftleben, who lives by herself on her plantation. I found her both ailing and depressed; I consoled her and felt strengthened by divine merciful guidance. Both she and I recognized my encouragement to have been through divine providence. God has meant it well with her in her past and present tribulations and, by trying her, intends to lead her to His Son entirely and to guide her away from this world's wickedness and from her own previous sins. When the heart has mellowed, then the gospel can enter it more easily.

Thursday, the 24th of May. On several occasions in the past, after Rogate Sunday and shortly before Exaudi, our miraculous

God has granted us the joy of receiving letters and gifts from our benefactors and friends in Europe; this year the same has happened. Yesterday afternoon, on the road close by the plantations, I met a messenger from Savannah. He gave me two packages of letters, some addressed to me and some to Mr. Meyer; and he brought news that three chests containing things for us had arrived. I had known this already because a good friend in Savannah to whom the chests had been delivered for us had written to me. Only one of the letters was for me, the others were for Mr. Meyer and his brother /Johann Georg/, and for several other people here. This time, no mention was made in any of the letters concerning the contents of the three chests; we think, however, that the gifts are partly things from Augsburg and partly books and medicines from Halle. We sent our boat to Savannah immediately in order to bring back as much as it would hold safely.

The letter addressed to me was by dear Pastor Maier in Halle, one of our most esteemed patrons and benefactors. For the past several years I had had no word from him and I was therefore most pleased to hear of his restored health and of his work; and his kind, fatherly letter gave me much joy. I also read several passages from the very friendly and edifying letters sent to Mr. Meyer and by Dr. Ehrhard and Mr. Laminit and found myself greatly strengthened in faith and encouraged to praise God. They not only wish our welfare but are also trying to contribute to our well-being by advice and assistance. May our merciful God reward them generously for their goodness! Today we remembered and celebrated Christ's Ascension in both churches and, through the preaching of the gospel, our Lord granted us much blessing for our souls.

Friday, the 25th of May. Today our entire community (that is, its male members) assembled for a meeting and, together with those present, I instituted the following: all people living in and around town as well as those living on the plantations are going to be grouped into seven districts or sections, and for each district a headman was decreed, referred to by the common English title of "tythingman." The tythingmen will not be a burden but a help in keeping good order and in helping with questions of subsistence. They will confer with the people living in their districts, in order to discuss temporal matters with them, as well as practical matters concerning food production. I, in turn, will meet with the tythingmen in order to consider their ideas and to make suggestions of my own. Upon the recommendation of the headmen I will also try to give additional aid to those in need. Some of our people manage their households poorly and do not lead orderly lives; it will be easier now to know who those are and to set them right. Others are hard-working but too shy to tell me of their difficulties, and in these cases it will be possible for me to learn of their needs in order to assist them properly and in time. Widows also will now know to whom to appeal; and, if vagabonds or other disorderly people come here, it will be simple to find them and to encourage them to leave.

From now on, if there is something which I need to make known to our community, it will be faster and easier to do so through these seven men rather than call a meeting of the entire community. Holding a larger meeting is usually very inefficient, and it hardly ever fulfills its purpose; most people are too shy to voice their opinions publicly. My main goal in this new arrangement is to receive, from time to time, the suggestions of these seven sensible men as to how subsistance can be improved for those among us who are worn out and overworked, and also to encourage the tythingmen to be the tools for trying this or that new thing.

Today I read in the latest edition of the newspaper from Charleston how much in demand and consequently how expensive the following are: cypress wood itself and cypress boards, as well as shingles and barrel staves made from white and red oak. I knew that already from a letter I received from Charleston. The reason that these items, which are indispensable in the West Indies, are so rare and so expensive here is in part due to the fact that not many oaks and cypresses that are both of good quality and also growing close to the water are left. In the past much of this useful timber was not treated carefully and economically. On our large island adjoining the Mill River, however, the land is as fertile as the best land in Egypt and has many excellent trees suitable for making a variety of wooden goods in great quantity that can be transported to market conveniently by boat.

I therefore advised our people to plant less and to spend more

time making shingles, barrel-staves, and the like, which can be
done in the shade and does not require too much physical
strength, considering the greater chance of profit compared to
the hard work of farming in the heat of summer. Another benefit would be that our people would be able to acquire goods from
the West Indies despite our shortage of ready cash since traders
from there prefer exchanging goods to using money. Also, I
read to them from the aforementioned newspaper how cheap
rum, sugar, and syrup (which is used locally for brewing a tasty
beer) are right now in Charleston, whereas these same goods are
sold at much higher prices in Savannah.

Our people's health would not be undermined as much from
work of this sort, since they would earn more and also would
have something better to drink than mere water. They would be
able to recover some of their strength as can be seen from those
who did less of the strenuous and not very profitable labor on
their farms and who switched to some other useful work. Work
on those farms which are already running smoothly would not
have to be abandoned altogether; the cooler hours in the morning, during the day, and in the evening could be used, for instance from five o'clock to nine in the morning and from four
o'clock in the afternoon to seven in the evening. During the hottest hours of the day, people could make various kinds of
wooden goods in the shade of the forest where it is considerably
cooler. If they were to hold to such a schedule then they would
have an easier time of finding and keeping good farmhands and
servants. Nobody can earn enough by farming alone to afford a
servant's wages and keep, considering the amounts commonly
paid in our area, but it is easy the other way. If the trees growing
on the large island between the Mill Stream, Purysburg, and Abercorn, which are of a very good quality, were to be felled regularly and their wood used in the manner suggested above,
then, eventually, the land could be transformed into fertile pastures and fields which would have a great advantage over all
those on high ground.

In past years people did not want to clear this very fertile
stretch of land because of the many trees; they felt they could not
manage without hired workers. However, I was surprised that,
even after the arrival of fieldhands, no progress was made in this

area. It would be impossible to build houses or stables on this island because of occasional flooding from the Savannah River during the winter or in the spring when the snow melts in the mountains. However, it would be possible for people who wanted to cultivate this land to live in town and keep their cattle there and use the island, which is about half an hour away from town either by water or by land, for growing their hay and crops. One acre there could easily return more than three or four times as much as elsewhere and easily pay for the work. In this way our town could grow; there would be space enough for several hundred families to live and farm here.

Sunday, the 27th of May. Today we held Holy Communion for eighty people. Our loving God granted us His word richly in both sermons as well as in our repetition hour, and we were all edified. It seems that some servants attend our services as well in order to meditate and to provide for their souls. They listen to God's word regularly, attend prayer meetings, and strive for a more orderly life than they lived after they first arrived here. One of them, who is the wickedest among them, promised me today that he would improve his conduct; and he asked me, in case he reverted to his old improper ways, to admonish him with utmost severity. He regrets having mocked our faith in the past, for which he and another man are at present under censure by the church. He promised he would avoid this man's company in the future.

Wednesday, the 30th of May. Three days ago, several urgent public duties made it necessary for me to travel to Savannah. This afternoon, praised be God, I returned in good health and in good spirits, having come to no harm. We might have had some problems concerning the payment for several thousand feet of boards which a certain merchant who lives in our neighborhood received from our sawmill a few weeks ago. Luckily, I went to see him in Savannah shortly before his departure for the French West Indies. We have to tolerate such difficulties. We lack experienced and practical people; possibly our friends in Europe can not imagine this fully. Honest people who do not have their own personal interest first and foremost in mind are rare in this country. Some among us might be willing to be more practi-

cal but do not act accordingly; especially, most of our people lack
the necessary knowledge of the English language. In Savannah I
received several letters from the Lord Trustees, as well as from
Mr. Broughton, dear Mr. N., and Mr. Albinus. All the letters
were friendly and had a most pleasant content. I wish to make
the following notes concerning them:

1. All the letters were already five or six months old. I especially regret the delay in the letters from the Lord Trustees because the time for silk-making is past now, in which we could
have made a significant advance toward the improvement of our
silk manufacture. They had bought silk worms seeds from Italy;
however, the seeds hatched underway and all the young worms
perished. The Lord Trustees encourage our silk-making here in
our colony according to our people's wishes as well as those of
some merchants in London. The merchants in London had such
a high opinion of the quality of the silk made and spun here that
they are even going to petition Parliament for support of this
enterprise, which may turn out to be of considerable importance
since the Pope and other Catholic princes and nobles in Italy
have forbidden the export of silk.

The English have no areas better suited for silk-making than
Carolina and Georgia, and it would therefore be most regrett-
able if the people of these two colonies did not apply themselves
to it, especially since they are being assisted regularly by sound
advice and significant contributions. Most Europeans in this
country, however, have a very harmful way of thinking, which
one learns from the other, namely, that of expecting to get rich
quickly by working only a little. The wages of Europeans are not
proportionate to the work they do. Consequently, they will refuse even the most important task if it does not promise a certain
large daily profit. Therefore, if they will not renounce this evil
principle, the silk manufacture will not progress or prosper,
even if the Lord Trustees encourage and support it.

2. Our dear Mr. N. had been too sick to write to us for some
time. Now, however, to our great joy, this has occurred. He continues to be one of our most generous benefactors, as is evidenced by the gifts sent not only to us but also to my dear colleague, Mr. Meyer, my children, and our community. In

addition to that, he sent us a good quantity of inexpensive articles of clothing which we needed urgently, as well as some seeds.
Praised be God!

3. To be sure, no letters arrived from either our esteemed Senior Urlsperger or from Dr. Francke this time. The chest from
Halle with books and medicines arrived in good order, even if it
has not yet been brought here from the ship. Mr. Albinus wrote
to me that the ship from Hamburg which had carried our chest
had sunk but that our chest was saved. God be praised for His
merciful protection and for having kept our Fathers and benefactors in reasonable health and having restored others who
have been ailing in this or that way.

4. Mr. Broughton recommended a very frail man to me,
whom the Lord Trustees had sent to Savannah to serve as
schoolmaster. The man is a midget, however, and is indeed not
suited to teach the children. Besides, Mr. Broughton writes very
seldom and then only very little. I received a very kind and inspiring letter from our dear Mr. Whitefield. He holds Mr. Ziegenhagen, the court preacher, in very high esteem.

JUNE

Friday, the 1st of June. In yesterday's evening prayer hour, as
well as today during the meeting on the plantations, I started to
read from the important and very kind letters from Europe
which arrived recently. This may be very helpful for our people
here, with God's blessing, since nearly all that our most esteemed
benefactors and friends have written to us this time is intended
for our spiritual and physical well-being. This past spring, our
loving God blessed our people here in Ebenezer richly by dem-
onstrating to us His mercy and loving care, and I was greatly
moved in remembering His goodness.

This afternoon, the seven tythingmen of our community, who
live in the seven districts into which our town and settlement
were divided, came to my house for the first time. The purpose
was to review their duties with them and to outline my own intention to work for the spiritual and physical well-being of our
community, and, concerning this undertaking, to pray to God,
who wishes that all things in our community be done in an hon-

est manner and kept in good order. The men are sensible, god-fearing, and willing. May God anoint them with His spirit just like the elders in Israel and make them worthy of their task so that my own duties will be made easier by this arrangement and that our community will benefit from their service as far as our physical subsistance is concerned.

Sunday, the 2nd of June. This morning Mr. Thilo and his wife[1] received Holy Communion in private. God granted us a fine treasure of edification through His word, our prayer, and this holy act. Mr. Thilo has been ailing for the past several months and was bedridden for most of the time. It seems this sickness will benefit his soul greatly.

Today I watched with pleasure as the silk spun by our people was weighed in my house and part of it was packed into a fairly large crate, which will probably weigh nearly one hundred pounds. The *plus ultra*,[2] which our most esteemed Senior Urlsperger, filled with confidence and faith, called out to us a few years ago when he heard that silk had been produced in our orphanage for the first time, applies this year, too, since this year our silk manufacture was increased by a significant amount compared to previous years. If the houses of some of our people had been better equipped for silk-making, we could have produced even more than we actually did because our supply of mulberry leaves was abundant. During the first phase of spring the mulberry trees and their leaves were delayed in growth by a long-lasting period of drought and by cool nights so that most leaves matured only towards the end of our silk-making season here.

The aforementioned *plus ultra* brings to my mind a Spanish type of coin, called Pieces of Eight, which is used in this country for currency, and which bears the words *plus ultra* in its legend. Besides the Sola Bills issued by our Lord Trustees, our people are paid for their work and products, as well as for their silk, with Pieces of Eight. May God teach us anew and make us more aware of the fact that we depend on Him for all things and that our prosperity has to come from His grace and can continue only through His goodness. May He make us grateful for His bountiful blessing!

Sunday, the 3rd of June. Today, our loving God let us live to celebrate yet another feast of Holy Pentecost. Yesterday evening

a preparatory sermon on the beautiful third article of our catechism was held in Jerusalem Church. It taught us sufficiently the
nature of the good intention of the dear Elders who decreed that
this feast be celebrated by Christians everywhere and what God's
purpose is in allowing us to live and take part in this celebration
once again. May He allow all of us to be strengthened in our
faith through the power of the Holy Ghost! Today, during the
celebration of the feast, we contemplated the Gospel passage
containing the important and comforting words on spiritual
anointing, starting from John's beautiful words "And ye have
been anointed from the Holy One".[3] We clearly felt the Holy
Ghost's presence and grace, and its powerful effect, both
through God's word as well as through prayer. May He continue
to give us the strength to lead a godfearing life by sending us the
kind of divine enlightenment which we received by the spiritual
anointing through Holy Baptism in the past and now through
the gospel.

Tuesday, the 5th of June. Today I had to go to Savannah in
order to bring those things before the Council which had not
been taken care of the last time I was there. God made my journey down a safe one, and He sent me great edification and joy
during the evening prayer hour when we and the German people who had come to attend our meeting contemplated the Pentecostal verse "If ye then being evil".[4] Each time these people
learn that a minister from Ebenezer is going to be in their area,
they eagerly come in order to to hear God's word being
preached. Mr. Altherr from St. Gall is a great supporter of the
good: he willingly provides the room, the benches, and the
lights so that the evening prayer hours can be held in his house.
He also frequently assists us and our people from Ebenezer
whenever we or they come to Savannah; I feel I can justly compare him to that Gaius whom John mentions in his third epistle.

Sunday, the 9th of June. I had a second opportunity to hold an
evangelical sermon for our German people explaining the
aforementioned beautiful Pentecostal verse. I felt strongly our
merciful God's assistance to me while I spoke, and I pray He may
bless this verse. The German people know that our crate containing books arrived from Halle; some of them would like to
have Bibles and hymnbooks. However, it will no longer be possi-

ble for us to give those away as presents. In the past, it caused
considerable difficulties when we gave away books for free
among people in our own community; and it was therefore decided to sell the various Bibles, hymnals, readers, and *Treasure
Chests*[5] at a very low price to those who could afford to buy them.
Only those who are less affluent or those who are completely
destitute will either receive books as gifts or receive something
towards buying them.

In the event that many Germans in our area and in neighboring colonies are fond of such very useful and quite inexpensive
books, then I will have more sent to us from Halle. I wrote a
letter concerning this matter to Mr. Albinus several months ago.
There are various important reasons which moved us to settle
the question of the distribution of the books we received in this
manner. A pious German widow had gone to Charleston and
then returned to Savannah; she brought me the unpleasant but
true news that people there devoted themselves to opulent living
and behaved proudly. They no longer adhere to the divine
word, give other people cause for complaints, and have a rather
bad reputation. Those are people who were poor when they arrived in this country and who became well-to-do; it is said of
such men, "The property of fools will destroy them."[6]

The chest from Halle contains books and medicines; all arrived in very good condition. May our merciful God, for the sake
of Christ, repay these and other benefactions richly! May He
also bless our Lord Trustees with His grace for the support
which they have shown once again to our community; especially
their encouragement of our silk-making by donating money to
us as well as by sending the ten cauldrons to our community for
preparing the silk for the spinning. May He also make us grateful for this.

Monday, the 11th of June. This summer there was very little
rain in our area; but in other places, especially around Savannah
Town, it must have rained a lot, because the waterlevel in the
river keeps rising. Our crops are doing fine, however, despite
the weather; and we hope for a plentiful harvest with God's
blessing. If God were to punish the faithless and the disobedient
among the people living in Georgia and Carolina by sending
them a bad harvest (which, however, God be praised, has not

happened since we arrived in this country) then this would, indeed, be a severe punishment since our supplies of food from the previous year run out or are no longer fit for consumption just after the time of harvesting. Flour made from Indian corn does not store well at all, neither does Indian corn itself. After only a little while worms invade it and it becomes very bitter.

Tuesday, the 12th of June. Today, our loving God showed us anew, and much to our joy, the signs of His fatherly care for us here in Ebenezer. Through His blessing, our people were able to produce about one thousand pounds of cocoons and seventy-four pounds and two ounces of raw silk from those cocoons which are not set aside for raising fresh silkworm seeds (counting each pound as containing sixteen ounces). For this, a little more than ninety-nine pounds Sterling was paid to them in cash. This is most welcome here, where things are so expensive; and the money will help them buy new clothing and some other things which they need in their households.

Each woman who has mastered the art of spinning silk received a vat and a machine as her own; in addition to that, two of them received five pounds and one of them four pounds Sterling as tuition money for fourteen young girls from our community who have learned to spin silk this year under their instruction. Each of those fourteen young women and girls, some married, some unmarried, received, in addition to the above-mentioned tuition money, a pound Sterling as payment for their hard work and the time they spent learning. Yesterday and today have been days for distributing the money and for marvelling at God's mercy, which we do not deserve, as well as for joy and the praise of God. For me, for my dear colleague, and for other pious souls here, it was also a day for the strengthening of our faith.

Through divine power this was impressed on us even stronger by the precious word of our Lord for yesterday and today, that is, for the 11th of June and for the 12th of June, as contained in our *Treasure Chest* on pages sixty-two and one hundred sixty-one. I can also see from this that our Lord is pleased to do good unto Ebenezer. This was further confirmed by what our esteemed Mr. Albinus wrote to me and by what I read with great joy from his letter in our weekly sermon today at the plantations. His

thoughts and words deserve to be set down here, for my own
edification as well as for that of our friends. He writes:

> I have trust in the Lord that the material circumstances of your
> community will improve with time, although it must endure its
> measure of tribulations. If only the people of Ebenezer do not
> spoil the blessings sent by our Lord by ungratefulness, com-
> plaints, and lack of faith. Ebenezer! "The Lord has helped us
> so far."[7] What we say today. Tomorrow we shall add: and to the
> end of our days into eternity! May our Lord fulfill our hope for
> the sake of Christ!

Saturday, the 16th of June. Our esteemed Mr. N.[8] remains a
generous benefactor to us and continues to show to our little
community here in Ebenezer his genuine interest for our true
well-being. Recently this became quite clear to us, to our great
joy, not only from the large amount of the most useful things he
sent to us but also from his noteworthy letters addressed to me
and to Mr. Meyer as well as from the very practical suggestions
he wrote to the Lord Trustees for improving the conditions of
our community with regard to its physical support. Another
very gratifying result from these beautiful letters, as well as from
the suggestions made to the Lord Trustees, is, in my opinion, the
change of heart which Mr. Meyer has undergone. He had decided, because of poor health, to withdraw from the trading
business he had started earlier, as well as from the offices of
agent and justice of the peace; and thus he put an end to our
hopes and expectations for a successful trading business.

I had put my trust in God and consoled myself with the
thought that I had a knowledgeable and reliable assistant in Mr.
Lemke, who is my very dear colleague, brother-in-law, and my
children's godfather. Then, when I least expected it, goods and
letters from our esteemed Mr. N. arrived, which moved Mr.
Meyer to change his mind and decide to resume the trading
business. We intend to assist him in this as much as we can, to
provide him with comfortable living quarters and to hire for
him a bright young man as a servant.[9] We are very pleased to
contribute our share to such a profitable enterprise which has
our benefactors' support. Today, against all my expectations, I
heard from Mr. Meyer himself that he would also be willing to

assume the offices of agent and justice of the peace again, if I would spare him the trips to the Council meetings held in Savannah.

Sunday, the 17th of June. Our merciful God has answered our prayers. Yesterday, shortly before sunset, He sent us a penetrating and fruitful rain, which filled us with joy and praise of His name. This time, I considered the unexpected rain an especially impressive blessing from our Lord. The reasons for this are: 1. that I consider it a merciful answer to my poor humble prayers; my faith was strengthened and I was filled with joy and confidence in divine mercy; and 2. that this great blessing from the Lord came at the closing of a week during which our dear God had shown us so much goodness from beginning to end.

On Monday, due to the unwavering assistance of my dear colleague, we had completed the extensive and complicated business of settling the accounts; in the afternoon we were ready to start paying out the money we had received for our silk. On Tuesday, in Zion Church, God granted us much common edification through the beautiful letters sent to us by Mr. Albinus. In the afternoon, with everybody present in high spirits, we continued paying out money to those who made silk, to the women who spun it, and to their fourteen apprentices. On Wednesday the silk which had been brought to my house was sorted, packed, and made ready for shipping. This work was made pleasant and easy for me by the good-will of the people who had worked together on the silk-making and by their genuine affection for each other.

I won't mention all the other spiritual and physical blessings we received from our Lord recently and in the past; among these blessings I count especially the remarkable strengthening of body and soul which I felt distinctly during the long hours of rather taxing work, and of writing letters, from Wednesday afternoon until Saturday evening. I submitted a detailed report of almost five folios on our progress and problems in silk-making, as well as other things pertaining to our community, in three letters, addressed to Mr. Martyn, Mr. Verelst, and Mr. Lloyd (a member of the Lord Trustees and the most vigorous supporter of our silk-making). This did not include the accounts which have to be submitted to the local Council as well as to the Lord

Trustees and receipts our people had to make out in duplicate and sign after receiving their money. I also felt obligated to answer the very important letter which our prominent benefactor, Mr. N., had sent and also the letter from Mr. Albinus and to write several letters to our most esteemed Fathers in Augsburg and Halle. After I had completed this tiring, although mostly pleasant, task, I felt almost stronger than I had before, through God's goodness (which is the reason I mention all these things here).

On Friday morning God granted us much edification through the pleasant letter from our dear Mr. N., from which we read aloud during a gathering at the plantations. I was very pleased by Mr. Meyer's decision, after he had considered Mr. N.'s wise suggestions, to resume the trading business, which had been begun and then discontinued. In the afternoon, eight householders and two widows came to my house; each received two pounds Sterling, as ordered by our most kind Lord Trustees. Altogether, I paid out twenty pounds Sterling in order to assist those people in building the kind of sheds which are necessary for silk-making. On Saturday morning I again asked our surgeon, Mr. Meyer, whether he were willing to act as the agent and justice of the peace in Ebenezer; and he agreed, on the condition that I relieve him of the duty of traveling to Savannah in business matters.

I also received word that my dear colleague's house and study had been repaired properly and that the construction of the house which we intend to use for holding school as well as for other purposes had been completed except for the kitchen. Finally, this parade of divine blessings was crowned by the much-needed rainfall. Therefore, in the evening, I was especially moved and impressed by the Sixty-fifth Psalm which our worthy Dr. Francke laid as a basis for his sermon on the praise and thanks due for the kindness and blessing of God that He had shown to the Orphanage for fifty years.[10]

At Mr. Meyer's request, I asked our community not to overburden him with minor matters but to refer these to the seven tythingmen or headmen serving in the seven districts of our community. They should appeal to him in only those cases which cannot be settled otherwise and bring before him only im-

portant matters and disagreements. If they had to write con-
tracts and other documents, schoolmasters and other skillful
people would serve them. In turn, they would come to Mr.
Meyer to validate the drafts during his bi-weekly court session.
During these two set days he would be ready to hear their complaints and attend to their affairs in general. On the other days,
however, people should spare him, except in emergencies and
very urgent matters. He also asked me to encourage people to
pray for him regularly, as well as for the other officials, which
would please God and also benefit them. Today we read, as is
proper, the sixth chapter of Acts, and I was impressed that, in
the first Christian church in Jerusalem, the Apostles, together
with the congregation, had appointed seven pious and experienced men to take charge of the community's secular affairs. I
pray that God may grant that same measure of wisdom which
had inspired these seven men to our seven tythingmen or headmen whom we have put in charge of keeping good order.

Tuesday, the 19th of June. Several of our servants are sick with
fever because the field-work is hard and the heat is great. I am
trying to care for them, body and soul, as best as I can. White
servants are treated with contempt in this country because they
get sick from the heat when they work the fields. I believe from
my limited experience that it would be possible, if people were
agreeable, for both householders and servants to succeed and
protect their health. It is too strenuous for white people to plant
local crops such as Indian corn, beans, and rice, because these
have to be cultivated during the hottest time of the summer and
some of the fields have to be located in the most humid and low-
lying areas where there are almost no drafts of fresh, cooling air.
People ought not plant these crops with the intention of selling
them. Rather, they should plant only as much as they need for
their own use; then the few cooler hours in the mornings and
evenings would suffice for getting the work done. Moreover,
people ought not to plant their crops in soil which has been used
over and over again; instead, they should choose the most fertile
land which is not too far away, since a small patch of more fertile
soil yields more than a much larger area of over-used soil does.
How profitable it would be if they joined forces and used the
above-mentioned island! It would definitely have to be a com-

munal enterprise, however, since a large area would have to be cultivated within a year and it would have to be guarded during the nights because of destructive vermin.

Wednesday, the 20th of June. In his letter of November the third of last year, which arrived here on the twentieth of last month, our esteemed Pastor Maier in Halle wrote to me the following:

> My most recent collection for Ebenezer was the sum of twenty Reichsthaler from a major's wife in Breslau, who wishes to remain anonymous. In sending me the money, however, she requests that, instead of getting a receipt on paper, she would prefer a more real one; namely that two children of your community be named Friedrich Karl and Anna Francisca when receiving Holy Baptism. We trust that her wishes will be remembered at the earliest possible opportunity.

The first child born here after the arrival of this pleasant letter, which illustrates so clearly the divine protection of poor parents and children, is a boy; he was delivered this morning and will be baptized in Jerusalem Church this afternoon. I had decided to distribute the gift we had received in the order in which God would let two children be born. The parents who are the first recipients are probably among the most needy of our people here; a few days ago they lost a cow and a calf, at a time when the new mother needed the milk more than ever. I gave ten shillings Sterling to the father of the child to help with the expenses for the care of his wife. If this gift is used properly, then I intend to add another sum, up to one half of the twenty Reichsthaler sent to us. The husband showed surprise; he considered himself a great sinner and quite unworthy of this gift. He did, however, recognize that God had granted him His unmerited mercy and protection, despite his own shortcomings, by relieving him of his worries concerning the midwife fee. Midwives here do not charge much, but for poor people it is difficult to spend even a small sum. I was therefore pleased to be able to help with the gifts sent by our Lord. The husband was also overjoyed at the beautiful name which his child was to receive as stipulated by the benefactress.

Sunday, the 24th of June. Our most esteemed Doctor and Professor Francke favored us two unworthy servants of the gospel, as well as our community, by sending us his written observations concerning the interaction of God's works in Halle and at other places. From them we can learn not only the state of our Evangelical Church and certain characteristics of our times, but also very rich material for a new awakening in Christianity and in our office, as well as for the edification of our listeners and the heart-felt intercession for His Zion. This Sunday, the second after Trinity, I felt so strengthened that, despite the oppressive heat, I was able to read aloud to our dear listeners some passages selected from the appendices to the year 1747 after the catechism and before common prayer. I made public the important news of how the truth is being persecuted in the Swiss canton of Lucerne.[11] I also started reading, explaining, and applying an edifying letter from a group of Protestants from Carinthia who had been transported to Siebenburgen and who, just like the people from Salzburg, had to endure hardships because of their adherence to the Evangelical religion.[12] I intend to continue the contemplation of this letter in the future.

Tuesday, the 26th of June. Because it has become known in our community for some time that I wish, God willing, to send my two boys, Samuel Leberecht and Gotthilf Israel, to Halle to attend the well-run schools of the Orphanage, one of our inhabitants here was found willing to accompany my children on this trip and to take along his own son, who is almost seven years old, and enroll him in the same school. For his age, this young boy has learned a great deal in our school in town; and he is ready to be sent to introductory Latin courses, if there is enough money for that. He is a very well-behaved child and quite promising; but he is still very young and needs the care of his mother. I therefore advised the father to keep his son here with us until he is a little older and able to make more progress in the subjects of writing and mathematics, and has learned more of God's word and our catechism. The father of this young boy is a pious and hard-working man who, in moderation and without over-taxing his health, has succeeded in earning good money by making boats in Ebenezer. He serves as an example for others to convince them that working with wood is of advantage in this country.[13]

My older son, Samuel Leberecht, asked me yesterday, almost in tears, to send him and his brother, Gotthilf Israel, to Halle as soon as possible; he would like to arrive there while our esteemed Dr. Francke is still alive. I encouraged him to pray for health and a long life for this dear man.

I intend to travel to Savannah towards the end of this week since it is time to preach to the German people and to hold Holy Communion for them. I also have business matters to attend to there because of our silk and the cowpen we purchased (our cattle ranch in Old Ebenezer); and I intend to send off the letters I have written. Our friend, Mr. Habersham, is a capable and hardworking man, who is eager and willing to serve our Lord Trustees and this colony as a member of the Council and the entire society in this country, but his efforts are hampered by numerous obstacles.

Friday, the 29th of June. Barbara Zorn, an orphan with neither father nor mother, was commended to my care by her dying mother a few years ago. Since then she has completed her time of service in Savannah and has arrived here in order to be instructed. God has so blessed His word and example in her that she has been converted to God with her whole heart and conducts herself in a way which is pleasing to Him. God shows her much goodness and will show her more in the future. She has been saved from great temptation because she is willing to listen to advice.

JULY

Sunday, the 1st of July. Two days ago I traveled to Savannah and arrived there in good health in the evening. There are so many things to take care of, both matters connected with my office and matters concerning this colony and our community, that I will probably have to stay for eight days. Unfortunately, as a result of this, I will not only have to delay several important matters at home but I will also be unable to hold Holy Communion, which is supposed to be held on the Third Sunday after Trinity. Yesterday evening, at a meeting of the German settlers, I continued to discuss the Ninth Commandment, after repeating some of the main points of the Eighth Commandment which I had explained earlier and by which our merciful God shows us that deceit, falsehood, and meanness fill the human heart. I had to hear confessions in the morning, one hour before public service, because Sunday morning was the only time some of the people from the plantations could come. I based my preaching on the Thirty-second Psalm.

In addition to this short sermon, God's word has been spread five times so far in this place. We also held one public prayer hour. In the morning, I explained the important verses Acts 26:16; in the afternoon I preached on Luke 15:1 ff. and in the evening on the important and very necessary teachings of true repentance; I felt blessed and inspired by the Holy Ghost. Mr. Zuberbuhler, the regular minister, preached to the Englishmen; and in the afternoon a student from the orphanage held an edification hour with much fervor on 2 Corinthians, 4:17.

Monday, the 2nd. of July. I had planned to deliver the silk made by our people, together with the silk-accounts, today, the first Monday of the month (on which day, according to the rules set by our Lord Trustees, the Council is to meet). However, neither the president nor the other members of the council came to the session. Nevertheless, I was able to use this time well since there was other business to take care of. Yesterday, during the sermons, our dear God moved the hearts of several people by His word; this became quite obvious from their looks and demeanor when they came to church and to the meetings held in the evening. In particular, one pious woman came to me after we had finished the edification hour and asked me to give her an opportunity to talk to me. I visited her today; she revealed her troubled soul to me and accepted instruction in God's word most eagerly and gratefully. God blessed our prayer and granted us both encouragement. She is an honest soul and is inclined to the Reformed religion. The state of her soul reminded me of the consoling Evangelical hymn: *Weg, mein Herz! mit den Gedanken, als ob du verstossen wärst,* etc., which I saw neither in her hymnal nor in others which German settlers had brought with them from their homeland; I decided, however, to make public its important and consoling text in our evening prayer hours so that our listeners may benefit from it; and I intend to spend an entire week on this undertaking.

Tuesday, the 3rd. of July. Today the members of the Council did meet in session. Already a few days ago I had outlined to two of them my method of paying our people for their silk, so the Council had agreed, even before I submitted the accounts, that I had been too thrifty in spending the money sent by our Lord Trustees and that I had paid our people too little money for both fine and coarse silk. Therefore, they changed my accounts in favor of our people; and I sent them back to my dear colleague so that the people could re-sign their changed receipts. Mr. Meyer took them back to Ebenezer; he had arrived here yesterday in order to attend to some business connected with our trading, as well as to send money to Mr. N. for the goods he had sent here. I thought that I had paid our silk-makers enough money; also, nobody had complained. Furthermore, I was unable to arrange money matters differently because the cocoons for which our Lord Trustees had agreed to pay a fine sum had already been spun off by the time the letters and instructions from the Lord Trustees arrived here; also they had not been weighed in the presence of Mr. Meyer or another reliable person. The original agreement had been that the cocoons should be graded best, medium, and poor; for each a certain bounty (premium) had been set by the Lord Trustees, and for each kind of spun silk, according to its worth, fourteen, twelve, or six shillings would be paid. This year no silk has been made either in Savannah or any place else, leaving me without any comparison as to pricing.

There was also another reason which caused me to use great care in spending the money sent by the Lord Trustees: namely, that they had already incurred considerable expense this year in supporting the silk-manufacture in our settlement. I was afraid that they might become dissatisfied upon being presented with such a large account (one hundred and eighty-six pounds), although in the past and at present such sums were paid upon their orders. What I had paid for fine and coarse silk came to ninety-nine pounds Sterling. The fourteen young women who learned how to spin silk received twenty-eight pounds, Christoph Rottenberger, who made the machines to fit the ten copper vats shipped here to be used in the spinning process, got fifteen pounds, and ten poor householders were paid two pounds each to assist them with the building of the sheds which are needed to simplify the silk-making. I won't even mention other sums of money which were spent on various necessities, following the instructions from the Lord Trustees.

The reason that the members of the Council decided to change my accounts in favor of our people is that they fear my thriftiness (which is not unacceptable to our people) in pricing the silk might be laid before the Parliament and might result in a more permanent lowering of the prices to a degree which is below that which the Lord Trustees had promised us in their last instructions to us. The Lord Trustees intend to go before Parliament to ask for the fixing of the silk premiums at a time when the Pope and other principalities in Italy would impose a general silk embargo and, as a consequence, English looms would be more idle than normal. Settlers here are not content with a modest bounty or encouragement; rather, they demand large sums of money without considering whether or not either the Lord Trustees or Parliament will be able to sustain such high prices for long. If in the future no premium can be paid for a given year, then they will stop making any silk at all, as past experience has shown.

Thursday, the 5th of July. I received a letter from a friend in Charleston, in which, among other things, he tells me that news has come via the sugar producing islands in the West Indies that, unfortunately, a serious rift between England and France may occur. The reasons for expecting such a conflict were not mentioned. May our merciful God avert this punishment from us in His goodness, even though we deserve such punishment and even more for our sins! Oh, how frequently am I reminded of the important first line of the hymn: "Lord, Thy loyalty is so great that we must marvel."[1] During this entire week, in our evening prayer meetings, I have been explaining to our congregation the most excellent hymn: *Weg, mein Herz, mit den Gedanken,* etc. Both I and our listeners felt edified; and we recognized quite clearly not only the proper kind of Evangelical penitence but also the powerful motives leading to it, as well as the reason why no poor sinner must despair as long as he is penitent. Everything is confirmed by verses from Holy Scripture. Praised be God! In the evenings my spirit, which is tired out during the

daytime, is refreshed and encouraged by song and God's word.
May God watch over us in the future as well!

Friday, the 6th of July. For the past few days, the members of
the Council, as well as the most prominent among the colonists,
have been busy composing a petition to the Lord Trustees and
the King. Namely, 1. that the union of the two colonies not take
place. This would also encourage the people to devote themselves seriously to silk-manufacture, as is the wish of the Lord
Trustees as well as that of the English people; 2. that the company of soldiers be replaced by a company of rangers or hussars
on horseback; they would be most effective fighting the Spanish
or the Indians. Although I do not have much insight in such
matters, I believe that the main purpose in this is to guard the
Negroes or to prevent their defection to the Spanish side, which
is easier done using rangers than employing infantry; 3. that the
taxation of the plantations, which is far too high, be made equal
to that customary in the Carolinas; there, people pay annually
only a few shillings for one-hundred acres, compared to the
taxes in Georgia where the amounts proposed are twenty shillings for some people and ten shillings Sterling for others. So far,
these taxes have not yet been in force, but they soon might be.
This last point, however, is not to be included in this petition but
is to be postponed for another time so as not to burden the Lord
Trustees with too many complaints at once.

Mr. Meyer returned from Ebenezer today at one o'clock in the
afternoon, bringing with him the new receipts signed by our
people. He also intends to sign the above mentioned petition. A
week ago today when I left from home, my wife had been sick.
Mr. Meyer brings me the news that three days ago, before he had
returned to Ebenezer, she had been so sick and weak that people
feared for her life. She had wished very much to see me; instead,
after Mr. Meyer had arrived, when she had heard that business
would keep me away for some time yet, her fragile mind and
body were taxed even more. Finally (as I see from a letter by
Samuel Leberecht),[2] she submitted to God's will and regained
her composure. Mr. Meyer assures me that yesterday evening he
had found her somewhat stronger in mind and body and that he
has some hope for her recovery. When I heard this sad news, I

was reminded of the words we had contemplated in yesterday's evening prayer hour: "He is, indeed, neither bear nor lion, who only," etc. and "His heart is accustomed to pure loyalty and mercy. God has a fatherly mind. Our suffering pains Him, our misery is His sorrow, our death troubles His heart."[3]

I wish very much that I could return home, but I have to obey God, since He, in His providence, orders me to stay here.

Saturday, the 7th of July. This evening the church in Savannah will be consecrated. I would have liked to stay here and preach to the German people the following morning. However, the sad news of my wife's dangerous illness forces me to return home. Yesterday, between eight and nine o'clock in the evening, I signed, together with Mr. Meyer, the petition drafted by the local authorities, the Council, and the most prominent of the colonists here. This petition is directed to our Lord Trustees, and concerns the matter of vetoing a merger of the colony of Georgia with that of Carolina and the matter of creating a company of hussars or rangers to protect the colony against Indian attacks; we left in God's name at three o'clock this morning.

While I was still in Savannah, my dear colleague had written to me that a certain master-builder is looking for work here; he is willing to undertake all sorts of wooden construction at low prices because he would prefer to live among us modestly and enjoy the quietude, God's word, and good order, rather than live somewhere else more sumptuously, especially since we pay cash here which is not the case in other parts of Georgia or Carolina. This builder had contributed to the financial ruin of the merchant Mr. David Zubli by constructing for him a fancy flourmill and sawmill, built to work like a large clock; at present he is in litigation with him. This young man /Brown/ arrived in this country from Scotland not long ago, where he was an apprentice. He seems to know his business and is an honest man, although he most likely is a poor judge of character and probably lacks the experience necessary to work as an independent master-builder. If our two carpenters, Kogler and Rottenberger, who are very skillful, were more serious and would not waste their time on minor efforts but rather pay more attention to their craft, then this man, who seems capable enough, could work under their supervision and direction; there certainly is no lack of work. We are eager to build a new sawmill; already last spring trees were felled to provide the necessary lumber.

Sunday, the 8th of July. Old Kiefer of Purysburg brought a young, twenty-four year old man to me. He told me that this was the orphan /Johann Paul/ Francke, who was one of our first four orphans here in Ebenezer. Although he had been treated very well by us, he left, first to join his poor mother in Purysburg, then to live among the Indians. He spent twelve or thirteen years with an Englishman, who sent him on trading trips into Indian territory, accompanying pack-horses loaded with various goods. He has forgotten both his native German language as well as everything he had been taught here. He confessed that he had lived for so many years among the heathens, although they had been baptized Christians, and that his conduct had been filled with sin.

Now, however, he desired to lead a proper life and was willing to be instructed in the Christian teachings. Since he no longer knows any German, as already mentioned, he intends to stay with Kiefer's family in order to reacquaint himself with his mother-tongue as well as to use the means of salvation together with them. Whether or not he is serious about this will become clear in time. For the time being, I suspect, he is one of those people who intend to reach certain goals and, as soon as they get what they want, they fall back into their old habits again. Kiefer thinks highly of him.

This Sunday, the fourteenth after Trinity, our locksmith Brückner fell ill in church during our public morning service; he was suffering from serious abdominal pains due to chronic constipation. He is an honest man and certain of his salvation in Christ; however, he is disturbed because he believes that he caused his condition by a certain carelessness. Several people are sick with a fever, especially servants who worked too hard in the fields. An older man, Conrad Baumann, died on Friday and was buried yesterday. His wife and child are still in Wurttemberg; about six months ago, he and Martin Burkhart wrote a long letter in which they asked their wives and children and some other families to come and join them here. He used to share the house with Matthias Brandner, a Salzburger and true Christian, who is a well-to-do man, who lacks nothing in either the spiritual or the material sense. While Conrad Baumann had been ill (as Mr. Lemke wrote to me in Savannah), he was seriously homesick; this might have contributed to his death even more than his illness itself.

I am surprised that people who lived in poverty while they were still in Germany think that in this country even a moderate amount of work is an unbearable burden. It ought to be obvious to them that, after completing three or four years of service, starting households of their own would turn out to be a more difficult task for them than any other ever before. In part, the large and almost unfair daily wages which are demanded by free people and are, indeed, paid contribute to this way of thinking; people add up what they could be earning even if they just got eighteen pence a day, which comes to more than twenty-four pounds Sterling per year. Some people here earn two shillings a day and get free meals on top of that. Of course, only merchants can afford to be that generous, because they simply charge higher prices for their goods to keep their expenses down. I am not surprised that even some of our people here prefer Negro servants to white ones.

Monday, the 9th of July. On the ninth of May of this year, the newspapers of Charleston in South Carolina reported the strange story of a Negro, Caesar by name, who discovered how to use two simple and easily obtainable remedies for curing the effects of the very poisonous bite of rattlesnakes; poisons induced by either food, drink, or other means are likewise rendered harmless by his medicine which, cleanses the blood. The Assembly or Parliament in Charleston, in recognition of his very useful remedy, put up the money and bought his freedom. In addition to that, they decreed that, for life, he is to receive for his support an annual amount of one-hundred pounds in local currency, which comes to fourteen pounds Sterling.

The governor and the other members of the Assembly must have been convinced of the effectiveness of his medicine; otherwise they would not have made the news public and they would not have spent so much money on this Negro. He uses only two herbs, roots included, which are cooked and their tea drunk; the English names of these herbs are plantain and horehound. He treats the wounds resulting from snake bites by dressing them with tobacco leaves which have been soaked in rum (sugarcane brandy). Until now, no known remedy for the bite from rattlesnakes existed, and many a victim died suddenly. If this very simple remedy indeed effects such an important and long-needed cure, then the above mentioned monetary reward is well worth spending. I feel sorry for the doctors in this country; they rely almost entirely on simple or mixed medicines from Europe and make no use of the herbs and roots growing in this country; if they only had the wish to be better doctors they would have ample opportunity to learn to do so.

Wednesday, the 11th of July. Hanns Maurer's pious wife came to me in tears and told me that her young son had eaten sand and raw rice; as a result, his body is bloated, and he seems to have swellings not unlike those of people who suffer from dropsy.[4] She had not been aware of his unhealthy eating habits because he had kept them secret, but now he confessed everything to her. His sister, who is about fourteen years old, did the same and, as a result, is also in poor health. When children eat unhealthy things, such as sand, dirt, charcoal, raw rice, grain, etc., it becomes quickly obvious that they are sick because they turn pale, their faces get bloated, and they gain weight. Recently I heard of several children who behaved in this manner. I promised to those who would stop, and whose skin would turn a healthy color again, various rewards; I repeated my promise in school on several occasions, and I brought and distributed gifts. However, the children are so voracious that they cannot control their appetites when they are alone.

Our most esteemed benefactor, Dr. E. from M. sent a letter to Mr. Meyer, giving us excellent advice on how to deal with this childhood disease; however, I do not believe it will be possible for us to put his advice into practice although both I and Mr. Lemke are more than willing to help by contributing money and other support. Some time ago I translated an article into German which had appeared in a London magazine, describing a cure. I also translated the newspaper article mentioned above, which reports how to cleanse the body of poisons and how to cure poisonous bites from rattlesnakes; I circulated my translation among our people here so that they could make use of it if necessary. I do not doubt that the two herbs, plantain and horehound, are available in this country; the newspapers talk of them as of well-known and ordinary plants.

Thursday, the 12th of July. After a long drought, which lasted for two weeks, we have had plenty of rain for the past eight days. Yesterday, and again today, there was a heavy downpour. Our main river, as well as the smaller rivers branching off from it, carry little water. Therefore, our mills are standing still; that is something which has not happened for a long time. We assume that up in the mountains, where the Savannah River originates, there is just as little rain as in our area because we heard that in some places the crops of Indian corn were spoiled; we do not expect ours to wither away. Early plantings may be damaged and may not yield as much as expected, because the time for their setting cobs and ears coincided with the drought; our rice, on the other hand, could not be better.

Rice and grain are very expensive in Georgia and Carolina and not easily obtained. Now, at the beginning of the Dog Days, the temperatures in the evening, at night, and in the morning, are as low as in the fall; people had better watch out for their health. Meanwhile, I read in the newspapers from Halle for the year 1748 that our all-powerful, miraculous, and just God afflicted various areas in Europe not only with a destructive war and great devastation, but also with cattle-plague, thunderstorms, lightning, floods, fires, and a plague of locusts, which even reached England. I feel obliged to praise His divine mercy and patience; He averted punishments of this kind from our country and our area and granted to our kingdom, as well as to other nations, a time of noble peace which may endure for a while. Letters I received from Charleston and newspapers printed there seem to indicate that a war between England and France is to be expected soon. Bloody conflicts between the English, the French, and those of the Indians who sympathize with the French broke out in Nova Scotia, which the English intend to colonize in earnest. These Indians do not recognize our king's authority in this country, and French supporters in Canada are aiding them secretly.

Friday, the 13th of July. Old Mitzcher died last night after several weeks of serious illness.[5] He was sixty-four years old; he had lived for a while in Purysburg and then spent the last few years with his family here in Ebenezer. His entire life was filled with sinning; even during his last illness it had not been easy to make him realize his trespasses. He would have liked to take Holy Communion a few weeks ago; however, I did not want rush him or be rushed in this matter, and finally he received Holy Communion at his urgent request two days before his death in the presence of his family. He repented his sins with all his heart and professed a great hungering and thirsting for the Savior of all poor sinners to whom he commended his soul as a poor worm.

Old Kiefer from Purysburg was present, at my request, because he was more familiar with this man's character than I am. Kiefer reminded him emphatically of his earlier life in Germany and in Purysburg; he commended to him that kind of order which grants grace to even the most hardened sinner. The dying man accepted all this so that pious Kiefer was able to vouch for him. Yesterday at his funeral late in the afternoon, I based my preaching on the edifying vita of the late Pastor Mischke, whom I hold in high esteem and I continued where I had left off last time. Strangely enough, I came across a passage dealing with his going to confession and attending Holy Communion. Since we also are going to take part in this Holy Sacrament, the day after tomorrow, we felt the text had provided us with a most welcome opportunity to prepare ourselves, with God's blessing.

Sunday, the 15th of July. We would have liked to hold Holy Communion fourteen days ago; however, at that time I happened to be in Savannah to take care of the German settlers there. Afterwards, quite unexpectedly, I found that the President and other members of the Council required me to stay for a full week with the result that Holy Communion could not be held eight days ago. Today, I and seventy-four members of our community shared its blessing, God be praised! It was the fifth Sunday after Trinity. Several people had indicated their intention to participate but were unable to come; I do not know what prevented them from joining us. Others were asked to abstain this time, with good reason. Widow Lemmenhofer and my own wife would have preferred to take Holy Communion together with the community if they had not been kept from doing so by their lingering ailments. May our merciful God, in His goodness, protect these and other patients; may He use physical sick-

ness in those who do not believe and use sickness in the unbelieving as a chastisement leading to salvation. Let us hope that those
among the adherents and friends of Christ who are afflicted
may not lack the consolations of the Holy Ghost; however, He
would certainly not allow that, for He loves them much too
much.

The heavy downpour is continuing. Today, especially today
since three o'clock in the afternoon, it has rained violently and
continuously; and this prevented us from holding our usual repetition hour. May our merciful God let this rain be a blessing
for us and not a punishment! So far, the thunderstorms have
been moderate; there are no reports of lightning striking or of
fires resulting from lightning. In all fairness, we ascribe being
spared to our Lord's mercy. In the forests there are many trees
which show the traces of being struck by lightning, some of these
are quite close to our town.

Monday, the 16th of July. Sad news reached us from Savannah: an Englishman from Frederica drowned after falling out of
his boat at night. A few days later, a German man sighted his
body in the harbor at Savannah and pulled him out. It is likely
that the Englishman had been drunk at the time of the accident.
People say that, as a practical joke, he set a trap in his boat so that
his friends would fall overboard when they got up; however, he
himself became the victim of his prank. May God, by this terrible
example, awaken others among us who sin so often!

At present, Creeks, Cherokees, and some French Indians are
involved in a heated war against each other, resulting in atroci-
ties being committed frequently. They usually torture their prisoners in terrible ways; for instance, first they play a long game of
cat and mouse, beating, pushing, and wounding their victims.
Then they tie them to poles and singe their naked bodies with
burning pine-wood torches, roast their skins, and revive their
prisoners from time to time, when they seem unconscious and
near death, by throwing cold water on them, in order to be able
to continue their cruel entertainment for some time longer. Indians who are executed this way or by other barbaric methods
are said to display no signs of pain during these tortures; they do
not flinch, nor do they cry out. I heard this not long ago about an
old man who was scalped while still alive and shot to death after-

wards; likewise about a young half-cast boy, born of an Indian mother and a European father, who was burned to death in the aforementioned manner by the Creeks. These heathens are otherwise cowards, but all the more cruel.

Tuesday, the 17th of July. Today, before my weekly sermon on the plantations, a Salzburger who arrived here with the first transport announced to me that necessity had forced him to buy a black female servant and that God had provided him with the means for doing so. His German servant was sick and wished very much to be free; he still had wife and children in Germany. He could not find a white female servant, he was badly pressed since he had three children, and both he and his wife were worn out from work and sickly. In the past, if anyone in our community spoke against using Negroes, then it was this man himself, a Salzburger named Leimberger; he probably would not have made this decision if he had not been forced into it by great necessity.[6] Our own servants never were of much use, in the past they were lazy or restless; and now most of them have stopped working because of sickness, thus causing their employers great expense and trouble. Therefore, I do not feel that I can object when people wish to introduce Negroes into our community; in this as in all things I trust in God, who will show us in good time whether or not this practice is of any advantage to our people here.

In his last letter, our esteemed Mr. N. shared with me some very realistic thoughts which I have considered many times since. He writes:

> Under these circumstances (namely, white laboreres asking such high daily wages and steep prices for their work), one can not blame the English for using Negroes as much as they do, since no workers are available cheaply. After all, goods produced here have to be produced inexpensively because of the cost of shipping them overseas; once exported, these goods still have to be competitive in price with goods produced by other nations.

Towards the end of his letter our benefactor promises to send an experienced winegrower along with a transport of servants, and he adds:

If this vintner does not succeed in finding cheap labor, then it will be no surprise if he, too, in order to keep his vineyards, calls for Negro laborers or else loses heart.

In this very important letter he approves of the small trading business started by Riedelsberger, for which I had lent him some money. Not only did this new business allow him to pay off his debts within two years, but he was also able to improve the state of his household and to do some building. In addition to that, he could afford to buy a Negro servant. Leimberger and another Salzburger on the plantations do no merchandizing; they rely on farming only, which is not profitable enough to afford buying male or female Negro servants. However, they were able to obtain the necessary money through various kinds of work connected with our mills. They had been hired to help with repairs, with cutting lumber and delivering it, with transporting some of our boards to Savannah, and with hauling loads from and to the mills for some of our people here. It goes without saying that their success is due to God's blessing, otherwise it could have gone with them as it went with Peter and his companions when they fished throughout the night and caught nothing.

I am not sure that I am right when I conclude that God, who granted quite a few of our people (actually, a large number) a good income without the use of Negro servants, will continue to grant them prosperity if we are able to increase the opportunities for working and earning enough money. We are planning, with God's help, to build a new sawmill for the benefit of our entire community. How easy it is for white people to make silk and to work with wood in the shade, now that this is getting underway! In the past, people had to work very hard to shell rice by using a wooden handmill; now we intend to build a rice husker next to the rice stamp, both run by water. In addition, our rice press and barley press are to be improved. Recently, in Jerusalem Church, I read the following beautiful passage from an account of a community of Evangelical Austrians who had moved to Siebenburgen:

> They live here under these conditions: some earn money as tradesmen or by skilled labor; those who have not learned a craft work as day laborers or get wages by the hour, and some

unmarried persons enter into service. All are accustomed to be
content with very little and they lead very limited, modest, and
simple lives.

At this point I made the following comment: "If the people here
in this country were more like those Austrians, then they would
succeed without the help of Negro servants." Afterwards I
heard that this remark of mine was ill received by several of the
people; they believe that, since their own physical strength is declining and their servants are of almost no help, they are entitled
to use Negroes. I have decided not to say one more word on this
subject, either for or against it, since God's hand could be involved in this matter. One thing, however, is certain: if Negroes
were to be commonly used instead of poor white people then the
latter's opportunity for earning money at the mills would de-
crease also if the mill-owners were to use Negroes, too, or if people were to send Negroes to work at the mills. But in this matter,
also, we trust in God!

Thursday, the 19th of July. A short while ago a new and quite
large house was built on public land, close to the old orphanage.
It has two large rooms and one smaller one on the first floor and
one very long and wide room upstairs. This house, which had
been in the planning for a long time, will be used for various
communal affairs, especially for holding school; Kalcher and his
family, who had stayed at the orphanage this year, will live there.
God will show us whether or not such a spacious and well-built
house, standing on a hill where the air is healthier, could be used
in the future to provide a home for widows and orphans or be
made into a hospital. Other considerable advantages of this
house are its good well, the barn, many mature mulberry trees,
and adjoining land where gardens could be planted. At present
and for the next few years we have no need for a house which
would serve these purposes; the reasons for this, however, I do
not wish to mention at this time.

When the last batch of letters from Europe arrived here, good
progress had been made in the building of this house but, it had
not yet been completed. When Mr. Meyer, in the best interest of
the entire community, had decided to devote himself again to
the commerce he had been forced to give up, and when he also

willingly agreed to resume the office of justice of the peace, he had mentioned that his old house, which had been built with money collected by Mr. Vigera, was too small. For the purpose of merchandizing, additional rooms would have to be constructed; and it was decided that the best solution would be to move Mr. Meyer into the new house rather than to rebuild his old one, which would have to be more spacious; another floor would also have to be added. Mr. Meyer agreed to this and moved into the new house last week. In turn, Kalcher bought, for twenty pounds Sterling, the house which was built by Mr. Vigera and which had been Mr. Meyer's home until now. Kalcher now has a good house of his own, with two large rooms and one small one, and he lives right next to Mr. Meyer, which means that he has the use of the good well and that he also may take advantage of various other things which are the property of the orphanage. He is willing to let us use one of his rooms, which has a stove, for holding school; and he is asking only very little money for it. When we have the necessary money, we plan to build a school-house next to the church.

Friday, the 20th of July. For the past fourteen days we have had much rain. It is a blessing for people and animals; not only our Indian corn, rice, and other crops picked up noticeably, but the grass on the meadows and hayfields grew very well and we have new hopes for a good hay harvest. The water level in the river has been rising steadily for the past six days; and our mills can be operated again, much to the relief of our people here as well as others. We would not appreciate our mill as much as we do if it did not occasionally lie idle (although the one with the double course fails us only very seldom in the year). In this country, God has been teaching us to be more respectful of wind, water, rain, sunshine, gristmills, and sawmills than people normally are; all of these things are indispensable blessings from God.

Saturday, the 21st of July. God-fearing Steiner is worn-out from too much hard work; his disloyal and strong-headed servants (a young married couple) stirred up much trouble for him and did considerable damage. Now he is forced to let Brandner, whose field-hand died recently, have them. It is to be hoped that Brandner will be able to discipline them since he has a clever wife who is quite experienced in running a household, and she probably will be able to keep these unruly people in check; Steiner, as a widower, did not do as well in this respect. He feels that his strength is dwindling fast, and he suspects his departure from this world is near. He asked me to take care of his three young sons and to take charge of their education in the case of his death; his household is deteriorating greatly because he lacks a wife or a housekeeper, and he is getting poorer and poorer. Only a few days ago he lost two good cows and three pigs to a very common disease. In the newspapers from Halle for the year 1749, number 18, I found instructions for preventing fatal sicknesses in animals; the author is a prominent and experienced man, and we are grateful for his advice. I am letting my sons write out several copies of this article to make the information known to our people. The preventive measures are inexpensive and easy to obtain.

Monday, the 23rd of July. It is surprising how cool the nights are during the dog days this year. The heat in the daytime is also moderate, and we can not complain. Several of the servants who were sick are recovering from the fever; and, since their employers nursed them back to health, they should repay their kindness with gratitude by serving them well. By working hard from now on they could probably lessen the financial burden brought on by their missing work and causing additional expenses. However, disloyalty and ungratefulness are among the main characteristics of our German servants here, as bad as ever seen in Negro servants. I am very sad that I can do so little with my office to improve these matters. From past experience I know that these servants only cause trouble.

I am not surprised that our Salzburgers have lost their confidence in white servants and do not wish to have anything to do with them in the future. These people are only a burden; and it would mean financial ruin for our people if they had to pay them or if they had to reimburse our Lord Trustees for paying their passage from Europe, namely, for each adult six pounds Sterling. They hardly earn their keep and clothing, and they are mostly unruly and ill-tempered. Other Germans here in this country contribute to this by corrupting talk and tempting them into disloyalty and dissatisfaction. A female servant who is of marriageable age can hardly be found any more because there are many opportunities for such women to get married quickly within our own community, or else they marry and leave us. If permission to marry is denied, nothing but considerable trouble results.

In this country, people do not hire free servants as is done in Europe; rather, servants are bought for a number of years, so little can be accomplished with them. We do not have much hope for improvement of this situation because there are so few white settlers in this or other colonies. The land for plantations costs next to nothing, and people have the opportunity to earn unreasonably high daily wages. Maybe this problem will improve if more Negroes come to this country. From experience we know that, when these unwilling servants regain their freedom and work for their own profit, then they usually do hard work well and fast, and they make excellent colonists.

If a solution could be found for our dear, over-worked Salzburgers concerning their subsistence, then it would be of advantage to this country if all servants could be set free with the understanding that they themselves would pay off the money laid out for their passage from Europe in time by making barrel staves, shingles, etc. Wooden articles of this kind are very much sought after in the West Indies, and the prices for those goods have gone up considerably in Carolina and other provinces where good oaks are becoming rare. We, however, have an excellent opportunity to make such things if we use the timberstands growing on our large island. The day before yesterday, a servant of Col. Heron again delivered a letter to me in which he asks my help in obtaining barrel staves, shingles, boards, etc. for his ship he has sent to Savannah.

Several of our servants bought their freedom from service, some of them in Savannah and some of them here in Ebenezer, with cash I lent them (because under the circumstances it had been in the best interest of our community). Two of them do work as carpenters and they are very loyal;[7] two others, at our request, started making clay bricks and firing them. I had been worried that their first serious attempt at this very difficult work would miscarry, since they knew how to make and fire bricks only from watching but had had no actual training themselves.

Furthermore, heavy and long-lasting rains had done some damage while the bricks were being fired. However, my dear colleague told me that, when the kiln was opened, the bricks looked so fine that both young men were quite encouraged to continue from now on with this very much needed and useful work, which is rather important to our community.

In Savannah only very poor quality bricks are being made, one thousand pieces cost between eighteen and twenty shillings Sterling, and they are stored at quite a distance from the waterways. How much more would it cost if those were bought and then transported to the river and then shipped to us by boat! Also, the more craftsmen and reliable workers we have among us, the more improvement is to be expected in our food situation. The conditions here are ideal for making bricks: down at the river there are veritable mountains and large expanses of good quality clay, water and wood are also near by, and there is plenty of both available. Furthermore, several thousand bricks can be shipped in one load for sale in Savannah. I wish we had a potter, too; we could make good dishes easily and sell them locally in neighboring colonies, and in Augustine.[8]

Several of our men tried their hand at tanning, but there are still problems. A man in Purysburg, out of greed and spite, is asking forty pounds Sterling tuition money. I wrote a letter to a good friend in Charleston, and at the same time to Pastor Brunnholz, asking them to teach us by correspondence how to make various kinds of leather; for we need tanners urgently. I am also asking those of our esteemed benefactors in Europe who read this diary to write to us and have a competent tanner teach us this skill by letter. The reason we do not want skilled craftsmen from Europe to come to join us here is that these people then insist on doing only what falls within the competence of their craft; we had trouble of this kind in the past. However, skilled craftsmen, like those mentioned earlier, are needed here if we are to make a success of trading, which is most important here, and if we are to improve our subsistence. I have no doubt that our Fathers and benefactors understand very well why I include such secular matters, which will not be of interest to all readers, in this diary.

I would like to speak briefly again of the four servants whom I

helped to buy their freedom: they are an example for the fact
that these people can contribute greatly to the community if they
work for their own profit and if they are free.[9] Other servants
would behave in a similar manner if they were given an opportunity to obtain their freedom; likewise the households in which
they work would be better off since people are fairly tired of the
problems with their servants, who do more harm than good.
Such a solution would also be in keeping with the plans of our
Lord Trustees.

Young Kiefer and his brother-in-law, Kronberger, both keep a
Negro at our place, and they planted good fields of Indian and
local crops. Our people here took notice of that; it seems that
they are all set on either buying or borrowing Negroes. We
would certainly not begrudge such an opportunity to our dear
people who can not succeed without help; it would be easier for
them to solve their food problems thus than if they were on their
own or had white servants. However, we will not become involved in the buying or selling of Negroes, even if they would
welcome it. If they like the idea of giving their servants their
freedom in exchange for six-thousand barrel staves made within
five months (and I hope that both our people as well as the servants will like this solution), then soon each household, or two
together, could buy a Negro in the near future without incur-
ring too many debts, especially if our people themselves worked
more with wood instead of concentrating on farming. In this
matter, too, let us trust in our benevolent Lord and His blessed
mercy!

Tuesday, the 24th of July. A single young woman and her il-
legitimate child were among our servants here. Yesterday, quite
unexpectedly, this child died and was buried today in the cemetery on the plantations. I have never seen any mother carry on as
she did during the funeral, screaming and crying; probably she
could not even hear the good things that were being said at the
funeral service. Both she and her child had been been lucky, living with a family of substantial and Christian Salzburgers; as I
heard, the child was also well cared for during its short illness.

Wednesday, the 25th of July. This morning I traveled to Goshen to visit the German settlers behind Abercorn. They met
quickly in order to hear a sermon on the noteworthy words from

Psalms 5:5-7; and I demonstrated to them, with love and seriousness, the extent and dangers of sinning and in which order they can extricate themselves from their temporal and eternal misery. These people show much affection for both me and my dear colleague and they listen, even when they are reproached for improper conduct. However, true conversion comes not easily.

When I returned home in the evening and was about to leave for our prayer meeting, I received the unpleasant news that the Indians, once again, had come and stolen a riding horse each from two of our people and taken them to Augusta; this had happened to other people in this colony before. One of the horses had been recovered by force; the better of the two, however, was speedily ridden off by the thieves; this horse was of greatest importance to Hanns Schmidt, a good man, who had bought it for ten pounds Sterling for his business in connection with the cowpen which had been purchased near Old Ebenezer. Immediately after our prayer hour I wrote a letter to several gentlemen in Mount Pleasant and in and around Augusta, asking them to take possession of this well-known horse if the Indians brought it in and to restore it to us. Tomorrow morning, one of our fastest messengers will be sent after these Indians on horseback, carrying this open letter. It could very well mean the financial ruin of Schmidt if he were to lose this horse, which is an absolute necessity to him.

Last week, a party of Indians had come to Savannah in order to get the presents which, by order of the king, they receive each year; clothing, blankets, linen, pretty boxes, woven cloth, rifles, powder, lead, axes, knives, and other household items. Instead of showing gratitude to, and affection for, the white people, these Indians first behaved disgracefully in Savannah; and then, on their way back home, they stole whatever they could find and take with them from gardens, fields, and paddocks. Usually, if they run out of meat underway, they shoot the best cows and oxen, take only the choice pieces and leave the rest to rot in the forest with the hide still on.

As a result of being treated so kindly by the English and after receiving so many gifts from them, these Indians have turned rebellious, and they have become impertinent and mean. On the other hand, the French and Spanish know how to keep them in check. The Indians know the boundaries between English, French, or Spanish territory very well; and they are crafty enough to let themselves be bribed by the French and Spanish into doing damage to the English. At present there is talk of a war between the English and the Indians, which seems to be unavoidable because the Indians take more and more liberties. In Europe, deer skins have become inexpensive, and traders can no longer afford to pay the same good prices they paid in the past. The Indians, on the other hand, insist unreasonably on being paid the same as before. This situation can easily lead to war. May God avert this danger from us!

A soldier from Frederica, together with his wife, has settled on a plantation on Ebenezer Creek; this year he planted its worst kind of land. In the spring, I saw with pity how scraggly his crops looked; nothing but a very poor harvest could reasonably be expected. However, since husband and wife both had worked very hard and said their prayers, God granted us good weather, especially in the area of their plantation. As a result, their crops of grain, beans, squash, and melons turned out as well as on one of the best pieces of land; both are filled with joy and praise the Lord. At noon today the wife, who lives in genuine fear of God, brought me, in a container she carried on her head, some fruit from their plantation, namely, a very large watermelon and several kinds of exceptionally good peaches.

Friday, the 27th of July. At the beginning of this week, when our shoemaker, Kohleisen, wanted to travel to Savannah, I sent word to him through his tythingman, or headman, to warn him not to get drunk again since, intoxicated, he would probably start some trouble, as, unfortunately, is his habit of doing. One of the people who took the same trip told me afterwards that, when he came aboard for the journey back home, he was dead drunk and fell into the river after they had left. No doubt he would have drowned, had it not been for the mercy of God, who allowed his traveling companion to save him most miraculously. After that, he was in great danger two more times. He has behaved this way ever since he came here, and word has it that he was the same way back in Germany. We have tried to be kind to him and we have tried to be firm, but we have succeeded only in preventing him from drinking excessively here in Ebenezer. He makes up for it at other places though, for example, in Purysburg or in Savannah, whenever he gets a chance to go there. So far, he has been an example of God's patience and mercy; I fear, however, that one day he will be made an example of divine justice and punishment, since he exhibits no signs of repentance. His wife is a pious woman; she has shed many a tear because of him and has sent many a sigh to God.

Saturday, the 28th of July. Our merciful God granted us very good weather which makes the fields fertile. A short while ago we had sufficient rain; now we have sufficient warmth and sunshine. The nights are cool, however; and we can sleep in comfort. Two weeks ago we believed that the river would rise a good deal (but the water level fell soon after that and we could not even use the lower millrun). Our people here as well as people in other communities would welcome it if our mills were rebuilt so that they could operate throughout the year, at least when using the lowest run. The water level usually falls after the wheat harvest and after the rye has been brought in, just at the time when we need the mill most.

Recently, my dear colleague has been giving some more thought to this problem; he is thinking of having a channel dug to bring in more water to the mill stream. Various other practically-minded people had thought of such a solution in the past; however, we have lacked both the manpower and the money for such an undertaking so far; and we still do. It has to be considered, though, that profits from running the mill year round would, hopefully, soon cover the building costs. As long as we don't have enough laborers, however, we can not start work on the channel, even if we had the money. Since our field hands arrived here, our farmers have started to plant larger rice and grain fields, so that public works do not benefit from these laborers.

Until now, much other useful public work could not be undertaken if God had not seen to it that the three Schubdrein brothers bought their freedom in Savannah, with money supplied mostly by us. Furthermore, we would not have a worker with his wife and five children in my house who, in addition to doing whatever needs to be done here, can also be called upon to work on public undertakings. Maybe these people can help dig the planned channel; on the other hand, we do not want to interrupt the useful progress of making and firing bricks. An impoverished English engineer, Brown, recently moved here to Ebenezer and asked us for work. For some time now he and Kogler have been busy making improvements on our rice stamp and barley press. Next to these, on the same drive-shaft, a machine will be mounted for shelling rice with great speed.

Brown also had some good ideas for constructing a windmill, which is to be used to separate the chaff from the kernels. We consider it a sign from God that we have received this knowledgeable, hard-working, and modest worker, who is content with little. People think that the work he did in Purysburg and in our rice stamp was well done; the fact that he is not very successful and poorly paid has its special reasons. Furthermore, here in Ebenezer, he will never work as an independent master builder; rather, he will work under Kogler's and Rottenberger's supervision, which he is quite willing to do. Since Kogler now has such an able assistant for building mills, I hope that very soon he will start the construction of a new sawmill, which is to be run by a small and easily accessible river. The preliminary discussions and work have been completed already. If God grants us success in this undertaking (as we trust and hope), then the food situation in Ebenezer will be much improved.

Monday, the 30th of July. For the past few days our schoolmaster on the plantations /Wertsch/ has been ill with fever; meanwhile I hold school in his place since my dear colleague is busy teaching the children in town. There is quite a difference between the schoolmaster we used to have on the plantations, and the new one. This can be plainly seen from the increased number of children attending school as well as from the fact that the children's education is progressing very well. The parents also say that their children love their schoolmaster like a father and are very eager to go to school. I enjoyed very much seeing for myself how well-behaved and well-taught our children are. Almost the only good thing that has resulted from the arrival of the transport of servants here[10] seems to be that we acquired a clever and hard-working schoolmaster, who also conducts himself properly. We also take good care of him.

Widow Lemmenhofer seems ever closer to death. She is suffering from dysentery and other ailments and her health is declining rather than improving. She is a good widow, as described by Paul, and she has had a good reputation in our community during all the time we have known her. Today, when I arrived, Mrs. Kalcher, a woman who is well-versed in the catechism, was with her. She was telling her about yesterday's consoling sermon based on the Seventh Sunday after Trinity dealing with those of the poor whose character exhibits the good qualities described in the introductory verses of Tobit 4:22 and the gospel.[11] We prayed together and I felt strengthened and awakened.

Tuesday, the 31st of July. It seems that the suggestion which I had recently made to some of our people concerning their servants, namely to give them their much sought-after freedom in exchange for making a certain amount of barrel-staves, is not very practical. One major obstacle is apparently that we do not have enough oak trees which yield wood suitable for barrel staves. Although many oaks grow on our large island, I hear that the trees have so many branches that only a small part of the wood could be used and that it would require a great deal of work at that. Some trees also have worm-holes and are useless for this reason.

On the good land on this side of the island most of the white oaks have been felled and then been left to rot away or were burned since this area used to be used as plantation land. We have, however, an abundance of very good cypresses; from which shingles, timber for building, and boards can be made, which bring a good price. There are enough white oaks on the Uchee land[12] and on the new plantations behind Abercorn, which our community will be able to use if they get more help.

AUGUST

Wednesday, the 1st of August. Whenever God lets me live from the end of one month to the beginning of the next, I become deeply aware of the progress of time; I try to benefit from this awareness in our communal meetings, while preaching on the divine word as well as while praying. The fleeting nature of time and our haste into eternity impress me greatly and cause me to think seriously upon my own death; various health problems, although minor, contribute to some extent to these feelings. This time, God in His goodness made the change yesterday from the last day of July to the first day of August a memorable one and granted great edification to my soul through my praying and contemplating God's word, first in my house, then in the one into which Kalcher just moved, and then in the school at the plantations, where, much to my delight, I now hold school in place of our sick schoolmaster /Wertsch/.

It would be too big a task to enumerate in detail all the spiritual blessings God has sent to us; I will mention here only how our loving God has granted a great deal of consolation to me and my wife, who had been dangerously ill for a long time. We both felt strengthened despite our circumstances, which are frequently oppressive enough, by the edifying contemplation of the passage devoted to yesterday, the last day of July: "Call upon me in the day of trouble"[1] etc., which is contained in Mr. Bogatzky's *Daily Housebook of the Children of God*;[2] while reading these edifying words it almost seemed to me as if the author had known of my wife's spiritual and physical difficulties and had set down his instruction and consolation for this day accordingly.

No two faces could be more alike than the similarities between my wife's spiritual and secular circumstances during her protracted tribulations and those described in this beautiful testimony to a woman who bears her cross steadfastly, like a person blessed in God. Shortly before that, we had been reading from the *Little Treasure Chest*:[3] "Restore unto me the joy of thy salvation," etc.; "As one whom a mother comforteth, so I will comfort you".[4] Afterwards, in our little room, we prayed together, simply and with all our heart, to God, our Father. I had returned to my work right after that, but then it occurred to me to consult the *Daily Housebook* in order to see which verse was dedicated to the day. When I saw what it was, I felt that God's promise had been fulfilled by this verse, together with our beautiful meditation "I will comfort you," etc.; and, filled with joy, I hastened to show this passage to my wife. I have no doubt that the time will come when God will let us offer our sincere thanksgiving to Him for all His help.

In addition to the books and newspapers, the chest from Halle contained selected verses for special holidays, printed in large letters on quarto pages; these I gave to the schoolchildren on the plantations today and they were overjoyed. I gave to each child one verse with which it had not been familiar so far; to the youngest children I gave the ones which were the shortest and the easiest, the older children received longer and more difficult verses; the children will memorize these verses at home and will recite them by heart tomorrow and the day after tomorrow. My dear colleague will do the same in the school in town tomorrow. Very recently I felt inspired anew by reading in the *East Indian Reports* about the great care our esteemed missionaries and their dear assistants there take to teach the children.[5] May our loving God bless them and their simple endeavors.

In Augsburg, some time ago, in complying with a humble request from us, the powerful evangelical words from Zechariah 9:9, "Rejoice greatly, O Daughter of Zion" had been copied on parchment most beautifully, decorated with edifying scenes and then framed under glass. The costs were met by several of our most esteemed benefactors, especially by our dear Pastor Schäffer in Regensburg. Unfortunately, during shipping, while still in the chest, the glass was broken, presumably by customs officials in London; in the past this prevented us from displaying these very beautifully written and painted pages containing the verse. Now, however, we were able to mount both pictures on the wall behind the pulpit in Jerusalem Church as well as in Zion Church, since this verse brought a joyous message to the Zion and Jerusalem of the New Testament. When a teacher is standing there preaching, they are visible above his head.

We also have several rather edifying etchings from Augsburg, done on large pages of best quality paper, depicting artistic and life-like scenes from the life of Christ from His birth to Ascension. Until now, we could not display them in church because we lacked frames; now we hope that engineer Brown, who works here, will be able to make some for us. They will be fine decorations for our church, and people will be edified by looking at them. Perhaps at some time in the future our dear God will send us such edifying Biblical pictures for our schools, which would enhance considerably the lessons taught to the younger and more simple children. I know from experience, since our catechism is illustrated, that the pictures are of value in teaching.

For several years now, some people among us who are knowledgeable in such things have been of the opinion that a rather long channel ought to be dug in order to increase the water level at our mill stream by about two feet, bringing in more water from the Savannah River. The advantage of such an undertaking would be that at least our flour mill could be worked at times when the water level is at its lowest. Nobody doubted that this plan would be practical, if only we had enough money and laborers to make it a reality. If we had not lacked both money and workers in the past, we would have gone ahead and undertaken this necessary and much wished-for task.

However, my dear colleague, Mr. Lemke, realized, on the basis of calculations he had been making yesterday and the day before yesterday, that, had we dug this channel, it would have done us great damage; he proved thoroughly and mathematically that, through this channel we had planned, water from our mill stream would have flowed back into the Savannah River rather than the other way around. These calculations did not turn out the way our people, as well as others, would have wished, since now there is no hope left that the water level could be increased in our mill stream, no matter how hard people were willing to work. Nevertheless, I consider it a benefaction from God and a sign from Him that we learned of the nature of these two rivers beforehand, rather than learning of it after having built a channel and spent even the least amount of money on it. May God allow us to submit totally to His fatherly guidance in all things from now on, and may He permit us to practice the *festina lente* in a Christian manner! May He also fill the hearts of all of our people here with gratitude for the great blessing of our mills. Although they cannot be worked year-round, they are still a worldly treasure for our community. Perhaps God will grant us a second sawmill soon, which, in turn, will enable us to construct a second flour-mill we are planning to build in a little river that is not as close by as could be wished but is deep and convenient enough, and which is fed by springs and rain, resulting in running water throughout the year.

Friday, the 3rd of August. Recently, N.N. promised to mend his ways, but now he has sinned again: in anger, he shouted incredible curses at his wife. I punished him for this yesterday, and I demonstrated to him from God's word how he would be judged. But it did little good. He threatened to run away and leave his wife and children. I did not answer because I knew well that he would not do that; he would not leave the children. Today I visited the couple again. To my great joy I found that he had asked his wife's forgiveness on his knees, and he had prayed to God, asking Him to grant them a change of their circumstances and to forgive them their many sins. He was embarrassed and depressed; he willingly listened to me when I showed him that he was in grave danger, and he promised to pray frequently, on his knees, and to keep his shortcomings in check. His wife was likewise reminded how to behave towards her hot-tempered husband and to conduct herself obediently, cleverly, quietly, and gently. We prayed together, and I left them the beautiful words Colossians; 3 12–15 for later contemplation.

Sunday, the 5th of August. Today, my dear colleague, who had held the sermon in Zion Church again, brought me the news that today, on the Eighth Sunday after Trinity, widow Lemmenhofer had been set free from her earthly pains and tribulations by a temporal death. Yesterday, after school, I had gone to visit her and had found her very weak and eager to leave this world. I asked her whether, in her heart of hearts, she was sure that her sins had been forgiven and that she would enter the heavenly kingdom. She had no doubts whatsoever. She had trouble in speaking because of her weakness and the pain. I reminded her of the words: "Look unto me and be ye saved, all the ends of the earth."[6] God had blessed her husband in church with these words not long before his death. I also recited for her the precious words of our crucified Savior: "Verily I say unto thee, Today shalt thou be with me in paradise."[7] This message filled her with joy. Finally I asked her whether or not she had put her worldly affairs in order and whether or not she had seen to it that after her departure from this world no quarrels and disputes would arise. She answered that Glaner knew her wishes.

She had lived on her late husband's small plantation close to the mill, and her household was always well-run; her neighbors, especially the aforementioned Glaner, helped her out regularly when she needed them. She had enjoyed living quietly by herself, and therefore she had never engaged any servants. The house she had built on the plantations was one of the best, built in the style of Salzburger houses, made of strong wood. She also leaves a good many head of cattle and horses and various household items and furniture. There are even rumors she may have left a good sum of cash. Glaner, her only relative by marriage, will probably inherit all, although I am sure she also thought of some of our widows and orphans and I do not doubt she left them something, too.

Monday, the 6th of August. Widow Lemmenhofer was properly buried today after school, which I am still holding myself while our schoolmaster is sick. God granted us a great deal of edification; we contemplated part of the vita of the late Pastor Mischke.[8] Many people had come, as always when a pious member of our community is buried; invitations are not necessary.

At present, with God's help, in my free time at home and on the plantations in the hours after school and before our weekly sermon, I am reading a very remarkable account of the missionaries in the East Indies.[9] God has granted me to apply the not inconsiderable benefit I derived from it to fulfilling faithfully my Christian duties and my office as a teacher. I found, among other insights, the following items especially impressive:

1. Missionary work and missionary institutions are sanctified by God not only through the fact that so many gifts are given in joy and with the blessing of many hundreds of honest servants and children of God but also by the fact that other very important tokens of divine mercy, all-encompassing power, and wisdom are revealed by Him every day; it would lead too far to enumerate these in detail here.

2. The genuine unanimity between the missionaries and their assistants.

3. Their untiring efforts in assuming their various tasks at home and on their journeys.

4. Their wisdom and quickwittedness in the face of so many serious incidents. The clever and Christian conduct of missionary Fabricius at Madras during the siege laid by the French and the subsequent occupation of the area after its fall ought to serve

as an example for the wisdom and strength given to these servants of God by Him and ought to demonstrate how much He loves their prayer and service.

5. Their exceptional patience and steadfastness in the face of the personal suffering they have to endure, both spiritually and physically, just like the first adherents of our Lord Jesus, as is written in 2 Corinthians 6;4-10.

6. The great care with which they hold Holy Baptism and Holy Communion; it shows most pleasantly God's assistance and blessing. I am taking note especially of the edifying signs of God's grace in those who were baptized, received Holy Communion, died, etc.; I intend to share these examples with my own listeners, partly in order to humble them and partly in order to enlighten them.

7. Their insatiable hunger and thirst for saving all people in those parts of the world; they need such enthusiasm as a means to help them overcome people's fears, stupidity, prejudice and other serious difficulties.

8. The humble and friendly manner in which they embrace even the poorest, least important, and most despised persons, following the example of our Savior.

9. Their Christian and most commendable custom of praying, of singing, and of holding funeral sermons at the funerals of their converted Christians in order to edify the survivors and the funeral attendants.

10. Their steadfast teaching of the dogma of sin, as well as of the blessed salvation from sin, through the powerful Savior of the world.

11. The frequent repetition of publicly held sermons.

12. The very useful effect of the schools built now and then for the heathens.

13. Their Christian thriftiness in distributing the gifts sent by European benefactors, thereby serving to spread God's word.

14. Their frequent visits to sick and dying Christians.

15. Their lively exchange of letters not only among themselves, but also their communications with rural parsons and teachers of the catechism, as well as their brotherly letters to their beloved brothers in Madras and Cudulur.

16. Their frequent prayer and teaching of God's word both at

the mission house as well as in the houses of newly-converted Christians. May God protect His servants and the good works done through them; may He send them among the heathens so that many poor souls can be saved! May He also bless the friends and benefactors of those missionaries and inspire others to follow in their footsteps!

Tuesday, the 7th of August. Last night, and also for some time during the day today, we had some rain; towards noon it turned into a violent downpour that lasted for the rest of the day and into the night. The water-level in the Savannah River is rising very fast now, and our mills can be worked again. Because of the bad weather I thought only a few people would attend our weekly sermon; however, in addition to the children, a good number of men and women came. God, through His word, granted me great edification. Our schoolmaster seems to have recovered somewhat from the fever; he held school himself again today for the first time since he fell ill.

Wednesday, the 8th of August. Since some of our people here have shown considerable interest in keeping slaves, after our servants arrived here, I, too, have been thinking about this. While I was considering the problem, God arranged matters so that, at the time I had to make a decision, I was reading the two appended reports of the East-Indies account, numbers sixty-five and sixty-six which had arrived in the chest from Halle. The following passages in these reports added to my information and influenced my thoughts: appendix number sixty-five, page 797: "Several heathens told one of the assistants, Joshua, that, in their opinion, the Patres in Trankenbar (as they call us missionaries) did so much good by putting an end to the slave trading there. They also said such good deeds were rare." From appendix sixty-six, page 1042: "Another heathen was very pleased that the slave trading had been stopped." From an edifying letter by Mr. Diego, a country parson, to Doctor Professor Francke, page 1072: "After I had left for Tanschauer, the Roman Catholics got together, went before the city sheriff, and accused me of having commited the crime of slave trading (which is a sin and very much abhorred by the heathens who, also punish it)."

Therefore, on Sunday (the 5th of this month), when I heard that young Kieffer had bought another young female slave in

Carolina for thirty-four pounds Sterling, I became very uneasy.
They now have one male Negro, two such black women, and a
young boy as slaves. At the closing of our prayer hour we sang:
Wer hofft in Gott und dem vertraut, wird nimmermehr zuschanden;
and: *Wer auf diesen Felsen baut,* etc.[10] People sang these words of
faith with so much enthusiasm that I was strongly impressed;
and I would have wished to write them down, using large letters
and the same style as our verses for holidays which were printed
in Halle, and to fasten these sheets on the doors of all of our dear
listeners! In the future, I will not say anything against keeping
slaves anymore, since our Lord Trustees allow it. Also, many of
our people here are convinced that slaves are necessary because
we lack capable and reliable servants I, however, sigh, for myself
as well as for others: Lead us not into temptation! People could
easily be tempted, if they are insincere about the preceding fifth
petition but, rather, fall even deeper into sin by obvious or subtle
conformity to the world.

I was positively impressed by what Mr. Lemke said to me on
Sunday: because the children of Israel did not know any better,
the Lord saw to it that the Canaanites remained in the land,
turning afterwards into a nuisance, leading to unrest and
punishment. The same could easily become true as far as Negro
slaves are concerned; there are many sad examples to that effect.

Friday, the 10th of August. The seven tythingmen or headmen of the seven districts in our community are of great service;
so far they had several clever plans and carried them out well.
Today, after school and before the time for our weekly sermon, I
met with those who administer the areas at the plantations. I
read to them a certain written document and also explained it; I
asked them to make the content of this document known among
the people of their district. This is quite important for me, for
my dear colleague, and even for the entire community. The
devil is ever on the alert to hamper attempts at improving people's circumstances; his work is all the more dangerous if it is
cloaked in the pretense of good intent, as is the case in this matter. However, when we learn the truth in time, things go well.

N.N., an honest man, had taken the side of a certain person;
in his anger, however, he had gone too far; and I had to remind
him of his duty and punish him. He was finally willing to listen

to me and followed my advice, otherwise the damage done would have been even greater. He regretted his temper, almost crying; and he told me something which I had to know in order to prevent certain irregularities which were about to take place in Old-Ebenezer. Conformity to the world occurred several times in the past, but I never know for sure what is in everybody's heart. This time it became apparent in several people who have business at our recently purchased cowpen.

Saturday, the 11th of August. God has sent a violent fever to Zoller, that mean servant of the wife of our clock-maker. It is my dearest wish that, harnessed by disease, he will take the opportunity and allow us to save him from his misery[11] and lead him to genuine repentance and to Christ. He is good at pretending; he acts as if he truly feels and regrets his many and serious sins. His wife, who has a better heart but who is quite ignorant,[12] says now that he has started to pray, using his own words and confiding his misery to God; she also says he asks her to pray with him frequently.

Sunday, the 12th of August. This Sunday, the ninth after Trinity, seventy-four members of our community and three people from Purysburg held Holy Communion. Several more had indicated their wish to participate, too; some did not come, for reasons unknown to me, others I myself asked, out of love for them, to wait a little longer in order to prepare themselves better. Several people from Goshen came and attended our public service, and we had quite a large gathering. God, in His mercy, granted us to spread His word vigorously, three times. He will surely not let it be without His blessing. I believe that God's word teaches all of us the path to life in such a simple and easily understood manner that, at the reckoning on the Day of Judgment, no excuses will be possible. God may have pity on those who, despite all attempts at enlightenment, warnings, and punishments, prefer to remain in spiritual death and seek consolation in the pleasures of the flesh.

Monday, the 13th of August. Yesterday morning I received several letters at once, some from Charleston and some from Savannah. Dr. Graham writes in one of them how happy he was to hear that a machine had been invented and constructed which promises to do the following: to make the shelling of rice fast,

cheap, and easy, separate the chaff from the grain, and to press
it, all in one process and with the use of one water-driven mill
wheel only. We also made several improvements on our old rice
press. God helps us in all things; strangers are surprised by this
and sometimes share our joy. If only all of our own people here
would recognize how much goodness, spiritual as well as physical, our Lord has shown to us so far; if only they would do their
part through prayer, good will, and honest and well-done work
in exchange for cash in order to contribute to various useful
projects.

Yesterday I spoke on the gospel dealing with the subject of
Christian charity towards the poor; at the end of my sermon I
asked my listeners to contribute lovingly their share through
prayer, good will, and work, so that we here in Ebenezer can continue to make plans for projects which will benefit our community further and to carry out some of these plans. This way
not only the poor among us would find an opportunity to increase their income but also those who would supervise them in
their work, and this, in turn, would enable them to help the
needy. Among such plans is the building of another millrun of
the kind which could be worked for the most part of the year,
even if the water level in the millstream is at its lowest; at present,
we have only one, and we can not cope with the amounts of grain
brought in for milling by our own people as well as by some from
other places, at the time when it is most necessary.

Another plan is to build, in the German style, a second sawmill
at a very convenient site; with God's help, we hope to obtain a
good income from such a mill. Since the previous batch of letters
arrived here, several strange problems arose to hamper the
building of this mill. I had attempted to deal with these difficulties by composing a written document (which I mentioned in
the entry for the 10th of August), and I hope it will have its desired effect. Col. Heron (the former commanding officer in
Frederica) wrote me a friendly letter from Charleston; he is asking for many boards, which he wants to ship to the West Indies
and to Charleston. These boards, especially those made from cypress wood, are so much in demand in Carolina that the merchants pay almost any price one asks, up to twenty shillings Sterling for one hundred feet. Mr. Heron informs me also that

definite news reached Charleston, namely that the government in our colony would change soon. He mentions that Mr. Habersham would be in a position to tell me more about it, but he did not write anything about that. Someone who had been at Port Royal heard there that Parliament had decided to strengthen this colony again with a sizeable regiment for its defense.

Wednesday, the 15th of August. Recently, during the dog days, our weather was moderate, partly because of the rain and partly because of cool winds. Of the people who have lived here for some years, only a few came down with fever this summer. Most of our servants, however, are sick with fever; they have to get used to this climate. The three Schubdrein brothers, who bought their freedom, have served our community well as free men. So far, despite the hard work they did, they had remained healthy, but now they are complaining of some ailment. They are honest people, and they are setting a good example for others. They are also well-liked and respected by most people of our community.

The youngest brother wishes to go to Germany as soon as possible in order to bring back with him to this country the rest of their brothers and sisters. This might be the opportunity I have been waiting for; and young Schubdrein could accompany my two sons, who wish to pursue their studies and who are eager to leave, to London and then on to Halle. May our dear God reveal to us His merciful and welcome wish in this matter! In taking such an important step no undue haste ought to be shown. Concerning the plans for my sons, I had written to Charleston as well as to our esteemed Mr. Albinus. Mr. Habersham's ship had to wait for the right winds and was finally able to sail on the 1st of August. Already several years ago I obtained the permission of dear Doctor Professor Francke to send the boys to Halle.

Friday, the 17th of August. Ruprecht Steiner, an honest widower, is weak and despondent, not only from too much hard work but also from bad luck; in quick succession he lost several head of cattle and some pigs. He also had to let go his two willful servants (a married couple); and his household has been deteriorating for quite a while now. He has three sickly sons; the oldest is about thirteen years old, and they do their best to help, but I would have preferred to see him keep the servants. He thinks, however, that the couple was a bad influence and he could no longer stand their quarreling and dishonesty nor could he discipline them. Servants of their kind need two masters, both the head of the household as well as a wife who can keep a sharp eye on them. Brandner will handle them better. I gave twenty shillings Sterling as a gift to Steiner because he was so ill and depressed; also, in keeping with the wish of the Lord Trustees to encourage silk-making, I gave him two pounds Sterling for that purpose as well as several large and well-developed mulberry trees. I would like to help him in other ways also, if only I knew how. I could assist him in finding light work, since he can not possibly run a plantation; I could ease his worries for his children, and the two older ones I could place with good masters for learning a trade. However, he loves his sons so much that he does not want to be separated from them.

Saturday, the 18th of August. This week the long bridge which leads to the sawmill and which is used for rolling logs up to the mill was repaired. Shortly before that, our new rice-mill had been completed; both undertakings are quite important for us and will benefit our community greatly. Today we held a conference with our most experienced master-builders and carpenters in the hope that they will come to a conclusion regarding the sawmill which we intend to construct. If the new dam is to be built the same way our present dam at the mills is built, then it would require a great deal of time and money; therefore we suggested another method of construction which would result also in a durable dam, but our expenses would be cut by one-fifth; and we convinced them all. God be praised for the signs of His merciful care for us and His guidance in this important undertaking! May He be praised also for the good will among our workers! May He continue to look upon us in kindness and may He bless this important task, which we will undertake in the very near future! We intend to work only for His glory and for the benefit of our community.

Monday, the 20th of August. I had asked a good friend of mine from Carolina, with whom I exchange letters regularly and to whom I lend books if he needs them, to send me Dr. Walch's *Introduction to the Religious Struggles of the Evangelical Lutheran Church*,[13] which I wanted to read. What I have learned so

far has made me quite sad; it is rather obvious how busily Satan
has been at work since the blessed Reformation took place, sow-
ing the seeds of discord among the members of the Christian
Church as well as in the hearts of many of its ministers, widening
the rifts of disagreements. I myself will do my best to pray with
all my heart for our poor and troubled church, which is being
maligned by its Papist and other enemies because of its problems; and I will strive, day and night, for peace and grace, without which no one will be granted to look upon our Lord. I find it
highly significant that our Lord Jesus, in His prayer as a High-
priest of His church, recommended peace and unity of purpose
with so much emphasis to His ministers and listeners; also, after
His resurrection He preached peace to His apostles and granted
it to them.

Tuesday, the 21st of August. Some of our people could not
come to terms with the fact that I had assisted those who run the
plantations and that I had, in a manner of speaking, forgotten to
take care of my own house and my own family's needs. Therefore, some time ago, without my knowing about it or planning
any of it, the President and the Assistants of the Council saw to it
that I was given a piece of very fertile land in Goshen, behind
Abercorn, altogether six-hundred acres, to be used by two of the
preachers for the community of Ebenezer. I could not have
wished for anything better. Also, a few months later, I was offered a plantation for my family of almost five hundred acres in
the same neighborhood, close to the Savannah River; there, I
would have our esteemed friend, Mr. Habersham, as a neighbor.[14] Doctor Graham also lives there; he is a member of the
Council and a friend of our community.

The land bordering on the western side of this plantation is
settled by German people of our religion; they gave the name
Goshen to this area which is extremely fertile and easily accessible. They would welcome me as their neighbor because they are
worried that someone would move there who would run his
plantation on a large scale with a great number of Negro slaves.
My plantation has many advantages: plenty of good soil, trees,
and pasture land. A creek runs through it, and on its north-east-
ern side it is bordered by the Savannah River, making it very easy

to travel to and from it; fish can be caught simply by immersing a trap made from wooden dowels.

If I had refused this property, I would surely have invited bad will; several people from Carolina were most eager to buy this plantation. However, the members of the Council were not too pleased at the prospect of having these people from Carolina settle there, but they could not have very well refused to sell to them, had I refused to accept. The cost for surveying comes to five pounds Sterling; and I am assured by the authorities that there will be no pressure on me to take possession right away. At present, my official duties, my other business affairs, my lack of experience in running a plantation, and especially my frame of mind, make it practical for me to remain where I am, for the time being, rather than to start working the land, which could, eventually, improve our living conditions.

My wife is constantly ill, and the servants here in this country are unreliable and cost more than their services are worth; furthermore, I cannot bring myself to buy Negro slaves. Also, I am almost forty-seven years old and I have to devote so much of my time to the everyday affairs of our community that, by necessity, I have to neglect some of the main duties of my spiritual office. It seems my wife will depart this world soon; both my older sons are willing and able to pursue more advanced studies; and, some time ago, they made their decision to serve the Church of Christ. As far as my two little daughters are concerned, I trust that our Heavenly Father will take care of them even without this new plantation. However, I am willing to spend the money for the surveying as well as the taxes should a larger sum be due soon. I think that this land could be used to the advantage of our community, or it could help some of our dear friends and assistants who might want to join us in the future; if not, then I feel sure that I will be able to recover the money I spent on it by selling out to someone who wants to work this plantation. My dear colleague, Mr. Lemke, does not wish to run a plantation, either; otherwise I would have let him have this property. Who knows what God intended by sending me this land in such a surprising way.

Yesterday evening I received a letter from Mr. Habersham.

He writes that he had been out on the plantation and had brought a surveyor along in order to fix the property lines for him and me; he asks me to come, too. I wrote back to him and explained the reasons for my not being able to travel just now; I trust in his honesty and friendship, and I am sure that he will have my best interests at heart.

Wednesday, the 22nd of August. God has punished unruly N. with sickness; and, as a result, his conscience is in uproar and his disgraceful behavior in the past causes him much grief now and he is in tears. Yesterday he poured out his distress to my colleague, and he confessed several sins which are especially severe and are burdening his conscience. Today he sent word to me that I might come and instruct him and help him ease the misery of his soul and conscience. I was most willing to do this; I talked to him, and we prayed together. I told him, however, of a woman whom I know in Savannah, who, just like him, came to recognize and regret her sins, especially her trespasses against the Eighth Commandment while she was sick, and who, after her recovery, fell back into her old bad ways.

Thursday, the 23rd of August. Our friend, Mr. Habersham, wrote me another letter, urging me to come to Goshen in order to discuss with him the surveying of our plantations. Although I have so little time and my wife is so dangerously sick, I had to leave this morning and travel there to see him. Towards noon, after an uneventful journey, I arrived at Dr. Graham's house, where he and his entire family are now living. However, I had to wait for him since he had gone up the creek in order to meet the surveyor and his assistants. He came back only a little after six o'clock. By then it was evening and it had begun to rain heavily, so I had to stay for the night. We concluded our business quickly, and we were both pleased with the surveryor's work.

Several people, honest and meaning well, had come; and they tried to convince me of the considerable advantages of using Negro slaves. It is quite obvious how much work gets done by these Negroes, not only in other parts of this colony, but also here, among us, at Kieffer's plantation and at that of his in-law, Kronenberger, who both have Negro slaves. However, my doubts are not on the question of whether or not Negro slaves are useful; rather, I doubt that a Christian should buy them with a good conscience and keep them in perpetual slavery. At this time, I seem to be completely against this idea; however, I wish with all my heart to be enlightened and to be able to form a more educated opinion.

Recently, a ship carrying three-hundred Negroes docked in Charleston; all the slaves were sold at very high prices. Until now, an adult young male fresh from Africa went for a little more than twenty pounds Sterling; now the price has risen to forty pounds. Who, except the very rich, could risk that amount on an unproven and still inexperienced slave? Several of our people who are practically minded are of the opinion that one should rather buy slaves who are already familiar with the country and the kind of work expected of them.

Friday, the 24th of August. I received a short letter from our esteemed Pastor Brunnholz; Mr. Meyer received a long letter from Mr. Vigera,[15] and he gave it to me to read because it contained a passage which pertained to Mr. Brunnholz. Among other things, I read the amazing news that last fall, N.[16] had brought a shipload of Germans from Rotterdam to Philadelphia and sold them there as servants, both male and female, strutting about in velvet clothes embroidered in gold, playing the rich merchant. His cargo also included a consignment from someone in Rotterdam, consisting of a great many goods for trading and a quantity of Rhine wine. He sold these goods in Philadelphia and then returned to Holland and Germany in order to pick up more people. His brother stayed in Philadelphia.

A German merchant, Mr. Heinrich Schleydorn, had the presence of mind to extract a promise from N.N., orally and sealed by a handshake, to make good the damages he had caused to our community and some of its members in the past. After that, apparently, Pastor Brunnholz had written to me, in order to ask me to delegate the necessary legal authority to this aforementioned Mr. Schleydorn so that he could attempt to persuade this man, at first in friendliness, and then, if kind words were to no avail, to coerce him to make good the damages for which he is responsible. This letter, however, did not arrive here. Who knows what methods N. used in Philadelphia to lay his hands on letters addressed to us? He is quite familiar with the handwriting of our friends and he knows where and when letters are sent back and forth between Philadelphia, Carolina, and Georgia.

In the past, he very cunningly intercepted and secretly opened my letters addressed to Philadelphia and did the same to letters sent to me by Mr. Brunnholz and by Mr. Vigera, without our noticing any of it for a long time. He had been worried, and quite rightly so, that his various schemes would have become apparent and been endangered if we had been able to keep each other informed through regular correspondence. Another circumstance which makes me think that he tampered with the letter sent by Mr. Brunnholz is the fact that since he left Philadelphia we have been receiving our letters on time again and none have been lost. Mr. Vigera writes that the so-called Prince of Wurttemberg[17] had become a soldier in Boston and then defected soon afterwards, masquerading as a preacher in Maryland for some time.

Mr. Vigera also writes that a skilled miller, Samuel Schröder from Danzig, had arrived in Georgia with the transport of servants from overseas; he went to see Mr. Vigera and shortly afterwards went on to Nova Scotia. Mr. Vigera had told him that he would have been better off if he had stayed in Ebenezer for a while, where he would have had the opportunity to serve God and his fellow-man. The miller had answered: "If I had known then what I know now, then I certainly would have stayed there." After his arrival, he had fallen in with some dissolute fellows; they all came to Ebenezer for a visit and left soon. He did not show even the least love for God's word; he was a good friend of the vile and treacherous Dippelian S.[18] who, as Mr. Vigera reports in connection with the aforementioned miller, traveled from Charleston to Philadelphia, using the land route in the middle of winter and barely escaped with his life. Mr. Vigera married an English lady who does sewing and tailoring for ladies.

Sunday, the 26th of August. Today, on the last Sunday of August, I should have preached and held Holy Communion for the people of our faith in Savannah; my trip to see Mr. Habersham because of our new plantations, however, made this impossible, since I was unable to return from there as quickly as I had planned. I sent word to these German people and informed them of this impediment; I made them a firm promise that one of us would come to them in eight days, that is, on the Twelfth Sunday after Trinity, God willing. Certainly, it would be rather desirable if some rewards of our office were to be reaped from among the people of Acton and Vernonburg, since we have worked with them now for several years to the best of our ability, through God's grace. Since they have neither ministers nor schoolmasters, they tend to quarrel; and there is considerable disorder among them which affects us negatively, too. Some of them are honest people and willing to accept God's word with an obedient heart.

Wednesday, the 29th of August. A few days ago, Col. Heron wrote a friendly letter to me from Savannah, where he stayed for several days because of his boat and because he had to take care of certain unpleasant matters. He asks me to come to Purysburg, where he wants to meet with me on his way back to Charleston in order to discuss some important business. Since I had to be in Savannah on business in any case, especially because of what Mr. Vigera had written to me regarding N.N., I preferred to meet him there rather than travel to Purysburg; in this way I was able to attend to two matters during one trip. Today, at noon, I arrived back home in Ebenezer, happily and in good health. On my way, however, I had witnessed the aftermath of a very sad accident which had taken place at a certain dangerous spot in the Savannah River between our plantations and Purysburg, where several mishaps had already occurred in the past. Yesterday a large merchant's barge, which had been on its way from Augusta carrying more than one-thousand pounds of tanned deer skins, got caught in the strong current and collided with a tree-trunk floating in the river, and overturned. The Negroes and the white people who had been aboard were in extreme danger of their lives; several of our people here, however, rushed to their aid and saved them.

Today, some people arrived from Purysburg to lend their assistance, too; and all were busy fishing for, collecting, and drying as many tanned hides as they could find. Most of them were lost in the river, and most of the ones brought ashore were ruined. Several months ago a very promising young man from Purys-

burg drowned at the very same dangerous part of the river; and
on a few occasions our boats and people, too, have been in grave
danger and have been saved by our merciful God. Our people
here would be willing to contribute their share to a communal
effort to keep this dangerous part of the river free of the many
floating logs if some people from Purysburg and some of the
merchants who use this river most were likewise willing to do
their part. Here, in this country, it is a major drawback that
rivers and creeks which are used for transportation are not kept
clean of floating obstacles. Once, when I spoke to an official
about this, he answered me that only a person who had felled a
tree could be held responsible to keep it out of the waterways,
and nobody else; people had better cope with this situation as
best as they can. The banks of the rivers here are densely covered with trees, which are frequently felled by storms; and sometimes the logs come to rest at dangerous spots in the water.

Col. Heron brought me the pleasant news that the Lower
House of Parliament in Carolina had refuted, using iron-clad
reasons, the opinion of the Governor that it be necessary and
useful to unite Carolina and Georgia and to have both provinces
under the authority of only one governor; rather, it was demonstrated that such a step would be of considerable disadvantage.
There is little doubt now that Georgia will remain separate from
South Carolina and North Carolina, even if the Lord Trustees
were of a mind to dissolve the government of Georgia, since only
recently the plan of unification had been rejected by the local
Council as well as by the most prominent citizens of this colony,
and their decision was reported to the Lord Trustees. If the governor of South Carolina were our friend, then a unification
might prove advantageous; however, rather the opposite is true,
and many colonists, especially the weaker ones, have to suffer
for it.

Thursday, the 30th of August. I received an answer to a letter
of mine from a benefactor from Charleston. He informs me that
he will not be able to supply us with silk-worm seeds from Portugal, as I had asked him to do, the reason being that at present no
ships from that country are sailing to our colonies or vice versa.
He advises me to write to London as soon as possible and to ask
the Lord Trustees for such seeds; it would be easy to obtain the

seeds that way since ships sail regularly back and forth between
Lisbon and London. Several weeks ago, when I sent samples of
silk made by Portugese silk-worms to Mr. Verelst, I told him that
I had asked this benefactor, Mr. Hector Beringer de Beaufain, to
get us such seeds and that I had no doubt that he would be able
to do so; now, however, I have to give up this hope. I do not plan
to write to Mr. Verelst immediately; the reason I mention this
problem here is, that I hope that our esteemed Mr. Albinus will,
as soon as he receives this diary, ask Mr. Verelst to obtain the
needed silk-worm seeds from Portugal for us.

SEPTEMBER

Saturday, the 1st of September. Once again, the passing of another month and season strikes me as something special and
causes me to reflect on the spiritual and physical blessings we
have received from God, and I welcome this occasion to praise
His great name and to admire His wisdom as well as His
ways of guiding us. And now, with the change of month and season, I consider it my duty as a Christian and as a minister to keep
this diary for our benefactors and friends in Europe who follow
God's works and rejoice in them, in order to inform and edify
them and, to the best of my knowledge and recollection, to set
down in this diary the examples of God's ways, works, and
blessings.

I shall start my account with yesterday, the 31st of August, and
I rightfully consider it a sign of divine grace that I received several very pleasant letters from our most esteemed Fathers, benefactors, and friends, in England and Germany. I had just sealed
a packet of letters to our worthy Mr. Albinus, in which were
some letters and the diary for the last two months, and I had
given it to my dear colleague, Mr. Lemke, for forwarding, since
he was going to Savannah on official business, when several
packets of letters and English and German writings were
brought to us from Savannah. What brought us rich material for
our hearty pleasure and for the praise of God consists of the
following:

1. The news of the life and tolerable health of our worthy Fathers and benefactors in London, Augsburg, and Halle. Our

dear Senior Urlsperger entered his sixty-sixth year on 20 August, old style; and therefore it pleases me all the more that he was still alive and in good health when he sent the last letter. That is precisely what we read in Mr. Albinus' letter about our prominent benefactor, von N. N., Court Chaplain Ziegenhagen, and Dr. Francke. In his pleasant letter of 8 May he writes thus:

> Our dear Court Chaplain is now, God be praised, as cheerful as one might expect. That is a great comfort for me. From Augsburg we have received news, thank God, that Senior Urlsperger and Mr. von N.N. are very well. Likewise, our dear Dr. Francke has, God be praised, gotten along tolerably well so far; but he has his many trials and suffering.

2. The news of the love, affection, and intercession of these and many other benefactors, who are also continuing so zealously to further the spiritual and physical welfare of the Ebenezer congregation before God and man, as is so clearly and abundantly evidenced by their letters as well as by the consignments of charities that have flowed together in Augsburg and have been sent to us. The names of our highly esteemed benefactors in the two said consignments are a good oder for our edification and shall be included in our intercession. Since they enclosed very pleasing gifts for the information of my children, my faith is strengthened again that our almighty and loving God will also care for them on the journey and in Halle, since I am planning to send them with the first safe and convenient opportunity to London and then on to the schools of the Orphanage.

3. Our dear Mr. von N. N.'s zealous efforts and his wise suggestions to the Lord Trustees and to Ebenezer for furthering our true interest, about which I read most encouraging examples in the letters from Mr. Albinus and Senior Urlsperger's letters as well as in the letters that he himself has written to us. I have been concerned that this highly esteemed benefactor might receive both from the Lord Trustees and especially from us more than one reason to withdraw his favor from us and no longer to devote his time and thoughts to the betterment of our physical conditions since his efforts with intercession, suggestions, and expenditures have already failed several times. We are assured, however, not only by Mr. Albinus of his continued af-

fection, rather it is now proved by his very useful and pleasing letters to me and to Mr. Meyer. May our merciful God, who has His pleasure in mercy and merciful people, continue to keep these His worthy and chosen tools, may He strengthen them in soul and body, may He keep them in health and life for the good of us and His church, and may He grant His spiritual and physical blessings to them, their families, and their descendants!

Among the proofs of divine goodness and care I also righfully count the edifying letters and writings from our other worthy benefactors and friends, which we have received with pleasure in the said packet, for example, from our worthy Counselor Wallbaum, from Mr. von Bonin, and from Pastor Wehlen in London, who wishes to begin a correspondence. We place our hearty and ardent wishes for the Lord's blessings on the German verses that our dear Mr. Albinus composed and printed for Mr. Ziegenhagen's birthday at the beginning of his fifty-eighth year; and we hope for much blessing from the printed sermon on the gospel for the Fourth Sunday after Epiphany. I agree wholeheartedly with Senior Urlsperger in his letter of 10 February of this year when he writes, "I especialy rejoice that God has helped our Court Preacher so far that he can again preach." May our loyal God strengthen him! Secretary Martyn has had, to be sure, an ailment in his eyes, yet he has written me a fine long letter in the name of the Trustees, which will redound to the great encouragement of our silk makers.

To be sure, Mr. Verelst wrote but little, but he closed his letter of 9 May with the lovely words: "Mr. Ziegenhagen having brought me the packets herewith seyt vion,[1] i have the Pleasure of forwarding them with my good Wishes to you & the People of Ebenezer, who are blessed & will be with Success in their industrious Undertakings under the Protection of that divine Providence, in whom they trust."

And thus God has revealed to us from the distance the footsteps of His goodness and care at the end of the summer and the beginning of the autumn. But when would I be finished if I should tell of all the proofs of God's grace and love that we have experienced and enjoyed all summer and especially during the last month? To them belong the tolerable health of the ministers and their parishioners in Ebenezer; the entirely bearable summer heat and the fruitful weather, the great blessings in the fields and gardens, the good condition and great usefulness of our mills, which are now in full operation again; further that just at the time that we are to begin construction of our new saw-mill, our loving God has let come to our hands such a joyful re-port of some charitable gifts that have flowed together at Augsburg.

The reason that some members of our community were reluc-tant to start building another sawmill and showed almost no en-thusiasm is that we still owe money on our mills. God, however, blessed both my oral and written arguments to the seven tyth-ingmen or headmen (I included a copy of it in the package which was sent off to Mr. Albinus yesterday); as a consequence, this very important undertaking was started cheerfully and en-ergetically a few days ago. Also, I am further strengthened in my faith by a very kind paragraph, written in Senior Urlsperger's own hand, which was included in the package we sent. He writes:

> My dear Mr. Boltzius! Once again, speaking for myself as well as for other benefactors and friends of Ebenezer, I can put your mind at rest regarding the debts accumulated before and after your demise. Let it remain at that.

Also the following paragraph from our so fatherly-inclined Senior Urlsperger is so full of love and friendliness toward me and my family that I humbly praise God for it and say, "I am not worthy of the least of all the mercies, and of all the truth, which thou hast showed unto thy servant."[2] Precisely this splendid evi-dence of our heavenly Father's loving care for me and my family through this dear man and many other worthy servants and children will make me wise, cautious, and once more loyal to employ all the charitable gifts we have received according to their purpose and to show all possible Christian caution for the maintenance and increase of useful institutions in our dear community.

If, as we hope, God also gives us the new sawmill, we should have no reason to incur any more debts; and, through divine blessing, we should be enabled through trade to pay off the great debts on our mills. Our most esteemed Mr. von N.N. understands only too well why, during past years, our expenses were big and our income small. If our God could make my Christian friends convince me that a Christian can buy and work slaves in good conscience, then we would be able to use slaves (whether bought or borrowed) also in communal work which would, indeed, keep our expenses down and increase our income, to the benefit of our community. It occurs to me just now what Mr. Martyn wrote on the subject of Negro slaves in his letter of the 3rd of May, which arrived here a short while ago: "The Trustees are pleased to find, you are satisfyd with the several Regulations, on which the Act for permitting the Use of Negroes in Georgia is to be formed. The People may be satisfy'd, that the Trustees have the Prosperity of the Province constantly in their View, & only hope in Return, that the People will have it in theirs also."

Among the blessings shown to our people here this summer we also rightfully count the fact that none of our servants have died of fever, excepting one very stubborn, over-worked man, who refused to take any kind of medicine and was unwilling to keep to the diet prescribed for him. My dear wife has been close to death several times; each time we were able to say: "Blessed be the Lord who daily loadeth us with benefits, and the God of our salvation" Praised be the Lord![3]

Other blessings which God has granted to us this past summer have been noted now and then in this diary. For example, the better arrangement of the new mill for shelling and pressing rice, or the fact that we are able to use the means of salvation in our churches and schools in peace, good order, and grace; further, that God protects us in His mercy on our journeys over land and water, where so many others perish, or that He inspires people to become our good friends and helpers, etc. I want to add one more example of divine care for us here, which I treasure especially now after the arrival of the English and German letters. Namely, at the end of the previous month I received five-hundred acres of land, which I described in my last installment of this diary.

Until now, land has not been especially valued in this colony because the Lord Trustees curtailed its use and ownership strictly, in sharp contrast to the practices in other colonies, which seemed to have been in accord with the British concept of freedom. Now, however, Mr. Martyn, the secretary, reports a change which, up to now, had been greatly desired by our people here, and which will offer the opportunity of settling and working land of the best quality within a short span of time. He writes: "That they may not have the least thing to complain of, the Trustees have resolved to enlarge all the Tenures of Lands already made to an absolute Inheritance, & that all the future Grants shall be in the same manner, & proper Deeds are preparing to free the Grants from these Conditions, which were necessary in the Infancy of the Colony, & could not properly be taken off during the war."

Other than using Negro slaves (which is allowed, too), Englishmen living far and near wanted nothing more than such a decision as the Lord Trustees have now made, as quoted above. I am not sure what I can do with the parcel of land which was allotted to me; however, since I obtained it through divine providence without any efforts on my part, I trust that God will enlighten me in the near future as to the proper use of this land. A short time ago, I and my dear colleague each received a tract of three hundred acres for the use of the parish; this property lies near my own five-hundred acres and is also entirely fertile land well suited for farming, except that it is not as conveniently close to the river. Only a few days ago I learned that it is against English regulations and English law for one parish or community to have the use of two glebes or to own any parish-land of double size. It was therefore decided that, on behalf of the church, Mr. Lemke and his family should become the legal owners of the three-hundred acres allotted to him as the second preacher of Ebenezer; the surveyor is to be paid three pounds Sterling for his sevices.

At the moment, Mr. Lemke is unable to spare this sum; the money will be paid, of course; but Mr. Lemke is not eager to own this piece of land himself. We do not intend, however, to let go of it and see it come into the hands of strangers; if the wrong person were to buy it, we could be saddled with a mean neighbor, and this would not be to the advantage of our community and our cowpen in the forest and its adjacent areas. God will reveal to us in time why He changed the minds of the members of the

Council and caused this good land to come into his possession. I wrote today's diary entry with great joy; after I had finished I went to see Mr. Mayer in order to re-read, together with him, some of the letters and pamphlets which had reached us. Also, I hoped to learn from him as much as was necessary for me to know, what practical suggestions our esteemed Mr. von N.N. had made in his letters.

In a certain letter to Mr. Mayer, Mr. N.N, had not only given us more good advice concerning the improvement of our circumstances, he had also, most lovingly, commissioned him to reply in detail to the various important points concerning the improvements of our households and the settlement of our district. This will serve as a means to inform this wise and experienced benefactor and true friend of our colony sufficiently and allow him enough insight into the actual conditions of our life here, into the obstacles we are encountering in settling this colony and into the reasons behind the great poverty of so many of our people. At the same time, he will have the information he needs for giving us even better advice for dealing with various difficulties and problems.

Since this prominent benefactor is well aware of my many duties and the fact that I am constantly under the pressure of time, he charged me only with one task: to describe to him in detail the entire process of silk-making, from beginning to end. I think I will be able to do this properly and easily, since a good quantity of silk has been manufactured for the past few years at the orphanage as well as in my own house and since my own wife is rather experienced in silk-making. May God guide us in all of our undertakings, for the sake of His glory, for the honor of Mr. von N.N., this most esteemed benefactor of our community, and for the honor of other friends as well!

Sunday, the 2nd of September. Today, the Twelfth Sunday after Trinity, I had to hold public service in Jerusalem Church all by myself, preaching twice and conducting our evening prayer hour. The reason is that my dear colleague went to Savannah in order to preach and to hold Holy Communion for the German people of our faith there. May God grant that he be able to prepare them well for eternity; these people, for the most part, lead rather disorderly lives. May God also bless the dear words which he has sown in the hearts of our own eager listeners here in Ebenezer! God has promised us this; He will keep His word.

Usually I make notes on my thoughts for Sunday's sermon at the beginning of the week since, during the week, unexpected tasks are likely to intrude. I had resolved, with God's help, to hold my sermon on today's gospel verses on the healing of the deaf and dumb, it being one of Christ's great works of love and grace. In reading through the text, I found these beautiful words which I intend to use as our introductory verses: Psalm 92; 5–7: "Lord, thou lettest me sing joyfully of thy works, and I praise the creations of thy hands. Lord, how great are thy works? Thy thoughts are so very deep. A foolish man believes them not, and a fool disregards them."[4] Our dear God reminded me so forcefully of His works of grace and love He has granted to us during the course of the past summer and the beginning fall, both through the change of the season and also through the letters which arrived from Europe; my mind is filled with astonishment, considering His mercy and blessings which none of us deserve.

I found it remarkable that our wise, miraculous, and loving God guided me in my morning sermon, so that, towards noon, I preached from a full heart, abandoning my notes, and not only used the aforementioned verses for my introductory verses, as I had originally planned, but made them the subject of my entire sermon. I spoke of God's great works and of man's varying attitude towards Him. I was able to tell my dear listeners what great blessings God, our Lord, has granted to us so far, according to the first, the second, and the third article, or, for that matter, in the realms of nature and grace. From the very beginning, He has blessed our community here, and we have to consider this: His thoughts, that is, God's intentions and plans, are inscrutable, as many of His works among us show.

In looking back, we sometimes realize His purpose. The cross is a mystery. We try to understand God's works properly, to admire Him, and to glorify Him (until it is time for us to enter the kingdom of His glory ourselves, we shall at all times honor His name and rejoice in Him, since we are able to share in God's thoughts concerning the governing and guidance of Christ's church on earth). In striving to understand God's ways, we have

:aken a warning from the bad examples of fools and buffoons, and we have been encouraged by the good example set by David. Most of the servants who had been sick were present in church, and I admonished them kindly.

Monday, the 3rd of September. The two older Schubdrein brothers, namely the carpenter and the mason, came to see me yesterday evening. They told me that they like our community all the better the longer they stay and that all three of the brothers have decided to settle here permanently. They well see the many spiritual and physical advantages that God has granted more to us than to our co-religionists and especially more than to many Lords in Germany; and therefore they would like to have all their kinsmen here with them. We would like to have many people like these three brothers at our place. They are not only knowledgeable, skilled, and industrious but also lead a good life. The youngest brother plans to travel to the fatherland as soon as possible and to fetch his family and other good friends.

Last spring a man in my neighborhood had a poor white mulberry tree next to his house; because it would not grow properly, he sawed it off eighteen inches from the ground and grafted a twig from a Spanish mulberry tree to it. This grafted twig had two eyes from which in six months two branches grew, one of them fifteen and a half feet high and five inches in circumference. The longest branches next to the trunk were cut off in the summer, otherwise they would have become longer.

Tuesday, the 4th of September. However tired I am of traveling, because of which I must neglect much of my regular official duties, I still could not avoid making another trip to Savannah today to attest our rightful demands against N.N.[5] in Philadelphia before the authorities and to fill out and send a legal plenipotentiary power to an Evangelical Lutheran merchant there by the name of Heinrich Schleydorn to demand, amicably or seriously, that the said N. repay the large debts he made here and the great damage he caused here.

Wednesday, the 5th of September. The Lord Trustees' letter to the President and his Assistants was communicated to me. It was almost the same as my letter from Mr. Martyn, except for the powerful reasons for inciting the gentlemen of the Council and, through them, the inhabitants of the country to make silk.

Among other things it was stated that Parliament, in ordering this year's sum of money, had its eye on silk manufacture and that the industry of the inhabitants in this so very much desired matter would contribute greatly to keeping Georgia a separate colony from South Carolina and letting her have her own governor and justice.[6] The new law rescinding the tariff on all silk from the English area in America will be passed as of last summer, and a copy was sent to us by the Lord Trustees. From it we can clearly recognize both the said benefaction as well as the conditions and cautious regulations concerning it, and likewise our lawful manner of exporting the silk. To be sure, I could not learn how much the duties or tariff had been on each pound of silk and has now been exempted. But it must have been no bagatelle because a special act of Parliament was passed concerning it, and the rescinding of this tariff is looked upon as a good encouragement for advancing silk manufacture.

Thursday, the 6th of September. As soon as I returned from my journey, I and my dear colleague opened the little chest, which had come to us at the same time as the letters for us in Savannah; and in it we found a pleasing treasure of many copies of some sermons and of a meditation concerning the Lords' Prayer. The title of the sermons is "The Right and Constant Use of Faith. A Word of Admonishment and Comfort for New Year's Day 1750. A Word of Instruction on the Right Manner of Seeking and Obtaining Grace from the Lord Jesus."[7] The meditation is titled, "A Short Explanation of the Lord's Prayer together with some Annotations Concerning It."[8] I have long wished to read something from this wise and experienced theologian, and it has grieved me whenever, in the accounts of missionaries, I read only the announcements of these important materials which the new missionaries brought with them in their hearts to London. May God reward His faithful servant for this and all the other spiritual and physical benefactions which we have received so far since 1733 from him and through his blessed service. May He also grant us the ability to use this treasure of good books wisely, here among the people of our community as well as among others, to fulfill the purpose He intended, namely, to find that on the Day of the Resurrection of the Just, the seed from his work here in America, too, has blossomed.

Friday, the 7th of September. Last night, God eased the intense pain suffered by the wife of Kogler, our saw-miller; and saved her life, which had been in grave danger. This encouraged her and other Christian souls to praise Him, who, even though He does send us tribulations, also relieves their severity and even protects us from death. She had given birth to a very weak boy, who died in the course of the night shortly after receiving private baptism. I asked for the details of how private baptism was administered and found that no mistake had been made. Together, in Kogler's house, we praised the Lord for this great blessing, namely, that He had allowed this weak child to live long enough to receive private baptism and that He had welcomed this child so soon among the blessed flock of other Christian children.

Saturday, the 8th of September. Yesterday afternoon I visited Mrs. Rottenberger and encouraged her to trust in God, to prepare herself for eternity, and to pray frequently, especially in view of her present condition. I also prayed together with her. This morning her husband came to tell me that she had given birth to a healthy baby girl last night; the child is to be baptized this morning. I had not known that her delivery was that close, but I was filled with joy that God, in His mercy, had guided me to visit her yesterday and allowed me to be of service to her.

Sunday, the 9th of September. Shortly before the ceremony was to begin, Rottenberger came to see me and asked me to suggest a proper Christian name for his little daughter. Bearing in mind the request of the anonymous, noble benefactress from Breslau who had sent twenty Reichsthaler to our dear Pastor Maier in Halle, asking that, in the way of a more real receipt than a piece of paper, two children of our community be named Fridrich Carl and Anna Francisca, I seized this opportunity gladly. I told the father of the loving request by this most esteemed noble benefactress and I explained to him that both names, Anna and Francisca, were beautiful and good names. He was pleased, and so was I.

First, seven weeks ago, Schefler's little son, Fridrich Carl, and now this child, Anna Francisca, have received Holy Baptism to my own joy as well as that of the parents and the godparents. These people are pious and honest, and the little girl is their only child; they will, no doubt, raise their daughter to fear and obey God. The little boy, or rather, his parents, had received a fine gift of money from this aforementioned benefactress; at the right time I will present them with an additional sum. Likewise, I intend that the little girl also share in the gift, and I hope that, in this matter, I acted according to the wishes of this esteemed and noble benefactress and followed the instructions of her dear pastor well.

Among the contributions from Augsburg which reached us very recently, we found a list of the names of our dear benefactors. Some of them stipulate that their gifts be used for a specific purpose; for example, one-hundred florins were designated for the much needed maintenance of our churches and schools. Both of our churches, in town and at the plantations, are built entirely of wood; and, since wood here in this country tends to rot quickly, we are constantly in the process of repairing and replacing damaged parts and thereby running up considerable expenses. We would like to construct a larger church in town, if God were to send us the means for such an undertaking! Our present church was meant to be used as a church only on a temporary basis; originally this building was to be our school in town and, at the same time, was supposed to house the schoolmaster. The money we received for schools and churches may also be used to pay the salary of our schoolmaster at the plantations, whom we have to support.

Monday, the 10th of September. Several years ago a weaver[9] /Held/ moved from our community to Carolina; afterwards he talked a great deal about Ebenezer and our people and about how much he and his wife had liked living here. Now he is impoverished and has accumulated debts, and he asked to be hired by our community to tend cattle. To his relief and joy, we agreed, after he had given his promise to lead an orderly life. I sent him a letter, which is to be handed on to an Englishman to whom he owes money, recommending that his debts be settled before he leaves for Ebenezer. There are more who would like to move here if we offered them work; however, we are not interested in people who are willing to come here only for the sake of earning money and who would be eager to leave after having achieved this goal.

A tanner from Purysburg came to see me and offered to teach his craft to two of our people for forty pounds Sterling. He estimates that he would have to live here for more than one full year, the time it would take our men to learn this trade properly. He thinks that our men would be able to earn about fifty pounds Sterling per year if they succeeded in mastering this profitable skill properly. We would have gladly paid eight or ten pounds Sterling to this man for his offered services, but the sum he is asking is much too high. Also, he would have needed to come here only once in a while in order to teach our people, since both are clever men and have already some experience in tanning. But these people are obsessed with gaining their own advantage.

Thursday, the 13th of September. My dear colleague learned that high-lying land was available near Purysburg on a large island which is separated from our large island, which in turn borders on the Mill River, by a very shallow creek. People could settle on this high-lying land while making good use of the surrounding low-lying land. Some years ago, four of our people set out to find this land, but without success. Mr. Lemke saw and inspected this land today, accompanied by several knowledgeable people; their description of the land could not be better. This island is located between the Savannah River and a wide creek that flows into our Mill River north of Abercorn. The land has a good elevation; part of it is densely covered by trees, which can be cut into wood for barrel staves and shingles; part of it is good grazing land. Some think that even the elevated parts of the land could be in danger of being flooded when the water level in the rivers is at its highest; others disagree.

There is also a spot well suited for building a good gristmill or sawmill. General Oglethorpe must have known about this island, and he probably had special plans for it. For this reason he stopped us from going beyond our island at the Mill River. If people from Purysburg or other people were to settle this land and to build a mill there, then we would be greatly disadvantaged. Therefore, I wrote a letter to a member of the Council (it is headed nominally by the President emeritus now)[10] and asked that he petition the other members on our behalf: namely, that the entire island be reserved for several people of our community, and especially for Mr. von N.N.,[11] our esteemed benefactor.

Mr. von N.N., together with Mr. Urlsperger, who continues to protect us with fatherly care, could suggest to the Lord Trustees that they settle the entire district around Ebenezer with Christian and hard-working people of the Protestant faith. It is possible that they have already done so, if through God's will a certain opportunity for it has arisen.

Our people have asked me, through their headmen, to help them acquire more land for larger plantations; at present they have fifty acres and they want one-hundred acres because they need more land for farming, raising cattle, lumber, etc. This island north of our island is located about three English miles from town by water and is even nearer by land. As soon as our boat returns I will receive news of what we may expect. At least I hope that this island will not be given over to other settlers before we have sent word to the Lord Trustees and received their answer. Our friends in Europe may well wonder why such a good piece of land in our neighborhood has gone undetected for so long; however, they have to bear in mind the following:

1. These low-lying areas, although very fertile, are so overgrown with larger and smaller trees, bushes, tall, thick and thin reeds, vines, and thorny bushes that it is difficult to see what lies beyond and even more difficult to penetrate on foot. For this reason, not even the surveyors themselves know any details of such land for certain.

2. The surveyors have no advantage from surveying such land; the work is very difficult and therefore nobody is interested in it.

3. From the very beginning, none of our Salzburgers were eager to explore the area around us, nor did they have the time. Also, because of the lack of money, they were not even able to clear and settle the island, which is located right at their own door step, so to speak. Some time ago, the members of the Council permitted me to have this island searched for high-lying land which would be suitable as church property; however, our people returned without having had any success.

4. Since Mr. Oglethorpe had reserved this island for his own purposes, as mentioned, our searches were bound to remain fruitless in any case.

God's grace is manifesting itself in a most miraculous way in the six-year old daughter of Zimmbernburg[12] to the great joy of her parents and other people. She has told her mother that God has allowed her, during school, to look straight into heaven; afterwards, she had difficulty recognizing her schoolmates after-seeing so much beauty. God has sent so many bitter tribulations to Mrs. Kogler that she no longer wishes to go on living once she is properly prepared for departing this world. I explained to her that she must not seek readiness for eternity in herself, but in Christ; all sinners are entitled to that. It is said: "I shall gaze after Thee, I shall press Thee firmly in faith to my heart."[13] Whoever dies in that manner, dies well.

Friday, the 14th of September. For some time now we have had plenty of rain; occasionally (as, for instance, today) the rain turned into a heavy downpour. God has granted us fine crops of rice, grain, beans, and squash; because of the heavy rains, harvesting is being delayed, and making hay is difficult, too. It is to be hoped that these crops will sell at a good price, because they turned out quite well, especially our grain, beans, and sweet potatoes. These crops grow well even in Savannah Town and Augusta; during the summer, news reached us from there that their grain was scorched practically beyond recovery. A man from Augusta offered to get our people a price of eight pence per bushel of grain if they woul agree to come there with a large boat. If they were willing, while going up the Savannah River, to take a cargo of oyster shells needed for lime-burning to a place about half-way to Savannah Town, they would get one bushel of grain for each bushel of oyster shells they brought, which is quite a profitable business. With a large boat, and three men at the oars, the trip takes ten days going upstream and four days coming downstream.

Salt is also rather rare there; and a few months ago a merchant told me that our people could get as much as six bushels of grain for each bushel of salt, which costs as much as three or four shillings in Savannah and sells for fifteen or sixteen pence in Charleston. Crops grow well up there and people keep quite a few Negroes; but they lack a market for selling their crops and use them mostly for feeding their many workmen who, accompanying caravans of pack-horses, are sent on trading trips among the Indians. I wonder whether it would benefit our community if we had a practical and hard-working man among us who would be interested in starting a trading business between here, Augusta, and Charleston. Grain is very cheap in Augusta and wheat is also inexpensive; if someone were to go there to pick up a boatload himself, he could get one bushel for under two shillings, compared to the asking price of four shillings here. The grain could then be ground into flour in our mill and sold in Savannah; our mills and our community would benefit from this kind of undertaking, and some of our people would get an opportunity to earn some money. Not all people like to do the same thing, for this reason we ought to encourage a variety of businesses in order to develop people's different talents.

We were able to start working our mills again a few weeks ago, and both our people here as well as people from other places are taking advantage of this; some bring their wheat to us from as far as Carolina and from the area around Port Royal, and we mill their grain as fast as possible. They seem to know exactly when our mills start working again, as if they got word by express rider; and strangers from far away arrive here at our mills with their wheat, rye, and Indian corn. This means good profits for the mills, even though we ask only two pence for each bushel we mill. People like to bring their grain here because we charge so little and mill their grain so fast, and also because we treat them in a friendly manner. Good people among us, together with their children, thank our dear God with all their hearts for our mills (as I was able to witness in a family only a few days ago), especially if they could not work the mills for one, two, or three weeks during the hottest part of the summer when the water-level in the river is low; after such an interval this blessing, which is so conveniently close to us, takes on a new meaning.

In my diary entry for the 13th of September I mentioned the letter which I had written to an important member of the Council in Savannah, in which I asked that we may be allowed to settle the beautiful land on the large island between here and Purysburg and that people from Ebenezer, our esteemed Mr. von

N.N., and Mr. Lemke may take land there. I regard it as another token of divine providence that he has sent me a very encouraging answer.

Saturday, the 16th of September. Continuing rains makes harvesting of crops and putting up hay very difficult for our people. Therefore, in last week's sermon, I told them that for the next two or three weeks I intended to suspend the sermons commonly held on Tuesdays and Fridays since this would give them more time for bringing in their harvests. They sent one of their headmen to my house to ask me to continue holding the sermons since they did not impede their work; so, today, I mentioned after my sermon that I would continue to hold our weekly sermons as before.

Sunday, the 17th of September. Today, the Fourteenth Sunday after Trinity, I felt very depressed and sad; however, our dear God protected me from any harm to my health, and I was able to hold my sermon and repetition hour properly. Moreover, He blessed my soul anew during the preaching of the divine word by Mr. Lemke and myself. I spoke on the gospel verses dealing with sickness and health and explained that we should strive to follow God's will in all things. My dear colleague presented to his listeners the verses Colossians 1:12–14, dealing with preparing oneself for becoming an heir to the saints dwelling in the light, a very edifying and blessed text. There were a couple of German, or rather Swiss, married people from Savannah here in Ebenezer, and they attended our public service three times today; I hope they were properly edified.

Monday, the 18th of September. From time to time many strangers arrive at our mill with their European and Indian crops.[14] In the past, our saw-miller Kogler and his family offered their hospitality to these people; but, as a consequence, they suffered considerable inconvenience and expense. It has become necessary now to build a comfortable house and to install an innkeeper. Since Schmidt, an honest man, became our foreman at the cowpen in Old Ebenezer, his house has stood empty for almost half a year; also, a good man was needed at the mill to supervise the servants there and to help with running the milling business. It seems that Kalcher, a hard worker and sensible man, and his family are willing to take on the obligations of acting as innkeepers and supervisors at the mills. Both I and my dear colleague were relieved to hear this; also, the profits yielded by our mills will increase now that the servants will be properly guided in their daily chores.

We had been forced to accept women servants who could not find support and work otherwise; after the harvest is over, we hope to find a large family willing to work at the mills. However, even a sufficient number of servants will not solve our problems if they are not guided in their work by a clever man. With the proper supervision, however, they could work at the sawmill, too, helping to make and move larger pieces of wood and carrying boards to the storage areas where they are kept before being shipped. This would be quite practical, especially since we are often at a loss to find enough workers for the various tasks which have to be completed without delay, not to mention that day laborers are much too expensive. Furthermore, it is not always possible to get the same day laborers to complete a certain work, and this often leads to confusion and problems.

The day laborers and carters at the mill have earned so much money during the past four years that, although I am glad for them, I do wonder whether or not they use their money properly. In the past, we have had a great deal of trouble getting carters and day laborers to work for us, and we have not always been successful in getting what we wanted. Now, we hope that Kalcher, this clever and hard-working man, will take care of most of this work himself and supervise the servants so they do things properly; such an arrangement was badly needed. The carters and day-laborers who worked for us sometimes in the past still have many opportunities to earn enough money, if they are willing to listen to good advice.

We also have another reason for making these changes regarding the situation of our servants; we plan to arrange their workloads and the problem of feeding them in the manner which I outlined in detail to our esteemed Mr. von N. in my letter of the 13th of September of this year; namely, they are to plant only as much as is needed for their own food; and they are to work in the mills, tend the mulberry trees, and spend the rest of their time as Kalcher does with wood-working, which, as we know from experience, is a profitable undertaking. Such a new arrangement will show us whether or not white servants deserve their poor reputation as workers. Just today I heard that some of them do not work hard enough to earn even their food, not to mention their clothes. Judging from the servants we have now, I can not guess how people with a background in farming would have done, who, from early childhood on, are used to hard work; the servants we have now are former bakers, shoemakers, masons, and members of other trades.

At present, not only Englishmen, but also most of our own people, are prejudiced against using white servants; therefore, no more industrious workers can be sent to this colony from Europe; as a consequence, our colony, as fertile as it is and as suited to farming, silk-making, the raising of cattle, wood-working, and trading, will be populated with Negroes, just as Carolina is; and this will result in a twofold considerable drawback. Namely, 1. We not only have powerful and dangerous enemies in the French and Spaniards on our borders, but also in the Indians, who are getting prouder and more impudent, and also in the Negroes; and they could become a considerable hostile force, with only very few white people here to rally to the defense; and 2. the original purpose of this colony, which our wise and merciful God sought to fulfill through the English nation and through the Lord Trustees, namely, to provide a safe haven and refuge for poor people of the Protestant faith, seems to suffer from these changes. These poor people are either not tolerated in their homelands or they are unable to provide for themselves and their families because of the many obstacles laid in their way. All English colonies (excepting Pennsylvania and, perhaps, New England), are heavily populated with Negroes; where they become too numerous, poor white people find themselves unable to prosper. If Georgia had been managed according to the original purpose, then there would be land enough for many thousands who would be able to feed their families easily, once they had settled in. I hope I made it quite clear in the aforementioned letter to our esteemed Mr. von N. that, if the workloads of the white servants could be arranged differently, these people could prove very useful and many other German people would be welcome to come here and make a good life for themselves.

It is a great tribulation for us that our servants are such poor workers. However, we should accept such tribulation with faith, patience, and hope (better than the Israelites in the desert); we should use these servants as well as we can until it pleases God to take this and other tribulations from us in His mercy. It is said: "Said I not unto thee, if thou wouldest believe."[15] Frequently, we sing these words: "Only faith is lacking on earth. If it were there, we would have what we need. He who can comprehend God in faith will not be forsaken by Him when all is lacking."[16]

In addition to a certain lack of faith and obedience on the part of our people, there are some other reasons (in my humble opinion) why, in the past, our servants did not do better. Some of them are not very good at running their households, since they left their homeland at a very young age, almost as children. Also, back in Salzburg, their servants had all been honest and hardworking; therefore, they are somewhat at a loss as to how to deal with the kind of servants we have now. The servants who have arrived here so far have a history of causing trouble in Germany, too, and of being sly and lazy. Their masters need a firm hand in keeping them in check, and they have to be on the alert in foreseeing and forestalling the various crooked schemes and secret plottings. In this respect, our people here are much too soft-hearted and too compassionate; they do not exercise enough severity with this mean and lazy riff-raff and rather dismiss than discipline them.

Tuesday, the 19th of September. Georg Philip Ports, who worked as a servant here a few years ago and who is a good and hard-working man, did, on the advice of his brother, settle last year on a plantation next to his near Goshen. He has worked so hard that he now has a good harvest of Indian corn, beans, squash, and rice standing in his fields. Since then, on several occasions, he has said how much he regretted leaving Ebenezer and pursuing a life filled with troubles and temptations. He also asked me to take him and his young wife back and to welcome them again into our community, he would gladly be a servant for the rest of his life; his wife is from here.

Today he came to see me twice. He told me that he felt so disturbed living on his plantation that he could not possibly remain there. Whenever he stayed in Ebenezer, his worries left him; and whenever he returned to Goshen, his heart felt heavier and heavier with every day. He asked me most humbly to assist them in returning to us, saying he could not possibly return to his land or work it.

I told him that our God was a God pleased by things done in good order and that it would be His will that he go back home in order to wait and see, but that he should definitely not let the good crops which were ripening in his fields go to waste and rot, since this would not only be a sin, it would also cause anger and hostility among other people and lead to bad talk about Christianity, me, and our community, of which he considered himself a member. I advised him to be patient for the time being, to harvest his crops, and to wait for his calling while praying to God with all his heart. If it were God's will that he move to Ebenezer immediately then He would send a sign by changing my mind in this matter and that of my dear colleague as well as granting us the means and opportunity to assist him in moving here. He left after we had prayed to God together, but he returned soon after that, telling me again that he found it quite impossible to return to his land, etc. I explained that what was happening to him, namely, the troubles he had to endure in body and mind had to be considered a temptation for disrupting God's order; if he gave in to that temptation, then the Devil would cause great damage to his soul, as well as impair the reputation of my office and my own person. Therefore, I had to tell him that, if he gave in to this temptation and let his ripening crops rot away, then I would have to withdraw any promise of helping him in the future or of allowing him to settle in Ebenezer again, since I had to avoid inviting unnecessary hostility and bad gossip to our community.

If, on the other hand, he were to resist his compulsion and his unusual whims and followed the advice I had given him while praying often and with all his heart to God, then I would be willing to help him come back to us. He went away after this explanation, and I hope he will do as I instructed him. He is an honest man who is earnestly concerned about his salvation. However, his neighbors and other people who know him think him a fool. He seemed angry and depressed; and I feared that, if I did not help him now (at least by giving him hope and a promise), he could slide into a miserable life and stray into sinful error.

I was called to visit Krause's maid-servant who, for the past several days now, has professed a need to see me. She arrived here last fall together with other servants; in Germany she had led a despicable life. God had begun to open the eyes of this woman; while she was still in good health, she had started to recognize her sins; and she often prayed by herself and in tears, on her knees, asking for mercy. Now, on her sick-bed, she continues in this manner. She has derived considerable benefit from listening to God's word; only recently she began to understand so much better than in previous years God's teaching of man's blessing. She has given thanks to God frequently for leading her to us, and she wishes the same could happen to all of the sinners in Germany who are still imprisoned by blindness and false security and who go on living irresponsibly until they suddenly face eternity. I was pleased by her confession, and I had not expected such good progress in her repentance. I have noted repeatedly that our servants are very receptive to what we teach in our sermons, they listen carefully from beginning to end to all the praying, singing, reading, and preaching. This has always pleased me, and I had hoped that the seed of the divine word would not be wasted on them.

Ports, whom I mentioned before, did not go home after all. He sent word to me that I might meet him at a place close to town. When I came, he said to me that he could not return to his plantation, even if it meant losing his life, except if I were to give him my solemn promise to get him back to Ebenezer. I promised and took him to my house for dinner. After that he went home much easier in his mind.

Mr. Whitefield writes from London that God keeps forever increasing the opportunities to convert large numbers of people from all walks of life. He asks me to think of a method to help the poor Negroes recognize and find Christ. He has a very high opinion of Court Preacher Ziegenhagen; he speaks of him in a very reverential and emphatic manner. He intends to come to America soon and to visit Georgia once more; he mentions in this letter again that he has always had high hopes that this colony would develop well and prosper after overcoming various initial problems. I hold him in high regard as one of Ebenezer's benefactors, as is my duty. However, I do not hesitate to express my own opinion to him clearly on some matters, just as I do to Mr. Wesley.

Saturday, the 23rd of September. Last night we had heavy rains, which continued into Sunday, although not as violently and with a few pauses between showers. We managed to reach and leave church almost without getting drenched. Unfortunately, our rice will be ruined; it was cut several days ago and then had to be left out in the rain. Fresh shoots are forming, and this batch is no longer fit for consumption. These and other problems in our community and in my own home sometimes threaten to make me lose heart; however, our steadfast and loving God has encouraged me today through His word during our preaching on the verses 2 Kings 6:27, which we used as an exordium: "If the Lord do not help thee, whence," etc.[17] as well as through the consoling gospel verses Matthew 6; 24–34. During our morning and afternoon sermons I had explained three important points of this text, proven them, and demonstrated their practical application, namely: 1. Mankind's total inability to care for themselves and other creatures; 2. God's all-encompassing power to care for mankind and other creatures, and 3. God's extreme willingness to care for all mankind and, especially, to care for all his children.

The sad history from which our introductory verses were chosen reminded me that God has sent our community its share of physical misery; however, He has spared us, so far, from more severe tribulations and suffering of the kind which His own people had to endure. We have, therefore, good cause to thank God, to use His blessing well, and to be content with His guidance. As is our custom, every fourteen days my dear colleague holds the sermon in Zion Church for the convenience of the people from the plantations, especially their women, children, and the sick, and they particularly welcome this during the wet season.

Sunday, the 24th of September. Glaner asked me to mediate between him and his neighbor's wife, which I did most readily. Glaner had foregone participating in Holy Communion several times because of their quarrel, but now he no longer is willing to do that. A short while ago he fell seriously ill, and the bickering between him and that woman, although mostly trifles are involved, weighed on his conscience. Of the two, Glaner is more to blame; I told both of them what I thought needed saying. May God grant him a better disposition and allow him to learn fully the deeper sense of the commandment: "Love thy neighbor as thyself". Sometimes one is surprised by what God reveals to us of other people's natures by coincidence. I believe it is very necessary for one to make the effort to listen to both parties. We prayed together, and they made their peace with each other in the presence of N.'s husband.

Monday, the 25th of September. The men who bought cattle from the herds of the Lord Trustees half a year ago are now obligated to pay off one hundred pounds Sterling; Our miraculous God gave them the opportunity to work hard and to try to save the necessary sum. Payment is due right after Michelmas. These men intend to present a petition to the members of the Council asking for assistance and requesting to be allowed to pay only fifty pounds since our cowpen is in very poor condition and certain ruthless neighbors continue to contribute considerably to the damage. The petition details their hard work, the high expenses they encountered, and their poor profits. Also, they do not think that they would be able to pay another one hundred pounds Sterling within another half-year. I myself will deliver this petition. Rather, from the beginning, we have had doubts as to the success of the cowpen planned by the Lord Trustees; however, for various reasons we felt we had to purchase it, since otherwise it could have meant the end of our community's cattle raising if this cowpen had been acquired by unfriendly outsiders.

Tuesday, the 26th of September. Soldier Dods, who arrived here from Frederica one-and-a-half years ago together with his German wife, is doing well among us. He has only one child; and he asked me today, in tears, that, for the sake of God's glory, it might be raised better than he himself was. He likes to hear how readily other children recite their verses and catechism in church and how well they answer the questions their teachers ask; he hopes to live long enough to see his own five year old son do as well as these children and to share this joy.

Wednesday, the 27th of September. Today I visited the German people living at Goshen; they had met in the house of one of their members, and I held an edification hour for them. As our text we used the beautiful, thorough, and edifying essay *Explanation of the Lord's Prayer*[18] by our esteemed court preacher Ziegenhagen, which we had received recently. Our dear God has granted me His blessing while reading from this text, both earlier at home and again during my sermon today; it is a thoughtful, edifying, and consoling essay for meditation. Oh, if only all of our listeners learned to pray properly, as instructed by these explanations of the Lord's Prayer! What a change we would all undergo! We would have heaven on earth and in our hearts! In reading this essay, one can not help but be filled with respect for the Lord's Prayer.

Before this aforementioned edification hour, I had to talk to a woman regarding a certain public nuisance which she had created for others by her quarreling and constant outbursts of anger; I admonished her in kindness and with strictness. I also reminded all listeners to treat each other with love, tolerance, and forgiveness and to bear God's word in mind, especially the important words of Christ which are printed in the aforementioned essay both immediately after the Lord's Prayer as well as in the beginning of the text. Quarrelsome and unforgiving people need not hope that their prayers will be heard, as these words of Christ show. On the other hand, it is well to be peaceful, eager to make peace, and peace-loving.

Thursday, the 28th of September. These few people at Goshen like to hear God's word; there are some, though, who think that I am too severe in my preaching. Some time ago, I had held a sermon on the text of Psalms 5;6–7: "Thou shalt destroy them that speak leasing: the Lord will abhor the bloody and deceitful man."[19] Afterwards, a woman came to me and complained that I had been too angry this time. She said she could tell from my face that I had been listening to ill-willed rumors about them and that I had never before, ever since they had come to this country, held such a severe sermon.

I had learned that a certain widow was dangerously ill; on my trip back I went to see her and talked to her of God's word. She told me that several times she had been very frightened in her conscience and had been afraid that she was lost. She added that she did not know why she should feel that way, she had never in her life committed serious sins, such as stealing, or lived an unclean life as some young people sometimes do. I told her that not only such obvious sins counted, but also that sins like original sin, that main evil, and the various sins of omission and commission resulting from it could exclude her from heaven; this she could see from the verse: "The sins of the flesh are manifest";[20] sins like animosity, discord, envy, and anger were among these.

I told her I thought that her fear of being lost was one of the punishments sent by the Holy Ghost and that she should pray to God asking Him to enlighten her as to her sins. She would then learn what is said in the verse: "For God so loved the world that, etc." and "whosoever believeth in him shall not perish, but have . . . " Finally, we prayed together; and then I explained to her the story of the fiery serpents.[21]

Friday, the 29th of September. God has answered our prayers. After so much rain He has sent us good, dry weather again. Our crops of rice, hay, and Indian beans can now be harvested while they are dry. Some of the rice did spoil; however, the damage is not too great. The water-level in the river is rising every day, and more than another eight or nine inches will result in flooding; some of the low-lying areas are inundated already, and it is a blessing that those of our people who live at the Mill River were able to bring their rice across before that happened. However, people settled on low-lying land around the rivers and creeks here are still better off than those in Augusta or Savannah Town, although there is much bragging about how fertile their land is and how abundantly their various crops grow.

The same is true of our low-lying land right next to the islands across our Mill River as well as the land on these islands themselves and other low-lying land. This land gets very wet in the rainy season but is not flooded by the rivers, although this means that these fields have to be improved periodically by either fertilizing or resting the soil; fields which are flooded regularly by rivers rich in silt need neither. I think of such land as the land of Egypt, which is irrigated and fertilized regularly by the floods of the Nile. I read that the same happens in the land around the river Gambia, which is settled by Negroes; despite the great heat they have good harvests. The main advantage which our low-lying lands have over those of Augusta and Savannah Town is that the flooding there occurs suddenly and unexpectedly; in our area it is predictable and happens gradually.

Upstream, the Savannah River is much narrower than down here in our area. Also, there are not as many small creeks branching off which can channel some of the overflow away from the main river. This is the reason that sometimes, in the course of only one night or twenty-four hours, the water rises by twenty or thirty feet, causing a sudden flood. Cattle and pigs often drown, and the crops are damaged. On the other hand, our people have enough time to prepare for a flooding.

Philip Ports, whom I mentioned in the part of my diary which I sent off recently, came to see me today and informed me that he has purchased a plantation close to the mill. It is easily accessible and fertile and includes a sturdy house; he paid a little over fifteen pounds Sterling for it. He is grateful to our Lord for fulfilling his wish to be a part of Ebenezer again and to live in his spiritual birthplace. I also prefer that he and his young wife have their own plantation, rather than being taken care off by me or by my dear colleague. A short time ago he had earnestly asked us for such an arrangement; in return he offered to work for us as a field-hand and his wife as a servant, and he said that both of them would work hard and serve us faithfully. He owns a plantation near Goshen; it is easily accessible and fertile as well. He does not mind letting it go but prefers the opportunity to live and work here. He is an honest young man and a hard worker, but not very strong physically and not really fit for hard labor.

Saturday, the 30th of September. Today, on the last day of this month (the Sixteenth Sunday after Trinity), seventy-three people went to Holy Communion. May the name of the Lord be praised for this blessing which He grants us in our pilgrimage so often and in such gratifying order! Since last Thursday I have been plagued by a persistent cold, and my throat is hoarse; yesterday I was unable to hold the sermon in preparation for Holy Communion in either Zion Church or Jerusalem Church; my colleague took over with great eagerness and ability. How fortunate that Ebenezer has two ministers, who, if necessary, can assist one another so that our community need not be disadvantaged or diminished if one is sick or has to travel. Since I was able to rest yesterday, God restored enough of my strength to enable me to preach today as usual and to repeat my sermon. I praise God's mercy with all my heart and thank Him for His assistance, which I do not deserve!

A German man from Savannah Town,[22] who recently lost several thousands of barrel-staves and whom I mentioned earlier, attended our public service three times; I was told he shed many tears during the sermon, and only God knows whether he cried because of his great financial loss or because the preaching of God's word moved his heart.

In our exordium we contemplated David's important words of prayer: Psalms 39;5, "Lord, make me to know my end," etc.[23] We preached on the subject of physical death, examining the gospel verses of the young man of Nain who died and was resurrected. My dear colleague spoke on Job 14; 1–2, dealing with the shortness of human life and its tribulations. May our dear God allow us to benefit from these precious words of divine truth until all eternity!

The aforementioned German man is from Danzig and is a follower of the Evangelical-Lutheran faith . He offered to give one of our people his land at Savannah Town in exchange for a plantation of one-hundred acres at the Mill River. He would spend more time working in wood and making things for sale than on farming. However, I believe that this trade will not come about. He told us that the commanding officer at Fort Augusta also had many barrel-staves made and had planned to send them to Savannah for sale; however, he may very well learn a lesson from this man's misfortune. One thing becomes clear from such business ventures: that the people there, who are so far away from Savannah, consider it worth their while to work in wood and to make things for trading with people from the West Indies. How much more would our people profit from such an undertaking, being so much nearer to Savannah! Barrel-staves made by our people, as well as shingles, barrel-hoops, and lumber for construction, as well as boards, could be transported easily and without any danger on the river, using the boards themselves as rafts. During our repetition hour it started to rain again; the dry weather lasted only a few days after all. The river continues to rise, and it looks as if all low-lying land will be flooded soon and our mills will have to cease work.

OCTOBER

October the 1st. On the first day of this month, I had to go to Savannah again in order to take care of our community's business; the weather was pleasant for traveling. As soon as I arrived, after eight o'clock in the evening, Mr. Zübli, the preacher, sent word that I should come to see him; he had traveled here from his parish in Carolina to visit the people of the Reformed faith in and around Savannah. He was very ill and had to keep to his bed; he suffered from a fever, chest pains, and a severe cough. He was rather troubled in mind and body. I consoled him and, together with other good people, prayed with and for him. I also gave him some of the medicine which I had taken along with me on my trip and took care of him as best as I could until Mr. Meyer arrived; at Mr. Zübli's request, I had sent for him by express boat. Mr. Zübli is a good, talented man; and our dear God will enlighten him even more through this physical tribulation, and make him ever more fit for his office. This incident as well as various others will prove to him more and more that I am his friend and have his best interest at heart. I hope he will recover soon.

October the 2nd. A chest from Halle arrived in Charleston aboard one of the ships which docked there recently. Just now, while I was in Savannah, a captain had it brought there. No letter accompanied the chest, but I assume that it contains the books and medicines which Pastor Zübli had sent for. I opened the chest, which was in poor condition and partly smashed, and found almost what I had expected. There were various useful bound books, larger and smaller ones, some for him and some for us, as I will explain shortly. The medicines were packed in a separate little box and addressed to Mr. Thilo; without opening this box, I took it along with me on my way back. May God be praised for this precious blessing, too! No letter and no instructions had been included; therefore, I assume that such a letter is still underway, or got lost before reaching London. We have all of the letters written to us by Mr. Albinus. Mr. Zübli was very pleased with the books; and I said to him, referring to this token of divine care for us: "I shall not die but live, and declare the works of the Lord."[1]

Several of our people have asked me to assist them in acquiring additional land for larger plantations; they wish to add another fifty acres to the fifty acres they already have, giving each of them one-hundred acres of land, preferably on the island on the other side of the Mill River and between Purysburg and Abercorn. They should be able to get good land not only on these islands, but also in other areas around Abercorn and on the Uchee land[2] wherever they find it acceptable to settle, if only they would move. Due to a mistake made by the surveyor and also due to a lack of good land close by, it happened, after we moved from Old Ebenezer, that, for the most part, three households had to be crowded into one plantation of fifty acres (and largely pine forests, at that) along the Mill River; their additional acres (of a total of fifty) were situated across the Mill River on the island. As a result of this, the plantation of each one household is very long and very narrow.

This arrangement, although made in brotherly love and by necessity, is rather inconvenient; in the future, the situation could even worsen when the present householders die. Therefore, several years ago I had started advising them to come to agreements with each other and to combine their three strips into one plantation again and for two of them to move in each case. For that purpose I had petitioned the Council in Savannah for good land around Goshen, which also lies close to our glebe and is settled mostly by Evangelical-Lutheran people. In order to encourage them to settle on this new land, I agreed to give two pounds Sterling to each one who would willingly let his neighbor have his strip of land; those who stayed on and got the land of their former neighbors, along with the houses and stables, would be obligated to assist their brothers and neighbors settling on new land by helping them with the work.

However, my advice and suggestion had not been accepted, although a few times it seemed as if people were willing to make such arrangements; in the end, they pretended that they would be unable to cope with the hard work. Now, such efforts will have to be made, or they will not get the additional acres of land they want; furthermore, they would be unable to obtain a land grant or a deed for their land, which is now splintered into so many little parts, in writing; they would also lose their pastures and other things necessary for securing better supplies. That miserable man, N., cheated people out of the good wood for barrel staves;[3] at present, there is almost none of it left on their narrow plantations. People did not understand the value of good trees, either; many well-grown stands of white oak were felled without any plan and then left to rot away or were cut up as firewood. Sometimes oak was used to make fence posts, when fir or other wood would have been good enough. Now, people are getting another chance to look for and obtain good oak for making barrel staves, offering them the potential to earn good money in a short span of time, as other Germans or Englishmen in this country do.

The reason for this good opportunity is that through the most extraordinary good-will of the members of the Council our people have permission to look for land wherever they want to, either on the aforementioned islands, or on the Uchee land, or behind or around Abercorn in Goshen. I will do my very best, with God's help, to support this advantageous enterprise by offering my advice and assistance.

The 4th of October. Yesterday evening I traveled from Savannah to Abercorn; there, despite the cold night, I had to make do with a very poor little inn run by a destitute Englishman, who means well. I noticed that the river had already risen here quite a bit; my suspicions were confirmed when I got to see that almost our entire mill land was flooded as well as the mills themselves. For the second time within twenty-four hours now, the water has risen very quickly to an impressive height. May God in His mercy, as He has done so far in the past, avert damage from the mills and our low-lying plantations!

The 6th of October. The Salzburger Glaner recovered from a severe sickness only recently; as soon as he was better, he fell ill with another ailment. When I entered his room, he said these verses to me: "Behold, thou art made whole: sin no more lest a worse thing come unto thee".[4] I knew already why he quoted these words to me. A short while ago he had confessed to me in tears the unworthiness of his heart; it is likely that after his illness, which God, in His mercy, sent to him as a reminder and punishment, he disregarded this divine sign so that our wise and merciful God found it necessary to punish him again. His eyesight is severly affected by a discharge, or something like it.

I talked to him of his spiritual and physical condition and explained in particular the beautiful example of old Tobias. For a long time now he has been a widower; he has no children and is quite alone. However, he could have saved himself numerous difficulties connected with the running of his household if he had followed the advice and opinion of Christian people and married his neighbor, widow Zant, who is a very pious and good woman and who was formerly married to carpenter, Pilz, an honest man. In doing so, he could also have avoided his poor health as well as the weakening of his Christianity. It seems, he will now follow this advice.

The 7th of October. A short time ago, Krause's maid servant was close to death. Today, I found her much improved; and there is hope for her recovery. I explained to her the great blessing of the period of grace, and I recited these well-known words for her several times: "Whosoever neglects this time and doth not turn to God, let him cry woe when he goeth to hell.[5] "Item, "Today thou livest, convert today, etc."[6] This fall, several people got sick with fever. May God let these ailments turn into a spiritual healing for those people! But laziness and a false feeling of security is widespread among them, notably in one certain man; and mere words fail in such cases. God himself, who loves our souls, has to punish such people by various means. Oh, may He succeed every time!

The weather has been dry and cool since the first of this month, although the days are still warm enough for processing our rice. The high water seems to be receding again, and we all hope that our mills will be operational soon. Several families who planted too late suffered damage to their rice crop through the flooding.

The 8th of October. The sixty-seventh continuation of the account of the missionaries in the East Indies[7] was among the books which Pastor Zübli had ordered from Halle. Once again, it contains much that astonishes me; and it fills me with joy to see the important missionary work continue with so much blessing. Although our Lord has called one or another dear laborer away from work and suffering into peace and eternal joy by physical death, He continues to support all the others who are in His service and who have resumed the task of those dear workers who have passed on. I am very pleased to see that our dear God enlightened three more men to go to the East Indies; they were honored by kind words not only in the preface of the continuation of the account mentioned above, but also in the last letter we received from Court Chaplain Albinus. In this letter, dated February the 27th of this year, he writes of them: "A short while ago, three esteemed brothers had been among us; they will go to the East Indies as missionaries. Their names are Mr. Schwartz, Mr. Polzenhagen, and Mr. Huettemann."

We can only hope that these men turn out to be blessed tools in the hands of our Lord, as they are honest and inspired men of great talents. May our Lord let them arrive in India under His protection and blessing! On January the 20th they left from Deal; after that they lay at Falmouth for four more weeks, waiting for the right winds. This was, however, also part of God's special plan, since there were violent storms (near London also a rather strong earthquake), and many ships, including one bound for the East Indies, which had left from Deal, were greatly damaged while they were still safe in harbor. He knows the proper hours for joy, etc.

The 9th of October. Old widow Müller has been sick with fever for several weeks now; she seems to have derived great benefit for her soul and her Christianity from this sickness. She keeps learning more and more about herself and her impure heart, and she repects now only salvation in Christ. I talked to her of last Sunday's exordium verses: "I know also, my God, that thou tiest the heart, and hast pleasure in uprightness."[8] I also explained to her the closing words of the last gospel: "Whosoever shall exalt himself shall be abased; and he that shall humble himself shall be exalted"[9] Previously, she had been lacking in genuine humility and in an honest heart.

The water level in the river, which has been very high, has begun to recede again during the past few days; tomorrow our mills will probably be able to resume work in sawing and milling. This time, the high water was to our advantage; and our community will benefit from it for many years to come, if God sends us His blessing. Many cypress trees grow in the low lying areas adjoining the rivers; and, so far, we have been unable to use them in our sawmill because people always claimed that the red cypress, which is a very durable kind of wood, would not float; therefore, it would have been too difficult to get the trees out of the low lying, swampy areas, which are the only places where they grow, by horse cart. Several of our people had given it a try and felled such red cypresses, but the trunks did not float. Boat-wrights and other people who ought to know confirm this also, namely, that every small piece and even splinters of red cypresses sink to the bottom of the water.

Last spring we hired several people and had them fell a good number of trees in an area south of the mill so that, if worst came to worst and they indeed would not float, the trunks could be transported onto high lying land by horse cart and brought to the mill from there during the dry season in the summer. Close to the town, and also north of the mill, we tried something similar; trees were felled and not only sawed into pieces of fourteen, sixteen, eighteen, and twenty foot length, but we also took the bark off the trunks and stored these pieces on top of several logs, so that they could dry out during the summer. Now, however, we know with certainty and pleasure that all the red cypress logs indeed float and that some of them have been brought to the mill. The trunks below the mill were brought to the high ground and can now be brought very easily the short way to the mill by cart.

This matter of the cypresses is a real blessing for our community because there are many of these trees alongside the large island as well as on the island itself, and in many other areas; now we know that they can be transported easily to the mill. The planks and floor boards made from red cypresses fetch a good price.

The 10th of October. Mr. Meyer, our justiciary, has been a widower for more than fourteen months now, experiencing the usual sorrow and practical drawbacks. Today he married a Christian young woman /Barbara Zorn/, who had never been married before; and, although she is an orphan without either father or mother, she is endowed with many fine spiritual and good physical qualities. Her mother, an honest and hard-working woman, had come from overseas, already widowed, together with my present colleague; she worked in his house as a servant and died there a few years ago. Her only daughter had not been living with her but was in service with the President of the Council, Col. Stephens; she could do nothing to change this situation, which had made her very sad, especially since it was denied to her to raise this child here with us and to instruct it properly in God's word.

When she was on her deathbed, she sent for her daughter; she impressed upon her most urgently to move to Ebenezer and to be prepared for Holy Communion here with us, after the time of her service had been completed. At that time, she showed little inclination to do this; she was a high-spirited young girl and preferred the so-called English freedom to Ebenezer's quiet and strict order. Also, there was no lack of meddlers and dispensers of bad advice. Her dying mother, however, designated me as the guardian of her only daughter in the presence of my colleague; I gave her my solemn promise to take care of the child to the best of my ability and to see to it that she would receive a proper education here in Ebenezer and would be prepared for Holy Communion by us.

After the mother's death I wrote to Mr. Stephens and informed him that I considered it my duty, because of both my office and my conscience, to think of her now as my own daughter; and I asked him, as her present master, to ensure her spiritual and physical well-being and to warn her earnestly against violating her mother's last wishes. This letter, which showed both love and sincerity, had the good result that she was released from her service earlier than expected and sent here to Ebenezer. My dear colleague had a position to fill in his own house, and he took her on. He instructed her faithfully, in his own home, in Christian dogma and taught her reading and whatever else was necessary as well. Together with other grown children she came to my house for the lessons in preparation for Holy Communion.

It became quite obvious how powerfully God's word did its work in her soul; she gained a thorough understanding and a healthy experience of Christian dogma, as she showed in her Godfearing conduct at all times. She quieted down and sought the company of pious, adult women and learned, in addition to proper Christianity, various female skills, which are absolutely necessity in running a household. Since her genuine conversion she excelled among other young women by her love of God and her virtuous conduct, without being conceited about it. Mr. Meyer has found a wife in her which God Himself designated for him, and for this precious gift he will be grateful to God for as long as he lives.

My text for today's wedding was Hosea 2;14, "I will allure her, and bring her into the wilderness, and speak comfortably unto her." The following verses also apply to this young woman: "When my father and mother forsake me, then the Lord will take me up."[10] Likewise, from the last gospel: "Whosoever shall exalt himself shall be abased."[11] Since our loving God rewarded this young woman for her Godfearing heart, her obedience towards her teachers and her betters, and her virtuous conduct in her earthly existence so markedly with a good match, we hope that other young women here will follow her good example. The marriage ceremony was held (as we usually do) in an edifying manner in Jerusalem Church, but without any worldly festivities, amusements, and expenses. Before we left church I read to the dear people who had gathered there a remarkable chapter from Proverbs; after that we fell to our knees in order to pray and to praise God. In church, before and after the marriage sermon, we sang and prayed; after the wedding was concluded according to the Augsburg Agenda we accompanied bride and groom to their home and finally took our leave with prayer and offering our good wishes. The bride's name is Barbara Zorn, and she is eighteen years old.

The 11th of October. The chest from Halle, which contained medicines for Mr. Thilo and books for Mr. Zübli, also brought us those parts of the *Harmonicum Antonianum* which had been so far lacking from our library. Now, we have the entire work, a precious and very useful treasure, for our edification and strenghtening of our most holy faith, as for that of our successors. May our loving God reward the esteemed Pastor Mayer, the editor of this work, and the orphanage in Halle for this blessing to our Christian church! From the orphanage, we received these and, in the past, many other books, frequently and free of

charge; may our loving God reward the people there also a thou-
sandfold and bless them spiritually and physically! We also
would like to add the writings of the late Dr. Spener[12] to our
library, if they are available.

What we have so far, is the following: theological writings in
German and Latin, consisting of reflections, writings on dogma,
guidelines for leading a proper life, thoughts of consolations
based on faith, and various necessities of actively practiced
Christianity, etc; Further, we have our catechism and tables related to the catechism and short sermons based on the catechism, for example, on the subjects of nature and grace, the true
milk of the gospels, complaints about Christianity, which has
been abused and neglected, etc. Further, we have instructive
writings on the blessed return to the Evangelical truth, and on
inner and spiritual peace.

The 12th of October. A year ago, many children in Carolina
and, to some extent, in Savannah, fell sick with the same disease,
namely, a rash covering the entire body, which the English call
measles (perhaps the same as our *Masern*). This fall, too, many
children in our community are coming down with such a rash,
which is similar to the purples,[13] and they also develop a fever.
Many are seriously ill, others are not as severely affected. Kalcher's oldest daughter seems to have suffered a relapse and may
be in some danger. She is a fine girl, Godfearing, virtuous, and
quite accomplished in various skills which are needed in running a household. It would indeed be a great loss for her dear
parents if she were to die in the bloom of her youth. She is one of
the three children born in Old Ebenezer who are still alive; all
the rest have died.

In my dear colleague's house almost everybody is sick; however, we must praise our God's mercy for letting him recover
from the fever attacks from which he suffered. His dear wife
also was saved from great danger and a most painful condition,
and his only daughter is likewise starting to regain her health
and strength again after being near death with sickness. Those
of us who are sick and weak are making excellent use of Richter's[14] medicine which we received from the blessed orphanage
in Halle and, as is our duty, we praise our most loving Father in
heaven for this very precious blessing. Based on my own experi-

ence (from my early youth on I was rather sickly and was attended by various doctors; and therefore I was frequently in a position, during times of illness, to observe the effects of treatments and medicines), I am firmly convinced that our medicines are not only some of the safest to use but also cure a wide variety of ailments; the sick need to be somewhat patient, of course, and they have to follow the instructions of their doctors. Many people are rather slack in the latter.

The 13th of October. Eight days ago yesterday, as is my duty, and with love for our community, I presented to our people the thoughts which I had outlined in this diary under the entry for the second of September. I offered my services and assistance in order to promote the changes which I proposed; I also gave them enough time to think things over and to discuss them with each other and to form plans for improving and simplifying that undertaking which has the blessing of the authorities and of all of our friends. Some people had made arrangements with their neighbors in the past, since they did not like it that their plantations (of a total of fifty acres) should be parcelled up into two and three narrow strips of land and that other people, selected by drawing lots, would take part in owning good land. They traded pieces of land among each other, thereby extending their property lines across the original narrow strips, others bought land from neighbors who moved away or settled on another farm, also with the effect of obscuring the original boundary lines of their properties.

Now, these pieces of land have to be returned, and the original narrow plantation strips which had been changed in time have to be restored. Otherwise, it will be impossible to obtain grants or deeds from the Lord Trustees in writing for land which has been splintered up into so many small pieces. I could easily convince our people on this point. They also recognize, for the most part, the suggested changes and the land which has been offered to them as an advantage for which they ought to be grateful. Together with me they think that not only our people here, but even the entire country, as well as the Lord Trustees, would benefit from such a useful arrangement; and they wish that it had been made at the very beginning, right after our arrival

here, or two years after that when we moved away from Old
Ebenezer to the present location of our pilgrimage.

If our people could be settled closer together, it would be in
their best interest, as far as the material circumstances of our
Salzburgers are concerned. They could help each other better,
their lives would be more safe and secure, and their Christianity
would prosper, too. They say, and they are telling the truth, that
their purpose in leaving their homeland was not finding an
easier life but, rather, to be able to take better care of their souls
and those of their children.

For a long time now ignorant people, and even some of the
authorities here in this country, have put the blame for the present situation of the narrow plantation strips on my shoulders.[15]
It is also rumored that after my death and that of the original
householders all sorts of confusion, disputes, and quarrels
would arise. Therefore, I suggested certain changes as early as
two years ago; and I shared my thoughts and motives with our
community, advising them to move.

At that time, nobody had been willing to do so; they were less
worried about being at a disadvantage as far as their properties
were concerned than about enduring a lack or a lessening of
their spiritual wealth, as for instance, going without churches or
school, which we have not only in town but also in the middle of
the plantations. The householders on our side of the long
bridge, on both sides of town, felt the same way; there each plantation is shared by two households. These issues were brought
up again because of the petition which I had filed with the members of the Council in the matter of adding land to some of the
plantations. I was instructed to advise our people to agree to the
changes which I listed in my diary entry of the second of September. This I have done, arguing most forcefully, as was suggested to me; however, I did suspect that our people would not
be swayed, as I learned today. Only two or three householders
seem willing to let their neighbors have their strips of land and
to move to other land close by; this would give us only two plantations for re-settling.

All the others believe that they lack the necessary physical
strength and temporal means to settle new land; also, they like to

stay close to the church and the school for the sake of their children. They are willing to take a chance as to whether or not the members of the Council will be willing to obtain for them, from the Lord Trustees, grants or deeds in writing for their long and narrow plantations of fifty acres. If the Council does not wish to help, then it is believed that the Lord Trustees will do it themselves, for the reasons cited above. After all, it may be all the same to them whether our people, their subjects, own fifty acres in lots which are long and narrow or which are shorter and wider. My opinion in this matter of our plantations which are so practically divided, is that, although this arrangement seems to go against reason and logic, God wished it to be so, even if ignorant people put most of the blame on me.

The 15th of October. Yesterday, the Eighteenth Sunday after Trinity, my dear colleague preached to the people living at Goshen near Abercorn. Nineteen people went to Holy Communion. May God bless His word and communion in all of them! On the one hand, they enjoy listening to God's word and also show considerable eagerness for partaking in Holy Communion; on the other hand, the results are less than we expect. Meanwhile, it is our duty, following the example of our Lord Jesus and His apostles, to continue with our prayer and preaching and to leave the rest in His hands. Some years ago, when I saw how little the Germans living in and around Savannah valued God's word, I believed that I could bring about a change in them by refusing, for a certain time, to preach to them or to hold Holy Communion. Dear Mr. Francke, however, reprimanded me sternly, since I had caused more damage than good by my conduct. Now I am wiser and no longer let an opportunity slip by to serve them with my office.

The 16th of October. A short while ago, sad news reached us from Savannah concerning a German who undertook to sail for the Sugar Island, Jamaica, in a small craft which he had built himself. On his way back, close to a Spanish island, he was shipwrecked and lost all of his cargo. His life and that of his crew was saved but they had all been made prisoners because they were suspected of smuggling goods on which the Spanish had an embargo, for instance, Brazil wood. Many of the sea-going people in this country have no conscience at all; otherwise how could they be so bold and, by force of arms, steal from other people goods such as Brazil wood, salt, and other things, and to bring them aboard their own vessels. People do a brisk business on the black market with the Spanish and the French, and the King of England gets cheated out of the tariffs due him. Good Christians abhor these practices and refuse to be a party to such goings-on.

I cannot understand that the conscience of some, who claim to be Christians, allows them to trade with such black marketeers. Germans living in English colonies are quick to learn to make illegal deals, even mastering these methods and perfecting them. Even though in the eyes of the world they may appear rich, such conduct is without blessing. A few months ago a large ship, badly damaged, sailed up our Savannah River. Its cargo was loywood, that is wood used in the dyeing process; the captain, under great danger, had smuggled it in from the Spanish West Indies. Since such people go out with the purpose of robbing others, they do not shrink back from murder. Furthermore, because they have to work very fast when they fell trees illegally, they can not afford to take much care and ruin a great deal of wood. I have heard that soon there will be very little left. One only has to look to this colony and to the neighboring territory to see how poorly people manage cedar, live oak, white oak, cypresses, and other valuable trees.

The 17th of October. Old Mrs. Landfelder sent for me; she was in need of hearing God's word and being consoled by it, and she requested assistance in her prayers. She seemed troubled about her salvation. God blessed me in my talk with her; I cited the gospel verses dealing with those who are racked by gout, and I explained to her what I thought was necessary and suitable in her circumstances, and I consoled her. She is old and worn out from too much work, therefore she thinks that her death is quite near. On the other hand, although she has very little money, she buys medicines from our doctor and is little perturbed about God's judgment of her. In the past, she has been rather self-righteous, and her attitude towards me and my preaching has not always been of the kind which befits a faithful listener. Today she asked my forgiveness for her past behavior. Another half-hearted Christian, just like her, did the same. If she had been willing to heed good advice, then she could have avoided her destitute circumstances in Savannah and Vernonburg and the great poverty of her family. But the eagerness to marry has brought her and others much suffering, especially if such a marriage was contracted with an unconverted man of another religion. She is very close to death; it is a token of God's mercy that she has been allowed, towards her end, to live and die at a place about which she used to spread lies and which she had formerly despised. She and her family realize this now.

The 18th of October. This week, two French merchants in Savannah caused me considerable trouble by their wish to have boards cut by our mill, a request which came very much at the wrong time. One of them came in person and asked me, and when I could not oblige him, the other wrote to me and tried to force me to do as he wished by sending along a rather large sum of money. Our friends in Savannah and Charleston had ordered so many boards of varying thickness that it is virtually impossible for us to fill other orders, as much as we would like to. Since people know that I supervise the work in the mills and that I am in charge of all correspondence in English, all too often the results are hard feelings towards me and unflattering remarks about my person. Mr. Meyer does not wish to take part in the running of the mills.

Our mills, especially the saw-mill, are earthly treasures for our community, and we derive more advantages from them than I can enumerate here. Although my dear, faithful colleague does most of the actual work, I must take a certain interest in such things; furthermore, I cannot refer strangers who come to us with their demands to him. There are also many reasons why it would not be practical to send quickly for a man from Europe whose sole responsibility it would be to supervise the work at the mills and the sale of our boards. To mention only one such reason: at present, we can not afford to spend the money on hiring such a man; partly because we still have to pay off our old debts, partly because we keep improving and repairing our mills, and partly because now we intend to build another saw-mill.

Among the people of our community there is nobody whom we could put in charge of the mill business. If, however, with divine blessing, we succeed in putting up a second sawmill (the dam for it has been completed already), then it will become necessary to find a foreman for that mill, especially since it will be somewhat out of the way; it will take approximately half an hour to reach it from our present mills, using a short-cut which was made recently. We can see quite clearly that God has given us His blessing for these very profitable undertakings; His blessing is the reason that they were protected from harm when it seemed unavoidable. Furthermore, in time, we have increased the number of our communal projects, and they have become more and more useful to us. Praised be the Lord!

From now on, it will make things quite a bit easier for us that Kalcher, this sensible, honest, and hard-working man, will be the supervisor of the women working at the mills, as well as our inn-keeper and assistant there. Very soon now he will move into his new house, which is rather well built, together with his pious and capable wife and his four well-behaved daughters who all show good promise.

The 19th of October. The Salzburger Thomas Bichler is not making any progress either in his Christianity or in the running of his household. His body is growing weaker, and he lacks sufficient supplies from time to time; it is his own fault. At first, he had been our miller; after that, General Oglethorpe, upon my recommendation, made him the commanding officer of the rangers. In addition to that, he kept an inn in town, raised cattle, and farmed. After the rangers had been dismissed, he was no longer interested in being either an inn-keeper or a farmer, and he asked to be installed as the foreman at our cowpen. In this position he received annually the sum of sixteen pounds Sterling, and his field-hand got ten pounds Sterling; in addition to that, he had ample opportunity for raising crops, as well as certain other advantages. He quit this job, too, and moved in with his mother-in-law.

Now, he has more troubles; he has a horse, which was the source of overweening pride in his days as an officer; his overbearing, sinful manner had been giving offense in our community. Due to his own fault, this horse kicked his only son, a good child, and injured him so severely that he died miserably the next day. This accident happened a little more than a year ago, in the presence of the father, on a Sunday during our afternoon services. At that time, both I and Mr. Meyer were unaware of an English law which applies in such sad cases; this law is called deodand (*quasi Deo dandum*). Therefore, nothing more could be done but to grieve, and to humiliate ourselves before God, asking Him to have mercy on our community by not burdening it with this child's blood. A good while after that, when Mr. Meyer had relinquished his offices as our justice of the peace and our trading agent, I had to read through the English laws in order to familiarize myself with them to an extent which seemed fitting for a justice of the peace. I made an excerpt for the purpose of reading it aloud to our people, and I came across the law deodand, which prescribes that a horse or other animal which kills a human being becomes the property of God and has to be given to Him or, by the authorities, to a community's poor.

Bichler was not present when I read the English laws to our people; but he heard about it from others and, in particular, of the law which pertained to him and his horse. He is determined, and calls it a matter of conscience, to keep this horse for his own use, and he has told me to obtain a judgment in this case from the authorities in Savannah. Since then, his good luck had been waning constantly; in this manner God intends to punish him. On the other hand, he is a capable, talented man, and a productive member of our community; he could be even more valuable to us if he were converted and in the process gave up his pride, short-temper, stubbornness, and belligerent attitude towards people in authority and if he could quit his self-righteousness. Almost everybody prefers to avoid dealing with him because of his character. His bad luck in the past he blamed not on himself, but on his superiors and on other people. At all times, I had sought to influence him towards his own best interest in spiritual and physical matters, and I still attempt to do this, against all odds. Secretly, he speaks ill of me, and in Savannah, in my presence, he was told that he was the worst enemy of me and our community.

The 20th of October. Four days ago I had to go to Savannah on business. Bad weather and many errands prevented me from returning earlier than today; I arrived here in the evening. My duties as our community's trading agent require the frequent traveling, and I pray that our dear God may forgive me whatever omissions may result from the fact that I have to neglect some things here at home as a consequence. May He not, for the sake of Christ, find fault with me for it. Last month, on the twenty-fourth of September, a drunken man fell into the river at Savannah and his body has not yet been recovered. Such accidents have happened frequently here in the past. It is not surprising that God makes an example of such people, since in this area sea-going men and boatsmen are in the habit of cursing and uttering disgusting oaths, and they drink far too much hard liquor. But they do not believe in God's anger, and they are not afraid of His wrath.

On that day (mentioned above), during the afternoon, an unusually violent storm and downpour occurred; one boat with a cargo of salt capsized, although the crew survived. A serving maid who arrived here with the last transport of servants, an orphan of our faith, has finally persuaded me, after begging me for a long time, to buy her freedom from her masters in Savannah upon certain conditions. The people for whom she worked are glad to see her leave because she is German. I was also encouraged to this step by Christian friends, who argued that, by coming to us, she would be saved from too much temptation, danger, and corruption, and that she would be led towards God's word. She will serve here, earning the money which was advanced, namely six pounds Sterling. Such poor people who come to us as the result of their own repeated asking, commonly consider it an advantage to live among us and accept our strict order more willingly.

It became rather cold after all the rain we had had; last night there was ice. I had met an old woman in Savannah who moved from Pennsylvania to Charleston recently, together with several German families. She had intended to visit her son, but learned that he, a habitual drunkard, had been found in Augusta last winter, frozen to death in the snow. She is Lutheran, and she praised the great work done by Pastor Muhlenberg and Mr. Brunnholz. Her husband and the aforementioned son who froze to death, and who had been to Ebenezer at one time, had been of the faith of his father; her other children, who are married in and around Philadelphia, have not chosen their religion yet. She told me more of their terribly confused state. She will now return to her family again.

The 21st of October. Yesterday afternoon, shortly before I returned from my trip, Mrs. Christ,[16] who had been very sick, died and was buried today before evening. I hope that our wise and merciful God, during the last days of her life which she spent here with us in peace and proper preparation for life eternal, has led her to His word, which she liked to hear in days of health and sickness alike. God certainly did not forsake her two young children; it was this dying mother's last wish that I should be in charge of the children's upbringing and education, and nobody else should be allowed to interfere. The brothers and sisters of these two children would like to take them and use them in their households. However, they would not be well provided for in such an arrangement, as the mother had been well aware. If she had stayed in Savannah or Vernonburg, or if she had not changed her opinion of Ebenezer, then these two poor orphans could very well have gotten into the wrong hands; there are many examples of such things happening.

The 22nd of October. Yesterday, the Twentieth Sunday after Trinity, my dear colleague preached in Savannah and held Holy Communion. In past years, I frequently suffered from a lack of physical strength, and I lost courage easily; I found it difficult to preach twice a day and to hold our evening prayer hour as well. Our faithful God, however, has come to my aid for several years now so remarkably that, to my own astonishment and to that of other people, my strength does not diminish, even when I preach several times a day and attend to the various duties of my office as well. God alone is responsible for that! May He be praised, most heartily, for His mercy, which I do not deserve at all!

Mrs. Bacher, a good woman who became our community's midwife a few years ago, is getting frail with advancing age, and it is not easy for her to go about her business. She has trained her daughter to be her assistant; the daughter is a sensible, capable and honest woman. She and her husband, a good man, live on her mother's plantation. The good women in our community will praise God for this blessing! We prayed to our Lord in this important matter and asked Him to enlighten us in His wisdom. Mrs. Bacher tells, praising the Lord, how God, on several occasions when she had to deal with particularly dangerous deliveries, heard her prayers, gave her courage, and granted a successful birth in order to strenghten her faith. She also told me that something I had said to her and her late husband several times had also come true: namely that God mercifully rewarded the work of the Egyptian midwives by building houses for them. Miraculously, and against her expectations, this had happened to her, too, and had greatly improved her circumstances.

The 21st of October. The last entry in my diary for this month, according to God's will and His miraculous ways, has to be the recording of an event which is the saddest in my life, excepting the death of my late colleague, although I am able to find some consolation in certain circumstances. Today, at five o'clock in the morning, it pleased our all-wise, miraculous, all-powerful, and merciful God to call my little son Samuel Leberecht to Him. He died after a painful agony, in his fourteenth year. He was our oldest son. He was very talented and especially obedient and God-fearing, which is most important. His pious conduct and his blessed, edifying end gave us strength; otherwise, our pain would, of course, have been much worse.

He was born here in Ebenezer on the second of January, 1737. It was a difficult birth, very painful and dangerous for his mother; at the time we had prayed most humbly and urgently for a successful delivery. Yesterday, and the night before, his unexpected and painful death gave us cause once more to offer Christian prayers to our Lord on His throne of mercy. Two weeks ago, he and his brother Gotthilf Israel, whom he loved most deeply and affectionately, had come down with the purples. Either they had not completely recovered yet, or the children went outdoors prematurely, but both became bloated, complained of a piercing pain in their sides and about stiffness in their joints. In addition to that, Samuel Leberecht's chest had become congested and he had great difficulty breathing.

Yesterday morning, while he was still in bed, he started to suffer from epileptic attacks. The convulsions were extremely violent and persisted until his blessed departure from this world; he did not respond even to well-proven medicines which we administered with utmost care. He was out of his mind with fever. However, even during this agonizing paroxysm he never said anything which was in the least childish or unfitting; his first words were only: "Lord Jesus, wash me in Thy blood and forgive me all of my sins". A few hours later, in the same painful paroxysm, he prayed in a loud and clear voice (but not being in his right mind) the Lord's Prayer, the Evening Blessing, the Christian Creed, and various other good prayers; he repeated those several times.

This morning, not long before his passing, he said to his weak and ill mother that he did not want to die, but he did want to go to his dear Savior. Shortly before his death he struggled to get up and said: "Papa will see it"; then he rolled over on his side and died suddenly. When I saw what had happened, we prostrated ourselves in mind and body: I, my other young son, Gotthilf Israel (who had wanted to stay day and night with his brother, whom he had loved so much), and the desolate mother. Once more, we commended his blessed spirit unto the wounds of his most precious and beloved Savior.

After I had finished writing all this down, I was told of a rather moving event, which I regard a beautiful sign of the workings of the Holy Spirit in the heart of this child, and I feel I have to share this edifying moment: at about one o'clock in the morning he said he thought he saw an angel before him. But he could not find the right words to express himself, and his mother tried to help him; she said, perhaps it was his beloved Savior. He seemed content and agreed that indeed it was his beloved Savior. Towards the end, his brother was on his mind, too, he seemed to feel that he had to help him. But he was no longer coherent.

The last few Sundays, while I was away in Savannah, he attended his ailing mother with much love, he read to her and they prayed together. She was impressed by his seriousness, his respect for God, and his eagerness for prayer and God's word. He liked very much to pray, to read God's word, and to listen to it; his conduct was exemplary, and all the God-fearing and honest people among us liked him well. He studied hard and he had made excellent progress in theology, Latin studies, geography, calligraphy, arithmetic, and drawing. He had made a good start in Greek and singing; God had endowed him with a rich talent, a fine carrying voice and much enthusiasm. He would have made faster progress if he had not attended the same lessons in Latin and Greek as his brother, whom he loved so much and who is almost three years younger; he wanted to study together with him and help him with the lessons, when necessary.

Both brothers had wished very much to go to school at the Orphanage at Halle; although young people normally wish for more freedom, both were more than willing to live under the strict rules and regulations at Halle; they both wished to leave as soon as possible. A long time ago, I had thought to enter them both into the service of our Lord, since He had granted both many good talents and a serious inclination for studying. God willing, I was firmly decided to send them, as soon as a safe opportunity offered itself, to London and from there on to Halle, either at the end of this year, or at the beginning of the next. I had already assembled the clothes which they would need.

He had an overwhelming, simple respect for our most esteemed Fathers in Europe; especially he felt drawn to Dr. Francke, who once had sent him and his brother a very pleasant and encouraging letter. He was afraid that Professor Francke would die before he got a chance to see him; this was one reason he wished to leave as soon as possible, he was longing to meet this dear servant of God while still alive and to see him in Germany in person, as he had seen his engraved portrait here in this country. I need not mention the remarkable workings of the Holy Spirit in him, which we had noticed from his earliest childhood on; I need not mention the great love which he showed his parents, and the complete obedience towards them and his elders, or his eagerness to help people, or his compassion towards the poor and suffering; describing his character in such detail is superfluous; it is not necessary.

Only the glory of God (who manifested His grace in him and through him) and my duty towards the benefactors of this blessed Samuel Leberecht and their plans for him could move me at all to write so much about this son, who showed so much promise for the future. These benefactors kindly contributed money and books; they made it possible for him and his brother to take private lessons from our doctor, Mr. Thilo, for two years;

this arrangement had been a blessing for the teacher, Mr. Thilo, as well, since he could make good use of the money, considering his poor income. I mentioned the talents of this son, who was such a joy and a source of strength to me, and God's gifts to him, in order to thank these benefactors; I wanted them to see that their kind support of his education was well placed and pleased God. I wished very much to send him to Halle, for the sake of our Lord, and to have him prepared for entering the service of our Lord. It is written in Isaiah 55;8: "My thoughts are not your thoughts, neither are your ways . . , etc."

In writing these lines, I wish to thank most humbly, and with all my heart, all of the benefactors in Europe, both known and unknown, for all the blessings, spiritual and physical, which they have shown to my late son and to his younger brother, who is still alive. May He reward them and their families for their goodness and bless them here on earth as well as in eternity! Although the main purpose of their benefactions, namely, to prepare this boy completely for the service in Christ's church, has not been fulfilled, it has nevertheless been fulfilled to a degree: he was dedicated to our Lord and was being taught to help me on many occasions and to make my work easier for me.

Personally, I suffered a great loss. However, since he was dedicated to our Lord and to His church, and since he was to leave for school in Halle, my heart had already been prepared for our parting. I no longer looked upon him as my son, but I considered him to belong to the Lord. Since our Lord, the Master over life and death, pleased to call him away from this world and to Himself, I feel quietly content and I say: "The Lord gave, and the Lord hath taken away; blessed be the name of the Lord"[17] Now he is beyond danger, he is in good care, and he is at peace; therefore, my tears are not tears of sorrow, but of joy. With this death, our kind Savior granted me and my dear wife His immense mercy.

In the morning hours of the first of November he was buried in a Christian ceremony. Our dear listeners came from town and from the plantations and congregated in Jerusalem Church. We sang two edifying hymns and read aloud a passage from the Holy Bible between the songs. After that, my dear colleague held the funeral sermon, based on the fourteenth verse of the

fourth chapter of the Book of Wisdom: "His soul was pleasing to
the Lord, therefore he took him quickly from the midst of wickedness"[18] My dear colleague had loved our Samuel as if he were
his own son and he had taught him most carefully. At the beginning of the sermon, we, the parents, were addressed with verses
from the gospel passage for next Sunday: "Thy child liveth."[19]
After the sermon, we kneeled and prayed.

After that (instead of reading his vita), in order to inform and
edify our people, the community was told some of the most remarkable events which had occurred in this child's life, suffering, and death. Then we accompanied the body quietly to the
churchyard. While the coffin was lowered into the grave, we
sang the beautiful song *Gott Lob! die Stund ist kommen*, etc. His last
resting place is next to that of his late cousin[20] and godfather,
Mr. Gronau, for whom he always had shown great respect and
whose blessing and prayers had been upon him. Finally, I
thanked our dear people for showing their love to me and to my
son by coming so willingly and in such great numbers to the funeral and by shedding their tears. I addressed them with the
verse: " Delight thyself also in the Lord, and he shall give thee,"
etc.[21] Only a short time ago, at his own initiative, my late son
wrote this verse in chancery calligraphy and pinned the sheet to
my door.

NOVEMBER

The 1st of November. Yesterday, the day the great change in
my life occurred which I reported at the end of last month, I had
gone out before evening in order to hold one of my soliloquies
with my precious Savior. While I was out walking, a thick
package of letters from Europe was brought to me; it had
arrived with the Germans whom the Lord Trustees had sent to
Ebenezer, partly as free men, partly as servants.[1] All letters contained good news; and just now, in my present tribulation, when
I need encouragement urgently, they are a source of considerable consolation to me. They are from our well-meaning authorities, the Lord Trustees, from our most esteemed Fathers,
and from other dear benefactors and friends. The fatherly letter from our most esteemed Senior Urlsperger began with the

words: "God has thought everything out well and done everything correctly. Praised be our God!"[2] Mr. Laminit, a true Israelite, sends his wishes to me through Mr. Mayer and he says: "We know that all things serve to the best interest of those who love God."

All German letters from the servants and children of God in London and Germany contain many beautiful evangelical expressions, which refresh my heart; and they contain so many signs of our Heavenly Father's care for me, my family, my dear colleague, his family, and our entire community that my faith is greatly strengthened in our Lord and King, who doeth all help that is done on earth. It is especially comforting for me and all of us that our most esteemed Fathers, Senior Urlsperger, Professor Dr. Francke, Court Chaplain Ziegenhagen, Deacon Albinus, and Mr. von N. are still alive and in good health and that they are continuing faithfully to pray for us, to work, talk, and write on our behalf. May Jesus Christ, our King of Grace, in His mercy, reward them on the Day of Judgment, the day of His glorious return, and even before that, in their lives, suffering, and death.

I did not know that so many true servants of Christ in so many different parts of Germany still remember me fondly and pray for me; some I had met during my days as a student in the service of our Lord. They wish me well; and they, too, praise God for all the goodness He has shown to our dear community here so far. I learned of this through several letters which I received from some of them this time, and I felt greatly encouraged. My belief in the Communion of Saints, of which, by God's grace, I am an unworthy member, is a great consolation to me. I am looking forward to joining this eternal Communion in Heaven. Once again, the letters of our esteemed Lord Trustees show considerable good-will towards me and our community here. They will send us another thirty-seven servants and it is to be hoped that these will be of more use than the previous ones who arrived here a year ago.

Last spring I asked for the iron parts of a sawmill near Savannah which is no longer in use; now, the Lord Trustees have given them to our community as a gift. Further, they are granting us fifty pounds Sterling towards the high purchase price of our cowpen, which we bought from them. I received twenty pounds for repairs on my house and another eighteen pounds to contribute to the expenses I incurred from supporting a large family of useless servants which had ended up with me. The Lord Trustees request a list of the names of our householders, together with the number of acres of their plantations in order to be able to send them an official letter and a deed of ownership. They also decided on a very useful change in the membership of the Council at Savannah; I am glad to say that Col. Stephens, who had become senile, was replaced by Mr. Parker, the highest-ranking council member, who was made vice-president, and Mr. Habersham, the youngest member of the Council, was installed as the secretary.[3] They also ordered that a general meeting take place next spring in the manner of a small parliament. Our community will be represented in it by two knowledgeable deputies. The intended purpose of this parliament will be to formulate resolutions reflecting the best interests of each community and of the entire colony; the resolutions will be sent to London for their ratification and their approval by the Lord Trustees. God willing, this assembly is supposed to take place from then on regularly in following years.

The 2nd of November. My dear colleague and Mr. Mayer went to Savannah in my place, in order to obtain clarification from the Council in the question of the Lord Trustees' intent concerning the German free colonists and servants.[4] My own thoughts on their settling I wrote down in a letter addressed to my friend Mr. Habersham. This morning, at my request, our householders assembled, both in order to discuss the problems connected with the arrival of the new servants, and in order to hear their opinions as to whether they preferred to stay on their old plantations or whether they planned on moving, as they had been advised to do by the Council, and to select new, good land for their plantations. They have first choice; people arriving now will have to be content with the best parcels of whatever land will be left over. Most intend to stay on the land which was given into their care through God's goodness: land close to the church, the school, and the mills; furthermore, the large, fertile island on the Mill River is almost at their doorstep.

Those of our original residents who did not have a plantation of their own up to now, either because of their trade or because they were minors at the time, or for other reasons, will take land close by, on the Uchee land. New colonists will settle near them, wherever they please. Up to now it was believed that the Uchee land consisted of many thousands of acres of fertile, good land; now, after people took a closer look, it turned out that there is only a modest amount of good land available. The best sections of land are supposed to be further up north along the Savannah River. This afternoon, I set down all these details in a long letter to the Vice-President of the Council and its other members, so that this time, as is the wish of our people, the question of the land for plantations will be settled properly for once and for all.

The 3rd of November. This morning I received the sad news that the youngest daughter of the late Klocker, a very well-behaved girl, took ill last night and may be in grave danger. Soon after the first messenger had left, he came back and reported her increasing weakness. I hurried to Mr. Mayer's house to visit her with the verses we had just sung in tranquility: "Just as a bird seeks a hollow tree";[5] but I could neither speak nor pray with her, for she had already died or rather fallen asleep. She, too, had had scarlet fever and then the very same attacks with bloating of the body[6] as our son Samuel Leberecht. Judging from the foam around her mouth, I assume (and Mr. Thilo, who was sent for soon thereafter, agrees) that, just as in the case of our own child, epileptic convulsions hastened the approach of death.

Yesterday she had still been well and in high spirits; she had moved back into Mr. Mayer's house from Mr. Lemke's, convinced of her full recovery; and she probably suspected nothing less than such a sudden change in her condition. Both of her parents had died young, and she was raised well and properly by Hans Flerl, a good man, and by his wife, also a God-fearing woman. After that, she had been in service in my house at first, and later in Justiciary Mayer's, until he got married. Mr. Mayer put her in service with Mrs. Lemke, taking the place of his new wife /Barbara Zorn/, who, until her marriage, had worked in the Lemke's household. Meanwhile, Mrs. Lemke got herself another maid; and, as mentioned, Mr. Mayer took the girl back into his house. We lost in her a rather fine, God-fearing, and sensible young girl, well versed in God's word and eager in her work. Often she had pleased our entire community by her clever and well-phrased answers in church, as well as by her conduct in general. In my home, as well as in Mr. Mayer's, she behaved in such a Christian manner and with such virtue that her blessed memory will be held dear by all of us.

God, in His wisdom, which we fail to understand fully, sent me such special tribulations this month; therefore, I turn to some of the remarkable and edifying sentiments expressed in the letters which we have just received and which were written to us by these servants of God (no doubt, as a result of His bidding). They strengthen me greatly and are worth being quoted in part in this diary to give food for thought and edification to others as well. They are as follows:

"We owe thanks to our Lord, for He continues to protect Ebenezer. Even if there be some little sadness, it will pass. Oh, how I will laugh! God is steadfast. God has also sent you laughter in the past. Since we welcome God's blessings, how can we refuse tribulations and sadness? . . . Without God's help it would be impossible not to lose heart and to continue the work, in these times of corruption and horrors. You feel its effects, nevertheless; yet you continue to work, and you believe that your work will not be in vain but, rather, will endure in the Lord. In time, when the passage through this vale of tears is completed and the Good Shepherd appears to us, we will be filled with unspeakable, glorious, joy. Meanwhile, we have to practice patience . . . Our Lord comes to our aid. In this matter also, as in all things, He will advise us. Lord Jesus, I belong to you, in life and death. Help me soon, I am but a poor soul! . . .

"Oh, how miraculously! How wonderfully does our Savior guide His servants and children! How right we are to follow His hand, even blindly, for in the end we will get to see His light and His grace! May our eternally faithful God grant to you and to your esteemed family ever more grace from His abundance; may He see to it, if possible, that the faith with which you discharge your office not be in vain and not a single soul of your community be lost during your tenure. . . . Our Lord, Lord, Lord, may He strengthen you in all physical tribulations, may He make life endurable for you, and may He make it possible for you to say, joyfully, at any time: Ebenezer, so far the Lord hath never forsaken us! He is faithful, He, who called you; and He will take care of you. He does as those wish who worship Him. He hears their cries and He comes to their aid. Yes, He does abundantly more than we ask of Him or understand."

An old, faithful servant of God in the principality of Anhalt sent me a catalogue containing a listing of all honest ministers who are busy upholding the peace and unity in dogma, in order to edify their people to promote the kingdom of Christ. He tells of a preacher, whom I know and whom I hold in high esteem, that he was born on the thirty-first of October, 1709, the day on which I and my late colleague received our vocations also my instructions.[7] This day has now also become the memorable day on which my oldest son died, whom I had dedicated to the service of God and His church.

The 4th of November. Our merciful and eternally faithful God has come to my aid and proven most impressively His power during this time of my great physical weakness; today, the twenty-first Sunday after Trinity, in the absence of my dear colleague, I was able to preach His holy word to my own blessing as well as that of my listeners, and I held the funeral services. In the morning we considered Abraham, this edifying example for Christian householders and families: Genesis 18:19. In the afternoon we contemplated the royal example from the gospel for the same purpose. Oh, how many good thoughts did our Lord let us speak and hear for our consolation and encouragement! My dear wife, who for many weeks now had been too weak to leave home and attend church, has been strengthened by God so miraculously that she was able to come not only to the funeral of her beloved Samuel Leberecht on the first of this month, but also to join us twice today at our public service, much to her great joy in our Lord and to the consolation of her soul. However, she regards this respite the calm before the storm and is preparing herself for it, by the grace of her Savior.

Before our service in the afternoon I received letters from the secretary of the Lord Trustees, Mr. Habersham, and from my dear colleague, in which they ask me to come to Savannah. I can not leave during the first days of this week; partly because I am very hoarse, a condition which set in towards evening; partly because I have to hold a wedding ceremony tomorrow, and also partly because of the poor health of my children and the children of my dear colleague. Meanwhile, I have finished my letters to these two friends concerning the necessary details about our people here as well as about the newly arrived colonists. These dear people lived through an especially difficult and dangerous voyage at sea; however, they did not complain, but behaved in a rather quiet and content manner.

The good opinion which my dear colleague and the two men of our community who had met them formed of them pleases me and encourages me to take care of them as well as I know how, to the extent of the abilities which God has granted to me. I also asked my listeners in particular to receive the new people with love; and I emphatically warned those of them who usually behave in a less exemplary manner to treat them properly and without giving cause for complaint. All of them are eager and willing to settle in Ebenezer. May God give His blessing to their arrival and to their new life among us!

The 5th of November. George Glaner (or Klammer, as he was incorrectly called in Memmingen) was married today to widow Zant, the former wife of Pilz, who was an honest carpenter. We chose a passage from yesterday's gospel: "He believed and his whole house." My God and Savior granted me a great deal of edification and hope for eternity during the ceremony; the small gathering consisted of the bride, the bridegroom, and some friends. Although this is a difficult time for me and my family, which has been sent to us according to God's plan and will, I felt strengthened and consoled through His word and our prayer. May His name be praised for this most humbly!

The 6th of November. This morning, our miraculous and merciful God called to Him our youngest daughter, Christiana Elisabeth, in her eighth year, during our, her parents' and our two remaining children's, prayer and tears; also present was a friend who loves Jesus and His children. For some time, she, too, had been suffering from a bloating of the body, and she had great difficulty breathing, just like her brother Samuel Leberecht, whom she had loved dearly. However, it had seemed that her condition had improved somewhat and responded to the medicine which she obediently and willingly took; she felt well and there was no restlessness, either during the day on Sunday, nor at bedtime. She went to sleep saying her prayers; and her loving mother kissed her good-night, hoping that she would get up the next morning healthy and well. Our miraculous God, however, had other plans.

Yesterday morning, she showed the same symptoms from which Samuel Leberecht had suffered; her chest was congested, she had great difficulty breathing, and finally the convulsions started; and they lasted, on and off, for the next twenty-four hours, just as in the case of our son. We felt her pain even more than she did, and we were greatly relieved at her release from all suffering. Towards the end, the convulsions lasted longer and longer (we could barely watch and were filled with deep pity for her, and we were most painfully moved); I read the eighty-first Psalm and the beautiful words: "Open thy mouth wide, and I shall fill it."[9] I tried to console my family, who were in tears and filled with grief witnessing such misery. I explained how God's heart and that of our Savior were eager for our salvation and how willing and ready He was to fill us and our dying child with the entire wealth of His grace and mercy. We kneeled before the Lord and prayed to Him in simple words, telling Him of our anguish and that of our child; and we asked Him fervently to open wide the mouth of the heart and the soul of this dying child and to fill it, and to end her suffering soon, for the sake of Christ, if it pleased Him in His wisdom. I had not expected how soon our merciful God would hear our poor prayers; however, it happened to our great consolation and strengthening our faith. She became suddenly quiet and passed away, praying, crying, and praising God.

Because of yesterday's wedding, many people kept coming and going at our house; and the dangerous illness of this child, who was quite gifted and liked by everyone, became known in town and on the plantations. As a result, this child was commended to the care of the Holy Trinity and our God both in and outside of my house through the intercession of Christ and through the prayer of many of our faithful during these past twenty-four hours. She was a dear well-behaved child; and she showed great willingness to die and to join her dear Savior (as she called him affectionately), both in the past, when she was still in good health, as well as towards the end, when she was still able to talk. Once, during one of her last severe convulsions, she called out to Samuel, whom she had loved even more than her brother Gotthilf Israel and who had loved her as much. Once, she asked for her catechism. My late colleague,[10] while he was still alive, and other god-fearing godfathers as well, had been pleased and had praised God, for immediately after receiving Holy Baptism she displayed a special and quite unusual friendliness, more as if she were the child of angels rather than of humans.

My dear late colleague, in his wisdom and Christian way of thinking, used this example for stressing the fact that Holy Baptism and the Articles of Baptism ought to be shown the respect due to them. He liked to quote the late Dr. Spener, saying: "Baptizing a child is more worthwhile than crowning an emperor." After Holy Baptism, Christiana Elisabeth, who had been in good health until then, became very sick and came close to death. Her sickly mother (who, while confined to her lonely bed during this last of her deliveries, had benefitted greatly from the gospel and the prayers in which the kind Abba and Father joined her often) had given her up to her Savior; she had then been overcome by unspeakable joy when she became convinced, most sweetly, that our loving God fulfilled His priceless, inscrutable and glorious promise, as is quoted from Isaiah 60,61, and 62 and noted on page 159 of the *Treasure Chest*.[11] He had fulfilled His promise partly on earth, in her child who had been baptized, and He would fulfill His promise partly later, completing it in Heaven, since the child had become, through Holy Baptism, a living member of the spiritual body of Christ and of His church.

We became aware of this edifying fact once more, deep in our hearts, since we remembered yesterday that her dear brother Samuel Leberecht had drawn a crown for her not long before his own sickness and departure from this world. At the time, I had not known this and had taken the piece of paper, torn it, and wrapped something in it. However, she came to me and told me that the crown was for her and took the drawing back. When we thought of this incident, which seems so childish, we prayed and cried tears of joy, remembering the beautiful words: "The righteous shall live forever, and the Lord is . . ."[12] and: "Therefore they shall receive a glorious kingdom and a beautiful crown, etc."[13] Now, it is as if she were calling to us from heaven: "O, you dear souls, your crowns, your psalms, your crowns of gold are ready. Be sure that you strive rightly for victory!

The 7th of November. Today, around eleven o'clock, many of our dear people came to attend the funeral sermon and the funeral of our dear little daughter. My dear colleague, who returned from Savannah only yesterday, held the funeral sermon on the previously mentioned beautiful words Wisdom 5; 16-17, dealing with the most exalted state of the righteous in heaven. In the introduction, to console us, he called out to us the word of our Lord Jesus, which He spoke in the house of the first preacher at Capernaum: "The maid is not dead, but sleepeth."[14] Like her brother Samuel, she looked so beautiful in the coffin that she appeared more like a sleeping person rather than a dead one. Both are alive in their Savior.

The 8th of November. I received a friendly answer from the members of the Council; in it they expressed their willingness to do their best for our community and for the people who arrived recently. They would like me to come and join them in their council session tomorrow. However, to some extent, they are aware of my situation; and they would be willing to wait, if I preferred to come at the beginning of next week. God will give me strength and allow me to do some more good, through His grace, during the short remainder of my life; I wish to do so with all my heart, and God Himself sent me this desire.

For the past fourteen days the weather has been very cold, both during the days as well as during the nights; as a consequence, our good colonists, who had arrived just recently, suffered much discomfort and endangered their health by traveling in an open boat to Savannah.[15] The people there did their best to assist them; and yesterday afternoon several families arrived here at the mill in a large boat; they were speedily provided with plenty of fresh and good food and then housed temporarily. The rest will arrive here probably tomorrow. The chest sent to us by those kind, dear people in Augsburg was unpacked in my house today and its contents were undamaged. God be praised most heartily for all the goodness He shows to us, despite our tribulations, from near and afar. May He reward those dear people who are His true servants!

The 9th of November. The blessing that our kind God let come to our hands in the large crate from the benevolent city of Augsburg, which consisted of pomesin, implements, linen, stockings, engravings, and all sorts of books, is great and marvelous. However, it cannot be distributed until the manifest of all these very necessary and useful gifts follows after it. May God be a rich Rewarder for them! He knows His people in all places, and He knows all our worthy benefactors of the present and past times, whom we humbly and confidently commend to His mercy and loyalty in our poor prayer. From the letter of our worthy Deacon Albinus I have seen that our miraculous God has also awakened for us a new benefactor in the region of Holland, who has put 25 £ Sterling into the hands of our worthy Dr. Prof. Francke. May He bless him for it in time and eternity and let him garner a rich harvest in everlasting life for this imposing gift.

Among the dear blessings we have just received we righfully count some selected sermons by our dear Court Chaplain Ziegenhagen, which have again reached our hands in a large quantity for our edification. May our gracious God strengthen this His proven and experienced servant for many years in strength of body and spirit and let the Church of Christ enjoy his service and prayer for a long time.

The righteous Kalcher, along with his family, has now moved to a newly built and convenient house at our mill to be the overseer and drayman there. Until now it could truthfully be said, "What He does turns out well"; and I do not doubt that his and his pious wife's service, work, and edifying example will also be blessed both for our inhabitants and for strangers. Because the new colonists have been brought from Savannah to the mill and will be provided for there initially until better arrangements are made, Kalcher and his wife are almost indispensable for us. For the provisions go through their hands, and he serves these dear strangers very well with his well arranged wagon. We are now trying to shelter them in the empty houses in town and in the homes of various christianly-minded householders so that they can get to know us and we them and so that we can see further to their shelter later.

Today Carl Flerl's little son, a sensible and skillful child, died of a sore throat. The father loved him so much that I thought he would be unable to resign himself to his death; yet he was very resigned and content with the divine will, especially since he knew that he had come to his dear Savior and to other pious children. Both parents fear the Lord; and especially the mother is an old and experienced disciple of the Lord, which I consider one of the greatest blessings for living and dead children. This afternoon I visited Eischberger's and Brandner's children, who are also afflicted with scarlet fever and, some of them, with sore throats. These children, too, cause me much joy through their proper and Christian behavior. They prove patient in suffering and they yearn, if it pleases God, to go where all pious people have gone for thousands of years, where we hear an everlasting "halleluiah" to the glory of our God. The righteous Brandner considers it significant that God began His chastisements over parents and children in my and Mr. Lemke's houses. He remembers that it went the same way some years ago with the cattle disease, which was first observed in the cattle of my late colleague. When people were astonished at that, the blessed man, he said, opened his testament and read from 1 Peter 4:17-19 the words: "For the time is come that the judgment must begin at the house of God," etc. I found this parallel and observation sad, to be sure, yet dear. From it I see how our dear parishioners profit in a Christian way from the things that occur among us.

The 10th of November. All last week, which was an extraordinary week of tribulation for me and my family, I was sickly and somewhat weak in spirit and had such a great hoarseness that I could not give any public sermon but could only visit some sick people. Necessity required me to hold the confessional on the plantations yesterday morning, when our merciful God noticeably strengthened me through His gospel while I was preaching it and made me fit enough to perform some external business at the mill and among the newly arrived colonists. My hoarseness also mostly disappeared last night so that today, the Twenty-second Sunday after Trinity, I could again preach to the old and new inhabitants about the right way of repentant sinners. Everything comes from thee, my God. We held Holy Communion with fifty-nine people. More than seventy registered, but very wet weather had come, by which several weak women and those who live on the most remote plantations were kept away. Also, some of them are on the large boat that is to bring the still remaining servants and colonists from Savannah to the mill.

Yesterday I waited for them all afternoon at the mill but could not wait long enough. My heart is very much concerned for the salvation and the physical welfare of these dear strangers; and today our dear God gave me the grace to show them from the above-mentioned text and from the whole psalm in what order they can expect pure good from God even in physical things, also what a blessing it is that, after having survived the sea voyage, they have come to our quiet Zion, where they have an opportunity to praise God and to keep their oaths. They listened very attentively. In the afternoon my dear colleague had as his text the dear words of Jeremiah 33:8-9. An honestly disposed planter in Carolina, who has corresponded with me for some time, reported to me in a letter some things that give sad examples of the great perdition of many people, probably of some ministers, too, in this region.[16]

The 16th of November. In the weakness I have felt so far I have had to take a trip to Savannah and remain there a few days at the demand of the President of the Council. I had to leave my dear family behind in a weakly condition; and, because I myself was not well, I suffered much disquiet and sorrow during all the business. Yet our merciful God strengthened me time after time and blessed my prayers and conversations with pious people, even if my renewed hoarseness and weakness did not permit me to hold a public sermon. My greatest sorrow is that I must neglect so much in my ministerial office because of these external affairs. I am writing this desire of my heart only in order that our worthy Fathers and friends will pray for me and my dearly esteemed colleague, who is my loyal assistant in everything and to whom I can truly apply what is written in Philemon 11:20-21.[17]

A young man named Neidlinger came over who should be an organist, musician, and scrivener; and our worthy friends in London hope that he will someday be useful to us at the mill and the sale of boards, as schoolmaster, and in other ways.[18] First of all we must test him. The new President, the Secretary of the Lord Trustees, and the Assistants of the Council showed me much affection[19] and made arrangements for the old and new colonists to acquire their land as quickly as possible, indeed, in such places and in such ways as pleases them best. The old inhabitants on the Mill River, also a few near town who are scattering and are leaving their very unsatisfactory plantations to their neighbors, are receiving a hundred acres; and the remainder, including the recently arrived, are receiving fifty acres. However, the old inhabitants must bear the expense of the surveyor, after that they will receive their written grants.

The 17th of November. Today I have been busy with visiting some sick and with setting up our servants, during which our dear God has granted me His blessing and assistance. It is now written in my heart: "Give us help from trouble, for vain is the help of man."[20] Some cannot help, and others will not, of which I cannot give any examples. The senior Eischberger's two children, a boy and a girl, have had violent paroxysms with their scarlet fever or red disease but now appear to be recovering, for which the pious old parents are humbly praising their good God. Their joy is especially great because they see good signs of God's grace on them, and since my last visit I have seen in them a hearty love for prayer, God's word, and the Savior.

Our dear and righteous Steiner is still weak and bedridden, and he will lose his life and his household if he is not soon helped. But it seems that our loving God, who never tries anyone beyond his strength, wishes to send him, like the said Eischberger, help and assistance through the present servants.

In the afternoon the householders from the plantations assembled in Jerusalem Church; and, after our communal prayer, I told them something of the joyful content of the letter from the Lord Trustees and of what I had been able to accomplish in Savannah for the good of the community with the President and his Assistants with respect to the enlargement and better arrangement of our plantations, for which we have God to thank. The important point concerned the finding of places for the recently arrived servants with Christian householders. There are many who wish to take the servants and maids, and even the children of both sexes, into their service; but there are not many single servants on hand. In this transport there are seven married couples, among whom there are some very small children.

A single servant and a maid were held back in Savannah, two young servants, an old carpenter, and a young woman died either on the very difficult voyage or in Savannah; and a family with two very small children (who are counted among the above-mentioned married couples) are lying sick in Savannah. After I had got to know them and had examined them as to which householder each person would suit as servant or maid, I wrote down at home, in simplicity and after submitting my heart to divine direction, the distribution of these servants. I first thought of who were the most needy and who should have the advantage for the good of the community. These are Mr. Mayer, Brandner, Kalcher, the said Steiner, and the senior Eischberger. Next in line came those who also need the servants very much; I offered to have them given by lot, but the inhabitants could not agree on this. Only one family, a man, wife, and child, was given by lot. And thus the entire transaction ended in love and peace and was concluded with a prayer.

The old and young tanners, Neidlinger, each of whom has a wife, etc., actually came here as servants. But they wish to begin their trade and are requesting an advance for this. We do not know yet how to use the organist Neidlinger. I am planning to settle two large families as free people on their own land with an advance of provisions; and the remainder, to wit, two families, one widower, one widow with two children, two servants, four maids, and three boys have gone into service with Christianly-minded householders. None was left over for the mill, except for a young and half-trained carpenter apprentice, for whom our worthy Court Chaplain paid from our Ebenezer fund. A man by the name of Birkholt, who paid for his passage in London, let some of his compatriots persuade him to settle with his wife and children some six miles from Savannah, which well-disposed and knowledgeable people regret for more than one reason. He did not come to me, perhaps because he owes two pounds two shillings Sterling to our fund, which was advanced to him in London and which I consider as good as lost.

The eighteenth of November. On this Twenty-third Sunday after Trinity during the preaching of His word and during the prayer our gracious God gave me back abundantly those powers of body and mind that I had lost on my trip to Savannah and in my business there. Oh, how I and my family and my dear colleague and his family praise our gracious God for all the good at Ebenezer in general and especially for all the blessings of the Jerusalem and Zion Churches, in which we preach His word and perform our communal prayer with great pleasure, joy, and blessing. Today Mr. Lemke prayed in Zion Church and I in Jerusalem Church; and this evening, although it was very cold, we held a public prayer hour with our old and new parishioners.

I was very pleased that so many had assembled. The parishioners heard a sermon of warning based on today's gospel, Matthew 22:15 ff., for I spoke on the three kinds of listeners. They are disloyal, malicious, and hypocritical listeners. In the introit from Hebrews 6:7-8 we heard something about the loyal and blessed listeners. May He bless this heavenly rain of His word in each and every one!

Concerning Carl Flerl I was told that he praises God sincerely for the blessed departure of his little son from this world, by which good has been done not only to the child but also to its parents. The father recognizes that he loved this sensible child all too much and would have sought the world and temporal things to better its physical care. Now that it is with its Savior in heaven, his heart has been torn by the grace of God from all visible things, the child died an edifying death.

The 19th of November. The condition of my family, my health, and my community prevented us from having our annual assembly in both churches after the harvest was garnered in order to praise our loving God communally for all His good in general and especially for the good harvest of this year. It was therefore announced yesterday in both churches that the parishioners in and around the town should gather today for this purpose in Jerusalem Church and the parishioners on the plantations should gather tomorrow in Zion Church, God willing. First I told my listeners something about the beautiful words of the 85th Psalm: "Shew us thy mercy, O Lord, and grant us thy salvation."[21] Then I laid as a basis for our edification the hymns of praise and thanks after a good harvest that are found in the new and well arranged Augsburg hymnal: *O GOtt dir dank ich allezeit für deinen reichen Segen,"* etc. This had happened to come to my eyes unexpectedly yesterday, Sunday; and from it our friendly God let much matter for the recognition of His manifold goodness and the praise of His glorious name fall into our hearts, and He let this praise flow humbly from our lips in humble prayer.

After we had offered our God prayer, intercession, and thanksgiving on our knees in the name of Christ, we sang our arousing final song: *Gute Nacht, ihr eitlen Sorgen, lass mirs Herze frey,"* etc. During that time I tenderly remembered my beloved and blessed Samuel Leberecht, who had copied this song very legibly for me and for others of our inhabitants and had sung it often with them in his mature and penetrating alto voice. He had also sung it shortly before his departure with his mother in her chamber to my great refreshment, along with another from our hymnal: *Lass dich GOtt,* etc. On the way to church another godly person tearfully remembered this singing of ours, which was so blessed by God.

In his letter of consolation to me a Christian friend from Purysburg attested having enjoyed similar edification in our church. This is being reported for no other reason than for the glory of God, who performed his work of grace in this child. I believe that, in citing this child's gifts of grace and works of love, I shall be reproved just as little by Christian friends who read this diary as was that pious widow in Acts 9, who showed the apostle Peter the coats and garments of the deceased Tabitha as evidence of her faith and love.[22] This comforting story was the last assignment that I read with Samuel Leberecht and his brother Gotthilf Israel from Castellio's Latin New Testment not long before his blessed death.[23] I had wished to stop earlier in the said ninth chapter of Acts, but he wished to have it expounded to the end, and this will impress me all my life. A righteous Englishman and his sincerely pious wife (my benefactors in Savannah) let the following comforting verses flow in their letter of condolence on the departure of our two children:

> And is the lovely Shadow fled!
> yet stop these fruitless Tears:
> He (she) from a thousand Pangs is freed,
> you from ten thousand Fears.
> Tho lost, he's (she's) lost to Earth alone,
> Above he (she) will be found
> Amidst the Stars & near the Throne,
> which Babes like him (her) surround.
> Look upwards, & your Child you'll see
> Fixt in his (her) blest Abode.

And who then would not childless be,
to give a Child to God?[24]

The 20th of November. In this vale of tears, sorrow and joy
always alternate, as I often experience both in Christianity as in
the performance of my office. Our dear God refreshed and rejoiced me yesterday and today in the harvest and thanksgiving
sermon; but today and yesterday He has let me experience vexing things from some young people of the last arrived servants,
which have both troubled and worried me. The friendly letter of
our dear Senior Urlsperger will give me an opportunity in the
prayer and weekday sermon to tell these people much for their
instruction.

The 21st of November. Our most worthy Court Chaplain
Ziegenhagen has given our Jerusalem Church an exceedingly
beautiful and costly painting, which is five feet high and four
feet wide, which has been cleaned today by a skillful man, like a
true painter, from some dust that had settled on it. It has been
placed very imposingly above the table against the wall between
two windows, where Holy Communion is always held. It presents, very animatedly and edifyingly, the Last Supper, which
our Lord Jesus held with his twelve disciples in Jerusalem when
he was betrayed. It not only gives our dear house of God a great
adornment but also makes an edifying and wholesome impression on those who gaze at it properly. Our dear Savior and His
disciples are so excellently adumbrated that one can imagine
nothing but true devotion and zealousness of heart in their most
important undertaking. Judas is also among them; and his
character can also, as it were, be read from his forehead and his
face. God be praised for this gift.

The 23rd of November. Our worthy friend Mr. Habersham is
very much concerned with advancing our community's physical
welfare in this country and through letters to the Lord Trustees;
and he is now requesting some reliable information about our
past and present situation, which I have given him this evening
in a detailed writing. God doeth all things well in His time. He
knows what we are lacking, but He also knows when and how He
should help us. From the fatherly letter by our dearest Senior
Urlsperger our loving God has granted us much instruction

concerning the mystery of the cross and the comfort of pious people during it, also concerning His merciful care for us and others.

The 24th of November. This morning I received the news not only that Carl Flerl's stepson, Johann Gruber, is dangerously sick but also that N.'s son and the senior Eischberger's little son are, too, and that Zoller's very weak little child, which was born two days ago, died last night. May God let these sorrowful events, which we have never had in this way in Ebenezer, make a blessed impression on both adults and children! May God especially touch the heart of N., who put too much work on him and thereby caused his premature death! Yesterday evening the surveyor arrived at the mill. He called on me today and promised me that next Monday he would survey the Uchee land, which, for a better name, we will now call the Blue Bluff, for some of the old inhabitants and for the newly arrived colonists. This pleased me very much. For the sooner these people are put in order, the better it is for them and me, since otherwise I must have all sorts of expense. For some time now I have had to expend so much money that it is now difficult for me to advance anything to these dear strangers and to serve the poor. The cowpen we bought also demands advances because the Lord Trustees' servants let it get into great confusion so that very little of it can be liquidated. Yet, at the express order of the Lord Trustees, 200 £ Sterling should be paid annually, 100 £ every six months. Still, this cowpen we have bought is a great blessing for the community, the reasons for which I have previously reported; and we hope it will be so in the future.

The edifying harvest and thanksgiving hymn and the sermon held on it seem to have made a good impression on my dear parishioners, and our loving God has let us hear much good after we presented the matter contained in it for vigilance in recognition and godliness. One of the new colonists requested a new Augsburg hymnal in order to copy out the hymn, and right after the sermon a godly widow also borrowed the said well-arranged book in order to study and repeat this hymn. In our congregation we have a very beautiful treasure of old and new chosen and edifying songs, which, through the blessing of God, contribute much to our edification in the public divine services and in the prayer meetings. Everyone of the adults who can read (there are few of them who cannot) has a hymnal to hand and joins in the singing according to his ability. No one has to fear that a hymn will be sung that does not stand in his hymnal because we all have one kind of hymnal. The newly arrived colonists and some of the grown children are lacking them, but we hope for a new supply from Halle.

The 25th of November. On this last Sunday of this church year our loving God has, to be sure, granted us cold, yet good, weather, good health and strength, and much edification and blessing from His word. When I see the church so full (as again today) and see the attention so great and constant before me, I often think of the well-known proverb: *Exitat Auditor Studium*.[25] I find this to be my case, yet I think that even a few, even if it were a single soul, are worth having the word of God preached to them willingly and joyfully. Many of the listeners come a long way from the most remote plantations and many come with a great hunger for the heavenly manna of the gospel; and we beg the Father of all Mercy to repay them all graciously for their love to Him and to His word and house and to let them return home well fed, quenched, and refreshed in a spiritual way.

When, shortly before my call to America, I was with the late very righteous Pastor Mäderjan in Thommendorff one Sunday, I was amazed that his listeners had already come several miles to church on Saturday evening and had visited all the prayer and edification hours, catechizations, and sermons so uninterruptedly and untiringly and had waited until the following Monday for their return home. I had not known of such hungry listeners previously except for what we read of Christ's listeners in Mark 8. But this beautiful and edifying behavior of the said dear people occurs to me almost as often as as I see it in certain souls among us. Now surely God has graciously repaid them for their love to His word on this last Sunday of the church year with a blessing and treasure from the holy gospel. For, both in the morning and the afternoon, everything we both preached to them with the strength of God was straight from the gospel.

In his introit my dear colleague repeated the incomparable promise of God in Jeremiah 33:8-9, about which he had catechized two weeks earlier; and today he had as the text of his catechization the excellent words of comfort in Psalms 91:14-16. Assisting, protecting, being with us in our need, extricating, and hearkening unto us has been the work of God among us in this almost-ended church year. He will also fullfil His remaining promises to us (even though they are too great and glorious for us poor, unworthy sinners) and reveal them to His glory and satisfy them with long life and His salvation. May He fullfil all the pleasure of His will in us with mercy for Christ's sake!

In the morning I had as my introit Psalms 60:13, "Give us help," etc.;[26] and from the gospel for the Twenty-fourth Sunday after Trinity, Matthew 9, I presented the mighty assistance of God to the needs of His children. The examples in the gospel and the now revealed matter was especially suitable for our dear listeners, who are immersed in all sorts of need, and for our present tribulations. During the sermon I also righfully mentioned something of the threefold deaths in one night that were mentioned yesterday and their burial on one day and in one churchyard and in one hour. There has never been such a sad event in Ebenezer, as a pious person remarked in my study.

That reminded me of the delicate expression that Master Lutz in Lindau composed in the edifying funeral hymn for the blessed death and burial of our dear Senior Riesch, who had such fatherly affection for us.[27] Our well known colleague Fels, who preached the major sermon on the last Feast of the Ascension at St. Stephens in rather good spirits, quite unexpectedly ended the course of his life and sufferings in the fifty-second year of his life and in the eighteenth of his ministerial office with a violent colic last Sunday morning at seven o'clock.[28] One hour later his dear friend and colleague, Senior Riesch, made his entry into the tabernacles of the fully just. A most painful and almost unheard of fate! Such a thing has not occurred here as long as the gospel has been preached, and it still resounds in our ears since it was first made known to us. Lindau, do not forget it!

I have wished to cite this sad event in Lindau diligently in the sermon for our people not only because it is remarkable in itself and belongs among the unfathomable ways of God but also because both of the two dear deceased men were Ebenezer's friends, intercessors, and benefactors and because their memory is blessed among us and because its renewal in these unusual circumstances will make a wholesome impression on the spirits of those Salzburgers from Lindau,[29] who have felt great reverence for this pious and diligent minister. My special purpose in this was to preserve my listeners, including the new colonists, from improper application of what God has done among us through the death of some children to humble us so that they will not ascribe it to the time, the land, our place, or secondary causes and thereby either sin or harbor unnecessary fears. Now there has been placed into our hearts and into our mouths the prayer, which stand twice *verbatim* in the Psalms,[30] "Give us help from trouble: for vain is the help of men." There we should not lack divine assistance in all our sufferings, labors, and doings, provided our prayer be made in faith. Immediately after that is written, "Through God we shall do valiantly."

The 26th of November. The senior Eischberger's daughter has the present children's disease, which some people call the "measles" with the Englishmen and others call the red disease or scarlet fever, and at the same time she is having severer paroxysms than her brother had. But he died, and today I found the little girl out of bed and rather healthy so that it appears that God will leave the old parents this their only child for some time as a helper. After this illness the children have an uncommon appetite, and one must always hold them back so they will not eat too much.

We encouraged ourselves mutually to achieve our salvation, and we praised God for all the blessings He has shown us and others. Because it was raining so hard that I could not visit any other people, I called on their neighbor, the pious Mrs. Straube and her children. She has had a very painful condition in her side for some days; and, because God has alleviated her pains and has shown the beginnings of an improvement, she wished to praise our dear God with me for His kindness. Therefore my visit brought her much joy and comfort.

Our butcher, Riedelsperger, began some time ago to trade with some people in Savannah Town and Augusta; and, because there is very cheap corn there, he went up there by water more than three weeks ago with some men who need much corn for their horses at the cowpen at Old Ebenezer. He truly gives such a description of the bad conditions of the colonists in the said region that the least and poorest inhabitant of Ebenezer should consider himself fortunate to live at our place. To be sure, everything grows there abundantly on the low ground (which is like our large island); but the harvest is very uncertain because of the unexpected flooding of the Savannah River, and this fall the inundation spoiled much corn and drowned many cattle. Except for Indian corn and beans everything is uncommon and three to four times more expensive than in our area. There is a lack of money; there is great uncertainty and great deceit in trade. Conscience seems to be outlawed there, and the people live in such sin that it could not be worse.

The 27th of November. In the assembly on the plantations yesterday I continued reading the fatherly letter from our dearest Senior Urlsperger; and we received, praise be to God, much material for edification and encouragement as well as instruction in the ways and dispensations of God. From it I also had a right desired occasion to bring much to the minds of our new inhabitants and to our last year's servants that may be advantageous to them for recognizing divine blessings and their conduct. The Lord Trustees had much pleasure in the new colonists after their arrival in London; on the other hand the ungrateful and ill-behaved conduct of our servants caused them no little sorrow. However, since for some time they have begun to be better disposed and to perform their work more loyally, I am sincerely pleased and the Lord Trustees and other worthy benefactors will rejoice, and this will bring them a blessing. How movingly and impressively it is written in the said fatherly letter for all our inhabitants, both free and indentured:

> My heart has much concern for all those among them who fear the Lord, walk the paths of good order, and take advice, for all Ebenezer, and for everyone who wishes to be saved, even if that has not yet occurred. That is known by the Lord, that is known by those who are around me. I shall now conclude everything in the words, 'Lord remember my Ebenezer fondly and all those whom I have now named.' We praise the Lord together for everything by which He helps Ebenezer, but we also participate in all misfortunes that they experience jointly or individually. Greet your new people for me heartily and tell them that they are now being brought daily to God with the old inhabi-

tants. They should just follow the words of their ministers, then they will enjoy the fruit from that in time and eternity.

The 28th of November. We have had dry weather for a long time, and this has been very convenient and advantageous for the construction of our new milldam. It is now almost complete, and all the work is approved and praised by all knowledgeable people. Last night we had rain with thunder and lightning, which is something very unusual at this time. Today it has been as pleasant by day as in spring. However, we assume that after the thunder we will have either much cold or else much rain. The wind appears to be veering to the west. The river water has fallen so far that the sawmill has not been able to go for two days. Today it is beginning to saw again. It is too bad that we have been unable to get any merchants for our excellently cut and durable cypress boards. To be sure, they bring a good price in Charleston, but it is an advantage only for the inhabitants there, while strangers must pay such a tariff that we are scared away from sending them there. In the West Indies they cannot be used as well as the pine boards. We are amazed that boards of such beautiful and durable yet easily worked wood are not exported to England.

Carl Flörl's stepson and Kalcher's second little daughter are dangerously sick, but it is written to the parents' comfort: "This sickness is not unto death, but for the glory of God, that the Son of God might be glorified thereby."[31] In both children the gifts of the Holy Ghost that are working in their hearts are so revealed that they cause joy and the praise of God. To be sure, my heart is very burdened by the tribulations that our wise God has visited on large and small in the congregation, especially since we have had to say from the last introit verse, "Human help is in vain." However, I shall still be comforted and refreshed when I see the good intention of our heavenly Father achieved in many of them. Surely He leads us on no other paths than those on which He has led the people of His covenant since the very beginning, through suffering into glory.

The 29th of November. The three Schubdrein brothers, who have not yet been a full year in Ebenezer and who arrived here in great poverty and debt, have established themselves so well here that they attest a burning desire to have here their parents and five brothers and sisters, who are faring very miserably in Nassau. For that reason the yongest brother /Johann Peter/ (a righteous Christian and loyal worker) has resolved with the approval, counsel, and assistance of his two like-minded older brothers, to take a journey as soon as possible into their fatherland and to fetch to Ebenezer not only his family but also some other useful people, who are faring badly over there, if he can get permission from the Lord Trustees. This settled young man, who has been born again in truth, is in a condition to report from experience the truth about Ebenezer and Georgia; and we can rest assured that he will bring no other people to Ebenezer than those who will fit here and love our order and arrangements. Also, because of his honesty, he will easily find trust among his compatriots for his tales and reports, for people in Germany are otherwise not without distrust, and for good reason. I am now seeking through my friends in Savannah an opportunity for this young man to go to London, and I am planning to recommend him and his cause as much as possible to the Lord Trustees.[32] Benefactions are very well applied with such people.

This week the surveyor is occupied in measuring our plantations for some of our old inhabitants and for our new ones on the Blue Bluff or mountain (formerly called the Uchee land), and today he received new instructions from Savannah to direct himself in his work according to my and Mr. Mayer's orders, also according to the mind and the desires of our colonists. He is doing this, too; and there is a great difference between the surveying in previous times and the present time. Formerly the poor people had to take whatever they were given, and now they themselves can choose what, how, and where they wish.

Indeed, the gentlemen in Savannah are offering those who are settled close together on the Mill River a new and very beautiful district at Goshen, which they have only now declared vacant and on which several can settle together very conveniently. There is no such fertile and well situated land far or near. Our glebe land and my own plantation lie in this region, and people of our confession are settled all around. Thus we hope that our dear God will gather a beautiful congregation here, which He can easily provide with a minister and schoolmaster. I loyally proclaim these advantages to our inhabitants as evidence of divine providence.

The 30th of November. A couple of months ago Mrs. Thilo requested Holy Communion on her long-lasting sickbed, but no day for it was ever determined for me. Yesterday evening at nine o'clock he sent to me to ask me to give her private Communion because she had unexpectedly become so weak that they were predicting her death. When I came to her, she spoke very well of her Savior's mighty help in driving out Satan and blotting out her sins and also of her living hope for eternal life. After saying prayers of repentance and confession she received Holy Communion. She had a difficult night, and today I found her very close to death.

DECEMBER

The 1st of December. Righteous Ruprecht Steiner was sick last week, but by divine goodness he has recovered somewhat; and we hope things will go better with him now that his household seems to be getting better arranged. The last servants, man, woman, and child, have almost ruined him. Because he has no housewife yet has three still unreared children, these servants have been disloyal in their service; and they cost him no little bit in upkeep. Now God has ordained for an apparently honest family of the recently arrived servants to agree to take over his plantation, to care for his house with cleaning, laundry, and repairs, and to give him a third of all crops and butter. Today the whole matter was discussed and concluded in my presence between Steiner and this family to their mutual satisfaction. I am advancing money for clothing and provisions, which these servants will gradually pay back from their produce. If they behave well and I reach my purpose with poor Steiner through them, they will enjoy many advantages during and after their period of service.

The 2nd of December. May God be heartily praised for having let us close another church year in this pilgrimage and begin a new one. On this first Sunday in Advent He granted His holy word to us abundantly in both churches; and, because our old and new parishioners gathered in large numbers for the preaching of His Holy word and for holy prayer, we hope that divine goodness will bless for their spiritual growth the spiritual seed we have sown. In this year I am planning (as we have always done so far) to lay as a basis for my sermon an important Bible verse in the introit[1] and then the Sunday and Holy Day gospels. My dear colleague, on the other hand, will catechize on the regular Epistle texts, whereas in previous years he has laid Bible verses as a basis for his catechization. If he preaches every two weeks in Zion Church (as he did today), he will also have the gospels and will build his sermon on a Bible verse in the introit.

Today I preached on the gospel of the righteous mind of the disciples of the Lord Jesus, to wit: 1, concerning its characteristics; 2, concerning the blessedness of this disposition. From the main verse from Romans 12:16, "Be of the same mind one toward another. Mind not high things, etc." I recommended to the parishioners the unity and humility of this mind of true Christians, and I did this to the best of the ability granted to me by God.

The 4th of December. On the 28th of last month we had a violent thunderstorm at night with rain and lightning. Then it became as warm as it usually is at the end of March. The river is rising very rapidly, and this is an indication that it has rained much more upcountry than here. The continuing dry weather is very bearable for the workers at the long and wide milldam; and we hope that this very useful, even though costly, work will come to an end this week. About twenty-four men are working on it every day, and they are using six carts and as many horses. And how much beautiful money our inhabitants are earning from it.[2] There is nothing like it in any place in this or the neighboring colony. May God let everyone recognize how many advantages they enjoy here.

In her poverty, a mother in our neighborhood has great joy in her three year old little boy because he falls on his knees voluntarily to pray, admonishes his parents, learns short verses and little prayers willingly, and sings while playing. Unnoticed, he has learned this and that good thing from his mother. In that regard I admonished her to show all Christian caution in her conduct, speech, and association with her husband because the child would learn evil more quickly than good when hearing and seeing. I gave her an example of a man she knew very well who, as a then wild and angry man, was accustomed to say to his wife, "Satan is looking through your eyes." The little boy very soon learned this monstrous and un-Christian speech and even said it to his sister. I am planning to give this mother and her child the lovely booklet, *The Power of God in Little Children*.[3]

The 6th of December. God has visited the righteous Brandner for a long time with a great cross, to which he has known how to resign himself well. For some years he has had a great bodily weakness, by which he has been much impeded in his business affairs. After he recovered somewhat, his industrious and honest wife and all four children became dangerously sick with scarlet fever and sore throats,[4] of which they have not yet been cured. This tribulation is all the worse for him because he has neither servant nor maid. To my great sorrow I read in the fatherly letter of 16 July of this year from our dear Senior Urlsperger the words: "Three months ago I wrote to Secretary Martyn and advised the Trustees at the time that they should at least reflect on some of the suggestions from Mr. von N.N."[5]

The 8th of December. Things are now going somewhat better for Mrs. N., but she still seems to be in considerable danger. We cannot discover what her sickness actually consists of. Some days ago, when she was near death and unconscious, she had attacks of epilepsy. She is warning others against postponing repentance until one's sickbed; and, because some of her acquaintances in Abercorn and Savannah are walking evil paths and have little regard for God in their malice, she let them be admonished to conversion and to a change of disposition. I have no doubt that she believes in the Lord Jesus, who has surely forgiven her all that others have found offensive in her. Whenever I visit her, she only listens to what I tell her from God's word, but she speaks little.

Several weeks ago young /Georg/ Mayer's apprentice had a slight case of scarlet fever;[6] and, because he went out into the air too soon, he suffered very serious attacks of swelling and short-windedness, and yesterday he had violent convulsions. It appears that he will soon be gathered unto his people, the communion of saints in heaven. He is a sincerely pious child who is a

very edifying example for other children and adults not only
through his devout behavior in church but also through his
zealous prayer and Christian conduct. Everyone who knows him
must give him the character of a true Christian. Yesterday
he complained of the weakness of his faith that arose from his
feeling of his sinful perdition. However, I presented him with
some dear gospel verses of a kind that are strong enough to
strengthen one's weak faith in Jesus, the Savior of poor sinners.
He found the following verses especially impressive: "The Law
recognizes sin and crushes the conscience. The gospel comes to
hand and, etc."[7] He wishes to die, but we do not wish to let him
go. However, it is rightfully said, "May the Lord's will be done."

The 9th of December. Last week three little children were
brought safely into the world with God's assistance, one on Tuesday (It was the 4th of this month) by Mrs. Simon Reuter, and
yesterday twins by Mrs. /Helena/ Hüber, a woman who arrived
here sick and miserable among the last servants yet became well
again through medicine and care, but especially through the
goodness of the Lord. She appears to be a sensible and Christian
woman, who loves God's word. She and her husband[8] are very
poor and need our help, which we give them as best we can.

In the afternoon of this Second Sunday of Advent the sincerely pious boy of sixteen years, Johann Georg Häfner, was released from all evil through a temporal death and was brought
to joy in his Lord, whom he has served with an upright heart.[9]
Now we have, to be sure, one less pious child, edifying example,
and zealous prayer in the congregation; yet we do not begrudge
him his blessed dissolution and are content with God's providence. His hand has not been shortened, and His grace is still
just as powerful for drawing even more inhabitants of our place
to Himself and to make them into zealous prayers. We detect
much good in our young people.

The 11th of December. This afternoon in my present physical
weakness my dear God granted me the pleasure of being able to
hold the burial sermon for the youth who passed away yesterday.
He was very much like the pious orphan in Bayreuth, Johann
Georg Stangen, whose last hours can be found in one of the *Contributions to the Building of the Kingdom of God*.[10] At the funeral I
acquainted the adults and children with something from these

last hours. Four weeks ago he had recovered from scarlet fever and would not let anything keep him from attending Holy Communion, and some people assume that he contracted his last sickness by going out. His master /Georg Mayer/ told me that in the last months of his life he took very little notice of the advantages of his trade and that this had been explained as inattentiveness, as if he had no pleasure in the work.[11] However, people noticed that he was excessively desirous of God's word and private prayer and that, whenever his professional duties let up even a little, he would seek out a hidden spot in order to speak alone with his Savior. From that one could conclude that, despite all his external work, his spirit was always up there where he always wished to be.

His righteous behavior and blameless and edifying conduct were known to most people, especially to the pious among us. Because of this deceased youth the matter of my sermon yesterday on Luke 21:25 ff. impressed me all the more when I presented to myself and to my listeners the end of sinners and the end of saints. In the introit we contemplated the important, partly comforting and partly frightening, words of Psalms 37:28. Because of this boy and the publication of the first part of the above mentioned "last hours" of the pious orphan boy in Bayreuth the memory of my Samuel Leberecht was renewed very tenderly in my heart. He was much like both of them in grace, and therefore he had a high regard for the blessed boy whom we have just buried. He has now been six weeks in the blessed loving and God-praising communion of all God's children, and he is enjoying perfectly in his soul what he wrote in red ink and chancery letters after the baptismal names of many children and young people: "Delight thyself also in the Lord; and he shall give thee the desires of thine heart."[12] He must have had a good impression of this verse in his heart, for during my absence on journeys he fastened it, with his mother's approval, on the door of my study, where it is still fastened and will remain fastened.

The 11th of December. Scarlet fever is still persisting at our place, along with the purples[13] in some people; and it is striking down not only children but also adults. All of them have painful, grave attacks, and it is a fatal sickness. God's counsel and God's hand are above us, and we should all humble ourselves under them. May He treat us with mercy, and not according to our merits! In addition to keeping the patients warm and inactive, knowledgeable Englishmen advise bloodletting and attribute the sad consequences to a failure to do so. It seems that way to me, too, according to my slight experience, for we have noticed that those children who have bled at the nose were greatly alleviated, indeed soon recovered, whereas in the case of the others, where nature could not break through, there has been great short-windedness, swelling of the limbs, sore throats, fearful vomiting, paroxysms, death, or long-lasting sickness.

Adults who have this scarlet fever say that there is an extraordinary movement of the blood as if it wished to break out of all veins. A grown girl had her first period during her paroxysm, but then it rose immediately to her breast as if it all wished to come out of her throat, and from this she suddenly died five weeks ago in Mr. /Ludwig/ Mayer's house. A pregnant woman in her first months was brought into mortal danger by the extraordinary motion of the blood in her body. However, because the blood broke out and she aborted, she soon recovered. A short time earlier another woman with the same scarlet fever had been bled and had had her period at the wrong time during her paroxysm. I have heard of these examples only from my wife, but there may be more of them. Oh, how necessary it is for all doctors to be well acquainted with nature and at the same time servants of nature!

The 12th of December. The widow Schweighoffer is the oldest person in our community. She came across the sea as a sick person with the first transport; fifteen years ago she was afflicted by a stroke on the right side while working hard with a cold. She had great spiritual doubts, great unrest, and sorrow because of her then still unconverted children; and she suffered much in all sorts of sickness and often from unnecessary worry. Despite that, she has so improved her life and has lived now for seventeen years in this land. God's word and prayer are now her meat and drink and her medicine and her everything in all incidents of this her pilgrimage. She marvels at God's patience and forebearance with which He has borne her so far and always given her time to prepare herself for blessed eternity, and she praises

Him for it. Now she is sick again and hopes that she will soon cast off her tabernacle. Her daughter, Mrs. /Maria/ Riedelsperger, is also often led by our dear God into the wilderness of the cross. Her physical suffering is the least for her, even though it is great for so weak a body. But her gravest suffering is that she must so deeply feel her old sins, the accusations of her conscience, her inablility to pray, her lack of faith and comfort, etc. I spoke and prayed with her.

The 13th of December. In addition to the above-mentioned pious boy our dear God has reminded us this week of our mortality through the deaths of three other children, who belong to the servants Seckinger and Hüber. Two were sucklings and one a little girl who was very swollen by a foul fever.[14] During the fever both young and old show no diet with respect to eating and drinking and the necessary steaming out,[15] and it is surprising that not more die of it. Despite all the sorrowful incidents through the chastising and disciplining hand of God, it is my comfort that it is so often written in Holy Scripture, "God's mercy endureth forever."[16]

Through this unending goodness of the All-highest, very many useful institutions have been made and maintained in Christendom for the care of the poor sick. Because this goodness is enduring and unending, I hope that it will gradually spread out over us or let so much material good flow to us that we can establish a spacious sickbay for poor people in our district, which, for various reasons, would be not only very necessary but also highly useful. To be sure, our all-generous Father in heaven has from time to time granted our dear Salzburgers and other inhabitants of our place their bodily sustenance by the sweat of their brow. However, because clothing, linen, and other necessary European goods are excessivly expensive in this land, very few of them acquire more than is absolutely necessary from their farming and cattle raising; and they live in poorly protected houses and huts and are not provided with sufficient blankets and quilts. Therefore, especially in winter, which is harder on them in this climate than in Europe, they must endure much in sickness, childbirth, etc. Their quick recovery is hindered, and they also contract long-lasting sickness and consumption. Doctors' fees are, to be sure, bearable among us because our physi-

cian and surgeon have received simples, medications, and other
things serving for cures from London and from the blessed institution of the Orphanage in Halle, also some from our dear
Augsburg. If, however, we had the means through God's dispensation and from contributions of Christian friends in England
and Germany to establish and maintain a spacious sickbay, much
good would accrue from it to the congregation and the whole
country under the influence of God's blessing.

For the initiation and establishment of such an institution a
sum of 2,000 pounds would, to be sure, be required. According
to my humble opinion its maintenance would not cost much
more than 100 pounds if one counted a kitchen and herb garden
to be laid out for it. If God should let the presently planned mill
construction turn out well and grant us a good profit from both
sawmills and gristmills, we would contribute as much as we could
to such a useful institution. The new milldam is very firmly built,
and everyone marvels at this construction. This imposing construction, which has lasted so far, was led by the very industrious
Joseph Schubdrein and, to be sure, in such good order that we
could not wish for a better contractor and overseer. He has, to be
sure, helped build gristmills, but he has never worked on a sawmill, because there are none in his fatherland because of the lack
of wood.[17] Because he had had no experience in the construction of sawmills himself, the completion of this important and
very useful work will be somewhat protracted. But God will
grant everything at the proper time.

Late in the evening two days ago it thundered, lightninged,
and rained, but it soon stopped. Since then it has again become
cold at night but tolerable in the daytime. So far the winter has
been very bearable, and the autumnal weather has been dry and
therefore exceedingly advantageous for our mill construction.
God be praised that this important work, and at the same time
the great expenses, will come to an end this Saturday. In contrast
only a few bearable expenses will be demanded to raise the sawmill, for which we have more ironwork in supply than we could
use for two or three sawmills.[18] It is no small benefaction that
even the weakest people among us have earned circa 73 £ Sterling cash money on this milldam since the harvest, that is in two
or three months, partly with their labor and partly with their

horses and servants.[19] How much is earned by our people who have lucrative jobs at our old sawmill and gristmill, either daily or on occasions and either with or without horses! That is why there is no cash money anywhere in the country but in Ebenezer.

The 17th of December. N. registered to come to the Lord's Table this coming Sunday and testified that he and his wife have again been shamed no little bit by their three year old child and aroused to a new seriousness and Christian caution in their Christian conduct.[20] She said, namely, that a discord had arisen between the two parents during which the child said to them, "You are wicked people, let us pray." They accepted this as a chastisement and correction of God through the mouth of a little child and were very humbled before God because of their sins. He had been a very wild and malicious man, whose heart, however, was made rather mellow and soft some time ago by the hammer of the divine law and by many chastisements. His resolutions and practices are very good. However, because of long practice the wicked emotions in him are so strong, especially when there is an outside cause, that he is often carried away by sin against his will. I warned him against further disloyalty against the working grace of God: otherwise, it will not turn out well. I gave him two edifying sermons by Court Chaplain Ziegenhagen.

Since Kalcher and his large family moved into the inn by the mill to be our host, overseer, and drayman, we have again had the desired occasion in this house to praise our almighty Creator of heaven and earth and also of our useful millworks, in the name of Jesus Christ, for His blessings. This was done this afternoon by me and some others who were called together. Until now N. has been one of the wicked servants; and recently he almost incited me to dismiss him from service at the mill, which would have pleased other people there. Today he attested to me that God had inclined his heart and that he had resolved to become a different man through the grace of God. Whether his resolution is true will be shown by his later life. As long as no crass excess or vexation forces us, we send no wicked person away but are patient with him according to the word and example of God. I know how useful this method was with the workers at the Halle Orphanage.

The 18th of December. Jacob Hüber and his wife told me with joy and to the praise of God that they have received many benefactions from good people in Ebenezer through divine governance. In her whole life she had never had such a good childbed or experienced such kindness. In all those who came here recently from the Territory of Ulm I find that they like to work and are content with what God grants them. I hope that they will gradually learn what they do not yet understand about housekeeping and farming, provided they do not wish to be cleverer than other people. It gives us a pleasure to serve them in every spiritual and material way. May God illumine and convert them all, then even the bad habits that we have observed in some of them will disappear. We must show patience, forbearance, and leniency. Most of them are still lacking recognition of truth for the sake of salvation; and they now have opportunity enough, through divine guidance, to garner what they neglected in this matter in former times. For that reason I would have liked to see them take up their plantations not far from the town and church. Only Scheraus is settling far away, for he is taking up his plantation several miles behind Abercorn on the boundry of Goshen, where, to be sure, there is the best land but no church, school, or mill.

The Salzburger Bichler is being humbled by God in many ways. He has tried all sorts of ways to support himself better than others. He has always aimed upwards and tried to get ahead of other people, but by this he has come into temptation, loss, and debts.[21] He has good understanding and other natural gifts but is now one of the poorest in the community; indeed, I believe that there is no one so poor as he. Today it pleased me that he has begun to recognize the humbling and crushing hand of God and to humble himself before it, whereas he had previously blamed his misfortunes on other people. In his great poverty he is also consumptive and incapable of work. Oh, if only God could achieve His purpose in him!

The 19th of December. This time more than a hundred people registered to come to the Lord's Table on the coming Fourth Sunday in Advent; and this week my sermon is aimed at instructing my dear parishioners, both the old and the new, how they should properly prepare themselves for this holy table through the power of the Holy Ghost. On the Third Sunday in Advent, after the introduction of the introit verses Romans 5:15 and Matthew 11:2, I treated the two major points of Christian dogma, to wit, the fall and the resulting great perdition of mankind, and at the same time the great grace of God in Christ.

Now, I know from God's word and from experience that many people, even among us, wish to be Christians and to go to Holy Communion but have not yet learned the first letters, the A.B.C.s as it were, of true Christianity and therefore stand in the fancy of faith, in trust in the *opus operatum* of prayer and going to church and Holy Communion.[22] These peope erect their own justification and go cheerfully into hell with the comfort of God's mercy and Christ's merits, or they let themselves be kept for a long time from true conversion, the core of Christianity, and from the imitation of Christ to their and other people's great harm. Therefore this week in the prayer meetings and weekday sermons I am treating the basic and principal dogma of Christianity from the fall and resulting great perdition of all men and of all human nature as clearly and sincerely as God is allowing me through His grace. For this purpose I am excellently served by the second and forty-first chapters of the first book of the blessed Arndt's *True Christianity* and by the heart and conscience examinations from the late Ambrose Wirth's *Confession and Communion Booklet*.[23] Because, through God's great goodness and providence, both books are in the hands of all our parishioners they can re-read and repeat the explicated and inculcated points again at home.

The 21st December. Yesterday evening our schoolmaster's wife asked me on the street to come to her as soon as my circumstances would allow me, and I did this today. She is a believing soul, who has often had a certain assurance of her state of grace through the witness of the Holy Ghost from the certain words of the gospel. However, her feeling of faith and the grace of God have disappeared, especially when she detects subtle disloyalties and moral lapses; and everything has become sin so that she well needs encouragement from the gospel, as she received today.

Old Mrs. Schweighoffer has recovered again and can again visit the prayer meetings and Sunday sermons, in which she is

almost exactly like the pious Hannah in Luke 2[24] and also like
the others who awaited the redemption in Jerusalem. She told
me to the praise of God and with a joyful heart how much good
the Lord has showed to her daughter in her sickness, from
which she had now recovered, and how seriously she had been
concerned about the true salvation of her still frivolous brother.

Yesterday and the night before we had a gentle and rather
warm rain. After it a very violent and cold storm wind arose,
which lasted all night and today with the greatest violence. I
often think now of the dear people of Luzern, who will surely
have left London already two or three months ago and will
therefore have come close to the borders of Georgia. This storm
wind, which has just come out of the west and is precisely against
the ships headed here, will drive them back very far; and, because it is freezing, it will cause them much discomfort. May God
be their leader, protector, and provider![25]

The water in the river has risen so high that it has stopped all
the mills. All the inhabitants and neighbors have surely been
provided with flour because we have had full use of the mills for
many months.

The 22nd of December. Among the last transport of German
people a young apprentice and an older unmarried serving
woman came to our place, who had behaved shamefully on the
voyage, because of which the woman is now pregnant. I reproached them several times with this shameful and vexing de-
filement, but they helped themselves with denials and then went
to Holy Communion anyhow. Finally they both acknowledged
that they were guilty of this misdeed and promised to convert to
God before they could be tablemates of the Lord Jesus. Yesterday evening they were with me again, and I spoke to them again
from the law and the gospel and bent my knees with them before
God. They both left me, first the woman and then a while later
the young man, with emotion and tears. They are both very ignorant in the necessary articles of Christianity, but they seem to
have docile dispositions.

A young man out of Wurttemberg, who has traveled about in
South Carolina and this land for some years with disorderly peo-
ple, showed up here a few months ago and hired himself out to a
Salzburger as a servant. He visited me a couple of times and ex-

pressed a disgust at his former life and a pleasure in good order. He had largely forgotten what he had previously learned from the catechism and the Wurttemberg confirmation booklet, but he promises to learn it again. I admonished him sincerely and prayed with him and gave him a New Testament along with the psalter that was bound with it. One must be very cautious with such people and go gently with them if one does not wish to drive them away. If they are here for a while and achieve a better understanding through the abundant preaching of the divine word, then they begin to love our place and good order and can all the better digest a necessary chastisement. May God teach us wisdom!

The 23rd of December. In these four Sundays in Advent it has been cold, to be sure; yet the violent wind has ceased and the sun is shining bright so that we are suffering no hardship or hinderance from the cold, especially during divine services in our well protected church. God has strengthened me and my dear colleague to preach His divine word to a large gathering. A hundred and twenty-two persons went to Holy Communion. Since the last German people came to us, Jerusalem Church, or the town church, is almost too small for us. When it is necessary, our dear God will surely see to a new one for us. The present church was not built too large because we have had the intention from the very beginning to change it into a schoolhouse and residence for the schoolmaster if the congregation increased so much that we would need a larger church.

If all the children who were born and baptized sixteen years ago in Old and New Ebenezer were still alive, how large our congregation would be! It pleases me and draws my heart heavenward that such a beautiful troop of chosen and transfigured children from the Ebenezer congregation are resplendent before God's throne, among them my blessed colleague Gronau (the friend of children) and two of his dear children. I, too, now have had two dear children up there for almost two months, where it is said, "Here it is good to be." Their withdrawal through temporal death has caused me and my helpmeet many afterpains, but the Lord always helps us up again. He will give us grace to hasten our journey to blessed eternity and will make us more and more certain of our salvation in Christ.

Now my Redeemer has borne with me for forty-seven years in this pilgrimage with ineffable patience; and even in this land He has granted me good health and strength, which I had lost in my young years through excessive study, harmful treatments, and all sorts of difficult circumstances in my poverty so that I (as my parishioners say) have almost become young again. I can also well feel that I have more strength of body and mind than in former years. Despite the good condition of my previously fragile body, I forsee my departure from this world every day and and concern myself with ending my course with joy as soon as it pleases the Lord. My dear colleague, the members of the congregation (with scarcely a single exception), my family, our dear Fathers in Europe, and many other friends wish me a long life, which I also recognize as a great blessing because I surely believe that in the still remaining time our Chief Shepherd and Savior will, through the Holy Ghost, make me very capable to serve Him and the congregation. This is my sincere desire and the content of my prayer. May my God never let me forget how much mercy and blessing He has shown me, most unworthy one, from His word and sacraments, from edifying writings sent after us, from the blessed letters of our worthy Fathers and friends, and in numerous other ways both spirituallly and physically and both near and afar.

The 24th of December. In today's evening prayer meeting I repeated something from yesterday's morning sermon from Isaiah 40:3-5 concerning the preparation of our hearts for the gracious coming of Christ, which is very appropriate at the present time. I showed the parishioners in many ways that the proper preparation demanded by our Lord consists of a change of mind and heart and how long those reveal themselves and hinder their true blessedness who shy from the true conversion that God Himself wishes to effect through His word or who postpone it from one time to another.

The 25th of December. On this first day of Christmas the dear gospel of the incarnation and birth of Christ was preached by me in Jerusalem Church and by Mr. Lemke in Zion Church. It rained most of the day, and therefore it was very convenient for the people on the plantations that they had their divine service nearby, namely, in their own church. Praise be to God, who gives

His word abundantly and who so noticeably strengthens us two, who must preach it. May He, for the sake of Christ, richly bless the precious seed that was sowed today!

The 26th of December. Also on this second day of Christmas we have had some unpleasant weather with fog and rain, by which, however, our parishioners did not let themselves be kept from public divine service. Toward evening yesterday my dear colleague traveled from Zion Church to Goshen behind Abercorn to preach to the Germans there and to administer Holy Communion. During this evening's prayer meeting he came back home safe and sound. May God be heartily praised for having strengthened us both in body and spirit during this holy period and for having assisted us with His spirit for the preaching of the gospel. In the evening prayer meeting we praised His name for that and likewise for His other spiritual and physical blessings, and we invoked it communally for a blessing on the word that was preached.

On the first day of Christmas I dealt with the gospel for that day concerning the conspicuously great mystery of the incarnation and birth of Christ, and on the second day I dealt with the Godpleasing behavior of our parishioners during and after the preaching of the gospel. After the holy days we are accustomed to repeat the content of the same sermons in the prayer meetings and in the first weekday sermon.

After the rain a strong and very cold wind arose in the evening, which again brought us a heavy frost. The water in the river has fallen somewhat again, which is good for the mills. Carl Flerl's stepson, a boy of about eleven years, was mortally sick. When he was very close to death, he said to his pious parents that a man had been with him, who told him that he would not die but would be able to help his weak and sickly mother with her work. One expected nothing less than that it would happen, yet it actually followed. We had him in our house during the holy days. His mother is a true friend of God and prays zealously, and she surely accomplished much with her prayer for this one and only child (for the youngest died recently).

The 29th of December. For the past three days there has been an uncommon cold both day and night, with which there was a violent west wind. What will our dear Protestant friends from

Luzern have to undergo if they are on the sea not far from the coasts of South Carolina and Georgia? May God stand by them! For a long time we have had no other wind but west and southwest, which is against those coming from England. Yesterday and today the sky has been entirely clouded as if it would snow, which at this season is something not entirely unusual. The last colonists, both free people and servants, have been so well sheltered in town and on the plantations that they can suffer not the least lack of warm dwellings and bedclothes or of foodstuffs. The mill was still for only a few days. What advantages these people have over the first, second, and third transports, who had to get along very miserably with their hard work in Old and New Ebenezer without mills, without good land, without dwellings, without boats, without wagons and horses, without meat and other healthy food, without good and knowledgeable advisors. I am often sincerely ashamed and bow myself before God that I was so very inexperienced in external economic matters concerning the plantations. Otherwise I would have been able to lighten many loads and difficulties for our colonists.

The 31st of December. Now that this old year is going to an end through divine goodness, my duty as a Christian and man of authority demands that I briefly advise our readers, such as Fathers, friends, and benefactors, dear to us in the Lord, about the major blessings the Lord has shown us in this newly ended year so that they in their place can help us praise Him for all His blessings.

1. We have enjoyed the jewel of undisturbed physical freedom in this year, too, even though it was said that the French wished to break again with the English. Especially, once there was almost a dangerous war with the Indians, which, however, our King of Peace changed into grace. We have had not the least trouble from Indians, Negroes, or other vagrant riffraff in town or on the plantations. Along with such external and physical peace we have also had the best peace and unity we could desire among one another.

We authorities, Mr. Lemke, Mr. Mayer, and I, as well as the seven tythingmen, stand in a bond of love and good understanding, on which the God of Love and of Peace has laid His blessing for the advancement of good order and subsistence. Churches and schools in town and on the plantations are used loyally by the ministers and parishioners for the purpose for which God granted them to us. We have nothing to complain of concerning the diligent and devout attendance at public divine services on Sundays and Holy Days, weekday sermons, and prayer meetings. Rather, they have shown themselves in such a way that we can believe that most of them have an upright love for God's word and the holy sacraments. I believe I can apply what is written in Acts 9, "Then had the churches rest throughout all Judaea . . . and were edified." Also, the divine promise spread to us, too, which He gave to his people who would attend divine services and leave their houses and fields alone and without any guard that He would take everything into His special protection during the holy days and during the divine services. Nor do we know of any grave vexation, and therefor no one has had to be legally punished.

2. God has kept us ministers in the church and teachers in the school in health so that we have not had to neglect any part of our duty because of sickness. He has given us the joy of performing our office among the people here and among strangers, in Goshen, and in Savannah not without blessing. In particular we have observed a noticeable change in the behavior of some young people who came here last year as servants.

3. The more our dear God spares me and my dear colleague from sickness, the more He has visited our families. His three children have all been dangerously sick, and He took two of mine within seven days through temporal death and thereby dealt me a wound that I still feel. Yet, to the praise of God, I must say that He is letting this tribulation do me much good. Many parents in the congregation have been visited in this same way through the sickness of their children or kinsmen, and possibly also through incidences of death. Yet not as many of them have died as in Carolina, but most of them have recovered again. God has granted us much edification and comfort during the sickness and at the burials of our dear lambs.

4. It is an especially dear blessing of the Lord that He has let us receive very pleasant reports of the health and life of our dear Fathers in London, Augsburg, and Halle and has kept us in their and other dear benefactors' favor and intercession and has often

caused us joy with their printed writings, through letters, through good counsel, and through material aid. He has also inclined the hearts of the Lord Trustees and of the praiseworthy Society to us live in love and benevolence. May He keep them and all our benefactors long in His blessing!

5. Our dear God has also inclined the hearts of the Lord Trustees to us to give willingly for our new sawmill all the ironwork that has lain in the storehouse in Savannah, which is a very great benefaction. There are more than two thousand pounds of good useful iron, of which we need only a little for the sawmill we are planning and most of which we will save for future use. God has not only let us know of a very good opportunity to build a new sawmill in our district but has also granted us the means to do so through the income of the previously used sawmill and grist mill and this iron that has been given to us. But we would not have been able to undertake this important and useful construction if God had not given us a capable and very industrious and well behaved carpenter among the servants who arrived a year ago.[26]

Joseph Schubdrein. See entry for Through his guidance and industry the new milldam was completed before Christmas, and it is an imposing and durable work from which most of our inhabitants have earned a sizeable sum of money.

If God grants health and blessing and the cold does not last too long, the mill construction itself should soon be undertaken. Sawmills and gristmills are not exceptional establishments in Germany, even though they are great benefactions; but here they are a special earthly jewel, for which we have great cause to thank God. Because of the low land no mills can be built far and wide, even though some have been begun in vain at great cost. We have to see to it that our inhabitants, who cannot live by farming alone, can earn something from time to time for clothing and other necessities. For this the construction, maintenance, and use of the mills are a great service. A large sum is earned and spent every year at the mills. For that reason cash money comes to our place, which is not found elsewhere in Carolina or in our colony.

To be sure, we have often been advised to use Negroes or Moorish slaves at the mills, through whose cheap labor and min-

imal expense for food and clothing the mill would have a greater
income. But where would the earnings be for the congregation,
for whom the mills were built? At the first mill we had to give out
much apprentice money, as it were; and through lack of experience we did not know how to use much wood and many boards
correctly. We also paid many expenses in vain, and we suffered
great loss through N.[27] However, for somewhat more than a year
it has begun to bring in good money, of which to a large extent
the milldam was built, which cost a considerable amount.

If the new sawmill is completed, as we hope, then, because of
the good location and very many matured, thick, and impressive
pine and cypress trees, we promise ourselves a great advantage
for improving our subsistence and advancing a useful trade,
which is as necessary for the community as the mill itself is.
Among the divine benefactions we have received this year I
rightfully count:

6. The discovery of an advantageous way to bring all sorts of
cypress to the mill in rafts at small cost, whereas it formerly
seemed impossible.[28] Such trees stand around the river in great
numbers and give the most beautiful and durable boards, of
which a great quantity have been sawed for the milldam and for
sale, even if we have not yet been able to sell them.

7. Among the pleasant signs of divine providence over us belongs the better arranged trade through the service of my colleague Mr. Mayer, for which our prominent benefactor, our dear
Mr. von N.N. in Augsburg,[29] has given much encouragement by
encouraging Mr. Mayer with word and deed. From the blessings
from the mill account a very spacious and very comfortable
house and store have been built as his dwelling and shop. A
kitchen, garden, and outhouses have been laid out, and everything has been arranged most conveniently for trade. Also, most
trade goods can be had for a reasonable price. This store is provided with goods at the expense of the mill account, and Mr.
Mayer is provided with a servant, whom he is to train for the
trade.[30]

Among the coins that are accepted here are pieces of eight, on
which stands the *Plus ultra*, which appears so remarkable to me
and which often encourages me to raise my heart to the praise of
God for the increase we have experienced so far and to sighs for

His continued productive blessing. During the Christmas service and during the repetition hour the day before yesterday my faith was greatly strengthened by the fact that the wisdom of God has so arranged it that Christ our Lord was born in the time of Caesar Augustus, who was called an "Augmenter,"[31] by which He wished to give us a sign that He truly wished to be our Augmenter in the realm of nature and grace. The blessing He merited and gave to us is an increasing good. This He has showed in the poorhouse in Augsburg and in the Orphanage and other institutions at Halle,[32] and I am greatly impressed and pleased that our late dear Professor /August Hermann/ Francke as founder and director of the said blessed Orphanage was named Augustus and that his worthy and pious son /Gotthilf August/ as successor in the theological faculty, ministry, and directorship of the Orphanage and of the *Paedigogium Regium* bears this same emphatic name.[33] In the Old Testament God ordained that the children of pious parents were given very significant names, whose true meaning and secret purpose were made known and became edifying only at a later time. Why did people in the New Testament not wish to recognize His careful purpose in this matter and thus rob themselves of a great advantage for the praise of God and the sincere enjoyment of His marvelous ways and ordinances?

8. Through the blessed harvest in European and local crops and through the purchase of the cowpen at Old Ebenezer our all-wise and thoroughly kind God has provided right paternally not only for our old inhabitants and their servants but also for the new colonists who arrived two months ago, by whom our community has been augmented. All of them can be provided at a reasonable price with grain from the harvest and with meat from the cowpen.

9. Through the heart-inclining power of God and through the affection of the Councilmen at Savannah our old and new inhabitants have received not only good but also more land than in previous years, to wit, a hundred acres instead of fifty. Since He has now begun to grant servants also, I hope that He will gradually let His blessing come to them for the better arrangement of their plantations and households and let them rest after so many trials and tribulations. Nothing is impossible for Him.

At the very time that He gave them more land through the service of the gentlemen in Savannah, the joyful news came from the Lord Trustees that all inhabitants would soon receive their grants, or sufficient written assurance concerning their plantations, and that they will possess an absolute power over their land, free of any previous restrictions, just as it is in England and all other colonies.[34]

10. Previously our righteous and clever Kalcher was a very useful manager and father at the orphanage. Recently, he assumed the calling as overseer, drayman, and host at our mills, which we hope will redound to greater alleviation and the advancement of good order. After Mr. Mayer moved into the above-mentioned new house, Kalcher bought the house that Mr. Vigera had had built largely with other money, but now he has given it back to me. This now serves us very well, for school is held in one of the rooms, which is provided with an iron stove, and the other part of the house is for a widow who cleans Jerusalem Church, washes its cloths, lights its lamps for the evening prayer meetings, etc. Also, space has been made for two families of the last colonists and their little children until they build something on their own land. Thus this house is a blessing in many ways, even though much money is invested in it and it will soon demand some repairs.

11. It seems a minor matter, to be sure, that some redeemed servants began burning bricks in town last summer and autumn with advances from us, but we do not consider it a minor matter. In addition to the fact that it has increased useful work and more subsistence among us, we have obtained bricks nearby for building chimneys and other useful things and do not have to bring them up from Savannah at great cost. With them the parsonage has been as well protected against fire as man can do.

12. As evidence of the kind providence of God over us I could also cite that the silk turned out very well last spring and summer and that the inhabitants have been encouraged to industry in this work by the cash they received for it. Many young women have thoroughly learned how to reel silk and have been provided with twelve cauldrons and machines for spinning off the silk. Likewise, the poor have had much opportunity to earn at the mills and elsewhere, the mills have almost always been in op-

eration, and many benefactions have flowed from Europe. A rice-shelling mill has been built, and now a tanning mill is being built for the recently arrived tanner, etc. But I will leave off with this evidence of divine goodness, wisdom, and omnipotence and will close with "Hallelujah"!

Appendix

HYMNS SUNG BY
THE GEORGIA SALZBURGERS
IN 1750

Hymns followed by F-T and volume and song (not page!) number are reproduced in Albert Friedrich Fischer—W. Tumpel, *Das deutsche evangelische Kirchenlied des 17. Jahrhunderts* (Gutersloh, 1916, reprinted Hildesheim 1964). Authors of all identified hymns are listed in (AF) Albert Friedrich Fischer, *Kirchenlieder-Lexikon* (Gotha, 1878, reprint Hildesheim 1967).

Gleichwie sich fein ein Vögelein in hohle Bäum . . . (Just as a fine little bird . . . into hollow trees), by Martin Rutilius. Nov., note 5

Gott hat alles wohl bedacht . . . (God hath considered all things well), by Gustav von Mengden. Nov., note 2

Gott Lob, die Stund ist kommen . . . (Praise God, the hour hath come), by Johann Hermann. p. 175

Gute Nacht, ihr eitlen Sorgen . . . (Good night, ye idle cares), probably a variant of *Gute Nacht, ihr eitlen Freuden*, anonymous, found in the Leipzig Hymnal of 1734. p. 191

Herr, deine Treue ist so gross . . . (Lord, thy loyalty is so great), by Johann Weidenheim. July, note 1

Lass dich Gott . . . (God let . . .), by Anton Ulrich, Duke of Brunswick and Lüneburg. p. 191

O Gott, dir dank ich allezeit . . . (Oh God, I thank Thee all the time), by Johann Rist. p. 190

Sieh, hier bin ich Ehrenkönig . . . (See, here I am a King of Glory), by Joachim Neander. p. 10

Was Gott thut das ist wohl gethan . . . (What God does is well done), by Samuel Rodigast or Benjamin Schmolck. May, note 1.

Weg mein Herz mit den Gedanken . . . (Away, my heart, with all such thoughts!), by Paul Gerhardt. p. 82

Wer auf diesen Felsen baut . . . (Who builds upon these rocks),
unidentified. p. 113
Wer hofft in Gott und dem vertraut . . . (Who hopes in God and
trusts in Him), unidentified. p. 113

UNIDENTIFIED VERSES

*Da will ich nach dir blicken, da will ich glaubensvoll dich vest an mein
Hertze drücken* Sept., note 13
Er ist ja kein Bär noch Löwe July, note 3
Er kann, besser als wir denken, alle Noth zum besten lenken Feb.
note 19
*Es wird die Sünd durchs Gesetz erkannt, und schlägt das Gewissen
nieder. Das Evangelium kommt zur Hand, und* . . . Dec., note 7
*Nur der Glauben fehlt auf Erden. Wär er da, müsst uns ja, was uns
Noth ist, werden.* Sept. note 16
Ohne Fühlen will ich trauen. Feb. note 4
Seele, was verzagst du doch. April, note 11
*Sein Herz ist zu lauter Treue und zur Sanftmuth angewohnt. Gott hat
einen Vatersinn: unser Jammer jammert ihn, unser Unglück ist sein
Schmerze; unser Sterben krankt sein Herze.* July note 3
Wer diese Zeit versümt Oct., note 5

Notes for the Year 1750

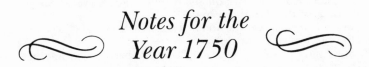

JANUARY

1. Even though Germany was divided into a myriad of squabbling little principalities and was also separated by religion and even by dialects, the people of the German-language area still felt a sentimental attachment to the "German Fatherland" and yearned for a united empire.

2. Oglethorpe's regiment had fulfilled its purpose by repelling the Spanish invasion of 1742. Now that the Spaniards were no threat, the regiment was no longer required. When it was disbanded, the Germans of German Village also left since their purpose had been to feed the regiment and to work on the fortifications.

3. These "Reverend Fathers," or patrons of the Georgia Salzburgers, were Friedrich Michael Ziegenhagen, Court Chaplain in London; Samuel Urlsperger, Senior of the Lutheran Ministry at Augsburg; and Gotthilf August Francke, the head of the Francke Foundation in Halle.

4. "Spinning off" (*abspinnen*) meant gathering a silk strand from each of several cocoons, forming them into a thread, and winding them on a spool. It was also called "reeling."

5. In this mercantilistic age, the British government wished to stop the flow of good English money to Piedmont and other lands for silk.

6. For the Pietists, "external business" (*äusserliche Geschäffte*) meant unimportant worldly matters, such as subsistence, civil order, and defense, as opposed to more important spiritual matters.

7. This is v. 8 in the King James version.

8. Bartholomäus Zouberbühler had crossed the ocean with the servants on the *Charles Town Galley* and, therefore, knew which ones to pick out for his own use.

9. Medieval theology, as well as miracle plays, taught that at death one is separated from kith, kin, and worldly possessions and is followed to heaven only by Good Works. It is surprising that Boltzius, who believed in salvation through faith alone, put such emphasis on good works, which were carefully reckoned in the Roman church.

10. See note 3, above.

11. Ernst Thilo, the physician, was then giving Greek, Latin, and musical instruction to Boltzius' two sons.

12. This was Jacob Mohr, a "Palatine" fr Purysburg.

13. This was Georg Eigel, who would not let his sons attend catechism classes.

14. The four Salzburger transports, or traveling parties, of 1734, 1735, 1736, and 1741, were gradually joined by Swiss and Germans from Purysburg and Savannah.

15. These valuable records, diligently sent to SPCK every year, have been lost or misplaced through the year 1755.

16. Boltzius means that the widow entertained thoughts of marriage too soon after her husband's death.

17. Since most travel was by water, "behind Abercorn" meant the land behind the village when one was on the river bank.

18. Schauer's balm was a panacaea manufactured in Augsburg by Johann Caspar Schauer.

19. *Sicherheit* (security) means the false assurance felt by people who think they can win salvation by good behavior and good works without a rebirth in Jesus.

20. "Customary sins" (*Gewohnheitssünden*, behavior accepted by society but considered sinful by the Pietists.

21. Johann Caspar Walthauer arrived in 1746 on board the *Judith* with a party of "Palatines," mostly from Wurttemberg.

22. Like all the other settlers, the people of Ebenezer complained against the law of tail-mail, which the Trustees had introduced in order to restrict the size of family holdings. It was designed to assure that each fifty acres maintained a yeoman farmer who could defend his soil.

23. This need not mean that he was ancient. In fact, he was only fifty-five. It means that he was the senior Gschwandel, even though surving records do not record a son.

24. *Friesel* is usually translated as "the purples" or "military disease"; but the symptoms described sometimes suggest scarlet fever, which was called *rothe Friesel* and was a scourge in the area until recent times.

25. John 14:6.

26. Isaiah 54:10.

27. Johann Peter Schubdrein was returning to his home in Weiher in Nassau Saarbrücken (Now Weyer in Alsace) to fetch his parents and other kinsmen.

28. Bichler had lost heavily because of of a swindler named Jacob Friedrich Curtius (Kurtz), who organized a big lumber operation but then absconded with the cash.

29. Johann Anastasius Freylinghausen, a professor at Halle, wrote a *Compendium Theologicum*, possibly the same as his *Compendium doctrinae christianae*, which appeared in German as *Compendium, oder kurtzer Begriff der gantzen Christlichen Lehre*. Halle 1726.

30. Even though Urlsperger has deleted the name here, it is easy to see that the neglected child was that of Mrs. Granewetter. See entry for 25 Sept.

31. Presumably Chrétien von Münch, an Augsburg banker who had commercial aspirations for Ebenezer.

32. This copious questionnaire was translated by Klaus G. Loewald, *et al* and published in the *William and Mary Quarterly*, 3rd series, Vols 14 and 15.

33. Now the term "the last German people" refers to the Palatine servants brought by Capt. Bogg in 1949.

FEBRUARY

1. Steeped in medieval economic theory, Boltzius thought that prices should be set not by the market but by Christian conscience. A price was fair (*billig*, which now means "cheap") if it would enable the seller to subsist without luxury and without rising in the world, these two goals being signs of greed and pride (*cupiditas* and *superbia*). He often uses the word "Christian price" or "Christian wages."

2. Boltzius conveniently forgets the sad voyage of the *Europa*, which lost half its Swiss passengers to "Palatine fever" in 1741.

3. Boltzius numbered the commandment against stealing as the sixth, according to Roman Catholic and Lutheran usage. In this translation all commandments are numbered according to Orthodox Greek and English usage.

4. *Ohne Fühlen will ich trauen*, apparently from a hymn.

5. For Pietists, "temptations" (*Anfechtungen*) meant the temptation to lose hope of salvation through faith alone. People who feared the law of the Old Testament more than they trusted the grace of the New were "legalists."

6. The text has *der* where one would expect *das*.)

7. See Jan., note 21.

8. *Cabinetprediger*, unidentified.

9. *Mitternachtgegenden*, "Midnight regions," a rather poetic expression for "north."

10. This was John Dobell, a former schoolmaster in Savannah.

11. Although this German trader is mentioned several times, he cannot be identified. It is probable that his name was completely anglicized. He may have been John Rudolf Grant, who appears occasionally in Purysburg.

12. See Jan., note 28.

13. The Uchi Indians, a small outcast tribe, were guaranteed ownership of all land across Ebenezer Creek. However, by now they had moved further up the river and had but thirty warriors, so the British were able to persuade the survivors to sell.

14. Only forty-some years later this little machine was displaced by a better one invented a few miles away by Eli Whitney.

15. *Fremde Sünden (peccata aliena)* were sins of leading or encouraging others to sin, or not preventing them from doing so.

16. Ambrosius Wirth, *Einfältige Anweisung... ec., etc.* . Nurnberg 1736.

17. This is the only mention in Boltzius' reports of the extensive silk business being conducted by his wife.

18. Boltzius must mean "as everyone knows."

19. *Er kann, besser als wir denken, alle Noth zum Besten lenken*, from a hymn. This is one of the many songs presenting the Pietists' theodicy.

20. The immigrants, being redemptioners rather than indentured servants, were free to redeem themselves for six pounds upon landing and could choose their own employers. The two servants in question were Daniel and Joseph Schubdrein, the brothers of Johann Peter. See Jan., note 8.

21. When the servants in Savannah served out their time, Col. Stephens encouraged the Reformed to settle in Acton and Vernonburg, where they would have Reformed services, while he encouraged the Lutherans to move to the vicinity of Ebenezer and Lutheran services.

22. Philipp Jacob Spener, *Evangelien- und Epistel-Predigten* .

23. The "literal recognition" (*buchstäblisches Erkänntniss*) meant an intellectual understanding of the articles of faith but not necessarily a rebirth in Jesus.

24. For the Pietists, "honest" (*ehrlich*), meant "accepting Pietistic tenets.

MARCH

1. According to medieval theory, the sciences were divided into the seven liberal arts, the seven mechanical arts, and the forbidden arts. The last were also called the "black arts," through a misunderstanding of the word *necromancia*, which meant "communing with the dead" but was construed as *nigramancia*, or "black magic." Those who practiced this were Satanists and in danger of the Inquisition.

2. The Salzburgers first settled at an inaccessible and infertile spot on Ebenezer Creek. When they removed to the bank of the Savannah River in 1736, the Trustees converted the old settlement into a cowpen or cattle ranch and also built an expensive lumber mill there, which was soon destroyed.

3. Boltzius calls this 3 John, apparently letting the Gospel of St. John count as 1 John.

4. Hebrews 13:5; *Was soll der Mensch thun?*, unidentified.

5. For boiling the cocoons to kill the worms before they chew their way out.

6. *Haushaltung*, like *Haushalt* and *Hauswesen*, denotes the housekeeping, the farming, and the whole domestic economy.

7. To make the pagan incantations respectable, Christian practitioners often crossed themselves or said the Lord's Prayer three time at their close.

8. Boltzius still refers to this useful building as an orphanage, perhaps for propaganda purposes, even though there do not appear to have been any orphans in it. The children mentioned a bit later may have been patients in the sickbay.

9. This was, of course, on the way down to Savannah. Returning in their boats, they would travel with the flood and rest during the ebb.

10. The three brothers, Johann Peter, Joseph, and Daniel came in 1749 on the *Charles Town Galley* with Captain Bogg. The Anglican pastor, Zouberbuhler, who was on the same ship, redeemed them for his own use, but Boltzius succeeded in obtaining them.

APRIL

1. The Salzburgers had the reputation of selling only the heartwood, while keeping the inferior outside slabs for domestic use.

2. William Stephens was the President of the Council, the magistry of the Northern District of Georgia.

3. Romans 10:10.

4. Samuel Urlsperger, *Schriftmässiger Unterricht für Kranke und Sterbende....*

5. Boltzius, as a British official, used the old, or Julian, calendar instead of the new Gregorian calendar, long since adopted by the various German states. Two years later, he, like the British, changed to the new calendar.

6. "Make haste slowly."

7. These symptoms were probably caused by malaria, to which everyone was subjected.

8. Those who came on the *Charles Town Galley* in 1749.

9. This was the family of Andreas Seckinger, which prospered and furnished Georgia with many fine citizens.

10. Unlike the South Carolina authorities, the Trustees decided to liberate all indentured children as soon as their parents had served their time, even though girls usually served until the age of eighteen and boys to the age of twenty-one. The Trustees had discovered that children would contribute more to the colony when working for their parents than when working for strangers.

11. *Seele! was verzagst du doch?*, from a hymn.

12. Wheat, rye, oats, and barley.

13. By chance this was about the same number as in Acton-Vernonburg and Ebenezer.

14. Ambrosius Wirth, *Beicht- und Communionbüchlein, ...*

MAY

1. This is an allusion to the hymn *Was Gott thut ist wohl gethan.*

2. Meyer had accepted the office of justiciary, or secular manager of the community, as well as that of justice of the peace.

3. Matthew 5:8.

4. Johann Caspar Wertsch.

5. In this context, "servants" means clergymen.

6. "Our religion" means the Lutheran religion. The old widow must have been Reformed.

7. This appears to be the family of Johann Caspar Waldhauer. See entry for 17 May.

JUNE

1. Nee Friderica Helfenstein.

2. "Still further, ever onward."

3. 1 John 2:20.

4. Matthew 7:11.

5. Karl Heinrich Bogatzky, *Güldenes Schatz-Kästlein der Kinder Gottes*, Halle, many printings.

6. Proverbs 1:32. Boltzius writes *der Gottlosen* (the godless) instead of *der Ruchlosen* (the wicked).

7. This was the meaning of "Ebenezer."

8. See Jan., note 31.

9. John Adam Treutlen, future governor of Georgia.

10. Boltzius is referring to the famous Orphanage (*Waisenhaus*) in Halle.

11. Lucerne, or Luzern, like the three other original Forest Cantons, had remained Roman Catholic.

12. At the same time the Archbishop of Salzburg was exiling his Protestant subjects, the Habsburgs were expelling Protestants from Upper Austria and Carinthia. Most of these were sent to Transylvania (Siebenburgen). Some of them, who had been residing in Regensburg, joined the third Salzburger transport to Georgia.

13. This was Theobald Kieffer, Jr. See "Two 'Salzburger' Letters from George Whitefield and Theobald Kieffer, Jr." (*GHQ* 62 (1978), 50–57.

J U L Y

1. *Herr, deine Treue is so gross, dass wir uns verwundern müssen, etc.* For author, see appendix.

2. Boltzius' older son, aged fourteen.

3. *Er ist ja kein Bär noch Löwe, der sich nur,* etc. and *Sein Herz ist zu lauter Treue und zur Sanftmuth angewohnt. Gott hat einen Vatersinn: unser Jammer jammert ihn; unser Unglück ist sein Schmerze; unser Sterben krankt sein Herze.* Apparently from a hymn.

4. The child was afflicted with pica, or clay-eating, a disease caused by dietary deficiency.

5. Johann Jacob Metzger, or Metscher, was a tailor in Purysburg who lost three children in a boat wreck. The other children moved to Ebenezer and prospered.

6. This must have been a good move, for, when Heinrich Melchior Muhlenberg visited Ebenezer in 1774, Leimberger's widow was the proprietress of a slave-operated plantation.

7. These were the Schubdrein brothers.

8. This was Boltzius' first reference to trade with St. Augustine, which, until recently, had been in enemy territory.

9. Col. William Stephens had already advised the Trustees that the German immigrants were of little value as long as they were indentured but that they were by far the most industrious workers in the colony when freed and working for themselves.

10. Boltzius is referring to the indentured servants who came on the *Charles Town Galley* in 1749.

11. The Book of Tobit is found in the Apocrypha and in the Luther translation, but not in the King James version.

12. The land across Ebenezer Creek was still being reserved for the Uchee Indians. See Feb., note 13.

A U G U S T

1. Psalms 50:15.

2. Karl Heinrich Bogatzky, *Tägliches Hausbuch der Kinder Gottes.*

3. Karl Heinrich Bogatzky, *Güldenes Schatz-Kästlein. der Kinder Gottes.* Halle, many printings.

4. Psalms 51:14. It is rendered differently in the King James version (51:12); Isaiah 66:13.

5. Like Boltzius and his colleagues, the Lutheran missionaries in India were submitting regular reports of their activities, which were published contemporaneously in Halle as *Der königlichen Dänischen Missionarien aus Ost-Indien eingesandte Ausführliche Berichte*, Halle 1735 ff.

6. Isaiah 45:22.

7. Luke 23:43.

8. Deceased Inspector at Halle.

9. See note 5, above.

10. Dr. Helmut Beck, Moravian minister in Hamburg, has kindly informed me that the first verse cited is v. 7 of the hymn *Wer hofft auf Gott und dem vertraut* (See appendix). The second cited verse is unidentified.

11. For the Pietists, *Elend*, which normally meant "misery," still had its original meaning of "exile," or "alienation from God."

12. In Pietist parlance, "ignorant" (*unwissend*) meant as much as "ignorant of Pietist dogma."

13. Johann Georg Walsch, *Einleitung in die Religionsstreitigkeiten der evangelischen lutherischen Kirche.*

14. This estate, called Good Harmony, was never developed.

15. Johann Vigera had conducted the fourth Salzburger transport to Ebenezer, where he had intended to settle. Finding this impracticable, he moved on to Philadelphia, where he married an English woman.

16. This was clearly Curtius (Jacob Friedrich Kurtz). See Jan., note 28.

17. An imposter who called himself Carl Rudolf, Prince of Wurttemberg. He claimed to have been kidnapped by Capt. George Dunbar and sold at Frederica. He sometimes posed as a Lutheran minister.

18. A medical student named Johann Christian Seelmann had come in 1749 with the Palatine servants on the *Charles Town Galley* but was *persona non grata* in Ebenezer because he was a follower of a dissident Lutheran theologian named Dippel.

SEPTEMBER

1. This typographical error remains to be explained.

2. Genesis 32:11.

3. Psalms 68:21.

4. The King James version differs greatly from Luther's translation.

5. See Jan., note 28.

6. When this proposal was made again during the Revolution, it was a vestryman of Ebenezer, Governor John Adam Treutlen, who defeated it by placing a bounty on the heads of the proposers.

7. *Der rechte und beständige Gebrauch des Glaubens. Ein Wort der Ermahnung und des Trostes am Neujahrstage 1750. Ein Wort des Unterrichts von der rechten Art Gnade beim HErrn Jesu zu suchen und zu erlangen.*

8. *Kurtze Erklärung des Gebets des HErrn nebst einigen Anmerkungen darüber.*

9. Hans Michael Held, a Palatine who arrived in 1738, had previously served as herdsman at the cowpen.

10. This was Col. Wm. Stephens, who had recently stepped down because of advanced age.

11. Chretien von Munch again. See Jan., note 31.

12. A typographical error for Zimmerebner.

13. *Da will ich nach dir blicken, da will ich Glaubensvoll dich vest an mein Hertz drücken.* From a hymn.

14. European crops were wheat, barley, rye, and oats. The Indian crops were corn, beans, and, apparently, also rice.

15. John 11:40.

16. *Nur der Glaube fehlt auf Erden. Wär er da, müsst uns ja, was uns Noth ist, werden. Wer Gott kann im Glauben fassen: der wird nicht, wenns gebricht, von ihm seyn verlassen,* from a hymn.

17. *Hilft der Herr nicht,* unidentified.

18. *Erklärung des Gebets des Herrn.*

19. The Luther version is more vivid: *Die Ruhmredigen bestehen nicht. Du bringest die Lügner um.*

20. Galatians 5:19. The Luther Bible says *Werke* (works) instead of "sins."

21. John 3:16. Allusion to the fiery serpents sent by the Lord in Numbers 21:6.

22. This was Christoph Vollbrecht, known in Georgia as Fulbright.

23. In the James version this is Psalms 39:4.

OCTOBER

1. Psalms 118:17.

2. See Feb., note 13.

3. See Jan., note 28.

4. John 5:14.

5. *Wer diese Zeit versäumt, und sich zu Gott nicht kehrt, der schrey Weh über sich, wenn er zur Höllen führt*, from a hymn.

6. *Heute lebst du, heut bekehre dich, etc.*, unidentified.

7. See Aug., note 5.

8. 1 Chronicles 29:17.

9. Matthew 23:12.

10. Psalms 27:10.

11. Matthew 23:12.

12. Philip Jacob Spener, Pietist leader and prolific author.

13. See Jan., note 24.

14. Christian Friedrich Richter was a professor at Halle and also a hymnist.

15. This was not Boltzius' doing. The "long lots" had been favored by German farmers since the early Middle Ages and had just been demanded, against the English surveryor Avery's will, by the settlers of Acton and Vernonburg.

16. A widowed daughter of Jacob Metzger who married the convert Gottfried Christ.

17. Job 1:21.

18. The Book of Wisdom is not found in the King James version. It is taken here from the Vulgate.

19. Both Luther and the King James version say "son."

20. Boltzius uses the word *Vetter*, although Gronau was only the child's uncle-in-law.

21. Psalms 37:4.

NOVEMBER

1. Some of the Swabians had paid their own passage and were therefore free; others borrowed all or part of their passage money from the Trustees and were to pay it off by working for the Salzburgers. The Swabians had been recruited in the territory of the Free City of Ulm on the Danube and had arrived in Georgia on 29 Oct. 1750 aboard the *Charming Martha*.

2. The opening verse of the hymn *Gott hat alles wohl bedacht...*, by Gustav von Mengden.

3. Col. Stephens must have retained the rank of President, even if not the office, for Henry Parker was named only vice president. As far as the Salzburgers were concerned, their friend Habersham was the most important councilman.

4. See note 1, above. The previous transport, that of 1749, were all inden-

tured, except for one family. Since the party of 1750 consisted of both free and indentured, Boltzius now distinguishes between "colonists" and "servants."

5. *Gleichwie sich fein ein Vögelein in hohle Bäum ...*, from a hymn.

6. It is not clear what Boltzius means by *Ausdünstung des Leibes*.

7. Boltzius means it was the same day of the month, but not of the year. In 1709 he was only six years old.

8. John 4:53.

9. Psalms 81:10.

10. Israel Christian Gronau.

11. See June, note 5.

12. *Die Gerechten werden ewiglich leben, und der HErr ist, usw*, unidentified.

13. *Darum werden sie empfahen ein herrliches Reich und eine schöne Krone, usw.*, unidentified.

14. Matthew 9:24.

15. From the offing off Tybee Island at the mouth of the Savannah River.

16. Hugh and Jonathan Bryan were the two chief Jeremiahs among the South Carolina planters.

17. This is an error for Philemon 1:20-21, since Philemon has only one chapter.

18. Unable to find a sedentary employment worthy of his talents, Matthias Neidlinger gave up in disgust and returned to Germany, much as the organist and schoolmaster Gottlieb Mittelberger did at about the same time.

19. Now Boltzius calls Henry Parker the President. See note 3, above.

20. Psalms 60:11 in the King James version, 60:13 in the Luther version.

21. Psalms 85:7.

22. In the Luther version she is called Tabea.

23. *Libra sacra latina*. Sebastian Castellio or Chateillon, a Burgundian Calvinist, made a new translation of the New Testament from the Greek to replace the somewhat erroneous Vulgate of St. Jerome.

24. This passage has been reconstructed from a very corrupt printing.

25. "The listener stimulates the lesson."

26. See note 20, above.

27. Samuel Lutz was a Swiss theologian of Pietistic leanings; Bonaventura Riesch, the Senior of the Lutheran ministry in Lindau, had taken particular interest in those Georgia Salzburgers who had been under his care during their sojourn there.

28. Pastor Fels of Lindau was mentioned previously in the *Detailed Reports*, but without a first name.

29. See note 27, above.

30. The word *Verbotenus* was the legal term for "verbatim."

31. John 11:4.

32. At Boltzius' behest, James Habersham wrote a very good recommendation for Peter Schubdrein, dated 2 Feb. 1750 Old Time. (PRO C.O. 5, 643)

DECEMBER

1. In previous volumes the word *Eingang* has been translated as "exordium." Now that it has been noticed that *Ein-gang* is an exact loan-translation from *intro-itus*, it is now translated as "introit," even though the latter suggests the Roman Catholic mass.

2. The financial contributions not only provided for the future by building mills, but also for the immediate present by providing an opportunity to earn cash, a rare commodity in Georgia, as Boltzius often attested.

3. *Die Macht Gottes an kleinen Kindern.*

4. *am rothen Friesel und bösen Hälsen.*

5. Chretien de Munch was then making suggestions for develping the mills and other enterprises at Ebenezer.

6. This was Johann Georg Häfner. See entry for 9 Dec.

7. *Es wird die Sünd durchs Gesetz erkannt, und schlägt das Gewissen nieder: Das Evangelium kommt zu Hand, und etc.* This hymn, like many others sung at Ebenezer, contrasts the Law of the Old Testament with the grace of the New, which enables even the worst sinner to achieve salvation through repentance and faith alone.

8. Jacob Hüber of Langenau, who died in 1756. See entry for 18 Dec.

9. He was the child of Pieta Clara, widow of Paul Häfner, a Palatine who had died at Vernonburg. She married Adam Straube before moving to Ebenezer.

10. *Beiträge zum Bau des Reiches Gottes,* a collection of religious tracts.

11. In Germany Georg Mayer had been a maker of silk purses, but in Ebenezer he was a tailor.

12. Psalms 37:4.

13. Boltzius contrasts *das rothe Friesel* with *das weisse.* The symptoms described, as well as the medical terminology of the time, make it difficult to identify the ailments.

14. *von einem verdorbenem Fieber.* The meaning is not clear.

15. *beweisen im Fieber fast keine Diet in Ansehung des Essens, Trinkens und der nötigen Ausdämpfung.* Not clear.

16. Psalms 106:1.

17. The Schubdreins came from Weiher in Saarbrücken (now Weyer in Alsace), where all land was under cultivation.

18. This hardware had probably come from the Trustees' destroyed sawmill at Old Ebenezer.

19. Money earned by an indentured servant went to his master.

20. See entry for 4 Dec.

21. Following medieval views, the Pietist taught that a man should remain in the condition in which it pleased the Lord to put him. The farmer should stay with his plow, the shoemaker with his last, etc. The desire to rise in the world was a sign of greed and pride, two mortal sins.

22. The *opus operatum* is the work or operation itself, the act of praying or attending church, but without spiritual involvement.

23. Johannes Arndt, *Vier Bücher vom wahren Christenthum.* Halle, 1731 ff.; Ambrosius Wirth, *Beicht- und Abendmahl Büchlein.*

24. This was the aged Anna in Luke 2:36-38.

25. No Georgia records mention any group from Luzern as coming to Georgia.

26. Joseph Schubdrein.

27. Jacob Friedrich Curtius (Kurtz), who swindled the Salzburgers in a big timber operation.

28. At first, the cypress logs would sink; but it was discovered that, if the trees were felled and the logs allowed to dry out for a year, then they would float.

29. Chretien von Münch, banker at Augsburg.

30. He must have been a good tutor, for John Adam Treutlen became a prosperous merchant before becoming Georgia's first elected governor.

31. The title *Vermehrer des Reiches*, "Augmenter of the Empire," a title bestowed on many Holy Roman Emperors, was last bestowed on Hitler.

32. The first Salzburger transport had been housed in the Protestant poorhouse in Augsburg while being recruited and prepared for the journey to Georgia. The institutions at Halle were the spiritual and physical model for Ebenezer, which tried to replicate them.

33. The *Paedigogium Regium*, or royal lycee, was a school for young noblemen.

34. The most disliked of these restrictions was the rule of tail-mail, which stipulated that only men could hold land.

INDEX

Abercorn, village near juncture of Abercorn Creek and Savannah River, mentioned, 10, 42; "behind Abercorn" = Goshen, 51, 52.

Abercorn Creek (Mill River), branch of Savannah River, fertile land along, 21, 66, 150

Acton, German and Swiss settlement near Savannah, mentioned, 123

Agriculture, see Crops.

Albinus, . . . , court chaplain in London, forwards gifts, 5. letters to, 14, 73, 116; letters from, 69, 70, 74, 76, 126, 153, 157, 185; mentioned, 125, 176; composed verses, 127

Altherr, Johann, Swiss from St. Gall, 72

Anhalt, German principality, mentioned, 180

Anton Ulrich, Duke of Brunswick, hymnist, 222

Arnsdorf, Andreas Lorentz, deceased tanner, 8

Arndt, Johann, Pietist author, 57, 210

Augsburg, city in Swabia, source of gifts, 2, 65, 136, 184–185, 207

Augsburg hymnal, well arranged, 190, 193

Augusta, city up the Savannah River, mentioned, 23, 59, 101

Austrian exiles, 94–95

Avery, Mr. Joseph, deceased English surveyor, 47

Bacher, Mrs. Thomas, pious Salz, mentioned, 44, becoming frail, 170, 171

Baptisms, see Births and Baptisms.

Barley press, 94

Baumann, Conrad, Salz, dies 87, 88

Beaufain, Mr. Hector Beringer de, South Carolina merchant, 125

Beicht- und Communionbüchlein, tract by Wirth, April, note 14

Beiträge zum Bau . . . , see *Contributions . . .*

Benefactions, see Gifts.

Bichler, Thomas, Salz, has consumptive fever, 13, a little stronger, 14, no progress in Christianity, 167, 168; being tried, 209; Jan., note 28

Bichler, Mrs., w Thomas, bears child, 15

Birkholt, immigrant, paid passage, settled near Savannah, 189

Births and baptisms: Bichler child, 15, German child at Abercorn, 42, English child, 63, Rottenberger child, 135, Schefler child, 135, Zoller child, 193, Simon Reuter child, Helena Hüber child, 203

Bloodletting, 205

Blue Bluff, new name of Uchee land, 193, being surveyed, 199

Bogatzky, Carl Heinrich, Pietist, author of *Güldenes Schatz-Kästlein der Kinder Gottes Treasure Chest*, 107; June, note 5, Aug., note 3; of *Tägliches Hausbuch der Kinder Gottes*, Aug., note 2

Bogg, Peter, master of *Charles Town Galley*, March, note 10

Boltzius, Christiana Elisabeth, d Johann Martin, dies, 181–183, buried, 184

Boltzius, Gertraut, w Johann Martin, makes silk, 29, ill, 91, 106, 119

Boltzius, Gotthilf Israel, s Johann Martin, to study in Germany, 80, 81; sick with purples, 171, loves brother, 172

Boltzius, Johann Martin, pastor at
Ebenezer (passim)
Boltzius, Samuel Leberecht, s
Johann Martin, to study in Ger-
many, 80, 81, letter from, 85, dies,
171–173, remembered, 191, 204
Bonin, Mr. von, benefactor, 127
Books, see Halle.
Brandner, Matthias, Salz, a true
Christian, 87, takes on servants,
96, 117, his children have scarlet
fever, 186, 202, receives servant,
189
Breslau, benefactress in, 135
Brickmaking, 98–99, 220
Bridge, repaired, 8, 117
Broughton, Mr., secretary of SPCK,
letter from, 16, 69, 70
Brown, Scots engineer, 86, 107,
working on barley stamp, 104
Brückner, Georg, Salz, ill, 87
Brunnholtz, Johann Peter, pastor in
Pennsylvania, letter to, 99, letter
from, 121, 122, praised, 169
Bryan, Hugh and Jonathan, S.C.
planters; Nov., note 16
Burkhart, Martin, Pal, writes letter,
87

Cabinet Preacher, Pietist tract, 22;
Feb., note 8
Calendar, printed in German in
Philadelphia, 24
Carl Rudolf, see Prince of
Wurttemberg.
Carpenters, in short supply, 49
Carters at mill, earn much money,
142
Catholic man, sick, 42, dies, 52
Cattle, Trustees to sell cowpen, 38,
49, 51, cowpen mentioned, 101,
176; March, note 2
Caesar, Charleston Negro, invents
cure, 88
Charleston, port in South Carolina,
(passim)
Charles Town Galley, ship; March,
note 10, April, note 8, July, note
10
Cherokees, see Indians.

Christ, Mrs., nee Metzger, w. Gott-
fried, dies, 170
Church in Savannah, consecrated,
87
Churches, see Jerusalem Church
and Zion Church.
Compendium theologicum, see Frey-
linghausen.
Confession and Holy Communion Booklet, religious tract by Ambrosius
Wirth, 26, 56. See Beichtbüchlein
Congarees, Congrees, settlement in
South Carolina, refuge of renegades, 22, 23, 56, mentioned, 52,
Lutheran people there, 55
Contributions to the Kingdom of God,
religious tract, 203
Cotton, grows abundantly, 25, cotton
gin, 25
Corn, see Crops.
Council, governing body in Savannah, consisting of a President and
five Assistants, convokes assembly,
instructs surveyor, 10, petitioned
by Boltzius, 19, 21, 72, 154, will
cede iron, 38, 47, in session, 83,
187, composing petition, 85, do-
nates land, 118, letter to, 137,
changes in, 177
Cows, Cowpen, see Cattle.
Creeks, see Indians.
Crops, barley; beans 139, 144, 150;
corn, 140, 144; rice, 139, 144, 150;
rye, 140; squash, 139, 144; sweet
potatoes, 139, wheat, 140
Cudulur, city in India, scene of
Lutheran missions, 111
Curtius, see Kurtz.
Customary sins, Jan., note 20
Cypress, see Trees.

Daily Housebook, see Bogatzky.
Deaths: widow Graniwetter's son, 11,
her other son, 27, N.'s oldest son,
15, Conrad Baumann, 87, Metzger, 90, illigitimate child, 100, wid
Lemmenhofer, 109, Mrs. Christ,
171, Samuel Leberecht Boltzius,
171, Klocker girl, 179, Christiana

Elisabeth Boltzius, 181, Carl Flerl's son, 190, Zoller's son, 193, Johann Georg Häfner, 203, a young woman, 205, Hüber child, 206, Seckinger child, 206

Deer skins, drop in price, 102, boatload lost, 123

Deodant, English law, 168

Diego, Mr., letter from, 112

Dippel, deviant Lutheran minister in Germany, 17

Diseases: pica (clay eating), 89, July, note 4; measles, 161, 196; the purples, 161, 204; scarlet fever, 178, 186, 196, 202, 204, 205

Dobel, John, English friend, Feb., note 10

Dogma of Penitence and the Forgiveness of Sins, religious tract, Drought, 90

East India, scene of missionary activity, 157

East India Reports, missionary reports, 107, 110, 156; Aug., note 5

Ebenezer, Salzburger settlement near Savannah (passim)

Ebenezer Creek, unnavigable waterway from Old to New Ebenezer, soldiers settle on, 1

Ehrhardt, Mr., letter to Mr. Meyer, 65

Eigel, Georg, Salz, obstacle to son's Christianity, 6; Jan., note 13

Eischberger, receives servant, 189

Eischberger, Ruprecht, his children sick with scarlet fever, 186, recovering, 188, 193

Englishmen, visit Ebenezer, 62

English inn keeper, 155

English soldier with German wife, 148.

Europa, ill-starred ship, Feb., note 2

European crops (wheat, rye, barley, oats), 47, faring badly, 55, recover, 60; Sept., note 14

Fabricius, Lutheran missionary in India, 110

"Fathers," Salzburger patrons, 1, 16, 77, 125, 176, 216. See G. A.

Francke, Urlsperger, Ziegenhagen.

Fels, Pastor, minister in Lindau, 195

Firs, see Trees.

First Swabian transport, 175, 177, 211, to settle on Uchee land, 178

Flerl (Flörl), Carl, praises lord, 190, his stepson ill, 198, 212

Flerl, Hans, Salz, mentioned, 178

Francke, Gotthilf August, s A. H.

Francke, Reverend Father and benefactor, collects gifts, 5, 185; mentioned, 77, 81, 116, 126, 164, 173, 176; letter from, 80, letter to, 112

Francke, Johann Paul, German from Purysburg, 87

French merchant in Savannah, 166

Freylinghausen, Johann Anastasius, professor at Halle, author of Geistreiches Gesangbuch, Compendium Theologicum 15, and sermons; Jan., note 29

Friesel, disease, Jan., note 24, Dec., note 13

Fruit, plum and peach trees damaged by icicles, 31

Fullbright, Christoph, Sept., note 22

Geistreiches Gesangbuch, see Freylinghausen.

Gerhard, Paul, hymnist, 223

German crops (= European crops), See wheat, rye, oats, barley.

German man from Pennsylvania, 59

German immigrants, arrive at Charleston in bad condition, 19

German people behind Abercorn (at Goshen), 51, 53, 61, 100, 114, 149, 164, 212

German people in Savannah, 3, 58, 72, 81, 123, 164

German servants in South Carolina, 4

German smuggler in West Indies, 165

German Village, at St Simons, Jan., note 2

German Reformed, see Reformed.

Gifts, collected by Francke and Urlsperger, 5

Gill, Captain, mariner, to take mail, 32

Glaner, Matthias, Salz, mentioned, 109, 110, 147, 155, 156; marries widow Zant, 181

Good Harmony, Boltzius' undeveloped estate, Aug., note 14

Goshen, fertile land "behind Abercorn," being surveyed, 20, 21; fertile, 25, 34, 61; mentioned, 53, 114, 144, 151, 154; Boltzius receives grant at, 119, 120; land donated, 199

Gospel and Epistle Sermons, by P. J. Spener, 35

Graham, Dr., neighbor of Salzburgers, 114, 118, 120

Graniwetter, Anna Catharina, nee Sturmer, Salz, wid Caspar, bears cross 22; her daughter ill, 9, 11, 62; her son bedridden, 11, dies, 12, other son dies, 27, she is ill, 62

Grant, John Rodolph, trader, Feb., note 11

Gristmills, a great benefit, 63

Gronau, Christian Israel, deceased colleague of Boltzius, remembered, 175

Gruber, Johann, Salz, sick, 193

Gschwandl, Thomas, Salz, he and his daughter dangerously ill, 13, 14

Habersham, James, merchant, member of Council, urges use of slaves, 12, 18; fears his ship has sunk, 15, mentioned, 1, 116, 119, 122; forwards mail, 32, effects improvements in Council, 58, capable and hardworking, 81; ship delayed, 116, a neighbor, 119, letters from, 120, 180; becomes secretary of the Council, 177, shows affection, 187, 192

Häfner, Johann Georg, sick, 202, dies, 203, 204; Dec., note 6

Hailstones, 45, 48, 60

Halle, East German city, home of Francke Foundation, source of gifts, 2, 5, 65; chests of books and medicines from, 70, 72, 73, 107, 153, 160

Halle Hymnal, 57, see Freylinghausen.

Halle Orphanage, mentioned, 77, 161, 171; June, note 10, source of medicine, 207

Harmonium Antonianum, musical text edited by Pastor Mayer, 160

Harris, Mr. John, partner of Habersham, fears his ship has sunk, 15

Haymaking, difficult, 139 , 141, being harvested, 150

Held, Hans Michael, Pal herdsman, returns to Ebenezer, 136; Sept., note 9

Helfenstein, Friderica, Pal, June, note 1

Hermann, Johann, hymnist, 222

Heron, Col., former commandant at Frederica, requests boards, 98, 115; letter from, 123, mentioned, 124

Hessler, Mrs. Christian, lying in, 10

Honey, wild, some poisonous, 39

House consecrations: Ruprecht Steiner, 43, Kalcher, 208

Hüber child dies, 206

Hüber, Jacob, Swabian, praises God, 209; Dec., note 8

Hüttemann, Mr., missionary to Indies, 157

Hymns, see Appendix.

Incantations, 37, 43

Indian crops (corn, sweet potatoes, rice), 141

Indians, capture renegades, 31; Creeks, Cherokees, and French Indians involved in war, 92; Creeks burn youth, 93, Indians steal horse, 101, demand old prices, 102

Instruction for the Sick and Dying, by S. Urlsperger, 52

Introduction to the Religious Struggles . . . , tract by Dr. Walch, 117

Ironwork for sawmill, ceded by
    Trustees, 38, 176, 217
Italian in Purysburg sells cocoons,
    43

Jerusalem Church, town church in
    Ebenezer, 107, 151, 160, 188, 190,
    212, 213

Kalcher, Mrs. Margaretha, w
    Ruprecht, weak, 19, well versed in
    catechism, 105
Kalcher, Ruprecht, Salz, mentioned
    7, 44, 45, 141, 142; lives in or-
    phanage, 95, acquires house, 96,
    receives servant, 189, consecrates
    house, 208
Kalcher, oldest daughter ill, 161, 198
Kieffer, Maria, w Theobald, Jr., ex-
    pecting confinement, 13
Kieffer, Theobald, Sr., Pal from
    Purysburg, gives witness, 91
Kieffer, Theobald, Jr., keeps slave,
    100, buys second slave, 112; June,
    note 13
Klocker, Gertraut, Salz, marries in
    Goshen, 53
Klocker girl ill, 178
Kogler, Barbara, w Georg, Salz, re-
    covers, 135, has tribulations, 139
Kogler, Georg, Salz, chief carpenter
    and sawmiller, mentioned, 8, 141;
    works on barley stamp, 104
Kohleisen, Peter, Salz, shoemaker,
    mentioned, 36, gets drunk, 102
Kronberger, Jacob, has slave, 100,
    120
Krause, Leonhard, Salz, his maid
    summons Boltzius, 146, 156
Kurtz (Curtzius), Jacob Friedrich,
    swindler, 25, 121; Dec., note 27

Laminit, Mr., patron of the Salzbur-
    gers, letter to Mr. Meyer, 65, 176
Landfelder, Ursula, wid. Veit, Salz,
    165
Last Supper, painting, donated, 192
Leimberger, Christian, Salz, buys
    slave, 93, 94
Lemke, Hermann Heinrich, assistant

minister in Ebenezer, mentioned,
    3, 88, 119, 141, 166; in Savannah,
    58, 125; a reliable assistant, 75,
    makes plans for dam, 103, 108; to
    receive land, 130, inspects land,
    137, attends Council, 177
Lemmenhofer, Maria, Salz, wid Veit,
    ill, 91, near death, 105, dies, 109,
    buried, 102
Lindau, city on Lake Constance, 195,
    196
Little Treasure Chest, see Carl
    Heinrich Bogatzky.
Lloyd, Mr., silk expert in London,
    letter to, 76
London, source of benefactions, 1
Long lots, Oct., note 15
Lord Trustees, see Trustees.
Lucerne (Luzern), Swiss city, exiles
    from, 80, 211, 215; June, note 11
Lumber industry: barrel staves,
    shingles, dressed lumber for West
    Indies, 17, 25, 31, 33, 66, 67, 98,
    152; boards in demand, 31, 48, 63,
    98; being cut, 36, cypresses plenti-
    ful on Abercorn Creek, 34, pine
    boards, 198
Lutherans, at Saxe Gotha, 55
Lutherans in Savannah. See German
    people in Savannah.

Madras, city in India, scene of
    Lutheran missions, 111
Lutz, Master, pastor in Lindau, 195
Mäderjan, pastor in Thommendorf,
    194
Maier, Pastor, patron in Halle, 65,
    letter from, 79
Martyn, Benjamin, Trustees' secre-
    tary, letter to. 76, letter from, 127,
    view on slavery, 129
Maurer, Mrs. Hans, mentioned,. 89
Maurer, . . . d Mrs. Maurer, eats
    sand, 89
Mayer, Johann Georg, see Meyer,
    J. G.
Mayer, Ludwig, see Meyer, J. L.
Mayer, Pastor, ed. of book, 160
Measles, see Diseases.

Memmingen, German city, resort of exiles, 181
Memorial and Thanksgiving service, 39
Mengden, Gustav von, hymnist, 222
Metzger, Johann Jacob, Palatine tailor, dies, 90; July, note 5
Meyer, (Johann) Georg, brother Johann Ludwig, his apprentice sick, 202
Meyer, (Johann) Ludwig, physician with 4th Salz trans, mentioned, 35, 153, 166, 177; still serves as judge, 40, resigns, 57, 58; reconsiders, 75, 77; to validate drafts, 79, to sign petition, 85, 86; receives new house, 96, receives letter, 121, marries, 158, 160, 178; receives servant, 189
Meyer, Magdalena, w. Georg, sick, 53
Milldam, well constructed, 207
Mill River, see Abercorn Creek.
Mills, must be fortified, 46, standing still, can run again, 112, 140, owe money, 128. See Gristmills, Sawmills.
Mischke, Inspector, inspector of schools in Halle, fondly remembered, 91, 110
Mitzscher, see Metzger.
Mohr, Jacob, youth from Purysburg, Jan., note 12
Mount Pleasant, fortress on Savannah River above Ebenezer, mentioned, 101
Mühlenberg, Heinrich Melchior, pastor from Halle, praised, 169
Mulberry trees (for silkworms), 9, 30, damaged by icicles, 31, in full leaf, 42, damaged by drought, 71, white mulberry, 133
Müller, Mrs. Christina, Palatine, w Fr. Wilh., ill, 157
Münch, Chretien de, Augsburg banker, Jan., note 31, Sept., note 11, Dec., note 29

Nassau, German principality, home of Schubdreins, 199

Necessary Combination, etc., religious tract
Neander, Joachim, hymnist, 222
Negroes, see Slavery.
Neidlinger, Johann, Sr. & Jr., Swabian tanners, 189
Neidlinger, Matthias, Swabian organist, 17, 187; Nov., 18
Negroes, see Slaves.

Oak, see Trees.
The Office and Authority of a Justice of the Peace, law book by W. Welson, 63
Oglethorpe, James Edward, founder of Georgia, his regiment disbanded, 1
Old Ebenezer, first location of Salzburgers, now the Trustees' cowpen, 38
Orphanage in Ebenezer, being repaired, 44
Orphanage in Halle, see Halle.
Oyster shells for lime burning, 139

Paedigogium Regium, lycee for young noblemen, 219
Painting of Last Supper, 192
Palachacolas, fort on Savannah River, mentioned 24
Parker, Henry, becomes President of the Council, 177; Nov., note 3
Pennsylvania, German from, 59
Pica (clay eating), see Diseases.
Pietist parlance, Feb., note 5, 24; Aug., note 11
Piltz, Andreas, deceased Salz from Rastadt, an honest man, 156, 181
Pines, see Trees.
Polzenhagen, Mr., missionary to Indies, 157
Port Royal, small port in South Carolina, mentioned 33, 48, 116, 140
Ports, George Philip, Pal, 144, 146, 151
Portugal, source of silk seed, 124–125
Power of God in Little Children, religious tract, 202

President, 51, 137, see Council.
Purysburg, Swiss settlement across and down river from Ebenezer, mentioned, 5

Red Bluff, site of Ebenezer, 28
Reformed, followers of Calvin and Zwingli, 5, in South Carolina, 56, woman visits Ebenezer, 60, see Zübli.
Reverend Fathers, Jan., note 3. See Fathers.
Rice, see Crops.
Rice stamp, 94
Richter, Christian Friedrich, professor at Halle, his medicines used, 161, Oct., note 14
Riedelsperger, Salz, has trading business, 94, serves as butcher, 196
Riedelsperger, Mrs., Maria, nee Schweighoffer, weak 206
Riesch, Bonaventura, pastor in Lindau, 195
Rist, Johann, hymnist, 222
Rodigast, Samuel, hymnist, 222
Rottenberger, Anna Franziska, d Stephan, born 135
Rottenberger, Catharina, nee Piedler, w Stephan, bears child, 135
Rottenberger, Christoph, Salz, makes machines 83, 104
Rottenberger, Stephan, Salz carpenter, names child, 135
Rutilius, Martin, hymnist, 222
Rye, see Crops.

Sachs-Gotha (Saxe-Gotha), settlement in South Carolina, Lutherans there, 55
Salt, scarce, 139
Sanftleben, Georg, Silesian carpenter, mentioned, 13
Sanftleben, Magdalena, nee Arnsdorf, w Georg, ailing, 64
Savannah, chief city in Georgia passim
Savannah River, river fronting Augusta, Ebenezer, and Savannah, et passim

Savannah Town, trading station near Augusta, mentioned, 23, 73, German man from there (Vollbrecht), 152
Sawmill, new sawmill to be built, 46, 128, 166; old sawmill productive, 47, a great benefit, 64
Scarlet fever, see Diseases.
Schäffer, Pastor in Regensburg, benefactor, 107
Schatz-Kästlein, see Bogatzky.
Schauer's balm, a medication, 11; Jan., note 18
Schefler, Fridrich Carl, s Johann, born, 135
Schefler, Johann, Salz, has son, 135
Scheraus, Johann, Swabian, has distant plantation, 209
Schleydorn, Mr. Heinrich, German merchant in Philadelphia, 121, 133
Schmidt, Johann, Austrian, changes plantation, 13, his horse stolen, 101, foreman at cowpen, 141
Schmolck, Benjamin, hymnist, 222
Schoolmaster, 112, see Wertsch.
Schröder, Samuel, miller from Danzig, 122
Schubdrein, Josef, Pal carpenter, builds milldam, 207; Dec., note 26
Schubdrein, Peter, still in Savannah, 14, could accompany Boltzius boys, 116, to visit Nassau, 199; Jan., note 27, Nov., 32
Schubdrein brothers, industrious, 49, 103; make bricks, 99, 104; ailing, 116, pleased with Ebenezer, 133, desire to fetch parents, 199
Schwartz, Mr., missionary to Indies, 157
Schweighoffer, Margaretha, old Salz wid, past sixty, 57, oldest person in community, 205, recovers, 210
Seckinger child dies, 206
Seckinger family, April, note 9
Seelmann, Johann Christian, medical student, 122; Aug., note 18
Servants, abscond, 40, 54, 56, disloyal, 97
Sharecropping, 200
Siebenburgen (Transylvania),

province in Hungary, refuge of Protestant exiles, 80, 94

Silk subsidy, 84, 134

Silk culture, 2, 9, 19, 27, 28, 30, 42, 69, 71, 74, 83, 124, 133

Singing lessons, 44, 49

Slaves and slavery: Boltzius opposed, 95, 119, 143; slaves offered by Habersham, 12, 18; rejected by Salzburgers, 20, being introduced, 29, Salzburgers urged to buy, 55, not to work on the Sabbath, 58–59, bought by Leimberger, 93, by Kieffer, 112, 120; Kieffers now have three slaves, 113, Kronberger has slave, 121, slaves land in Charleston, 121, Trustees' decision, 129

Smuggler, see German smuggler.

Snow, unusual, 3

Society, see SPCK.

Soldiers, settle on Ebenezer Creek, 1, 33, 102

Spener, Philip Jacob, Pietist leader, 35, 161, 183; Feb. 22, Oct., note 12

SPCK (Society for the Promotion of Christian Knowledge), missionary society in London, support Salzburger ministers, 25

Squash, see Crops.

Stangen, Johann Georg, pious youth in Bayreuth, 203

Steiner, Ruprecht, Salz, cedes plantation, 42, his house consecrated, 43, dismisses servants, 96–97, weak, 116, 117, 188, recovers, 200

Stephens, Col. Wm., Trustees' secretary in Georgia, President of the Council, letter from, 54, mentioned, 159. steps down, 177; Feb., note 21, April, note 2, July, note 9, Sept., note 10, Nov., note 3

Stöller, Mr. of Koethen, daughter deceased, an edifying life, 15

Straube, Adam, Lutheran from Vernonburg, moves to Ebenezer works diligently 74; Feb., note 6

Straube, Pieta Clara, wid. Häfner, w Adam, ill, 196

Superstitions, see Incantations.

Surveyor, in Abercorn, 10, returns to Savannah, 12, surveying in Goshen, 21, 120; to be paid L 300, surveyors have hard task, 138, Blue Bluff being surveyed, 193, 199

Swabians, see First Swabian Transport.

Swiss immigrants, arrive at Charleston in bad condition, 19,

Swiss man comes from Congarees, 52

Tail-male rescinded, 130; Jan., note 22

Tanners, needed, 99, tanner from Purysburg, 137

Thilo, Christian Ernst, physician, mentioned, 35, 153, 160; receives private communion, 71, gave lessons, 173–174; Jan., note 11

Thilo, Friederica, nee Helfenstein, w. Ernst, receives private communion, 71, 200

Treasure Chest, Pietist tract, 73, 74, see Bogatzky.

Trees: oak, cypress, pine, and black nut trees now scarce, red cypress very durable, can float, 158, white oaks on Uchee Land, 105, white oaks wasted, 155, water oaks present, 25, firs of excellent quality, 50, not well protected 66, cypresses on Uchee Land. See Mulberry trees.

Treutlen, Johann Adam, future governor, June, note 9, Sept., note 6, Dec., note 30

True Christianity (*vom wahren Christenthum*), Pietist tract by Arndt, 57, 210

Trustees for Establishing a Colony in Georgia, offer to sell cowpen, 38, will cede iron, 47, letter from, 69, well meaning, 175, mentioned, 197

Tybee, island at mouth of Savannah River, Nov., note 15

Tythingmen, a great help, 65, 66, 113, visit Boltzius, 71, carry message, 102,

Uchee (Uchi) Indians, neighboring natives, Feb., note 13

Uchee land, tract across Ebenezer Creek, mentioned, 25, 154, to be occupied by Swabians, 178, named Blue Bluff, 193, being surveyed, 199

Ulm, Territory of, city-state on Danube, home of first Swabian transport, 209; Nov., note 1

Urlsperger, Samuel, Senior of Lutheran ministry in Augsburg, mentioned, 52, 71, has birthday, 126, letter from, 175, 192, 197; April, note 4

Verelst, Harman, Trustees' accountant, letter from, 2, 3, 9, 16, letter to, 76, mentioned, 125

Vernonburg, Swiss and German town on Vernon River, mentioned, 123

Vigera, Johann, of Strassburg, leader of fourth Salz transport, mentioned, 96, letter from, 121, 122; Aug., note 16

Vollbrecht, Christoph, from Danzig, 152

Walch, Dr., author, 117

Wallbaum, Counselor von, benefactor, 127

Walthauer, Johann Caspar, Pal, husband of widow Graniwetter, 9, 11, 61; Jan., note 21, May, note 7

Walthauer, Mrs., see Graniwetter.

Watermelons, see Crops.

Wehlen, Pastor, benefactor in London, 127

Weidenheim, Johann, hymnist, 222

Welson, W., author of law book, 63

Wertsch, Johann Caspar, teacher, sick, 104, 106; May, note 4

Wesley, John, English clergyman, mentioned, 147

West Indies, market for lumber, 25, 31, 33, 36, 48, war expected, 84

Wheat, see Crops.

Whitefield, George, English evangelist, letter from, 70, 146

Wirth, Ambrosius, author, 26, 56, 210; Feb., note 16, April, note 14

Woodworking, see Lumber.

Wurttemberg Confirmation Booklet, 212

Wurttemberg, Prince of, imposter, 122; Aug, note 17

Wurttemberg, young man from, 211

Zant, Sibille, nee Bacher, wid. Piltz, wid Bartholomäus, marries George Glaner, 181

Ziegenhagen, Friedrich Michael, Court Chaplain, Reverend Father of Georgia Salzburgers, aids German immigrants, 40, esteemed by Whitefield, 70, 146, mentioned, 126, 176, has birthday, 127, sermons by, 185, 208, donates painting, 192

Zimmerebener, Ruprecht, Salz, 139; Sept., note 12

Zion Church, church on plantations, mentioned, 76, 107, 109, 147, 151, 190, 212

Zoller, Balthasar, mean servant, 114, his son dies, 193

Zorn, Barbara, German orphan, being instructed, 81, marries J. L. Meyer, 158, 160, 178

Zouberbuhler (Zuberbiller), Bartholomäus, Swiss, Anglican minister, retains indentured servants, 4, preaches to English, 83; Jan., note 8, March, note 10

Zuberbiller, see Zouberbuhler.

Zübli, David, Swiss at Purysburg, father of Johan Joachim, mentioned, 86

Zübli, Johann Joachim, Reformed minister, tries to visit ship, 19, summons Boltzius, 153, orders books, 156, receives books, 160

PLAN Von Neu EBEN=EZER verlegt von MATTH. SEUTTER Kayserl. Geogr. in Augspurg

PLANTATIONES
PLANTATIONES
PLANTATIONES
PLANTATIONES

A. Haupt Straßen. B. Marckt Plätz. C. Mittle Gaßen. D. kleine Gäßlin. E. Store Kauß. F. Pfarr Wohnungen. G. die Kirche. rer ein jeglicher Zehen Wohnungen faßt. So in einem Kauß Hof u: Garten bestehet. L. ein Schindel zaun Sechs Fuß h. welcher ebenfals eingezaünt. P. Höltz. Q. Eigenthumlichs Land einer kleinen Nation Indianer. R. die Mühl. S. Kähre. Land wo die Saltzburger ihre Vieh Ställe haben. Y. Sind 20 Kauß Plätze zwischen drey Straßen. so Hr. General O.

This plan of Ebenezer first appeared in Urlsperger's *Ausfü*
A tinted copy is in the De H